ALGREN AT SEA

CENTENNIAL EDITION 1909–2009

ALGREN AT SEA

Who Lost an American?
&
Notes from a Sea Diary

travel writings

Nelson Algren

Seven Stories Press

New York • London • Toronto • Melbourne

Seven Stories Press
140 Watts Street
New York, NY 10013
www.sevenstories.com

In Canada: Publishers Group Canada, 559 College Street, Suite 402, Toronto, ON M6G 1A9

In the UK: Turnaround Publisher Services Ltd., Unit 3, Olympia Trading Estate, Coburg Road, Wood Green, London N22 6TZ

In Australia: Palgrave Macmillan, 15–19 Claremont Street, South Yarra, VIC 3141

College professors may order examination copies of Seven Stories Press titles for a free six-month trial period. To order, visit http://www.sevenstories.com/textbook or send a fax on school letterhead to (212) 226-1411.

Book design by Jon Gilbert

Library of Congress Cataloging-in-Publication Data

Algren, Nelson, 1909–1981.
 Algren at sea : Notes from a sea diary & Who lost an American?: travel writings / Nelson Algren. — A Seven Stories Press 1st ed., Centennial ed., 1909–2009.
    p. cm.
Includes bibliographical references.
ISBN 978-1-58322-841-8 (pbk.)
I. Title.
PS3501.L4625A78 2008
813'.52—dc22

                                              2008038735

Printed in the USA.

0 9 8 7 6 5 4 3 2 1

CONTENTS

Who Lost an American?

For Simone de Beauvoir

The author wishes to thank the following publications for permission to reprint articles: "Rapietta Greensponge, Girl Counselor, Comes to My Aid," first published in *Harlequin* under the title "Whobody Knows My Name or How to Be a Freedom-Rider Without Leaving Town." "The South of England," "The Banjaxed Land: You Have Your People and I Have Mine" (under the title "You Have Your People and I Have Mine"), and "There's Lots of Crazy Stuff in the Ocean" (under the title "The Moon of King Minos") were first published in *Rogue*; the poem on pages 77–78 was first published in *Rogue*, under the title "The Bride Below the Black Coiffure"; © *Rogue Magazine*/Greenleaf Publishing Company 1961. "Barcelona: The Bright Enormous Morning" and "Seville: The Peseta with the Hole in the Middle" appeared originally in *The Kenyon Review*, under the title "The Peseta with the Hole in the Middle." "The Night-Colored Rider" originally appeared in *Playboy*, under the title "The Father & Son Cigar"; © 1962 by Nelson Algren. "Down With All Hands" was first published in *The Atlantic Monthly*. "They're Hiding the Ham on the Pinball King" was first published in *Contact*. "When a Muslim Makes His Violin Cry, Head for the Door" was first published in *Nugget Magazine*. "Almeria: Show Me a Gypsy and I'll Show You a Nut" was first published under the title "Dad Among the Troglodites or, Show Me a Gypsy and I'll Show You a Nut" in *The Noble Savage*, No. 5, a Meridian periodical, published by The World Publishing Company, 1962.

Permission to quote from the following publications has been granted by the publishers: "Cocktails for Two" by Arthur Johnston and Sam Coslow, © 1934 by Famous Music Corporation; copyright renewed 1961 by Famous Music Corporation. Passage from *Green Hills of Africa* reprinted with the permission of Charles Scribner's Sons from *Green Hills Of Africa* by Ernest Hemingway, copyright 1935 Charles Scribner's Sons. Selection from "An Impolite Interview with Hugh Hefner," in *The Realist*, May 1961. Excerpt (page 54) from Borstal Boy by Brendan Behan, Alfred A. Knopf, Inc. "Tricks Out of Times Long Gone" by Nelson Algren first appeared in *The Nation*, September 1962. Excerpts from "Playboy's Number One Playboy" by Peter Meyerson, *Pageant*. Excerpt from *The Hive* by Camilo Cela, Farrar, Straus and Company, Inc. Excerpt from *Chicago Sun-Times* reprinted with permission.

NEW YORK

RAPIETTA GREENSPONGE,
GIRL COUNSELOR,
COMES TO MY AID

When I recall today what a mark I must have appeared, before Rapietta came to my rescue, I have to smile. It's a wonder somebody didn't take me for a fool.

Legally speaking I have held my own ground ever since. The house that stands on the ground is, of course, in Rapietta's name—but what house by the side of any road could have found a better friend to Man? Bless the day, I say, when first I shook the firm small hand of Rapietta Greensponge, Courageous Counselor: Bless that hour.

"Are you putting that expression on to match the style of your shoes or is it real?" Rapietta inquired of me with a forthright smile, when I first appeared in the offices of Doubledge Deadsinch & O'Lovingly, shaking my hand forthrightly.

"The expression is as completely my own as the shoes," I assured her, referring to the ankle-high white sneakers I had earned, some years before, by making a bet on a Cuban middleweight. Naturally I call them my Ked Gavilans.

"I don't believe it," she told me, "but if you can hold it, we'll bury them."

"Might I ask whom we may be burying, ma'am?" I inquired, watching my grammar as this was my first visit to New York.

Rapietta tiptoed to the door, opened it softly, peered down the corridor, closed it as softly, and tiptoed back to confide in me.

"The jackals who are trying to take advantage of you, my friend."

I tiptoed to the door, opened it softly, and peered down the corridor. Sure enough, the jackals had gone into hiding.

"Any jury with eyes in its head can see advantage is being taken of you by *somebody*, so it must be *them*," she revealed. It was the first time I had seen the judicial mind at work.

"In event of a bench trial before a blind judge," she explained, making allowances for the fact that I was only a layman, "we'll demand a change of venue."

It was during my first change of venue that an Indiana sheriff led a motorbike posse to my door and read an eviction notice aloud to me. I did not ask him to let me read it myself as there was not a moment to lose. Excusing myself, I rolled my stamp collection into my G.I. blanket, mounted my British lightweight bicycle made in Duesseldorf and, with the cry of *"Sink the* Bismarck!" broke through the cordon and sped swiftly down the Indiana Turnpike till I came to a tollway. There I abandoned the bike and made my way on foot to Chicago's West Side.

Quick thinking had thus salvaged several valuable items as well as a portion of my dignity.

When the weather turned cold the hallway in which I had taken refuge, pending word from Rapietta, developed a draft. I didn't mind walking up and down swinging my arms until dawn; but when the weather turned icy I began to slip on the frost. I bumped my head just once too often. The suspicion then came upon me that either advantage had somehow been taken of me once more or the hallway was too small for sleeping purposes.

Reluctant as I was to get a representative of law and order into trouble I determined, nonetheless, to advise Rapietta of my situation. I set out for the Eastern Seaboard with my Eastern-Seaboard-English dictionary under my arm.

Exchanging cheerful handwaves with motorists along the Pennsylvania Turnpike was jolly fun, particularly when a light snow was falling. Then I could pelt merry fellows driving to town. One fellow got into the spirit of the thing so well that he stopped and invited me to ride beside him.

I accepted readily and was about to thank him when he struck me with a rubber gearshift handle with great force and pushed me into a snow-bank. As I didn't wish to make a nuisance of myself around a clinic, I waited until the blood from the gash had coagulated before setting out once more.

Six days later I was riding through the Holland Tunnel singing

> *Don't throw bouquets at me*
> *Don't laugh at my jokes too much—*

and in no time at all I was opening the door of Doubledge Deadsinch &
O'Lovingly. I simply could *not* remember to knock.

Rapietta Greensponge was with a hearty fellow who looked so familiar
to me that I felt I must have encountered him somewhere before.

"Three guesses," The Hearty Fellow offered, causing me to warm to
him. Nobody enjoys playing "Guess Whom" more than I. I guess I'd
rather play "Guess Whom" than ride a passenger train.

"Only offer him two," Rapietta counseled him. I gathered he was her
client as well as myself. We already had something in common.

"I don't *need* three!" I boasted, "*I* can guess in one—Have you been in
a Bwoadway Pwoduction wecently?" I asked The Hearty Fellow, cleverly
emulating Mr. Bennett Surface.

"No," he confessed, falling into my twap.

"Then you are Zewo Mothtell!"

"You're getting warmer," my new friend assured me.

"Come *on,* give us a clue, kid," I cajoled him, for he was a regular fellow.
He turned back the lapel of his coat and revealed a sheriff's badge.

"Duke Wayne!" I cried.

"You're getting even warmer," was my hearty friend's hearty response.

"No more guesses," Rapietta cautioned, "he's *really* getting warm."

"Oh, tell *anyhow,*" I pleaded.

"Next time I see you," my mysterious friend promised as he shook my
hand, and left.

"Wemember—you pwomised!" I called gaily after him. Then I became
my old thoughtful self.

I told Rapietta how I had been evicted and had saved myself by quick
thinking and the cry of *"Sink the* Bismarck!"

"Where is the bicycle now?" she inquired.

"I traded it to a tollgate guard on the Indiana Tollway for an extra pair
of Ked Gavilans. *He* won *his* by betting on Chuck Davey."

"You're putting me on," Rapietta told me, waggling a finger playfully at me.

"I needed them to keep my feet dry," I explained, "in event it rained on the
Pennsylvania Turnpike. Last time it snowed and I got a gash on my forehead."

Rapietta's admiration gleamed in her eyes but there was no time for
that. Wasting no time in useless indignation, she handed me a document
prepared for the contingency we now faced.

I read it swiftly and had to protest.

Passing ownership of the house to herself was a shrewd legal stroke—but what was to become of my stamp collection? Even now it might be endangered by another motorbike posse. I demanded that Rapietta assume guardianship of it lest it be seized as I slept. My clever demand put her on the defensive.

"I can only assume guardianship in perpetuity," she dickered. I snatched the papers and signed them before she could change her mind, and once more we had eluded my pursuers.

"What does 'in perpetuity' mean, Rapietta?" I inquired later.

"It means that your stamp collection is now protected forever by a little somebody," she assured me modestly.

"Then that was a neat ruse," I boasted.

"It certainly was," Rapietta agreed generously, "and half the credit belongs to *you.*" She emphasized this by tapping the top button of my weskit with her forefinger.

The honor of the thing fired my ambition. "What do I do *next?*" I asked eagerly, jumping in and out of my sneakers. "How am I to get *full* credit for something?"

Rapietta put her hands on my shoulders to calm me.

"Bring five hundred in small bills to my apartment after twelve," she advised me; "we are facing a *new* contingency."

"Then we will have our first lunch together!" I realized.

"Twelve *midnight,* you wild thing," she taunted me gently while shoving me with her powerful forearms into the spick-and-span corridor of Doubledge Deadsinch & O'Lovingly, Selfless Solicitors—"and bring your toothbrush so we can *both* get some sleep."

Rapietta slammed the door softly in my face. Little did the innocent creature fancy that at that very moment my G.I. toothbrush was hanging about my neck cleverly concealed by my collar. For, since suffering the theft of my Dr. West's in the 178th Field Artillery I have never been able to bring myself to hang it up in a civilian bathroom. Needless to say I was honorably discharged. So much for World War I.

Shortly after midnight the contingency Rapietta was facing came to a head.

"What do I do now?" I asked sleepily, for it had been a trying day.

"Hit the road by the backstair," she explained, "and write me *par avion.*" And slipping into sleep as easily as she had slipped into French, the dear girl began snoring noisily.

Swiftly translating her message into my mother tongue, I hurried down the stair and picked my way through Central Park in search of a friendly drugstore where I might purchase a *par avion* stamp. A friendly officer interceded, inquiring why I might be walking barefooty in New York after the sun had set. Although I had noticed that the streetlamps were lit, I hadn't noticed that I'd forgotten my shoes. Thanking the officer courteously, I hurried back to Rapietta's to recover them.

She did not answer my knock. But when one of my Ked Gavilans came through the transom I concluded she must therefore be half awake, and knocked again.

The second shoe caused me to wonder whether it were Rapietta throwing, as the shoe that came through this time was a size 13 British walker. It made a snug fit.

I peered through the keyhole in order to see why Rapietta was getting her footwear confused with mine, and sure enough, she *was* wide-awake. Never a man to spoil somebody else's good time, I withdrew tippytoe.

Returning across the Pennsylvania Turnpike, however, I didn't make as good time as I had in coming because the walker has a higher heel than a sneaker, which has no heel at all.

My spirits picked up on the Indiana Tollway, and I began striding along while humming contentedly

> *I'm a Dingdong Daddy from Dumas*
> *'n you oughta see me do my stuff.*

I was first in line at the General Delivery window in Chicago the following morning. My reward was a night wire from New York.

Had something gone wrong in the week I'd been gone? I opened the wire with apprehension. Sure enough, it was from Rapietta:

TIDE HAS TURNED STOP WE HAVE JACKALS CORNERED

Western Union had italicized a telegram for me! It was my first time. I wired back:

MISS YOU STOP COMING BACK TO HELP CORNER JACKALS

By taking a shortcut through Grant Park I reached the monument to Stephen A. Douglas on Twenty-ninth and the lake by noon. Bundling my clothes neatly, with my oddly matched shoes inside to keep them dry, I struck out into the lake at Thirty-first and came up, dripping but happy, on a sand-bar only a quarter-mile offshore just as day was breaking the following morning. Now all I had to do was find the Indiana Tollway in order to make the Pennsylvania Turnpike so I could again negotiate the Holland Tunnel. I *so* much wanted to see Doubledge Deadsinch and O'Lovingly once again.

A motorist driving a Bentley with a Nassau, Bahamas, license, picked me up at Harrisburg and made me get out in front of the Shredded Wheat plant at Niagara Falls. After admiring the colored lights on the falls while eating a Shredded Wheat biscuit somebody had discarded on the grass, I was once again on my way. In no time at all I was striding cheerfully along the Palisades, humming:

> *In some secluded rendevous*
> *That overlooks the avenue*
> *With cocktails for two*
> *As we enjoy a cigarette*
> *To some exquisite chansonette*
> *My head may go reeling*
> *But my heart will be obedient*
> *Most any afternoon at five*
> *We'll be so glad we're both alive*
> *It may be fortune will complete her plan*
> *That all began*
> *With cocktails for two*

until I reached the offices I loved so well.

"Tie a rubber band around it and toss it through the transom, Needlenose," Rapietta's voice instructed me from within.

Nobody had ever called me Needlenose before.

It was my first time again.

"I don't have a rubber band," I explained through the door. After looking carefully about to see whether I'd brought somebody along.

"Use your shoelace!" she instructed me.

"Which shoe?" I countered.

"The longest!"

I had a problem: my laces were of equal length. Quickly solving this puzzler by cutting one short and using the other, I called—"Ready!— What I do wrap it *around?*"

"The *bankroll,* Melonhead."

"I don't have a bankroll, Rapietta."

"Oh," I heard her mutter, "it's him," and she opened the door. "I was expecting a Britisher named Walker," she explained. "What the hell do *you* want?"

"I felt we should be together while the tide was turning, dear," I explained.

"The tide ebbed yesterday," she explained crisply. "Now *they're* suing *us.*"

Rapietta handed me a morocco-bound sheaf of 399 pages of single-spaced figures. Adding them up to see if they came out right was interesting work. I had never done addition before. It was one more first time.

"Get up off the floor," she reproached me.

"But what does it *mean,* dear?" I asked.

"It's your bill as of the fiscal year ending today at 1200 hours. Four researchers, five shysters, Morris Ernst and an alley-fink have been working night and day in your interest, compiling your account."

"Why, I thought Doubledge Deadsinch & O'Lovingly took my case on *contingency,*" I protested.

"Where is your compassion?" Rapietta reproached me, "Are Doubledge Deadsinch and Pyrhana to be pauperized by a legal technicality? Is a layman to impoverish men of good family? Is that their reward for giving of themselves selflessly in your interest?"

"When did Pyrhana join us?" I inquired.

"When O'Lovingly retired," she informed me, and turned her back to me. I felt *awful.*

"I didn't mean to hurt you, Rapietta," I tried to explain, approaching her. But she kept her back to me. It was a swivel chair.

"I'm putting it up to you," was all she would say.

She was putting it up to me.

"Not to mention a C.P.A.," she reminded me over her shoulder. I heard the catch in my counselor's voice. When I put my hands on her shoulders they were quaking.

"You are a brave girl," I told her; "you haven't mentioned yourself."

Rapietta captured my hand and clasped it between her own. When she turned her eyes to mine they were shining.

"*I* am yours on contingency," the self-sacrificing girl confessed. And, taking me by the hand, led me into her inner office, opened a drawer, and from it withdrew a document which she handed me.

It was a one-way passage on the SS *Meyer Davis,* departing from Pier 86, Tuesday, at 1600 hours.

"What does it all *mean?*" I wanted to know.

Rapietta's face grew stern. "It means that our opponents have discovered that you marched in a demonstration protesting the bombing of Ethiopia in 1936, or somewhere along in there, and you have to get out of the country before you are subpoenaed. If this evidence comes to light they will be able to establish that if you had a mind you'd be dangerous! Our defense will go sky-high."

"But I have never been at sea before," I protested.

"You've been at sea for some time," Rapietta told me.

I wondered what she meant by *that.*

"Can I *afford* an ocean voyage?" was my next poser.

"Candidly, you can't afford a trip to the drugstore for an airmail stamp," she told me candidly.

"I already made that trip." I revealed that my memory, at any rate, was still functioning. "Now I'd like to go somewhere else. But I'd like to return someday."

"We can't chance that," she informed me. "You'll have to stay abroad until things blow over."

"How will I know when they have blown?"

"You will receive a message *par avion*—that means 'Welcome to Paris,' dear boy."

And wasting no time in useless indignation, she drew a document from her desk she had already prepared, in order to avoid losing even more time in useless indignation.

"I have completed arrangements for you with my trustworthy cousin, Trustworthy Ex-Naval-Eye Roger Blueblade of Blueblade, Suckingwise, Scalpel & Tourniquet, Trustworthy Publishers, whom I deeply admire, as he comes from the venal branch of our family."

"I admire Venal Roger Blueblade, Ex-Naval Eye, too, Rapietta!" I assured her with an eager cry.

"You preposterous *nut*"—Rapietta was suddenly put out with me—"you don't even know the sneaky little usurer and you're *admiring* him—for *what?*"

"Keep your voice down, darling," I felt forced to reprove her; "there is no need of getting rowdy simply because I happen to know that, as Mr. Blueblade has published some of the most trustworthy volumes in circulation, hence his name of Trustworthy Roger is not unearned."

This speech, delivered with an aloof take-it-or-leave-it air, raised me in Rapietta's eyes at the same moment that it reduced her to sitting down heavily. The judicial burden she was carrying on my account was almost too heavy for her childish shoulders, I perceived.

"Let us look at it this way." I took a kindlier tone. "People who really matter hardly ever enter a Chicago hallway. But there is no telling whom a first-class passenger may meet. I might even meet Abraham Ribicoff."

While Rapietta had her back turned to me, I signed the papers swiftly to make certain she would not change her mind. When she turned about and handed the papers to me to sign, I shook my head stubbornly.

Rapietta paled.

"What is the *meaning* of this?" she asked sternly.

"Oh, I just don't *want* to," I teased her.

Rapietta sneered.

"Look at yourself," she told me, "standing there in one British walker and a button-down sneaker and no socks, *presuming* to impose a layman's judgment upon legal counsel."

Though shaken, I held my ground. I did not make PFC by happenstance. I just happened to be inducted when the army needed cowards in that classification.

"If you don't sign you can't have a *Bon Voyage* party," she informed me with finality.

"I don't *care*." This was turning out to be a real fun day.

"You won't get to meet Abe," she threatened me.

I gave ground.

"Say *please*," I demanded.

She refused. It was a test of strength between two strong souls.

"A *Bon Voyage* party!" I suddenly caught the picture. "For *me?*" I asked, and began jumping in and out, as both shoes happened to be unlaced.

"What *does* it all mean?" I cried.

"It means you will soon be rubbing elbows with '*celebs*,'" she informed me quietly.

"'*Celebs*'? Such as people seen wecently in Bwoadway pwoductions by Tennessee Rilliams?" I inquired, getting myself under contwol.

"Such as Chinless Kilgallen, Hedda Eczema, and Norman Manlifellow, Boyish Author."

Rapietta put her hands on my shoulders in event I should begin jumping again, but I was feeling too faint for that.

"Do you mean Norman Manlifellow, Boyish Author, might come to a party for *me?*"

"*Might?*" Rapietta scoffed. "He wouldn't *dare* stay away."

"And what of Leon Urine, author of *The Whole World Looks Jewish When You're in Love?*"

Rapietta touched forefinger to thumb in the gesture employed by the fast international set to indicate Leon was in the bag.

"And shall we play *Verités?*"

"No, dear, Françoise won't make it. But Giovanni Johnson *shall!*"

My breath caught.

"You don't mean *Sixteenth Arrondissement* Johnson, America's greatest gift to Mecca since Ahmad Jamal?"

"None other."

"And will he wear his fez?"

"I *guarantee* it."

She was too late to hold me down. I got in six jumps before I could stop.

"Roger Blueblade is our man!" I cried, coming down for the last time. "Give me the papers, dear girl, dear girl"—and I reached for the shining sheaf.

Rapietta snatched it back.

"You've already signed them when I wasn't looking, you mischievous marmoset," she taunted me. The clever creature had been on to my game all along!

She flung herself across my lap in a burst of *gaité Parisienne* but slipped through my knees to the floor with her dirndl tumbling capriciously under her armpits. This was a woman I had never glimpsed before.

"Is that what is called a *foundation garment,* sweetheart?" I made bold to ask.

"Why do you *ask,* awful boy?"

"Because it's raking the hell off my sternum, awful girl."

"It's a *foundation* garment alright," she chuckled merrily—"a *Guggen-heim* Foundation garment—Yuck! Yuck! Yuck!" and in an access of womanly passion she grasped me to her change belt.

I extricated myself from her grip and filled two long-stemmed glasses with imported manzanilla, taking care not to spill a drop.

"There is one question I *have* to ask, sweetheart," I told her seriously.

"You have only to ask."

"Did Ethiopia finally get free?"

"They *must* have. They now belong to us."

"Then here is to Haile Selassie," I proposed, clinking my glass against hers although she was nowhere near it.

"The Lion of Judah!" Rapietta responded, seizing her glass and flinging the contents full in my face.

Taking me upon *her* lap, the changeful creature dried my face on her doeskin bag while reproaching me for not keeping my knees together when *she* had sat upon mine. As her fingers kept trailing the catch of my change purse, I had to shift position now and again.

Yet in trading a cabin-class hallway for a first-class stateroom on a first-class ocean, I could not help but feel I *must* have outwitted somebody.

"I feel I've made a shrewd move for a layman," I assured my friend and legal counsel, Rapietta Greensponge, Decorous Public Defender.

"Son," Rapietta confided in me, "you are *all* layman."

So much for World War II.

If all that was needed for a successful *Bon Voyage* party was one clever move, I'd already made it by buying a gallon of sauterne for $2.98, putting it under the soda recharger until it fizzed, and then pouring it into bottles labeled "Mumm's." Because if there was one thing I wanted my New York friends to have, it was the aura of success. I didn't wish them success itself—in fact, I longed passionately for the total ruin of them one by one—but I did want to arrange some sort of aura for them.

"How does a hack like that manage to serve champagne at all hours?" my New York friends often marvel. My Chicago friends don't bother with that. They just say, "Where'd you get the cheap wine?" and toss the remains of their drink in the sink. So much for bobsledding at Garmisch-Partenkirchen.

My next move was to snip whiskey ads of Scotsmen playing bagpipes and glue them onto old root-beer bottles, into which I poured the contents of a curious brew distilled on Amsterdam Avenue to which nobody has yet given a name, probably because it has to be got down without fooling around or it won't go down at all. Labeling these "The Best Scotch Procurable" would, I hoped, raise the fascinating issue of where one might purchase the best scotch that is unprocurable; thus providing even inarticulate guests with a topic of conversation.

Rapietta arrived first, as might have been expected, with the excuse that she had news so good it couldn't wait.

"I am as much for good news as your next client," I reproached her, "but couldn't it have waited till you'd finished dressing?"

"Just because a person's girdle snags on her navel is no sign a person isn't well dressed," Rapietta pointed out.

"A flimsy alibi," I had to tell her, for she is the only counselor in the jurisdiction of New York State with a dollar-shaped navel.

"Any jury that has eyes in its head," she began, but I cut her off. "I *know*, I *know*," I told her quickly. I just didn't want to go through that blind-judge routine again.

New York was sharpening me up, as the reader may have noticed.

What the SS *Meyer Davis* could do for me remained to be seen.

"What I want to know is how much we're going to wipe them jackals out *for*, Rapietta," I demanded.

"A good round sum," she assured me. "I am dropping a writ of *Non Compis Barracuda* into the hopper, and when it hops out we will be legally entitled to bone our opponents like a fish."

"Then that's one of the best kinds there are," I realized, doing a *Bon Voyage* jig even though the party hadn't begun.

"Now slip me five hundred in small bills, and into the hopper she goes," Rapietta invited me.

"Five hundred?" I asked, bewildered anew.

"For *Non Compis Bonefish* just like I said," she reminded me.

I lacked eleven dollars of five hundred, but Rapietta, generous friend, drew the balance out of the dollar-shaped navel, accepted my Parker 51 as collateral at 40 per cent, and glanced at her watch to check the hour of the transaction. A moment later we were friends again.

But where were my guests?

A rich Old-Plantation contralto came wafting up the cotton-pickin' stairs. It mounted ahead of the singer flight after flight:

> *Dis train don't carry no gamblers*
> *Dis train*
> *Dis train*
> *Dis train don't carry no ramblers*
> *Dis train*
> *Dis train*
> *We's ridin' to Freedom on de Freedom Train*
> *Gonna git to Freedom on a daisy chain*
> *Dis train*
> *Dis train*

"Giovanni is here!" I cried, and I had barely cried it when a small, sandpiperish person, wearing a fez, and deeply tanned, sandpipered into the room.

"Où sont tous les garçons?" He skipped gaily about. *"Allons-nous jouer?"* He stretched out on a divan, put his fez under his head for a pillow, picked up the phone, crossed his sandals, and dialed languidly.

"Hello, Da-aady," he informed the phone, "still angwy with me? No, I *can't* see you; I'm flying south, and one goodbye is enough. Yes, I'm holding Roy Wilkens responsible for my nephew's well-being while I'm gone. No, I don't have to worry about my niece; *they* take care of themselves. Of *course* I don't like my nephew as well I do you; it's a different thing, like *related—oooo*, aren't you the *dzealous* daddy! Did I tell you Normy has decided to be mayor, and I'm *infuriated* with him, sacrificing himself that way? Why should *he* be responsible for juvenile delinquency and technocracy and all like *that*, Da-aaady? Isn't that Jack Kerouac's job? The first thing you know, he's going to want to be *president* of something, I don't think he cares of what. But what I say, let *that* to somebody who is ready for the responsibility, like Eddie Fisher. Well, kiss-kiss and huggy-vous, see you in the *Seizième Arrondissement*, Daddy-doo. *No. Don't* bring Faulkner." And he hung up.

I was pleased to see a young man devoted to his father but I didn't understand why he didn't want anybody to bring Faulkner.

"For the same reason I don't want anybody to bring Hemingway," he read my mind; "Faulkner is full of soupy rhetoric, and Papa wrote a novel that is boyish and romantic."

"What we need is more novels that are girlish and unromantic," I hurried to agree, because I saw his point.

"No!" he refuted me fiercely, "all we need is as much truth as we can bear!"

He stood up, the better to look commanding. I quailed.

"I can't stand much of *that* crazy stuff," I had to admit. "Can *you?*"

"All *I* can do," he informed me proudly, "is attempt to prove, by hard precept and harder example, that people *can* be better than they are!"

"Oh, good for *you,* Giovanni Johnson," I exclaimed, "and I'll *help* you—between us we'll make the rats better than they are whether they like it or not! We'll cram goodness down their stinking throats! By *God,* you and I are going to show the scum a few tricks—in three months we'll *both* be rich!"

"Where's the booze?" he asked me quietly, "you *nut.* "

And it is a pure wonder how many people you've never met will go out of their way to wish you a pleasant journey if you'll only keep liquor on hand. In the space of several minutes there were more people partying about me than I could have hoped to meet in a year on Milwaukee Avenue.

"Have you been in a Bwoadway Pwoduction wecently?" I would ask a guest, and then move to another. When they began replying, "You've asked me that twice," I refused to be offended.

A fellow wearing a sandwich-board advertising himself approached me.

"I am Norman Manlifellow," he introduced himself, sheathing a nine-inch jackknife, "Hemingway never wrote anything that would disturb an eight-year old." He began working the lighting of the board by a battery concealed in his pocket, with the result that his candidacy for the Presidency of American Writers was spelled out alternately in red and blue lights. I realized that I was dealing with none other than the boyish author of *The Elk Paddock,* or *Look, Ma, My Fly Is Open.*

"It's a nice thing if a fellow can hold down two jobs," I offered, thus intimating that I knew he was running for two offices, but before he could pick up the intimation someone began kicking the door in and I had to hurry there before the hinges gave way.

It was Ginny Ginstruck, whose own hinges gave way some decades ago.

"I *may* stagger—but I *never* fall down!" Ginny trumpeted tri-umphantly, swinging her handbag heavily at my head. Ginny *may* hold onto that bag when she swings it. Then again, she may let go. As it holds a one-pound jar of Pond's cold cream and a fifth of Haig & Haig, you're better off if she lets go. Somebody farther off is more likely to go down then than yourself.

They never stagger. They just go down.

"I may fall down," Ginny explained, knocking guests sidewise and every whichway, "but you can't pinch me without a warrant!"

It's true that Ginny has never been pinched. Ever since forming a lit-erary agency with Zazubelle Zany, in fact, she has been picking victories out of defeat.

"We may have returned that rotten book to the wrong writer," is the view of Ginstruck & Zany, "but god*damn* it, *we got it in the mails,* didn't we? Alright, so that rotten novel got thrown out with that rotten *Sunday-Times Book Review* but god*damn* it, we got the rotten carbon around the joint *somewhere. Ain't* we? Alright, maybe we *did* sell something to Hol-lywood without asking some idiot's permission, but god*damn,* that agent *acted like he was drunk too."*

Typewritten pages fluttered across the floor every time Ginny opened her bag to take a drink. She fell across the divan, using a dozen crumpled pages for a pillow.

"Did you misplace these, Ginny?" I asked, after I had assembled sec-tions of a treatise entitled *Cerebrum to Cerebellum: How We Think,* the lifework of a brain surgeon whose own mind had recently snapped. Or he wouldn't have dispatched it to Ginstruck & Zany.

"I never lose *nothin',* you sonofabitch," she reassured me; "they just keep saying that so their rotten friends won't think a publisher turned them down. Get me a drink, you rotten crook; get out of my sightline, Whoever-You-Are; I done everything I could for you, you cheap ape; the least you can do is get a lady a drink, you lickspittle baboon. Who the hell let *you* in?"

"I'm the fellow the party's for, Ginny," I reminded her. "I invited you to show you there weren't any hard feelings on my part just because you lost that book and gave away the other one and told me you'd sue if I got another agent."

Ginny pulled herself up by holding onto a floor lamp. I stepped on its base to keep it from falling, as Ginny weighs three pounds more than a porpoise.

"You invite me to a party 'n' then you *bee*-rate me in front of your snooty friends," she told me, looking terribly hurt. " 'Come up to my house and see a boob'—is *that* what you told them?" She broke into tears.

"Don't cry, Ginny," I asked her.

She reached for her handbag, so I got out of the way. When I brought her a water glass of straight gin she drank it down in one try and lay back.

"I'm leaving on the SS *Meyer Davis,*" I told her. "Aren't you proud of me?"

"I don't give a goddamn if you're climbing into a nose cone," Ginny told me. "When are you going to get me a drink?"

I have to give Old Ginny credit. Losing a few lifetime treatises doesn't dampen *her* spirits.

A fellow in horn-rimmed glasses helped me to prop Ginny against the wall with a Manhattan Directory at her feet to keep her from sliding. I thought it would take a Queens Directory as well, but he thought one book was enough. I told him I knew Ginny longer than he: when she started to slide, one Manhattan book wasn't going to hold her.

The horn-glassed fellow introduced himself as Kenwood McCowardly, Chief Junior Editor of Doubledeal & Wunshot, a subsidiary of Ethical & Entity. Mr. McCowardly was interested in my transaction with Blueblade & Scalpel, and I had just gotten to the good part, where I swing a first-class passage on a real ocean liner simply by signing over ownership of everything in perpetuity.

"*We* wouldn't have taken advantage of you like that," Mr. McCowardly informed me; "we would have limited out rights to ninety-nine years. We're an *ethical* house."

At that moment Rapietta took Mr. McCowardly by his ethical elbow and led him into the bedroom and shut the door. I was flattered to see that one of our leading junior editors was represented by the same coura-geous counselor as myself.

Sure enough, Ginny began to slide, so I had to get another directory. While holding her ankles, a young woman, seeing the difficulty of my position, came up with a Bronx and a Yonkers book too. With her help we got Ginny blocked so she couldn't inadvertently trip anybody.

The helpful young woman introduced herself as Denise Paperfish, wife of Alfred Paperfish, Leading Footnote King. I inquired whether Alfred was on hand, having long been an admirer of his authenticity; not to mention his footnoteship.

"I left the old fig home," Mrs. Paperfish assured me, "I *loathe* him."

"I'm sorry to hear your marriage didn't turn out well, Demise," I consoled the poor child.

"Oh, I loathed him long before I married him," she explained. I didn't follow the explanation but assumed it had something to do with Literature.

"Nobody but a square would marry a man she didn't loathe," she cleared matters up; "right now he is doing a paper revealing that Lewis and Clark were forced to make their expedition because nasty talk in Washington had made it impossible for them to be alone together anywhere except in the Northwest Territory."

"I begin to see what you mean," I assured her.

"I treat him like so much dirt," she added proudly.

"Don't worry," I comforted the woman; "on Alfred Paperfish dirt isn't noticeable."

Then we stood merely looking at each other.

"Well, Mister Man," she broke the silence, "it's *your* move."

"Mine?"

"I have just time for a quickie," she explained.

"I think we should come to terms with the Technocrats," was the only move I could think to make for the moment.

"Furthermore, Mister Man, my name is not 'Demise.' " She concluded our little discussion and turned away to seek elsewhere for a quickie.

"Lean white cat vs. lean black cat!" I heard Giovanni make a curious challenge. Sure enough, it was Norman Manlifellow he was challenging.

"Lean white boy meets lean black boy!" Norman replied.

I looked around to see if I was hearing right, as the better word for Giovanni would be "puny," and Norman's physique is closer to Buddy Hackett's than to that of a jaguar.

But Giovanni, tossing his fez to one side, balanced himself like a ballet dancer, strangely upon one leg; and Norman executed a similar posture with equivalent grace.

I was about to witness the first arabesque Indian-wrestling contest in the history of American letters!

"Is this for the black or the white supremacist title?" I inquired eagerly, hoping to get a bet down.

Ginny sat up and boggled about. "Liberace can whip you both!" she announced, and sank back upon the divan.

Norman, apparently discouraged by this comment, broke the contest off. "I'm a writer, *not* a performer," he explained with disdain of attention-getting devices, and thereupon stood on his head; revealing, as his trousers slipped to his knees, that one of his socks bore the legend "Look at me!" and the other the plea *"Keep* Looking!"

Actually, I believe his withdrawal from the contest was provoked by an unwritten ethical law among New York writers never to run for public office against one another. Except, of course, for the Presidency of American Writers.

At this point he resumed an upright position and began jumping up and down with drinks in both hands, shouting, "I'm getting mine! Getting mine!" As he was already wet from previous drinks I didn't see the need of spilling more on himself.

Giovanni, left in the ballet dancer's attitude, got tired of holding it. He got back on tippytoe and tippytoed right up to me.

"You look like you're from nowhere," he informed me. "Are you really from somewhere?"

"Chicago." I had to admit it.

"Do you realize you are responsible for the race riots of 1917?" he informed me, placing his forefinger on the tip of my nose.

"I was eight years old at the time." I tried wriggling out of the accusation.

"You are an honorable, well-meaning white square," he informed me; emphasizing his point by tapping my nose lightly.

"Yes, sir."

What else could I say with my eyes crossed? I didn't ask him to take the finger off as I knew this would be to deprive him of personal dignity.

"In short," he summed the situation up crisply, "you flatly deny that Negroes are lynched, jailed, cheated, corrupted, flogged, degraded, debauched, deprived, dehumanized, alienated, isolated, disaffected, locked in, locked out, smoked in, smoked out, outcast, outlawed, knocked down, strung up, run over, banjaxed, castrated, jillflirted, stomped, harassed, jeered at, vilified, despised, warped"—he paused to change fingers, as he tires easily—"pulled apart, soldered, molded, transfixed, invaded, pursued, abandoned, orphaned, aborted, disemboweled, and are last to be hired and first to be fired?"

"I know you pay higher rents." I gave an inch.

"And you call yourself a *Christian?*"

"I can't call myself a Christian. I'm not ready for the responsibility."

"Ah! You take *no* responsibility. I could tell that by looking at you." I broke.

"I was the kid who put the ten thousand dollars under Eddie Cicotte's pillow," I made a clean breast of everything, "later I burned down the Reichstag. What can I do, just short of killing myself, to atone to the human race?"

Giovanni relented. He removed his fingertip from my nose tip. I was grateful. A new resolve filled me. My eyes were wet as I grasped his hand.

"Let me join you and Norman in your struggle against the established order," I begged him for a chance to strike a blow against oppression. "Let me hail squad cars and pretend I thought they were taxis! Let me help snarl the system by defying local traffic ordinances! Let me lead a wade-in into Buckingham Fountain!"

Norman came over to us.

"Have *you* ever written anything that would disturb an eight-year-old?" he demanded.

"I can't remember."

"Then don't bug *me,*" he instructed me, and walked off.

"Don't bug me either," Giovanni added. *"I'm* going south."

I held him by his sleeve. "Take me with you to Atlanta," I pleaded.

He removed my hand. "The south of Corsica, *Baby,*" he corrected me, and turned to leave. I followed.

"But aren't we going to fight for the downtrodden everywhere?" I wanted to know. "Isn't that our *responsibility?*"

Giovanni turned so swiftly on me I almost lost my balance.

"Ours?" he asked, as though he had not heard aright, *"ours?* Why can't you understand that, as you represent white power, you have deprived me of the *right* to take *any* responsibility? Oh, *no,* Baby, you aren't putting *that* on me *now. I* am a victim of society! You have to make everything up to me."

"I will! I will!" I leaped at the opportunity. "I'll immolate myself in the Negro race! I'll pull a Jim Crow in reverse! I'll be a white James Baldwin and you be a black Eisenhower!"

Giovanni looked disgusted.

"Go tell your troubles to the Reverend King," he advised me. "Now ta-ta and huggy-vous. See you in the Seizième Arrondissement, Daddy-doo"—he gave me a small delighted shriek and whirled about. "Normy, you *dreadful* boy! You *goosed* me!"

"Boss Johnson can't cut the mustard!" Normy challenged him, and fled out the door.

A merry chase! Down the steps went Normy with Giovanni right on his heels, trying to catch him, and I was right on Giovanni's heels, trying to catch *him*. At the Fiftieth Street entrance to Central Park, Giovanni almost caught Normy when Normy ducked around a hansom cab and Giovanni did a U-turn on him. I guess he would have caught him at that if I hadn't gotten between them. That was *all* that saved Normy.

The last I saw of him he was heading toward the carrousel in the park with Giovanni gaining on him. I couldn't follow because I had lost my Ked Gavilan. It was under the cabman's horse, and when I went to pick it up the horse reared, waking up the cabman. He leaned over and gave me such a crack with the butt end of his whip that for a minute I forgot all about my sneaker.

"What the hell do *you* think *you're* doing?" he wanted to know, and I couldn't blame him.

"I was just trying to be some kind of supremacist, sir," I explained as best I could.

"Can't you do that without getting under a horse?"

"I just got carried away, sir."

"If I give you another crack as good as the first, you'll be carried away alright," he told me, fingering the butt of his whip.

"That first one was pretty good, sir," I complimented him. "I want to thank you for it. It cleared my head."

A policeman came up at that moment, and I was pleased that he did. He was the same one who had scolded me for looking for a drugstore in Central Park without my shoes. I was relieved that I had one on now.

"I see you're back," he congratulated me. "Where's your other shoe?"

"It's there under the horse, sir," I pointed out.

"Then get it and put it on."

I looked at the cabman. He still had a good grip on his whip.

"Are you waiting for me to pick it up and put it on for you?" the officer wanted to know.

"No, sir."

"Would you rather go to the station with one shoe than two?"

"No, sir, I'd *rather* wear both. If you give me my rathers."

"Then *get* it."

"The horse don't want me to," I explained. I didn't want to get the cab-man in trouble.

But the cabman was a regular fellow. He came down off the cab and got the shoe for me. They both watched me putting it on. I tied a neat bow so they would see I was sincere.

"Are you deformed, son?" the officer asked.

"No, sir. It's just that one shoe is a British walker and the other is a Ked Gavilan."

My friends exchanged glances.

"Don't take him in, he's harmless," the cabman suggested.

"I wasn't seriously thinking of taking him in," the officer decided in my favor. "I was just curious about his plans," and he looked at me inquiringly. The cabman looked curious too.

"Why, come to think of it, my plans are to sail from Pier 86 in an hour and a half," I recalled, checking the hour and hopping into the cab.

"To Pier 86!" I instructed the helpful cabbie, and we were off at a rollicking gallop.

"Are you going aboard without baggage?" he asked me over his shoulder.

"Stop at the first hockshop. I'm glad you reminded me," I thanked him.

On Eighth Avenue I purchased two traveling bags and a secondhand electrified typewriter the salesman assured me was a real bargain. "And I'll throw in an electrified tie," he offered.

"I'm traveling first class," I demurred. "I don't want to be conspicuous."

"Nothing conspicuous," he reassured me. "Something in a dark blue with a gray pencil stripe."

He snapped a vermilion tie around my neck, one with two Chinese-red polka dots which lit up gloriously at the touch of the battery in my pocket.

"And I'll throw in an extra set of batteries in case the salt-air damages the set attached," he told me.

And he was as good as his word.

DOWN WITH
ALL HANDS

THE CRUISE OF THE SS MEYER DAVIS

At Pier 86 a blue-uniformed baggage-hustler took both bags and the typer off my hands, and I took the elevator. "How much does a baggage-hustler get per bag?" I asked the elevator guy.

"He gets what you want to give in your heart," the guy instructed me.

"I don't want the man to work without shoes," I explained. "How much does he get per bag?"

The elevator guy stopped the lift between floors. "Let me tell you something," he reproved me; "the intelligence you breathe, that you were born with, let *that* be your guide."

Then we continued going up.

I gave the bag-hustler a two-dollar bill and stood waiting for change. "That was a deuce I just gave you," I reminded him.

"It's mouse eat mouse," he informed me.

"Easy come, easy go," I warned him, glad to get my bags back. But were I going to keep count of people who were out of their minds and those who were in them on this trip, the kooks would already be lapping the field.

However, I wasn't dismayed to learn it was mouse eat mouse and every man for himself now, more than it used to be; because whatever we have lost in brotherly feeling I am confident we have made up in spitefulness. Things work out best for everybody in the end if you just look at things right. Prospects for mice are particularly bright.

I had never crossed the Atlantic first class before. It was my first time.

My ticket assigned me to Stateroom S-1, meaning sundeck and first to chow, but a fellow in a seafaring cap told me to go to U-68. United States Lines had put me on a submarine was what I assumed. But the gangplank led up to some sort of seagoing department store that had three decks below water level, so I went down. What traveling first class means, I gathered, is that you may be sent to the galleys but you still don't have to row.

I kept going down until I hit the engine room. As long as I was there I figured I might as well inspect the turbines and the rest of that crazy stuff. It looked in better shape for crossing an ocean than myself. The pin that kept my topcoat from flapping made me self-conscious among such well-groomed engines. I went upstairs to see if the captain would take time to sew a button on for me.

In U-68 my bags were waiting but there was nobody home. The vice president of U.S. Lines had left a personal message for me on the dresser, however:

> "There is little need to describe the charm and attractiveness of this gay lady of the seas," the V.P. informed me. "There is an atmosphere of ease and relaxation about her that seems to rub off on all who stroll about her wide promenades and enjoy themselves in her roomy salons."

I fell asleep on the gay lady of the seas and dreamed that so much ease had rubbed off on me that I was strolling around trying to rub some off on a roomy saloon. Until someone wakened me by hollering All Ashore That's Going Ashore outside my door. I got up and looked out of the porthole, and what did I see but the whole New York literary scene moving past me as if I were being towed.

I'd never see that scene again nearer than now. The people I had known there were being towed away too.

I had come to know two New York crowds: one that took its cut off the traffic in horses and fighters around St. Nick's Arena, and the other that took its cut off the traffic in books. Plungers and chiselers alike, I'd found, were less corrupt than Definitive Authorities on D. H. Lawrence. The corruption of the sporting crowd was that of trying to get two tens for a five off you, but the corruption of the throngs of cocktail Kazins went deeper. They were in need of something more than two tens for a five. The fight mob possessed that spirit and humor that comes of being oneself. But lack of any inner satisfaction in being alive had left the paperfishmen feeling deprived. They owned the formulas for morality, but couldn't make them good personally. All they carried within them was the seeds of their own disaster.

Each had had his own seed. Ambitiousness had made them inventive in making footnotes. And so, like paperfish, they became transparent.

I was watching vigilantly for a glimpse of the Statue of Liberty out of the wrong side of the ship when a deck steward entered. I told him that the object in the brown metal box was a typewriter so he wouldn't try to feed it, and he urged me to go up on the sports' deck.

This was good news. "I didn't know you had one." I thanked him, and went up to look around for a couple of sports. A young man and young woman were leaning on the rail with their arms about each other, plainly waiting for the gaming to begin. I leaned beside them. If they wanted action they'd have to speak first. Neither one spoke. I finally had to.

"You look like a couple of bad losers," I told them, and left them for a part of the deck where losers aren't allowed.

I took a turn of looking at the Atlantic. I remembered when I had crossed it along with some four thousand other Americans, on *The Dominion Monarch,* in convoy. It had taken us seventeen days to make Liverpool. And seventeen years had passed since that day.

Memories made in the seasons of war are the most enduring.

I remembered the time, as though it had been but a week before, in Camp Twenty Grand, that MP's had pinched a chaplain for auctioning off an ambulance. And not even the chaplain could account for the Indian GI in the back, so drunk he could not tell the name of his own outfit. The chaplain hadn't known that, in auctioning off the ambulance, he had auctioned off an Indian.

Or trying to find my way back to the motor convoy, late at night, a snoot so full of chianti, and no pass, that I got lost out of bounds in Marseilles. I heard sea-bells under the Egyptian streets and sea-bells rang the walls.

The street I got lost on was the Rue Phocéen. The street of the Phoenicians. Its narrow heights were lit that night by a lion-colored moon. I stopped for a moment to lean against a wall. And felt a baby's fingers entwine themselves about my little finger.

Looking down I saw an Algerian child, no more than eleven or twelve. She looked up at me with darkly solemn eyes. "Come," she told me. "Come." As though "come" were the single word of English she knew.

She led me down the Rue Phocéen to a door the moonlight lay across, whose knob was no higher than her head. She went in before me, and I did not follow. At the foot of a staircase I could see only dimly, she turned and stood with her back to an unshaded bulb.

She did not ask me again, but merely waited. I shook my head, "No." And went on down the Rue Phocéen, with a great length of time seeming to have elapsed since she had taken my hand. And the moon burned darker now.

When I looked back, the door she had entered was still standing open.

Or the time that, feeling well fed, well groomed, and well endowed, the epitome of the successful private, one who had come through the war (for the war was then done) without being court-martialed, and wearing a wallet on either hip. I was on my self-contented way, at 1800 hours, to see Humphrey Bogart in *To Have and Have Not.* I stopped, in the after-chow light, to pick up the dice at an acey-deucy table. And returned to my tent at 2400 hours with both wallets emptied, feeling ill fed, badly groomed, and sadly endowed. And never have gotten to see *To Have and Have Not* yet.

Or the time the Tennessee private on the cot next to my own got the letter from his wife saying, "Honey, Don't Come Home." Upon which he said simply, "Absence makes the heart grow fonder for somebody else," and tore the letter in two.

I went down to U-68 to ask the steward how much he'd gotten for my clothes.

Apparently he hadn't had a decent bid, because all he'd done was hang up my topcoat, a new experience for the coat. If I had a needle and thread I'd sew you up myself, you sonofabitch, I told it, so at least you'd hang straight; you're trying to make people think I'm a bum. I went to the mirror and, sure enough, I'd made it.

It wasn't because I needed a shave so much that I made my next move, but from curiosity about the rapport of my electric razor and the bath-room current. It worked fine. I cleared the dresser, took the typer out of its kennel, and plugged it in. At the first jump of smoke I thought, Women and children first, but after I got the plug loose it kept jumping smoke at me, and if that wasn't lead I smelled burning I can whip Chico Vejar. A lucky thing I didn't bring a dish dryer, I thought; half the crew would have been washed overboard.

"Your dirty current blew up my nice typewriter," I accused the stew-ard, who had, it was plain, anticipated that event.

"Lots of people do that lately," he assured me contentedly.

It just wasn't a friendly ship; that was all there was to it.

Should evening ever bring you the need of an apple at sea, either go to bed or keep your fat mouth shut. All I did was to make some casual inquiry about where I might buy one, and went for a short stroll. To find, on returning, a basket heaped with apples, three hues of grapes, pears, bananas, oranges, kumquats, and litchi nuts. My first thought was that I must have an admirer aboard, probably the captain.

Now, if I could smuggle this heap down to tourist class, I thought, I might make the price of my ticket back in the greatest seagoing financial coup on record. Finally, I felt I was being treated better than I, or anyone else, deserved. A feeling from which I recovered by eating my way through the heap down to the wood. It didn't occur to me that this could happen twice in my life. Actually, it happened thereafter every time I left U-68. I couldn't take a ten-minute stroll without returning to find a basket of flora transported from the gardens of four continents to rot in my stateroom. Either I was being secretly watched or the stuff was growing out of the wall.

Once, however, I became accustomed to the admiration implicit in the presentation of these baskets, it was a back-hand slap when one basket showed up definitely short one kumquat. Let the chef collar the clown who perpetrated this cruel mockery or come in and be flogged himself, was my thinking. Yes, and be damned to the cowardly rabble traveling second and third class over my strictly first-class sea.

Had I only been able to sustain this high-wheeling mood I might have qualified as a literary critic for *Partisan Review* or a mutuel clerk at a fifty-dollar window. I might even have been able to hold both jobs. Presentable people are needed in both these lines. But the mood was melted by the strains, faint yet clear, of Meyer Davis's orchestra swinging *Drink, Drink, Drink to Old Heidelberg*—it was teatime in the cocktail bar and teatime in the lounge! Teatime in the powder room and in the hearts of men! Who can hold bitterness in his heart when music like *that* comes along?

Oh, good for *you*, Kindly Meyer Davis and your kindly orchestra, I thought, and hurried to the lounge.

I loved that lounge because it was there that the most right-thinking people aboard were to be found, drinking tea as the evening sun went down. I didn't even mind when that evening sun sank. Because then the

lights came up and I could see them all better. In fact, I was so moved by
the consciousness of being among these great-souled men and women that,
when the music stopped, I planted myself directly beneath the orchestra.

"As for Meyer Davis's orchestra," I announced, "I say *hurrah!*"

The ladies joined me in three rousing cheers for Meyer Davis, and I
retired, confident that Mr. Davis was pleased to have found so frank an
admirer aboard his ship.

Everyone wanted to know, in a sort of teatime huff, What is she so *quiet*
about? Why don't she *say* something? Why they figured the poor broad
should make more noise than anyone else because she was a duchess I
couldn't quite catch.

But there she'd be, evening after evening, waiting for the duke to finish his creamed spinach so she could get started on her sirloin. The duke
had had his quota of sirloins by the time she was born and must have been
over the hill before. Now only God and creamed spinach were keeping
him pasted together.

But for some reason he didn't want to actually fall apart till he was
eighty-two. If he had more than three days to go his reasoning was faulty.

Nobody held the duke's extreme age against him but myself. It was the
little broad that had the nerve to sit there as if she wasn't yet thirty, when
everyone knew she was every day of thirty-four, that made the ladies so
salty. Myself, I didn't dare to say she hardly looked twenty-six.

In fact, I approved of the match from her standpoint, which seemed
to be the only tenable one. What was the difference who spooned spinach
to the duke the last week before he was buried? was how I felt. Either he
had had it or he hadn't; and if he hadn't, not even Meyer Davis could help
him. If I pulled a chair up beside hers to ask, "Baby, exactly what are your
plans?" it would show her whose side *I* was on. But I never got around to
it, being too diverted by the carryings-on of my own table.

At the head of it, in full command, was a seagoing Fatty Arbuckle, a
ship's officer who looked like he lived on gold braid and some of the
threads had caught on his sleeves. Since he was at the head and I was at
the foot, there was no chance of pasting him one without knocking over
the flowers. He took an immediate liking to me too.

"Try the gin-ger, it's *tan*-gy." Fatty would recommend a dish of sweets
to Mrs. Di Santos, and then leave his mouth hanging, tongue thrust into

his cheek. I got a better grip on my fork in case he tried to close in. I thought he was after my salad. When you're a victim of overprivilege you have to be ready for anything.

(The way you know you are traveling first class, *really* first class, is by the way the olive looks up at you when the glass is gone dry, with its own special appeal, saying, *"Please* eat me." Another way you know is by the way the waves back off bowing. Across a strictly first-class sea. It may look a bit rough and wild for the brutes two decks below, and if it isn't, the crew is entitled to knock them about a bit. Otherwise, what am I paying for?)

Mrs. Di Santos, a dazzling blonde from the headwaters of the Amazon, sat at the officer's right. She never showed up till evening, and by that hour was so zonked she had to be strapped into her chair. Everyone, for that matter, had to be strapped, with a view to prevention of personal-injury suits should the tub take a sudden dip, but Mrs. Di Santos would have had to be strapped in a bowling alley.

By the time she came to dinner she had just sense enough left to put stuff in her mouth—if it ran down the inside of her neck, she swallowed it. If it didn't run she chewed it. She was a healthy young sot who liked the stuff that ran down the inside of her neck better than the stuff she was forced to chew. I think she had real class when sober but I never saw her asleep.

On Fatty's other side sat The Connecticut Child, a twenty-year-old of six foot one and a half, poor child, for I took her walking around the deck and she wasn't wearing high heels. My private guess was that someone had sent her in hope she might gain spirit and elegance. God knows she needed a touch of both. But I couldn't see how she was going to pick up either by sitting at our table. There was nobody there to pick up from. All she could learn was how to pass ginger that wasn't *that* tangy.

Beside The Connecticut Child sat the Rear-Echelon Liberal, one of the best kinds that there are. A real boy-barrister, a Fearless Philip of that vigilant breed who are forever breathing down the necks of others to see that others are as fair-minded as themselves. They have to keep you from joining the dark forces gathering against Mankind.

These dark forces are forever trying to put Shylock on TV or Fagin in a movie, while the forces of light realize that Fagin was a cockney all along. After all, the cockneys never suffered a pogrom like us—poor us—and to tell the truth neither did we. But we had relatives in Warsaw (a city we never saw) and are thus entitled to practice cold-caulking shysterism with immunity. Behind the legal barriers of the law and the moral barriers of liberalism.

This was the line Fearless Philip got on right off, conveniently dividing humanity into forces of darkness and light with no doubt whatsoever about what side *he* was on. Actually, he didn't give a hang for "The Human Condition," as he was fond of putting it, his only real concern being the condition of certain loans he had made at 12 per cent out of bank funds borrowed at 4. But this type of operation requires a moral tone with which to protect itself, and that's the tone of your Fair-Minded Liberal. (First Class, I ought to have told you before, was. purely loaded with fair-minded persons, all of whom had paid their first-class passage out of the proceeds of usury, blackmail, fraud, double-loyalties, decorous finkery, and the whole pervasive entanglement of Rapietta-Greenspongism.) I was elated to discover that I couldn't have found a better table at which to observe the judicial mind at first hand.

This was demonstrated by Fearless Philip himself, making a decision on whether he wanted *filet avec champignon* medium, on the rare side, rare on the medium side, or just five-eighths between rarefied-medium and mediumed-rare. As every cut had a toothpick stuck through its hide I couldn't see how the difference was that crucial.

What made him really appealing to everyone, however, was that he didn't mind keeping the rest of the table waiting at his chamber doors while he took the waiter into consultation. With one judicial finger on the menu designating the ultimate steak of his ultimate choice, the waiter leaning forward attentively, pencil in hand, the Rear-Echelon Liberal would frown in thought while the tension around him mounted and spread; till even the duchess, at the next table, would feel it and crane her head about to see what was affecting her neck. When he had everyone's attention, he would hand his verdict down: *"Meeeee-deeeee-yummm ray-err."*

It was done. Tension relaxed, conversation picked up.

He was the real thing in front-line finks as well as in rear-rank radicals. I still wonder how he got his start.

Then it would be my turn, and since The Connecticut Child seemed to expect something from me, I'd sneak a bit of spit on the ball myself. I'd hold the menu close to my eyes, one eye nearly shut, and ask, "What is *poissonnière?*" Immediately everyone would shout in chorus, *"Fish!"* Especially Mrs. Di Santos.

"Yeah," I'd answer shrewdly, "but which one?"

That menu was an honor roll of the Vasty Deep. Everything that disports itself in the trough of the waters or hangs upsy-downsy by eyeless suckers to the roof of the deepest sea-sunk cave, that scuttles sidewise across the sands, leaps in a spout of welcome to swimmers off Cape Cod, or comes smiling down the Gulf Stream on its hunkers with no thought of tomorrow was on that *carte.*

"Nothing much in the line of seafood tonight," I'd mutter, making it plain that the one chance a gourmet like myself had to have an edible supper was to go out and harpoon something himself.

"Do try the gin-ger," Goldbraid Fatty coaxed The Connecticut Child; "it's *tan*-gy."

"What do I say *now?"* she asked me in a lowered voice.

"Ask him if he'd like to jump ship with you," I suggested just loudly enough to be overheard at the head of the table.

Pale fruit, blue flowers, and sequined hats loaded the table where we sat, the night that the Gala Captain's Dinner arrived at last. Meyer Davis's aides stood ready on the festooned balcony above us. Goldbraid Fatty had fitted the most comical hat of all onto his head—and even at that the fun had barely *begun!* I hadn't seen a table so loaded with goodies since the last time I'd played Pin the Tail on the Donkey.

This was *it.* We were traveling first class at last. We were almost too gay to bear.

The musicians struck up a chirpified tune. "They're playing *Bluebird of Hoppiness,"* Fatty explained, letting his tongue hang for the usual effect. Then, without re moving his comical hat or putting his tongue back where it belonged, he began hacking at a swordfish as if it had tried to attack him. Mrs. Di Santos began dipping shark's fin with sherry down her neck in a way that made me glad they'd taken the trouble to pour it into a soup bowl first. They *might* have handed her a fin and a bottle. If this one ever sobered up sharks wouldn't be in it with her.

The Rear-Minded Radical conducted preliminary inquiries on the red-snapper situation. Had I been the waiter I would have made some inquiries about *him* to a red snapper.

Between the red snapper and the lobster, he trapped himself. He had committed himself verbally to red snapper in an announcement made to the entire table the day before, and now he wanted a change of venue—*if* the lobster were fresh and not frozen—but the waiter could not swear, beyond a reasonable doubt, whether the brute were frozen or fresh. He therefore arranged for lobster upon the contingency that it was fresh and *that* contingency was contingent upon *how* fresh, and just as I decided to solve everything with one straight shot to the jaw, Fatty dispatched the waiter to the research department to discover the hour at which the lobster's heart had ceased to beat.

This production so intimidated The Connecticut Child that she was afraid to order anything at all lest she be committing a misdemeanor. I told her she would impress everyone by ordering jellied eel, my thinking being that the kitchen might be working with a blacksnake who'd leap out of the jelly and sink its fangs into Goldbraid Fatty so deep we could tie a ribbon onto its tail.

THE PLAN appealed to The Connecticut Child.

"How do I *ask* for one?" she wanted to know.

"Go to the rail and holler—maybe one will give himself up," I suggested.

The waiter returned with good news for everyone—a lobster was just putting in his death throes under the auspices of the chef, after having gotten the latter's promise that he wouldn't be served to any but a first-class passenger. In that event, our right-wing progressive decided, he'd take lobster instead of red snapper. *He'd* had a choice, but what choice had the lobster had between being scalded or frozen to death? If you can live on contingency at sea you've got it made, men. That's what it's like when you're traveling first class.

Now it turned out that Goldbraid Fatty had fixed things with the kitchen for a *surprise-du-chef.* So long as I could defend myself, I resolved quietly, I wasn't going to be taken by surprise by a seagoing fry-cook. "If you can keep your head when all about you," I recalled, "are losing theirs and blaming it on you"—

Soufflé Grand Marnier would be the *surprise-du-*fry-cook, Fatty announced. And taking up a deflated balloon, he began stretching it in a fashion that might not have been suggestive had he not shut his eyes and the balloon not been as pink as skin. With his mouth open and his tongue deriving pleasure from the touch of his own lips, the effect sustained was definitely one of minor rapture. I simply couldn't see why it should be necessary to put all *that* into so simple a task as balloon-stretching.

"I take it you've been at sea a long time, sir," I suggested in a friendly tone, implying that nobody could have achieved such sureness of touch in handling balloons who had stayed on dry land.

Fatty blew the balloon up, tied it, and volleyed it toward me in a taunt as contemptuous as it was gentle. I fought down an impulse to push half a banana into his puss and say, "Call *this* tangy." As it was, I had no choice but to volley the object just as gently back. But if I didn't get the hell out of there before that soufflé arrived, I realized, they would find me hiding in the hold writing "Catch me before I kill more" on the underside of a turbine. All I wanted was to be alone with the smoldering remains of my Smith-Corona.

I fumbled with the belt that held me to my chair. The waiters were clearing the tables of dishes bearing the remains of haddock, eel, salmon, whale, sole, clam, whitefish, oysters, octopus, herring, crabs, and sword-fish and here it was only the middle of the week. Would there be enough left out there to go around come Friday? Well, no news is good news.

I was still trying to unstrap myself when the ship hit a long swell; the duke's chair with the duke in it started sliding downgrade away from the duchess—yet how proudly the old man held his little dish of creamed spinach high as he went! Like a man who knows too well how much spinach is left in his life and being careful not to lose a drop. Two waiters rushed to retrieve him, though it struck me that they might just as well have walked. Then, as they almost had him, the back-swell took chair—duke, spinach and all, sliding him right back to where he belonged. The duchess didn't look up.

She didn't know he'd been gone.

But the duke held his little dish high to show everyone he hadn't spilled any. There was a polite scattering of applause. Meyer Davis's aides burst into an encore of *Bluebird of Hoppiness.* I got free at last.

"Won't you wait for the *surprise-du-chef,* sir?" Goldbraid Fatty inquired politely as I stood up and the others eyed me strangely, "—it's *tan*-gy." Closing his eyes, he let his mouth hang in order to run his tongue across his lips.

"I'm going up on deck to look for Moby-Dick, sir," I explained. "The moment I see white water I'll let you know."

That night I dreamed that every passenger aboard, first class, second class, tourist, and cabin, all sat at some gala dinner at the same long board. I saw Goldbraid Fatty rise at the head, strangely promoted to Captain.

He did not speak, but chewed some pink sort of gum instead, with a fork gripped firmly in his right hand. Chewed slowly, with a theatrical effort, exactly as though the point of the occasion, the reason for this assembly of right-thinking persons, was to study the procedure of a ship's captain in the chewing of pink gum.

Then I sensed, with a slow apprehension, that there was more to it than this. For a meaningful bubble began to form on our Captain's lips, that grew into a pink-skinned balloon. With a snap of his tongue like a command to all hands, the officer took his lips from the balloon and blew lightly to launch it. It floated straight up, as in Zero-G gravity, and I think that at that moment we all felt a little weightless too. For every eye followed, as every eye knew, that whether the ship were to continue on course or to plummet to the bottom taking down all hands, depended upon our Captain's next move.

And with one firm stroke he plunged the fork into the balloon.

It did not burst. It gently deflated yet did not fall. It held itself above us by a special chemistry, turning itself slowly into a barely visible dust. Never growing smaller yet ceaselessy spilling: a barely visible green-gray dust. Over flowers long faded, over favors age had dried, over fruit decayed to a scatter of seed and faces gone eyeless in their dry skulls; that since time out of mind had been those of our Captain, the Rear-Echelon Radical: Mrs. Di Santos: The Connecticut Child.

And downward and down through deeps ever darker, sun-green to death-green to ultimate black, in the shroud of the waters I felt the hull seeking its sea-bottom home. I felt the hull touch, that gradual impact: then the slow cutting sand-spraying slide through coral and anemone, along the sea-drifted sands.

And lost in vast oceanic ages where, wandered by waters where no fish swim, the voice of the duchess came to me grieving:

"What are your plans *now,* Daddy-O?"

THE BANJAXED LAND

YOU HAVE YOUR PEOPLE AND I HAVE MINE

Flying the Irish Sea by Aer Lingus on a secret mission for the Irish Republican Army is serious business, especially so when the I.R.A. hasn't been let in on the plan. Although my papers, consisting of a signed photograph of Victor McLaglen and a character recommendation from ex-Mayor O'Dwyer, were cleverly concealed in the spare battery of an electrified jazzbow tie purchased on Forty-Sixth Street, I remained outwardly calm despite the altitude.

The Irish stewardess did give me one bad moment, however, when, leaning over to fasten me more securely into my seat belt, she threw me a glance of ill-concealed lust. The woman was on the verge of losing her self-control, I perceived.

When she bade me goodbye on the ramp I merely tossed my head and never saw the bold creature again.

I had come to Dublin to have a fast glance at that Irish Republican felon who would rather detonate Lord Nelson than ride free on a passenger train, a house-painting jackeen who used no ladder, and that very same party who, put before American television, had once blown a bit of well-dressed dust called John Mason Nothing off the screen.

The name was Brendan Behan, a terrible fellow in height six-foot-twelve, to be seen only maddened by drink, prone in the street or battling gendarmes on the *Rue des Martyrs*.

The panel on which this dangerous stud had disposed of the highly expendable Mr. Nothing had been billed as "The Art of Conversation," and the essence of Mr. Behan's opening thought was: "The art of conversation is dead and you Americans have murdered it as you are murdering everything else worthwhile in the world, so I'll now sing you *Kevin Barry—*

> *"And before he faced the hangman,*
> *in his dreary prison cell,*
> *British soldiers tortured Barry,*
> *Just because he would not tell,*
> *The names of his companions,*
> *And other things they wished to know,*
> *'Turn informer and we'll free you'*
> *But Kevin proudly answered 'No'. . ."*

"The art of conversation isn't the only thing dying around here," the swift Mr. Nothing (who is nothing if not swift) nipped in but didn't quite get out.

"You have your people and I have mine," the slower man replied cheerfully, "so I'll now sing you a bit of *The Dublin Brigade*—

> *"The boys of the column were waiting*
> *with hand grenades primed on the spot*
> *And the Irish Republican Army*
> *Made muck of the whole mucking lot"*

—or words to that effect. Mr. Ed Murrow then pulled the shade for the network on both conversationalists, one for being in his cups and the other for not knowing what cups were for.

"That was a better job of detonating the Art of Conversation than you did on Her Majesty's shipyard, Paddy," I decided, "and a faster trip back from Liverpool, too."

At I.R.A. Headquarters I was informed that Behan no longer carries his Sinn Fein conjurer's suitcase, and, indeed, has no present plans for blowing Lord Nelson off his pedestal overlooking O'Connell Street.

This news came as a blow, for I had brought along a camera and flash with which to catch the blind adulterer going sky-high about 4:00 A.M., as I understood that that is the hour that Behan is at his liveliest.

Needless to say, I had no intention of scaling the pedestal myself, because of the danger of falling off. There was no help for it—I would have to appoint someone else to the chore.

An I.R.A. officer wrote a name and address on a card, to which he referred as that of a youth of ancient Irish lineage whose mind had been touched by a year spent in the Department of Humanities at Yale University.

"The very man for you, and that's the lot," he added, pushing me gently onto the street.

A man who had lived a year without seeing a human face made Behan's term in Borstal seem a jolly romp in a sunny meadow, so I hurried to meet this Dublin Valjean, by name John Montague, realizing that after such an experience the man would welcome a chance to go out as a martyr.

I was confident that my appearance at 6 Herbert Street would come as a complete surprise and I have seldom been so completely surprised. Mr. Montague greeted me with a warmth recalling the passion of Buster Keaton. "We don't want your Coca-Cola culture around here," he welcomed me; "our Ancient Nation is not on the market for cool sound."

"That's *my* ancient nation you're talking about, Bud," I informed Mr. Montague, as I consider it my mission to defend culture even in its most curious forms.

"Let him in, John," Mrs. Montague suggested; "a button is missing on his old weskit."

"Can you sew in a doorway?" Mr. Montague asked her.

"We won't be able to warm up the house for half an hour," she pointed out.

"Won't you come in?" Mr. Montague invited me.

I knew they would like me in Dublin.

Mr. Montague closed the door behind me; I stepped into a small but comfortable apartment; he opened another and I stepped through that into the backyard of MacDaid's Pub. Entering by a rear door, I had ordered a Guinness when Mr. Montague came through the front accompanied by a massively constructed, slightly stooped man of fifty-three wearing double-lensed glasses and an overcoat that would have made Charles de Gaulle a better fit, if De Gaulle didn't care what he wore any more.

"Meet Patrick Kavanagh," Montague introduced the gentleman with the N.S.F. sign on his forehead.

Mr. Kavanagh squirrel-eyed me, then roared, "I'm a delicate cray-ture!" Where he had gotten the idea that I wanted to fight him I'm sure I don't know, but Kavanagh's voice is a foghorn gone mad. What it was when he had both lungs I don't care to consider but am content that I wasn't in Dublin at that time.

His voice is also that of the best Irish poet since Yeats. But he is a peasant, and has none of Yeats's grand self-dramatization.

"So be reposed and praise, praise, praise
The way it happened and the way it is."

He is the poet of the way it happened and the way it is; very close, in his celebration of man's ordinary hours, "the arboreal street on the edge of town" or the bleakness of a hospital ward, to Walt Whitman.

This is a poet to whom love is nowhere debarred. One who "the common and banal heat can know." Yet he is no mere country bird watcher in love with the countryside: his reverence is as sophisticated as that of Gerard Manley Hopkins.

He is in praise of sensuality, of "the explosive body, the tumultuous thighs" where down some country lane he sees Miss Universe—"though she is not the virgin who was wise."

Patrick Kavanagh, his poems inform us, is a poor man, a bachelor, one who has suffered illness and is acquainted with desperation. But who is saved by his gift of loving and the contentment he has drawn from undramatic days, where, "leafy with love-banks and the green waters of the canal" he finds redemption in the will of God—"in the habitual, the banal," growing with nature again "as before I grew."

"A sad thing," I observed, taking care to make my voice sound weighted with melancholy, "to think that the Irish are vanishing."

"Too good to be true," Mr. Kavanagh decided, and began a headlong row with a bartender by demanding that his vanishing credit be restored by a check signed in Erse on an English bank. I shared the bartender's fear that the check would bounce signed in any language, and Mr. Kavanagh made no effort to defend the check's soundness. His view, rather, was that any bartender who would not help to force the English banking system to a decision on the legal acceptability of Erse was plainly a successful business man from Belfast. Kavanagh isn't called the last peasant poet of Europe for nothing.

These things matter in Eire, a country with an N.S.F. sign on her forehead.

"We want no part of the Twentieth Century," Mr. Kavanagh decided as though I were forcing something on him; "we wish to belong only to ourselves." It struck me that it isn't too hard a task to disassociate oneself from something to which one doesn't belong anyhow.

When the Guinness had begun to affect Mr. Montague's mind, I inquired his frank opinion of Lord Nelson. He merely replied that he could live content without the monument overlooking O'Connell Street.

"If you scale the pedestal I'll get the gelignite," I offered quickly, before he could back out of my trap. But I was overeager. Mr. Montague pleaded inability to scale the pillar upon which Nelson stands. It looked like shameless cowardice to me, one of the worst kinds that there are. I excused Mr. Montague with ill-concealed scorn.

"Don't be a martyr, then," I told him; "*be* an old stick-in-the-bog."

"Not every Irishman craves martyrdom," he replied, but I think he was exaggerating.

"'They went forth to battle/ But they always fell/'" I quoted, "'Bravely they fought and nobly but not well/ And on the hard-fought field they always fell.'"*

"A man belongs to himself," was his reply, groping for Kavanagh's escape route.

"You belong to nothing but Guinness," Mrs. Montague, strictly a non-escapist, only what was she doing in Ireland after having been born in France, told her husband. Then added, "And neither does this other pseudointellectual," putting me in front of her broom as well.

"Nobody in Dublin belongs to anything but Guinness," she went on, sweeping all reason aside; for they also drink whiskey in Dublin.

Mrs. Montague is the only person in Dublin who doesn't drink. Inasmuch as there is nothing in Dublin for a Frenchwoman to drink, this is not a spectacular virtue.

"Would you like some black pudding?" Mrs. Montague asked, and I began to dress for dinner immediately. If black pudding was to be the main course—just fancy what the *surprise-du-chef* would be!

The *surprise-du-chef* was that same black pudding, something that everyone ought to try on a day when everything else goes wrong. It explains why no restaurant on earth features Irish cooking. Simple: there is no Irish cooking.

"It's too bad the French didn't win Ireland," I observed; "at least they would have taught you people to cook."

"We cook very well," Mr. Montague insisted, "we merely lack the in-gray-dients."

---

* *Studs Finnegan's Wake*, by Molly Bloom.

I hadn't thought of that.

So we walked as night was falling to see the swans come down The Grand Canal.

They came like ghosts of swans, silently, one at a time.

John Montague spoke the name of each as it passed, softly, in some tongue I had never heard; as though he had known each when they were men.

Through the perpetual dark green mists that forever abide, we walked the banks of The Grand Canal.

"That tree looks like a palm," I observed to John Montague.

"That is because it *is* a palm," he informed me.

I had not known palm trees grew in Dublin.

They do. It has something to do with the Gulf Stream, and they are the only things in the town that aren't potted.

When we returned to 6 Herbert Street, I succeeded in wedging myself into the doorway with Montague, so as to preclude being left outdoors. But the doorway of 6 Herbert Street is narrow and we were wedged so fast that neither of us could move despite a good deal of shoving. Mrs. Montague had the presence of mind to butt her husband in the small of his back, thus breaking the wedge, and I came in second.

Montague, once I was inside, became his old gracious self, opening a door that looked as if it led to a guest room but didn't.

"The last time I went through that one I wound up between Patrick Kavanagh and a bartender," I reminded my host, stubbornly holding my ground. "How about that *other* door?"

"Why don't you try it and find out for yourself?" he invited me, a peculiar huskiness in his voice.

"It's raining out, John," Mrs. Montague reminded him, and opened a passage through which I passed and, what do you know—I was in a wee bedroom with a wee bed where a wee fire burned in a wee stove, with wee bars on a wee window! I always like a window with bars as it keeps creatures of the night from seizing me in the dark.

That night I dreamed I was walking up a ramp to board a plane, and saw an Aer Lingus stewardess at the top of the ramp who smiled down at me with a look so steady I understood she didn't like flying anywhere without me.

I was strong for joining her, and tried to hurry. But it's a tiring climb up a ramp that has no end with the old sky darkening.

I had time only so long as the steady girl kept smiling down. "Haven't you flown with me before?" she asked, extending her hand for mine to touch—and dream stewardess, dream plane, and dream turned slowly onto its side at a very great height.

To leave me adrift in those perpetual mists that forever drift: along the banks of The Grand Canal.

It rained all night and it rained all day and then Mrs. Montague said, "It's time to have fun," and I thought so myself.

Only, how would a thing like that be done in a rain-sodden black-pudding town?

On a sea that just *might,* some night, swallow all down, Ulster and Belfast, the orange and the green, shawlie and culchie each alike, bogman and Fenian both the same, doubting priest and believing doubter, lovers of Jesus and lovers of Joyce, the National Farmers Association along with the *Amharciann na Mainistreach?* So long as I did not hear them keening from forty fathoms down I would not mourn too long.

Yet in such a great wash Siobhan McKenna might also be taken, and for that reason alone I stand firm as Bray Head against Ireland being washed into any sea.

People who find it hard to put up with the Irish should consider, for one moment, the job Brendan Behan has had his whole life with no relief but for a few years in Borstal. And there were Irish there too.

"The Last Dive of Dublin" was the name of the fun-place we found. A dozen aimless-looking women and girls sat about two jukes, one green and one white; as though all had been waiting for days for someone to come by and drop a dime in the coin box. If this is a dive, it came to me, Ireland already has vanished.

Or did it ever truly exist outside of the few Days of Easter Week, when it came onstage and then went off; having presented a drama, if not a revolution, to a world that has always loved Irish theatricals?

Waiting for the fun-things to begin, I danced with Mary, a girl of twenty, who was going to America to work as a domestic "in a place called Pasadena."

"I'm fed up here," Mary told me, putting my cap on her head to pretend she was now having fun.

I might as well tell you right here that, when she did that, we had both had the peak of the evening.

"I hope you don't get fed up with Pasadena," I voiced a hope while concealing a doubt.

"I'm already fed up with Pasadena," she told me; "I hate the very sight of the place." Under the cap her eyes turned inward to a dark hollow no Pasadena would fill.

It isn't hard to see how a young person would feel fed up with a nation unable to offer its young women more than a life between the shafts of old drudgery's two-wheeled cart forever going uphill and then the snifflers coming around saying, "She's happier now she's in Heaven."

> ". . . for such is the condition of man in this old world (and we better put up with it, such as it is, for I never saw much hurry on the part of priests in getting to the next one, nor parsons nor rabbis, for the matter of that; and as they are all supposed to be experts on the next world, we can take it that they have heard something very unpleasant about it which makes them prefer to stick it out in this one for as long as they can)."

—writes the man who was once forced to a very hard choice between his nation and his faith.

I was reaching for a drop of wine when the glass was snatched from my hand by the proprietor's stout wife, seizing all glasses empty or full, out of hands of drinkers thirsty or dry. Under the tables went the lot. Everyone sat up straight as in church with nothing before them but ashtrays.

Two inspecting officers entered from offstage, where they had been waiting their cue. Now they were seriously bent on discovering evidence of drinking in teetotaling Dublin.

This isn't the last dive, I thought; it's simply the end.

The officers inspected the ceiling, clothes racks, flowerpots, tabletops and juke boxes without finding evidence.

Everyone in the bar felt pleased with himself, after the officers left with a warning, for having outwitted the law. It struck me, however, that the Dublin Police Department is not so well organized as that of Chicago, where an owner would have had a full hour's warning of a raid instead of ten minutes.

Then the music began and the dancing began and the drinking began and the singing began, with the green juke taking the lead—

Goodbye, goodbye, County Mayo

"Fed up," Mary repeated, "everything."

But this time just to herself.

I'll Take You Home Again Kathleen They Must Have Made Angels in Ireland for My Mother Came from There—the whole tinpan vale of Glocca Morra, along with the Vale of Tralee, doesn't work anymore. The young Kathleen Mavourneens as well as the Mikes pack up overnight and leave Dublin as though they had never had a friend there; and never write home as though they had never had a home.

"Gone to America" is the word some leave chalked on a broken farmhouse.

Broken farms left to turn to earth on the great unused stretches of Irish land that there is none to work.

"Gone to America" is the unseen legend left above the Dublin tenement door where some girl who says "Fed up," gets fed up at last.

Ten millions of people once lived in a country that now supports less than half the population of Chicago: a people whose fresh magic was a wonder and a light are going into that good night.

The Germans, whom the world could better spare, may bring in neighborly little Volkswagens to distribute from Ireland's ocean ports, to make more work and better pay for many Marys and Mikes, as well as effecting great savings for German enterprise.

If The Ancient Nation says good night in a Volkswagen, that will be a prettier sight.

I can't wait till Mary sees Pasadena.

Dublin is part city and part high-noon sky whose clouds as white as ocean sails veer changefully between sun-wave and rain across a changeful sea.

Till evening cracks Heaven with the sad hues of old stained glass. Then mad saints long-martyred, and the memory of them among men, seem equally cracked. This twilit sky is the work of painters of holy dusks, everyone drunk or cracked. However so holy, all drunken.

All cracked.

To subdivide this sky for television, partition it for air rights or pierce it with a skyscraper, partakes of blasphemy here. But "blasphemy is the comic verse of belief" the aphorist Behan comments. The Irish are already sufficiently apprehensive about the world about them. Though they name their apprehension reverence.

So when the low roofs are huddling in the cold like shawlies at prayer, bolder souls go to MacDaid's to challenge pope, priests, and saints—it is dark in there and MacDaid won't inform on them.

Dubliners divide their lives largely between pew and pub. Some are faithful to both, going drunken to Mass and atoning later in Guinness.

"If a man is horrified by another's sins," Behan believes, "it is because he is uneducated, inexperienced and a hypocrite. Certain things must be restrained in the world for our convenience—but for our convenience only. Why can't we let it go at that?"

I had come to Ireland at the time that the Liverpool whores were coming over the water to see Ireland whip Wales at rugby. The subject of the day, everywhere, was Ireland's chances.

It was a very important contest, I understood from Mr. Montague, because of the present low state of Irish morale, what with Scotch outselling Irish whiskey in New York. Yet, in the highly unlikely circumstance that Wales should actually win, please to bear in mind that Gaels, true Gaels, never play rugby at all. That being a sport devised by British begrudgers.

The Irish squad was therefore made up wholly of players from the North Counties, every begrudger of them a Black Protestant. Thus a victory by Wales would be a blow to Ulster: hence a triumph ardently to be hoped for by true Gaels. It was by now quite plain that no one in The Floating Ballroom could lose, whatever the result of this crucial contest.

Then again, what did it matter who won between Protestants? Either way, Eire was in.

Beneath their certain faith that Ireland could never lose lies a faith equally certain that she must finally fail.

"The Floating Ballroom" was so named by Behan's Aunt Maggie, who was present, as well as was Behan's mother and that star of American television, Brendan Behan himself.

Aunt Maggie occupies a special fame in Behan's heart, as she does in hearts of others, because of her moment of truth, where the dead lay against the dead before the P.O. Then she materialized in the midst of gunfire to inquire of her husband, among the holdouts inside, "Are you going to work this morning or not, Mr. Tremble?"

Mrs. Behan recalled another occasion when Behan had given her ten pounds and she had subsequently been so deceived by Guinness that she had wakened wearing only one boot. "It's a lovely drink," she assured her glass that she held no hard feelings for its deception.

Nevertheless Ireland has a very good rugby team despite the fact that true Gaels don't play rugby. They play Gaelic football, an entirely different diversion.

I didn't ask whether the Irish Gaelic football team had yet won a match, as I was outnumbered.

The capture of the American liquor market by Scotch whiskey, while Irish whiskey has failed to scale the wall, struck Mr. Montague and Behan as a monstrous irony, since Irish drinkers in New York outnumber Scots at roughly fifty to one. What were the people of The Ancient Nation drinking in New York bars for the love of God, both men marveled.

"The last time I saw the Oak Room Bar," I recalled, "the people of The Ancient Nation were drinking Drambuie. The only customer drinking Irish whiskey was wearing kilts. But, since you raise the question, I once knew a man named Guinness who would touch nothing but champagne."

"That's surely odd," Behan remembered; "I once knew a man named Champagne who would touch nothing but Guinness. "

The great game of The Floating Ballroom is to discover a triumph of Irish sporting life to redeem the country's economic defeat.

In this I tried earnestly to help by recalling my father's memory of John L. Sullivan and how proud Dad had always been of having once shaken the hand of The Boston Strong Boy, for had it not been for my father grasping his hand, The Boston Strong Boy would have fallen on his face, he was then that weak from the drink.

The company appeared curiously unimpressed by this colorful legend from life's other side, so I told how my own mother had once taken me, a mere tot of eight, to hear Honeythroat Reagan sing *If He Can Fight Like He Can Love / Good Night Germany!*

My friends remained unmoved.

Then there was Kenny Brenna, I added, for I perceived that my friends were eager to hear more, who used to sing *O Why Did I Pick a Lemon in the Garden of Love / Where Only Peaches Grow?* And Doyle the Irish Thrush!—a fantasist who billed himself as a heavyweight pugilist but was retired after knocking himself out on a ringpost at Madison Square Garden and yet he married well.

"It's a lovely drink," Mrs. Behan observed.

"I'm also a friend of Roger Donoghue," I now clinched some lasting friendships, "the last Brooklyn-born fighter whose father still speaks with a brogue. In fact I was at ringside the night Donoghue was knocked out by Solly Levitt."

"It is not a momentous occasion for a fighter to get knocked out," Mr. Montague observed.

"For anyone to get knocked out by Solly Levitt was a most momentous occasion," I was forced to correct Mr. Montague.

Although it was a day of driving wind and slating rain, with fog coming in from the sea and mist coming up through the floor, it was sunny enough in The Floating Ballroom withal, and the sun shone even more brightly at news that local parties had thrown a sleeper across the rails of the train to Belfast and derailed it that same afternoon of slating rain. Every time the I.R.A. tosses a sleeper across the rails in hope that whoever gets his back broken may be from Belfast, The Ancient Nation is that much closer to unification, I gathered, looking at my Guinness a bit closer.

"You don't necessarily achieve a goal by stepping *directly* toward it," Mr. Montague sensed my doubts. "Look at the Algerians."

I hadn't realized until that moment that the F.L.N. was going about matters indirectly. Yet I had gotten wind of an address made in French by Behan, appropriately enough on the *Rue des Martyrs,* demanding that the F.L.N. begin to emulate the I.R.A. Meaning, I take it, that they should give more thought to the possibilities of dramatizing their revolution for the European stage. Less people get hurt onstage than in street fighting.

"We've been banjaxed," was how Montague put it.

"Fughed," Behan explained, "from a height."

Run over by the British economy like a truck over a biscuit tin.

For the Irish dissipate their violence. They make war like the American Indian, like schoolboys, blowing up monuments that no longer stand for anything and then going home; as though unable to sustain a hostility. They upset everyone with their skirmishes, while the English keep a general goodwill on their side by the control they exert over their own violence. The fact is that the English are a much more violent tribe than the Irish, but the Irish have all the bad manners.

"I can tell a Protestant half a mile off by his walk," Montague disposed of all issues in one.

"O death where is thy sting-a-ling-a-ling," I hummed, *"O grave where is thy victory?"*

"If that tie is el-ectrified," Montague accused me, "when is it going to light up?"

"I'm told the Irish are a vanishing race," I replied, "but I don't see anyone here leaving."

"She has one son dead and the other vanished"—Mrs. Behan nodded toward Aunt Maggie—*"vanished."*

The great Irish trick is to take care to hate most that which is farthest; so as not to be obliged to do anyone harm. Had the wise old warning, "Hit him again, he's Irish," not been invented before Brendan Behan was born, it would have been needed at that moment. Where most men have a chin Behan has a challenge attached to a face constructed deliberately for provoking blows. Thus it deploys defiance while concealing pity. And hence his intellectual belief in the class struggle is modified by his emotional conviction that the only class is Mankind.

Not so many people get hurt that way either.

"I was nearer to them," he tells of the English inmates of Borstal who, like himself, had come from working-class homes, "than they would ever let Ken be. I had the same rearing as most of them, Dublin, Liverpool, Glasgow, London. All our mothers had done the pawn-pledging on Monday, releasing on Saturday. We all knew the chip shop and the picture house and the fourpenny rush of a Saturday afternoon, and the summer swimming in the canal and being chased along the railway by the cops.

"But Ken they would never accept. In a way, as the middle class and upperclass in England spend so much money and energy in maintaining the difference between themselves and the working class, Ken was only getting what his people had paid for, for he was more of a foreigner than I, and it's a lonely thing to be a stranger in a strange land."

For some reason unclear to myself, I launched into a long discourse on the career of The-Man-Who-Could-Throw-Harder-Than-Anybody—one Boom-Boom Beck—an athlete who pitched for the Chicago Cubs in Hack Wilson's day.

"Boom-Boom could throw so hard," I told the company around me, "that if he hit you on a fingertip you'd go down. He could throw so hard that his catcher never had to use signals. There was nothing to signal for.

Boom-Boom had no drop, he had no slider. He didn't even have a noth-ing-ball. He just threw harder than anyone else on earth.

"Sometimes he threw so hard the ball got past the batter, and when that happened the backstop would be pulled onto his hunkers by the impact.

"Fortunately for the Cubs' catching staff, this seldom happened. The bat itself, it seemed, was what Boom-Boom was aiming at. Boom-Boom's throw would streak back like a falling meteor into the right-field stands. In event of a direct hit, it would zonk against the big white E that topped the center-field scoreboard. If a batter ever caught the pitch square it was almost as sure as mortar fire to kill five or six workmen tarring a roof two miles away. Well, that was why they called him Boom-Boom."

The company remained unimpressed.

Another thing Mr. Beck had in common with Mr. Behan, that I did not mention, was that if he wanted to have a drink, he was going to have a drink. And if he wanted to have two drinks, he was going to have two drinks. And the more drinks he had, the more stubborn he would get; the more stubborn he would get, the more drinks he would have. And the more drinks he would have, the harder he would throw the next day for being that mad at himself for having been so stubborn the day before.

And, of course, the harder he would throw, the harder he would get hit, and the harder he got hit, the more he wanted a drink, and if Boom-Boom wanted a drink he was going to have a drink and if Boom-Boom wanted two drinks—his manager summed the matter up in one phrase —"He looks like a twenty-game winner between line drives."

Yet nobody managed Boom-Boom, least of all himself.

No one, least of all himself, manages Brendan Behan. "The first duty of a writer," he has expressed the conviction, "is to let his country down. He knows his own people best. He has a special responsibility to let them down."

"I once had occasion to drink with Dylan Thomas about the time God got him by the short hairs," I recalled. "I asked him why he hit the stuff so hard and he said he didn't know. But I'm still sure that the world at the bottom of a whiskey glass is a different world than that at the bottom of a cup of tea."

The Dublin house painter with the fighter's mug leaned across the table and touched my tie tentatively, with a faintly incredulous smile. I pressed the bulb in my pocket and it lit up fine.

He lifted his glass, holding nothing but water, and clinked it against the Guinness in mine.

"Fugh the bedgrudgers," was Behan's toast.

The Irish have a very good rugby team.

That was soundly thrashed by Wales.

The following morning I walked up the ramp of an Aer Lingus plane and was pleased to see, smiling good morning down at me from the top of the ramp, an Irish stewardess waiting there expecting just me.

"Haven't you flown with me before?" she wished to know.

"No, Baby," I told her, "but I'm ready to fly with you now."

Farewell, picturesque Dublin, quaint metropolis of Old Erin, where the poor contrasts with the very poor and the old contrasts with the prehistoric. And the fairly sober contrasts with the stinking drunk.

Adieu and farewell, bustling capital where the world at the bottom of a glass of tea contrasts with that at the bottom of a glass of Guinness.

Goodbye, County Mayo, goodbye.

THE SOUTH OF ENGLAND

THEY WALKED LIKE CATS THAT
CIRCLE AND COME BACK

Now, I had once been most comfortably stationed on the drowsing coast of Wales in the dreaming town of Tenby in the sleeping slough of Penally.

For all the seasons of war.

And it had been a better country for our knowing, by bulletins tacked to morning reports, that elsewhere bombs were falling.

Elsewhere sirens told disaster, elsewhere great walls fell. Elsewhere V-1's violated the sheltering sky.

But that was only upon a location, a device, a mythical nation called "South of England." A make-believe site invented by Winston Churchill permitting the *Luftwaffe* to unload its bombs harmlessly and hurry back home to Old Heidelberg. Some *Luftwaffe*.

This dreaming air, this sleepwalking rain, this land of ancestral mists reminded me so much of Champagne County, Illinois, that I was content to be anywhere up North. For up North was where wars were never fought.

Surely the proud Federals bivouacked, in equal proportion of home-sick hillbillies and Chicago alley-finks of which I was a leading member, had simplified the life-and-death struggle of Western Civilization to a matter of staying in good with our nurses. Again I was a leading member.

We liked our nurses because their contempt for our officers supported our own agreement that they were jerks to a man. Indeed, our nurses' disdain for their fellow officers made the EM mind to boggle. We *admired* the nurses.

Therefore when they challenged us to a softball contest we accepted with pleasure. We were flattered.

When they whipped us, 10-8, in the tenth inning, we congratulated one another upon having forced officers into an extra inning to beat us. We were proud of our showing.

And even more proud of our first baseman, who had been sufficiently gallant to keep his big foot off the bag long enough to let the tying run get on first. However, in letting a grounder go through him to put the winning run on, we felt that he had gone too far.

As I had not let the grounder through me through gallantry, I protested, claiming honest ineptitude. My claim was accepted so readily I was shocked. For though the TO listed me as a private of no class at all, my real rank was Infielder, Very First Class.

Subsequently, when the nurses offered the EM another chance, the public humiliation of being busted to right field faced me.

I had an escape hatch. The Service had been pressing me to accept a pass, in token recognition of the steadfast fashion in which I had held my position on the TO without shooting through the ranks, and now was the time to accept the distinction.

That the English girls were becoming impatient to see me I was well aware, but my plan was to make their hearts yet gladder by bringing each a tropical goodie. Such as a Sunkist California orange.

These I stole under cover of KP duty from our mess hall, and boarded the train the following morning with a dozen beauties cleverly concealed in my overcoat.

"I'm going to the North of England, sir," I informed the train conductor briskly, realizing it would cheer up the kindly fellow to know he was the one bringing me.

"No, son," the surly old bore assured me, "You're going to the South of England."

Well I be dawg. So *that* was it. I was heading for Sunny Soho, bustling metropolis of sea-washed Piccadilly where they pick bomb fragments instead of cotton and the train was already in motion.

It was raining in Soho. It was raining in Hampstead. It was raining in Kent. In Piccadilly there weren't enough doors for the girls on the game. There weren't enough gaffs for the matter of that. That was the kind of war winter was waging on women in Soho.

Theirs was the Dunkirk of which no one spoke. Yet they had come by all available craft.

To walk like sisters, pairing off under parasols of summers past, or a cheap winter umbrella, through the rain.

They walked like cats that circle and come back. Slowly wheeling, in an encompassing circle, the black taxis of Piccadilly outflanking them.

That wheeled like little hearses and came back. When evening came the women fell into ranks, for all came from a single nation. Enlistees of the eldest republic, whose citizens live by the sweat of their sex.

Enlistees who look straight ahead without knowing name, rank, or serial number of the enlistee beside them.

By the sweat of their sex. By the tools of their trade.

The woman pressed into prostitution by war is more at ease with herself than the one who has had no more than the complicity of peace. That men are to blame for her hard lot is more plain then. So when she puts the issue straight to the soldier, he has to feel, if he's any sort at all, that her need is the only real consideration.

For she comes like a sister in the rain.

The American GI who carries himself with conscious superiority of the natives is, at the same moment, secretly uneasy because his superiority depends upon access to cheap toothpaste. He carries his PX card wrapped in guilt. Or his guilt wrapped in a PX card, as you will. This makes him a setup for sister. Especially in a rain.

For what is a big grown man doing toting a box of nut-filled Hershey bars around, whether it comes from the PX or was shipped by Mother? Who does he think he is, in a fish-and-chips country, to be eating chocolate?

Actually he doesn't feel like eating the sickening junk himself; yet it's sweeter than money to the girls of Piccadilly. If he hands it to one and walks off, he's really a mark. If he trades it off for love, she's the mark. Then too, what becomes of his promise to Mother, to return to her as pure as the day he was inducted? The soldier is wisest to pay the girl in pounds, and put the candy on her as a fringe benefit. Let Mother be the mark. She always was.

It was the only fun Mother ever had.

Candy or oranges, I happened to have no particular problem about Mother. The only promise I'd ever made her was not to give anything of value away without getting something of greater worth for it. She had gotten into this rut through Pa's uncanny knack for coming off poorer than ever. Had it not been his toil, sweat, blood, and tears that had filled me so early with a determination to be a bum? Now neither God nor Patton was going to interfere with *my* career.

Bringing goodies to hungry London made me feel benign. After all, these weren't those puny Florida growths, all seeds and wrinkled peelings. These were California dandies, paunchy as a producer of B-pictures but not so pale, burned a deep orange streaked with red. (The coloring is applied in the Imperial Valley.)

The girl fortunate to win me as well as an orange would have to be a nicely sliced mandarin herself, it goes without saying. I wasn't about to be trapped by somebody's old blind hair-covered owl of a grand-stepmother.

Fleeting as fireflies under eaves, tiny flashlights revealed a woman's shadow in every nook. Click on and click off, now you see her now you don't. More than one grandmother owl never had it so good, doing better by flash than she would have by day. And blessing the Germans every night that good times were here at last. Praying a bit that they might last longer even if it cost her her son-in-law, a bombardier in the R.A.F.

"*There's* a notion for a shrewd free-lance journalist," I reminded myself, peering shrewdly, like a free-lance journalist, and consequently seeing nothing at all. "R.A.F. flier on hospital pass picks up a girl in pitch-dark London, goes to her hotel with her where she switches on the light. 'Turn it off,' says Bombardier Cathcart, for he recognizes her as his estranged wife, Bess Cathcart. He himself is unrecognizable as he has had plastic surgery after coming down, full of night-fighter pills, in flames over Slough-on-West.

"He uses her in a fashion sufficiently vile and then declines to pay her a shilling. 'Not a shilling, Bess my girl,' he tells her, switching the light on while buttoning himself, 'for I am the honest lad who married you at Slough-on-West! Heah! Heah!'

"'And I am the sensible lass who divorced you at Fugh-the-East,' she assures him, hooking her bra without his help, 'and I recognized you on sight because on you plastic surgery isn't noticeable. Now hand over four pounds tuppence you bloody cheap officer toff or I'll have Four-F MacHeath, my mighty Bulgarian ponce, dash your head in on the ceiling and then bone you like a fish. *Theah! Theah!*'"

This epic of passion in war and peace was interrupted by a girl who bumped into me deliberately, as I had no idea where I was going.

One who had the grace to throw the light of her flash on her own face instead of upon my own. A heart-shaped face with wide-spaced eyes burning green and a smile that lit up small flashlights all over town.

She led me into a Mack Sennett, where I sat upright, being correct. She leaned against a corner of the thin upholstery, sniffing. There was a distinct scent of oranges in the air.

'What's in the sack, Yank?"

"Oranges."

"Air-enjez? Whut the bluidy hell you tottin' *air-en-jez* around London for?"

"I'm very fond of the fruit," I assured her primly. I peeled one and offered it to her primly to prove it.

She shook her head. "I haven't eaten a brute like that in years, Yank. It'd make me deathly ill. Now if you have a bit of chocolate—"

I pitched the peeling into the dark.

"Is it much farther to your apartment, Miss—"

"You're *in* my apartment, Yank."

"If we have to go about Piccadilly again it'll cost you another half-crown, Sandy," the driver helped out.

On the other hand the meter was clicking like mad. Was he working it with his foot?

But as we circled Eros we began to pick up speed and were going at a really breakneck rate when we smashed headlong into a shattering *bloooo* that rocked the town and brought the cab to a wobbling halt with myself on my hunkers on the floor.

"Sink the *Bismarck!*" I exclaimed. "What was *that?*" Either we'd smashed into something in the dark or this was an unusual girl. It had left me feeling curiously weightless where I sat.

The odor of oranges was blown off by the scent of an ashen debris like the very smell of weightlessness.

"Just the disgustin' Germans up to their dirty business," she assured me from the dark upholstered corner.

"Less is known about weightlessness," some scrap of newspaper knowledge blew through my mind, "than any other stress man is likely to encounter." I sat on the floor of the cab until my weight returned. Then I got up and sat beside the girl. Together we peered out at the dark, lit momently by flashbulbs as before—but with a difference now. Now we were like people who had been blown off the earth and back and would never forget that moment when we did not own our own weight.

"What *was* it?" I finally dared to ask.

"Just a V-2, Yank."

I had come to the South of England. A pitch-black nation where pay-ing for love with Sunkist oranges made the *Luftwaffe* mad as all get-out.

Later in a dim café called the Café Cypriot, the girl told me that just the scent of the things had made her ill.

"I'm very sensitive to smells, ever since I was buried, in the time of the V-1's," she told me.

She had come to London from Birmingham and had been caught, on her first date with an American, below a falling wall near Paddington Station.

"That was all for my poor chap, whoever he was, but all I got was bruises. *Frightened?* Here I was hearing the diggin' blokes chattin' it up and what would Mum say if I were found dead with an Amerikun? Mum wouldn't minded my bein' found dead with a British lieutenant, but with an Amerikun and him not even an officer. I've never been so frightened since, Yank.

"I couldn't bear those nasty screaming V-1's, where I had to run and hide even though I hadn't hurt anyone. Why should I be ducking under-ground when I've done nothing wrong? It's much nicer now with the V-2's. If you hear it hit you know you're alright. If you don't there's noth-ing to worry about."

Later I kissed Sandy good night and she walked off into the dark. She was hardly out of sight when I started after her, sensing an inner wave of loneliness I wished to fend off. I made a complete circle of Piccadilly, try-ing to find the Café Cypriot again, thinking the people in there might tell me where to find her. But there was no Café Cypriot.

I tried all the side streets leading out of Piccadilly Circus, and finally began asking M.P.'s. Nobody had heard of the place.

I hired a cabman who assured me he was acquainted with the place and knew Sandy.

"This is it, Yank," he finally told me.

The place I got out in the dark was the same place I'd gotten in. Nobody, neither M.P.'s nor British police, had ever heard of the Café Cypriot.

I searched, by cab and on foot, for her and for the Café Cypriot until I had just time to get back to the vasty train shed.

The lights on the night train to Wales went out whenever the little train rocked. It was on and off, awake and asleep, the whole rocking night. I felt strangely emptied of love and desire.

Yet asleep or awake on that cold returning my mind returned again and again to the girl.

During the week that followed I became the biggest sport in the PX. I bought a woman's comb-and-brush set, a bracelet, a cigarette lighter, a tiny scissors, and a bottle of *Cuir de Russie,* purported to be a Paris perfume.

The EM had beaten the nurses in the return match, and in the playoff game I played errorless ball, handling one flyball in right field without mishap. We lost.

The bulletins tacked to the morning report continued to report bombings in the South of England. But it was no longer a make-believe land to me.

Storing Sandy's gifts in my duffel bag against the day I would get another pass, the South of England became my own country.

On the last day of the year the Order of Departure was posted. The Channel train left in a misting rain.

It was raining in Soho. It was raining in Piccadilly. It was raining in Wales.

In the years that followed my tour of the South of England, in the time of the V-2's, my life turned purposeful; as though cabled to a diesel-powered destiny.

Then strangely in dreams I began to walk between small stars; strung on a moment through some pitch-black undismayed town. Stars that lighted human figures, in doorways of lodgings and old cafés, before they flickered out. I would see myself standing before a café with a name that had been painted over. In dreams I sought a place whose name was altered; yet inside nothing would be changed. And in the end, wherever I walked, I would have to go through this remembered door.

Thus through dreams I came to know that I was still riding a taxi with dimmed foglights, looking for someone I would never find.

Wherever I got out it would be before the Café Cypriot.

In the cold light of London of 1960, the South of England was gone for keeps.

In its place, a city of neon towers climbed. Topped by one in which I was welcomed by one MR. BRANDYWINE. Who greeted me by racing down a line of colored lights to fetch me, then glancing over his shoulder as he raced back to see if I were following. He wished to show me new wonders, I understood.

I had seen the new wonders. I wanted only to see old Soho.

The Underground was still an iron hole down which escalators moved to an English Hell. The guardian lions of Eros looked much shrunken. The British were apparently still trying to shake the Irish off their backs, as I judged, by signs saying IRISH GO HOME TO A BOOM IN JOBS.

SINK THE *Bismarck!*

billboards demanded all over Piccadilly.

What, I thought, do we have to go through all *that* again?

A press, an international multitude, moved all day around the guardian lions. When the red night-lights of London fell, I saw the guardian lions stir.

The evening neon moved their hearts.

Taxis no longer circled ceaselessly. Instead, they waited, still like so many hearses, in a line down the center of the street. They still looked like they should be horse-drawn.

I climbed into one and off we went on a four-shilling ride to Half-Moon Street, where I gave the driver a twoshilling tip. He said it was alright but thought I was going it rather strong. Only an English cabbie would resent being overtipped.

It looked like he was going to make a scene, but I remembered the George Brent movies just in time, where the big scene is when George turns his back on the woman he loves and says, "When I turn around I want you to be gone," and when he turns around she's still there.

"When I turn around I want you to be gone," I told the driver, and when I turned around he had beat it with my two shillings, the bloody Piccadilly bandit.

If he'd had a spark of dramatic instinct he would have left one on the curb. Or *both!*

I was on some little lonesome half-street where low-slung strip-tease caves seemed barely surviving. A Spanish girl came through the pushing gloom and offered me a card—

COME TO THE SPIDER'S DEN

"Who sent you, honey?" I asked her.

She shrugged and took back her invitation. Whoever had sent her had taught her to shrug in English but never to speak it.

This Spanish con is as corny as the American hard sell or the Irish blarney. The decoy puts on pressure right away—"You like to stay in my house tonight? *Very* cozy."

When her large boyfriend walks in it gets even cozier.

The Irish blarney is just as sad—"You're such a darlin' man your blood is worth bottlin'."

The English con works better because it doesn't try to con; it merely disarms. The decoy stands in a doorway like a statue of indifference. A neon sign above her says *Casino de Paris.*

Wow.

"What's going on in there, baby?" you have to ask.

"Couple gels chattin' a couple blokes up is all, luv."

In the *Casino de Paris?* Who does she think she's fooling?

The stairway behind her begins to look sinister. She barely moves aside to let you pass. At the top of the stairs two janitors with a dustbin between them are coming down.

And conversation *is* all that's going on inside. A bright, metallic-looking girl sitting before a glass with a false bottom is only a make-believe whore. Her payoff depends upon how many glasses she can get you to order before you catch on. Her racket is not sex, but conversation. When nobody from the first-person world is left, and third-person persons are running things, sex may come to just that—conversation.

These clubs are flourishing in London for the same reason that the key clubs are doing so well in the States: They remove the responsibility of passion. And a responsibility is what, to these utterly demoralized men of distinction, in whom life has been reduced to protecting oneself at all times, passion has become. The clubs offer them the appearance of being playboys, sports, and regular fellows without the risk of love.

Take this sensible-looking, well-dressed, pleasant chap: he has that infirmity. Should he dream of a woman's arms around him in a naked embrace demanding physical fulfillment, he'd have his afternoon appointment with his analyst moved up to the morning hours, for he would feel life closing in. He pays the analyst to keep life away.

The analyst, of course, has his own troubles. Last night he dreamed he went into a washroom in Madrid and saw the sign on the door had not read *Señores,* but *Señoras.*

So much for World War III.

The men who own these clubs, like those in the States, are businessmen, not hoodlums. They are the same investors from the suburbs who, behind the front of a banking, insurance, or investment-counseling firm, use a go-between to buy a piece of a crap game or a whorehouse. These are the same parties who own broken-down but well-paying tenements by proxy.

They are not members of "The Mafia," "The Brotherhood of Evil," or "The Syndicate." They are members of no syndicate save the international one of Make-a-Buck-and-Shut-Your Face. And what is a businessman, anyhow, but a hood who cuts corners when splitting a score? After all, isn't the end product of General Motors not electric appliances, but price fixing? And isn't the end product of the square who gets squarer and squarer, a fascist? Isn't it always the man who goes about neighbors' homes, on Sunday mornings, with a petition banning unescorted women from drinking in the local tavern, always the same bird the girls have so much trouble getting to leave on Saturday night?

I kept on my way along the little lonesome street, plainly an American waiting to be accosted; until accosted I was.

She handed me one of those thin, ladylike pencils usually attached to a note pad beside a phone—this was attached by a cord of some sort around the young woman's neck. She was very young even for a young woman—no more than seventeen—who dipped into her coat pocket and put a note pad under the pencil as I held it suspended.

Her finger jabbed the pad: a mute girl wearing black gloves.

A deaf mute at that. For, when I spoke, she shook her head quickly and showed me a smile that meant *that* did not matter. The finger jabbed my breastbone, then pointed to herself.

You and me.

I wrote on the pad:

"How much?"

She glanced at the pad, took the pencil, crossed out the question, and wrote:

"Name please."

I wrote:

"John. How *much?*"

She took the pad back and wrote:

"You can trust me. John."

I was pleased that John trusted her. I certainly didn't. I'll trust an unattractive girl in an expensive coat or a beautiful girl who is badly dressed. But this combination of a deaf-and-dumb beauty wrapped in a mink that would have paid my fare by jet back to Chicago was a little too good to be true. I took her arm, a cab wheeled to the curb as though it had been waiting down the block, and we were off to Ipswitch-on-Bagel-and-Hop-in-the-saddle come what may.

We drove toward the south of England, my sense of direction told me, and disembarked at a bar that had no sign, but seemed well lit. My friend, who had written her name as "Emma" and was no more an Emma than I was a John, permitted me to pay her cab fare. But I let her enter her hangout first. I'd trust a bushman ahead of an Englishman and a bushwoman before both. In fact, I just wasn't too damned sure Emma *was* deaf and dumb.

We were in a cocktail lounge with an American décor, two bartenders and a dozen couples sitting around without making a sound. The couples were jabbing their fingers at each other, tapping themselves and making small circles to dot their "i"s. I caught the bartender's eye, and he asked, "What's yours?"

That was a relief.

It was a relief, but it wasn't right. The other bartender was a deaf mute too.

"Give me a dummy on the rocks," I told the bartender who had all his senses. If I stuck around here I was going to lose mine. Which was why I had been brought, my instinct told me.

If the bartender with his senses had smiled when I made a funny I might have stayed. But he frowned, so I made him ask again before I told him I'd take Scotch—"And give my friend Guinness." I saw a way out. She grabbed her pad and scribbled:

"Whiskey, please."

I grabbed the pencil, and wrote:

"Thank you for an interesting ride," finished the Scotch while she read my farewell, and got the hell out of there. No, it just didn't *feel* right.

Yet here and there, beside a juke in an all-night restaurant, the honest British whore still survives.

The barrage balloons are long down, but she still makes it here and there, forever on the dodge.

Like the woman who called herself Chantelle—perhaps because the café had a French name. She came up in a first-person war and will do first-person time on a penal farm if caught peddling her goods on the streets.

Little ferns, in rusty pots, were caught between the double-panes of the café. It was the only café on this street permitted to stay open all night.

"Were you ever buried in the time of the V-1's?" I asked.

The small ferns are neither outside nor in; their life is lived out between panes and they don't look at all well.

"It begins to seem so now," was her answer.

The press of the throng between the Regent Palace and the Hotel Piccadilly, the ceaseless hurry-hurry of MR. BRANDYWINE, and the urgent demands to resink the *Bismarck* later began to confuse me. I bought two bags of peanuts—I let the oranges go this time—from a huckster near the Regent and returned to Room 916.

When I got inside, my telephone was ringing madly. Although I knew not a soul in that whole vast city, anticipation leaped in me like a sailfish in the sun—England had been expecting me! I was ready for dinner in Hampstead or Kent or to fly back to Dublin if the party were already starting.

"918?" a male voice asked.

"916."

"So sorry. Would you mind jumping the small bell up and down there's a good chap?"

I jumped the small bell up and down like a good chap to recall the operator, but she paid me no heed. I could hear the other good chap breathing into the phone. He wasn't as young as he used to be anymore either, the other good chap. Time and The Goat will get you breathing harder over the prospect of a light date than you once did in handling a heavy one.

"Have *you* ever been buried alive?" I asked him.

"What's that, Old Chap?"

"I say have you ever been buried alive? A lot of people have, you know."

He seemed to be thinking about something else.

"Would you mind stepping down the hall and telling the lady in there John is on his way down?"

At any rate I'd gotten him off the "Old Chap."

Down? On his way *down?* We were on the top floor as it was. But if Old John liked living on a hotel roof it was alright with me. I hurried down the hall, as I wanted to be back in time to see him scaling that wall. It was pretty wet out there.

At the door of 918 I noticed I was still carrying one bag of peanuts. I smoothed out the wrinkles in it before knocking as I wished to make a powerful first impression. The woman who opened the door wasn't Simone Signoret.

But she wasn't a brute either. Just one of those five-foot-eleven Marylebone Road blondes with a pile of hair that made her look six-three.

"John is on his way down," I told her, feeling short.

How I happened to know so much about her affairs she didn't bother to get being astonished about. Lazy girl. Too lazy to ask me inside for a drink. I actually had to *filter* in, by explaining that I had been in London in 1944. This entitled me to a passkey to any room in the hotel.

"You'll excuse me," my new-found friend asked. This kid needed someone like me to restore her confidence.

"I came over on the SS *Meyer Davis.*" I sprung the surprise I'd been holding out. She stayed unstartled. She had good control.

Her apartment had a continental, I might almost say apartmental air, and was four times the size of the broom closet in which I had been cowering. A cheerful lived-in air. Taking off my tie, I started to live in it. A nice water color by somebody named Duffy hung over the mantel.

"I painted that," I assured her. Anytime I can't paint as good as an Irishman, you let me know.

She threw me a look.

"What I mean is that I have the same painting and once drew one of my own by tracing it."

"John is on his way down," she pointed out.

"I'm the one who told *you*," I reminded her.

She sat on the bed and began drawing on a pair of black woolen stockings that didn't go with her hairdo. The stockings looked like she was going skiing. Was *that* how John was coming down from the roof?

"I asked John if he had ever been buried alive," I reported.

"Why in the name of Heaven did you ask *him* that?"

"Just to make conversation," I explained, "but I knew some people who actually were when I was here in 1944. A girl named Sandy."

"Oh, you were a soldier," she announced as though I had been elected to that position by a runoff in the House of Representatives. "It was all a bit before my time, of course."

"I was close to Patton," I referred to an occasion when he had been driven out to where we were pinned down and told us that the way to clear a minefield was to go through it, then went home and went to bed. We were grateful to him for not having slapped us. Some Patton.

The Marylebone Road Brute stood up and drew a babushka about her face.

"I know," I told her, "John is on his way down. May I knock on your door tomorrow?"

"You may knock on every door in the hotel if you wish, and the day after as well," she gave me an opening.

Whoever said the English aren't friendly?

Down these antiseptic English halls every chambermaid looked like a mother cop.

A lanky old geezer stood beside the lift, smiling as though he'd been expecting me.

"Would you mind tieing my shoelace, old boy?" he asked.

Would you mind if I hit you a clean shot in the teeth despite your age? was the answer that went through my mind. I didn't express it. I didn't express anything. I'd just never been up against a polite request to tie a stranger's shoelace before. I know there is a first time for everything, but why it had to begin with keeping somebody else's shoe from falling off I couldn't see.

"I have an arthritic hip," he explained with self-satisfaction.

So there I stood with both hips in place while he stood with one hip out of the game. I tied the lace with care, making a knot that would spring his good hip when he tried to undo it. I must hand it to the old gent for not kicking me in the teeth when I was in position for it. He could have gotten every tooth in my head but restrained himself out of lifelong habit.

"One good turn deserves another," he strangely thanked me.

"Absence makes the heart grow fonder for somebody else," I assured him.

That's what it's like in Inner London, Men. That's what it's *really* like.

One side of the placard on 916 said DO NOT DISTURB and the other read MAKE UP BED. I could never decide which was the greater thrill. Now, when I returned, somebody had turned the MAKE UP BED sign around to read DO NOT DISTURB. That disturbed me. Especially when I found I'd locked myself out.

A chambermaid who looked like another soft-clothesman threw me a glance of an ill-concealed lust to pinch me before she'd let me back in.

I drew the shade to shut out the gloom, but it did no good: the stuff wasn't pushing in from outside, it was seeping up through the floor. Either the management manufactures the stuff in the basement and distributes it to all the hotels in Piccadilly or it was fallout. I stretched out on the bed, and in no time at all was asleep in a litter of peanut husks and broken possibilities.

In sleep I saw the guardian lions and the guardian lions remembered me. Under neon like a doom they turned to a fire-fed red. Something stirred their hearts.

A line of small black hearses circled endlessly, and the driver of each had a peanut face. Down Regent Street I saw a throng, an international multitude of peanut faces. All Earth's peanut-faced people came thronging, begging me, pleading with me—

"*Sink the* Bismarck! *Sink the* Bismarck!"

It was up to me.

Beside me on the bed the number on my key read "918." I was in the wrong room. Someone tapped the pane.

John was on his way down.

I got up and switched on the light. Someone had placed the room card against the mirror: DO NOT DISTURB. I turned it about: STEP INSIDE. SEE THE MAN WHO LOST HIS WEIGHT, it said. Again the warning tap against the pane.

Someone was trying to tell me that, unless I came awake, I would never get my weight back. I woke up waving my arms as if trying to push off an oncoming sea.

It was raining in Piccadilly. It was raining in Soho. It was raining in Wales. It was all new and green in Ireland, I felt sure—it was all green, all sun and white-blue clouds in Dublin.

My watch began ticking as if trying to get my attention: 11:00 p.m.

They would be bringing dustbins down from joyless rooms above a neon sign reading:

Casino de Paris

"The Captain will let you know when to fasten your seat belts by lighting up the sign 'Fasten Seat Belts,'" read the pamphlet I picked up off the BEA seat the following morning just before taking off. I was willing enough to fasten my own seat belt, but I *had* hoped the Captain would come down and ask me himself. I covered my disappointment bravely.

"In the event of an emergency landing, the Captain will first of all announce 'Prepare for an emergency landing.' In this event please keep calm and carry out the following instructions: Loosen neckwear, remove glasses, dentures, and high-heeled shoes, and empty pockets of sharp objects. When you hear a whistle blast lean forward, cradling your head in folded arms. Be prepared for more than one impact." If it was the stewardess's arms that were going to cradle my head I was ready for several impacts.

I loosened my tie but decided to wait for the first whistle blast before removing the bridge with the two powerful molars attached lest it frighten her off.

Somehow the old boy who had asked me to tie his shoe returned to my mind. It came to me that the reason the English think so little of asking kindness of total strangers is that they think so little of granting such kindness themselves. If I am to believe my own sightline, these are the only people on the face of the earth who actually believe in kindness.

Not believing, as we do in the States, that we believe in it by attending a movie about Kindness certain to gross a million dollars. The English *legislate* it into their daily lives.

The spectacle of a great country, such as our own, demonstrating greater concern for the profits attached to the illegal drug traffic than for its victims is abhorrent to the English. Yet it is sufficiently plain that, if our concern for human beings was as large as that for investments in heroin, we surely would not assign its solution to men whose only qualification is a capacity to carry out orders. While the English use their medical men to rehabilitate addicts, we hand them over to policemen whose duty, as they conceive it, is to drive all offenders into the underworld.

What was that the sixteen-year-old Puerto Rican told the arresting officers? "Put me in the electric chair; my mother can watch me burn."

The plane's doors locked, the big zoom lifted me. I felt myself losing weight and began to smell oranges. After struggling since the twenty-eighth day of March, nineteen hundred and nine, to get a semblance of dignity into my existence, all my good work was undone.

At 60,000 feet I struggled against the seat belt, resolved *not* to be a Zero-G Gravity man. "My weight is my own!" I cried out in my mind, clenching my fists against this final outrage. "I *forbid* you to take my weight! This must not happen again! *Never!*"

But my voice slipped out with the slipstream.

Into the vasty silence of Zero-G.

PARIS

THEY'RE HIDING THE HAM ON THE
PINBALL KING *or* SOME CAME STUMBLING

There are sad little sights of Paris
After Metro lights go dim
There are strange flowers woven of rain
That scatter like petals on the Rue Tiquetonne.

Great trucks haul peaches all night from Rouen
All night workers are stacking crates
And the odor of peaches, rain and perfume
Mix with drivers' cries on the Rue Tiquetonne.

Café chairs were stacked to the bricks
Peach crates were stacked to the wall
Sacha Distel sang *Ah Quell Nuit*
The *Dracula Cha-cha* kept banging away—
It was very late on that curious street
And later than that in the juke café.

Peaches that year were rather high
Yet girls came strangely cheap
An excellent year for *Champagne 'pernay*
But a tough one on old tarts.

I saw the girl with the black coiffure
Against a wall of the Rue Tiquetonne
Turning a parasol under her arm
And how the grass between the stone
Grows a brighter green on the Rue Tiquetonne.

For she stood less tall than the piled crates
When the clocks of St. Denis cried each to each—

tique-*tonne!*

tique-*tonne!*

A light rain (she told me)
Brings men to a room
A hard one keeps them home.
She did not say each drop of rain
Is a drop of regret on the Rue Tiquetonne.
For, buyer of peaches or buyer of flesh
You pay up your money and spit out the pit.

Peaches and girls both grow a light down
You don't touch either one without money down
What you don't have in money you save in regret—
Maybe peaches are better. You can spit out the stone.

Seller of peaches or seller of flesh
Wish each other in Hell, then cheat on the weight.
The stair smells of soap and wine and old leather
That men climb to feel their deaths with pleasure—
Death costing little in such weather.

These are small sad thoughts of a Paris street
Where coiffures are costly though death comes cheap.
Yet above a bed on the Rue Tiquetonne
Two lamps keep burning each to each.

*Trapped in a network of night-leaves, a moon of the night-trees kept trying
to rise. Between the bridges of Paris, both banks of the river, amber lamps
were tethered deep in the waters.*

*Through green-gray glimpses of the moon, couples strolled below the lamps.
Till an evening cruiser white with light moved noiselessly downriver. The people aboard it looked out, through glass walls, at the lovers strolling. Some waved.*

*Their white boat severed the tethers of light but the green moon of the
night-trees could not get free. The lovers didn't wave back.*

But all the lamps of Paris began of a sudden to burn too bright. As if with desires too strong for themselves; desires that could not last the night.
Leaving the waters darker and deeper than before.

I first saw the city of Paris from the top floor of a five-story tenement overlooking a street called the Rue Bûcherie. Notre-Dame's heights were just out of reach. Behind its gray spires the white light of Paris fell.

All day long.

One morning rain kept making ready yet did not fall. The traffic that war had halted was picking up below. Cheap music came up from a jukebox café where Algerians met. Postmen and housewives and shopgirls and children, old men and old women and drunks moved along as though each felt his own life to be just beginning.

It was a time of beginnings.

All of my friends in that city were making beginnings.

My friends were Jean-Paul Sartre, Simone de Beauvoir, Jean Cau, Boris and Michele Vian, Juliette Greco, Mouloudji, and Olga and Jacques Bost.

Of these the most memorable face is that of Greco. She was then under twenty and had come to the cafés of Saint-Germain-de-Près from imprisonment.

Hers was a face as old as time and as young as herself. She had come to the cafés wearing her hair as black as a shroud to her shoulders. A face of great strength and no pretense, in a girl whose manner was made of grief.

Yet the small songs she sang in a voice none too good, when the lights began to come on in the night cafés, were often lighthearted. In her voice, also, there was no pretense. Greco was then a woman who had been made by times in which there had been no hours to spare to pretension. So she sang gravely, without change of expression till a song was done. Then she smiled.

She smiled. And the lights in the room came up a little.

That was Greco in 1949.

Mouloudji. Who was he? Like Greco, he emerged from the kind of winter that war makes upon children, one when the only heat in Paris was that of the café. Sartre, sitting with others, saw the Arab face looking in. It was plain enough, in that long face, that the boy did not have the money to come inside. Sartre invited him in. Mouloudji began to sit among Existentialists as a kind of mascot; whose payment was a cup of coffee and a croissant.

He was the son of a French mother who had lost her mind, and an Arabian father who peddled on the streets. He could barely read and write. So he listened, instead, to the makers of books around him. In the spring that followed that winter he said suddenly, "I too will write a story."

"About what, Mouloudji?" someone asked.

"The Mexican disease."

"What is the Mexican disease, Mouloudji?"

"Death."

"But death is not a disease. And is common to all. Why Mexican?"

Mouloudji had a logic all his own. The book *The Mexican Disease* proved a sound artistic success. He followed this with *Death in Barbary,* a novel of equal originality. Then he lost interest in writing and began to paint.

His painting, like his writing, was primitive but striking. Mouloudji had some direct source to the wellsprings of man's being; which ignored problems of technique. Sartre's group realized he was a painter of talent. Yet, when he had painted well, he put that aside also.

Mouloudji began to sing in the cafés, and as in writing and painting, immediately drew a small public to himself. He sang his own tales of the streets of Paris.

The versatility of Boris Vian was not the spontaneous reaction of Mouloudji, but an advised act. Vian was an intellectual, bright but shallow, who conducted a band devoted to American jazz; and who also wrote thrillers, after James M. Cain and Mickey Spillane, under an American name. He had great success with *I'll Spit on Your Grave,* and then turned out a small biographical novel of his own childhood. This book had purity and simplicity, and no success at all. With its publication Vian learned that in France, as here, the fast applause goes to the writer who performs publicly rather than to the one who merely stays home and writes.

While Vian's interest in American jazz appeared to derive from its facility, the interest of Michele Vian derived from the emotion behind the music. She was "The Golden Zazu" of whom Mme. de Beauvoir once commented simply, "The Zazu cares for people."

Cau was a student who had come to Sartre without being sent for. He ran Sartre's errands, de Beauvoir's errands, my errands, The Zazu's errands and Boris Vian's errands. I don't know who ran Bost's errands.

Cau *liked* running errands. If nobody had one to send him on, someone would think one up and tell him to take his time coming back.

The manner of Cau at this time was precisely as though he were rehearsing for a part in Dickens. I never saw him without hearing someone say, "Oh, I *am* 'umble, Master Copperfield. "

Sartre's surest friend was Jacques Laurent Bost. Bost had been wounded in the defeat of France and had written *Le Dernier de métiers,* a foot-soldier's story of France's defeat that remains one of the most genuine literary works to come out of World War II.

Had I passed Sartre on the street as a stranger, I would have taken him for a cheerful tradesman, cheerfully failing in the trade in men's pants. Unprepossessing in both appearance and dress, he was ugly as well. One eye out of focus and with a dryly amused air, he appeared to be more a waiter not above snatching of another waiter's tip than France's most dangerous thinker.

Most dangerous because of his total commitment to the nature of man and his opposition to formal assaults, from left or right, upon the nature of man.

This could, of course, be said with equal truth of Camus. But Camus never became a danger to the state, as he never implemented his conscience in action. When decisive action was needed, Camus remained the intellectual at the point that Sartre exposed himself to charges of treason to the state.

Although his public answer to all uses of oppression was always an unfaltering NO, his personal answer to any small scheme upon his works, his time, or his pocketbook was always an unfaltering YES. As he was the public man who never said Yes, he was the private man who agreed to anything, as the quickest way of disposing of the matter.

While walking down a Paris street with him shortly after he had returned from Haiti in 1949, he made a sudden U-turn and fled into a café. What had come over him was the sight of a girl who had asked him to bring her a toy electric train from whatever country he was going to, and he had promised it simply to rid himself of her. This was not a girl toward whom Sartre had any obligation, but only a café idiot who liked toy trains. Now Sartre had to avoid her until he could buy such a train in Paris to make his promise good!

He was at this time being sued by two parties for the same dramatic rights to the same play, having signed contracts with both parties the same day. A French court later resolved the dilemma by nullifying both contracts and then appointing a member of the court to referee Sartre's financial life. When the appointee later made off with most of the money, Sartre merely shrugged; as though he had assumed there could have been no other result.

His emotional life was, apparently, conducted upon the cheerful premise that it is better to say yes to a woman than to disturb her by saying no; with the result that his work was much infringed upon by women's demands.

And since these demands were made upon him at the same time that he exposed himself to arrest by encouraging French youth to refuse to bear arms in Algeria, he discovered, as he always discovered, that both matters would be happily solved for everybody if the De Gaulle government would imprison him. Then he would be able to have the peace essential to completing an anthropological essay; and, at the same time that it would keep the demands of women away, he would be serving a political purpose to the best interest of his country.

Simone de Beauvoir's eyes were lit by a light-blue intelligence: she was possessed by something like total apprehension. Her judgments seemed a fraction sooner than immediate and her decisiveness shook the *arrondissement*.

"Now, tell *me* about Existentialism," a male interviewer once settled himself down to amuse himself, and get a story too, at a café table where she sat; with pencil and notebook ready and self-contentment coming out of his ears.

"You do not care about Existentialism, you do not care about anything"—and, taking her own notebook and pencil from her handbag, she bent to her own work. The interview was over.

She did not even bother to glance up when he left.

Yet to the fool trying not to be a fool, to the perplexed or the half-maddened, to the man or woman in trouble, to all those making an effort to understand themselves, she put down her own work with the same immediacy and struggled with others' problems as though they were her own.

Friends sometimes had to remind her that it might be just as well to hang up last winter's dress, midsummer having come to France. Most Parisian of Parisians, she was least the *Parisienne*. As a court had to prevent Sartre from blocking the French economy, Castor's friends provided her with needle and thread and buttons. Nothing more was then needed except a volunteer to sew them on.

"If one gives time to trivial things, the important matters will never be settled," she disposed of all sewing of buttons, all washing of dishes, all sweeping of all floors, all shopping, all cooking, all childbearing—she not only did not know one end of a broom from the other, but was actively opposed to other women differentiating between either end. It was understandable that she should resent husbands honoring themselves with the freedom to drink and chase the girls while wives lived between bed and stove. But I worried a bit about how the human race was going to perpetuate itself once Castor took over. She struck me as a bit preposterous.

And, indeed, in 1949 her one-woman opposition to the single standard *was* preposterous. It was preposterized in every newspaper and magazine edited by the French bourgeoisie. She was cartooned, ridiculed, sometimes made gentle fun of and, at other times, reviled with no restraint.

When I came again to Paris, in 1960, there was no more laughter: she was feared. She had broken through the defenses of the bourgeoisie, of the church, the businessmen, the right-wing defenders of Napoleonic glory, and the hired press. She was, at once, the most hated and the most loved woman in France. It had become plain: she *meant* it.

"The difference between a desert and a paradise is not as great as generally assumed," she wrote upon returning from her first visit to the States; "in the gardens of Fra Angelica or the Sahara there is nothing for men to do. . . . The young American is in a world that others have created for him, a completed world. I do not say there is nothing for him to do, far from that: America is not a paradise, it is a living part of the earth of men. But to discover what is to be done, a human interrogation has to put the world to question. They feel the abstractness of a contentless freedom: it makes them giddy; they look for a way out. The American is afraid of that dereliction into which man falls when he has to split off from what is given. The individual has to assume the task of being what he is in the jeopardy and glory of his lonely freedom; only then can the world in which he thrusts himself have a human character and value."

She had been awed at the possibilities she perceived here; and dismayed at the uses to which these possibilities were reduced. The American conviction that happiness consisted of a house, a faithful mate, no passions and no cares left her cold. The common possession of an automobile looked to her as though it brought only a chance to a great many more people to drive at greater speeds to nowhere.

She had then perceived the necessity of giving content to our civilization, lest its technical triumphs come to no more than a race between drivers who did not know they were dead.

She herself was not waiting for death. To have a house, a faithful mate, no passions and no cares; to take no risks and never to play the fool was not the way Castor ran her life. Existentialism, to her, was not a philosophical complex of Hegel, Kierkegaard, Kafka, and Kant, but a means of living in the world with freedom and joy.

"A man tied to a fertile soil which he obediently cultivates," she wrote, "is not free. Nor is the man abandoned in a desert and told to go where he likes."

She had seen the particular abandonment Americans endure; of how common it is to become an expatriate without leaving town. She had seen those Americans' faces that seem to lack responsibility even to themselves. They had looked to her like the faces of occupying troops, capable of cruelties they would not risk at home.

They had no home on the streets where they were born. Their lack of connection with the world of men had left them unconnected to themselves. Since they did not know the name of their world, they did not know their own names. How could they know who they were when they did not know to whom they belonged?

This was the beginning of that strange change of Americans from first person to third: instead of seeking to impose his will on the world, he contrived to defend himself from it in an emotional isolationism.

"The American fears that dereliction into which man falls when he splits off from what is given," Mme. de Beauvoir had observed. Her observation has since been confirmed by the man paying fifty dollars for a tin key with a bunny on it, upon an assumption that he is purchasing a unique personality. (That twenty thousand keys may be sold the same month to men suffering the same sense of inadequacy doesn't, apparently, modify this assumption.)

Stripped of philosophy, the question asked a decade ago by Existential-ism was, simply, "Why not?" Meaning that, to multitudes who despair at risks involved in living, it offers the answer that not to try is to die. It answers that there is no alternative but to assume the responsibility of giv-ing oneself: That the only way to be alive was to belong to the world of men.

A decade later it appeared that the American key-holder had decided death preferable to risk.

"The only spot on Achilles' body which was vulnerable was where his mother had held him," another French scold* writes. And it began to appear that the American's mother had literally encompassed him until he was old enough to own his own key. He was then set free and imme-diately ran away from home by buying himself into the sanctuary of a key club where he could look at nude women without getting involved with them. For the understanding within the club, however tacit, was, "If you'll let me stay a little boy I'll let you stay a little girl."

And was not this pervasion of the emotional life of Americans by the values that had once only been employed in business—never sell till the price is right and then try to get a piece of the commodity back along with the profit—precisely the result of what the French philosopher had observed in saying, "The cult of money which one encounters here expresses the fact that the individual is unable to commit his freedom in any concrete realm"?

The shift in emotional values from first person to third appeared to have followed a similar shift in the philosophy of business: the investor no longer put his life savings into an enterprise and went for wealth or went for broke: now he invested the money of others. And so, in love, he invested only the emotions of the other party, and contained his own.

Thus the anonymous nude performed for him the thrill without the risk. And, as nothing is happening in the private life of the third-person man, he feels an increased appetite for the private life of others. Which the omnipresent camera now supplies us through *Life* and *Look* and dozens of other mindless rags.

What the key-holder—and multitudes who cannot afford fifty dollars for a key but remain key-thinkers all the same—has settled for is to remain uncommitted, by taking no risk of exposing oneself to another. It

---

* Henri Motherlant, *Sur les femmes.*

means never being *for* another. In short, a flat refusal to be fully human. His answer to the question "Why not?" is "No. Never."

Existentialism directly opposed this view by going to its source, to the ancient biblical warning that to gain the world is to lose oneself, and to give oneself to the world is to gain one's self.

This was the beginning my French friends were making in 1949.

The people partying through the rooms were Americans who wished to be helpful but didn't know how. This was the spring of 1960: They were the first wave of a summer inundation that had broken early in April on Saint-Germain-de-Près.

It had been in April, too, that a thirty-year-old Algerian woman, an attorney named Gisèle Halimi, had come to Mme. de Beauvoir with the story of Djamila Boupacha.

On the night of February 10, 1960, Djamila Boupacha, twenty-two, a member of the F.L.N., was arrested and sent by the French to the camp of El Biar. Arrested with her was her father, Abdellaziz Boupacha, seventy; his pregnant daughter, Néfissa Boupacha, eighteen; and his son-in-law, Ahmed, thirty. The pregnant girl was put in solitary confinement but suffered no violence. Her husband and father and Dajmila Boupacha were tortured.

Mlle. Boupacha was told, "If we raped you, you might take pleasure"— and was thereupon impaled on a bottle in the hands of a French soldier. Mlle. Boupacha was a virgin.

Mme. Halimi's plea, for Mlle. Boupacha to Mme. de Beauvoir, was to have her client transferred for trial to Paris, both to prevent further torture and to obtain a fair trial. Mme. de Beauvoir's account of the story in *L' Express* was subsequently seized in Algiers, but it broke in the American press and the story was out. Although Mme. Halimi has not succeeded in getting her client to Paris for trial, there are no indications that the girl has been tortured further.

The people partying through the rooms had come from places like Fort Dodge and East Jesus, Kansas, because they had found Fort Dodge and East Jesus unbearable. So they had immediately set up small Fort Dodges and East Jesuses on the Left Bank in order to Keep Paris Away. The last people they wanted to see were the French, who had troubles nobody was concerned with in Fort Dodge and East Jesus. They had come to see other people from other Fort Dodges and other East Jesuses in order to talk about how things used to be in Fort Dodge and East Jesus.

One could hardly blame them for believing in an acquisitive economy which enabled them to live without feeling acquisitive. But now they didn't know what else to do with themselves. By and large, they seemed to be people whose feelings had been hurt because they had only one of everything while others owned two. All the same I was happy to meet them, because I suspect American affluence has come to depend upon a fundamental corruption to which I felt capable of contributing. I hadn't been driven to Paris by disenchantment over the Black Sox scandal so much as I'd been drawn by rumors of lonely Americans looking for dinner guests who were bilingual. I speak both English and Chicagoese.

Already I had introduced myself to several film writers who were frankly disapproving of a nakedly competitive economy unless it gave them a head start. One of these, wearing a sweat shirt on which his initials had been sewn, was particularly scornful of any economy in the hands of French waiters.

"What *they* call *breakfast* in this country! What they call *coffee!*" he warned the assembled expatriates—"it took me forty-five minutes to get ham and eggs this morning!"

Of course, when you write for the movies every minute counts, but why did this thinker want to get up before Darryl Zanuck? I had once seen his picture in *Time,* routing the foe with a samurai sword bought in Manila after the war, but I hadn't read the book. All the same, the picture had left me with a strong impression that at last America had a novelist who could slice off your head at a single stroke without going on safari. I haven't gotten around to slicing off somebody's head but am willing to give it up if the other side will. This fellow didn't strike me so much as being a downright expatriate as he did a fellow who was afraid he'd go broke before he was ninety-two if he stayed in the States.

What had made him think he wouldn't have to pay for his meals if he moved to Paris I don't know. He was pretty hot about it.

"They don't even know what a toasted cheeseburger is! *Try* to get a chocolate malted!" This Pearl Harbor Paul Revere circled the room spreading the alarm—"the hell with serv*ees* compr*ee!*" He looked over at me but saw I wasn't wearing a napkin over my arm so he didn't charge. I wondered why anyone would come such a distance just to be made a fool of by French waiters.

Yet I once knew a fellow from East Jesus who fell in love, and the girl failed to mention that she'd once had a roll in the hay with the pinball champion of West Jesus. The new beau caught the scent, challenged the earlier conqueror to a pinball tournament, and then punched him silly over a pinball technicality.

And to this very day the pinball champion of West Jesus thinks he was whipped just because he was outweighed. It wasn't him who put two pounds of sugar in the new beau's gas tank the next day, I happen to know. It was just the girl's way of showing she still thought of her first hay-roll fondly.

Was this fellow who had hacked his way through the jungle single-handed for *Time* this type of athlete or had he made sergeant on sheer ability? Is the pen *really* mightier than the sword? Should the spitball be made legal? Can Missouri remain half slave and half free? If Jerry Lewis, Jr., and Norman Mailer actually *are* two different persons, how come nobody has ever seen them together? These and other problems now perplexing Western civilization crossed my mind while I worked my way toward another shot at the Scotch.

On the other side of the room an unescorted woman, wearing horn-rimmed glasses, was growing hysterical over the difficulty of finding a mate. If she took off the glasses and pulled her skirt down over her knees she might do some good in the few years remaining to her was my figuring. But, as it turned out, it wasn't a mate for herself that was giving her concern, but one for her ladylike boxer.

"I won't have my Mimi made a fool of!" she warned everybody, as though the room were full of people who planned to have their Great Danes seduce little Mimi, "My Mimi is going to be *properly* mated!"

Although they owned apartments and children and cars, these people seemed strangely to feel they'd been left out when the *real* goodies had been passed around. Each seemed like an only child that was trying too late to learn how to play.

There was something about the way they ate that would give you a weak streak right through your middle, particularly if you were hungry too. They ate as though they were in need of something more than food, and I'm sure they were.

The athlete in the sweat shirt was eating everything that wasn't moving, so I kept shifting from one foot to another so he wouldn't splash mustard over me. I wasn't hungry myself and so limited myself to things that weren't big enough to bite back.

Somebody mentioned a friend who had missed a plane by five minutes and was still arguing with a reservation clerk about it when the plane came down in flames on the other side of the field.

"I *never* have that kind of luck," the pinball fellow complained at this news, "Oh, no, not *me*—*I'd* have been on it," and walked off grieving over his premature demise, his work half finished, his songs half sung. Still and all, he appeared to have been well brought up and I suppose that's where the trouble began. He came over to me holding a loaf of bread half the size of himself, stuffed with something that was wriggling to get out, yet he kept a firm hold.

"I don't buy this serv*ees* compr*ee* deal," he let me know.

"You don't *have* to tip, Zane," a girl lying on her side, reading a letter, glanced up to inform him and she wasn't lying on her side for fun. "As a matter of fact, you don't have to tip at all. It's just a little something extra."

"PAR-DON-AY-MWA, *Madame,*" the witty chap excused himself, "but since when did anyone ever give *me* 'a little something extra?'"

Buddy, it occurred to me, if this is your old lady you have certainly been given a great deal extra and the benefit of the doubt as well, but I didn't express this notion as I was on a tight schedule myself. Till the bar went dry.

The girl held out her Martini glass to him and he peered down into it, thinking she was offering him a drink; only, the glass was dry. He couldn't figure that one out. Then he saw the olive and it came to him that she wanted him to eat it. He popped it in his mouth. At least they weren't hiding the olives on him.

"She wants another Martini," I explained, not wishing an expectant mother to tire herself by holding out her arm indefinitely from a prone position.

"You had one, honey," he remembered when they had first met.

"That was for Baby," she explained, "now get one for Mother." He finally got the idea and wheeled off as if gin were going out of style. I'd been wondering which of the paralyzed embryos stalking her premises this girl had gotten careless with, but now I didn't have to wonder any longer.

I liked her approach to motherhood so much that I sat beside her to see what else I could do for her.

"I'd like to read your mail," I told her.

"It's just from an ex-fighter in a fix," she told me, folding the letter.

"I know all the ex-fighters in a fix," I assured her, taking the letter from her, "and some people who can't blame it on boxing. I even know one ex-fighter who has never been in a fix. Do you know Roger Donoghue?"

This is a standard gimmick I employ, in tight situations, about a fellow who used to fight around New York, in order to avoid being crushed by such issues as whether the service is better on a Dutch or a French line or What Would *You* Have Done If *You* Had Been Mary McCarthy When Françoise Sagan Came Along? As long as I can stay clear of serious subjects, I may add, I can be a dangerous conversationalist.

"I saw Roger Donahue the first time he fought Flores," the girl told me, "he won."

"He won the second time, too," I informed her, "he always did have color."

"He wasn't *all* color," she corrected me, "Roger really *could* fight."

"The night I saw him he wasn't forcing himself," I remembered, but I was just egging her on. Pregnancy had put a silver bell in her voice and I liked hearing it tinkle.

She was no beauty but she was a beauty all the same. She was the only person around who didn't seem to feel that she was being made a fool of if she couldn't get a filet topped by a mushroom the size of a baby bison in four minutes flat. Anybody who didn't like her on sight had a mind that had recently snapped.

"He seldom forced himself," she told me, "because he seldom had to."

There was something to what the girl was telling me, because this Donoghue, at one time, might have been welterweight champion of the world were it customary to give the title to the most articulate contender. Actually Roger Donoghue was the unrecognized champion of the world at not getting hit, but there now they don't give the title for that either. The fact is that at one time nothing stood between this athlete and the welterweight title except four fellows named Young, Graham, Vejar, and Gavilan. Young and Graham were ready to concede as they were furious about being shifted around in the rankings every other week and Gavilan was out of town, so nothing stood between Donoghue and the title except

Chico Vejar. But instead of matching him with Vejar, the people behind Donoghue let him take on an unknown to whom Donoghue lost with such sudden grace that he was immediately advanced in the rankings from sixth to twenty-third, thus breaking the world's record for the longest leap ever made backward by a welterweight from Brooklyn sponsored by Budd Schulberg. This unexpected windfall gained young Donoghue his choice of carrying his own bucket or writing for the movies. Long past his prime at twenty-two, the sensible youth made the right decision and has never been heard from since.

"Roger was the last fighter wearing a shamrock on his trunks who could whip top contenders," she told me. "Could he have whipped Gavilan?"

"No, but he *could* have whipped Chico Vejar."

"Then I could have gotten a draw!"—I leaped up, keeping my left in Chico's face, the right cocked and ready to cross, only the girl pulled me back down. She was a very strong girl. Anybody who didn't admire her inordinately was no longer among the living.

"What happened to Donoghue?" I wanted to know. "Did we get to fight Vejar? I've been away for some time."

"We never got to fight Vejar," she told me gently, "they got us an opponent who wasn't even ranked in his own family and he knocked us cold almost immediately."

"At St. Nick's?" I asked, trying my very best to remember.

"What's the difference?" she asked, "It was Solly Levitt, who used to come out saying, 'Keep punching, Solly,' to himself so he wouldn't forget what he was there for. Roger hit him twenty straight lefts, but Solly still knew what he was there for. Roger leaned in with the right but he leaned too far and when he came to he thought he'd been dancing and one of the chandeliers had fallen."

"I once knew another fighter who could whip top contenders with ease, *nonchalantly—one-handed,*" I recalled, "but *always* had trouble with opponents. He fought Satterfield in Chicago after Satterfield had been kayoed by Rex Layne, of all people, and got himself knocked out *twice* in one night. In fact, this fellow did this sort of thing so often they finally had to put him in a jail—and right there is another funny thing, because every time this fellow went to prison and everybody would say he was through, he would come out a better fighter than when he went in. The reason for this was that, outside of jail, he never went to bed, whereas he always did time in prisons where the warden put the men to bed early."

"If you're talking about Vince Loman," the girl told me, mentioning a former heavyweight whose name isn't Vince Loman, "the letter you're holding is from him. I used to date him. You had to be careful not to leave money around when he was drinking, because he would tear it up. Vince really *liked* to tear up money."

I was pleased with myself at swinging the conversation to a fellow like Vince Loman who could get himself knocked out twice in a single night whereas the best Roger Donoghue had ever done along those lines was once in a night and to this very day never tears up money.

Fighters who go into the tank leave my interest in boxing undismayed, because I feel that so long as our businessmen stay corrupt our fighters will continue to do their part.

Apparently the girl shared this clever view, as she began to tell me how the fellow whose letter I was holding once went into the tank for the champion of Inner Soho.

"Vince *really* stank the joint up that night," she recalled with genuine pride in Vince. While Soho was running up and down hill strengthening his leg muscles, Vince and his manager were training with two hookers from Piccadilly. They had to do this to protect the ten grand apiece they had bet against Vince, to keep him from getting into shape. They always shared fifty-fifty on tank jobs arid were already sharing the redhead and the blonde.

"The DO NOT DISTURB sign was out, but they'd left a call for noon of the day of the fight to give Vince eight hours to strengthen *his* leg muscles. But all four were sleeping the sleep of the stewed, so nobody heard the phone until late afternoon, when the redhead knocked it off the hook and the clatter woke the blonde, who shoved the manager off the bed because he was snoring. He landed on Vince, who had been sleeping on the floor for two days. Somebody looked at the calendar and, between the manager and the two girls, they got Vince into the shower and into his trunks and into his corner, where he started falling asleep again.

"The sixty-second buzzer woke him, the bucket-man pushed him out and what Vince saw scared him, he told me later, because it was something like a double-image out of a TV screen coming right at him. He threw a right-hand shot and hit the correct image and there was the correct image on the floor and the half of Soho hollering 'Heah! heah!' and Vince's manager hollering something else Vince couldn't quite make out, but it sounded like 'Pick him up! Pick him up!' so he went over and tried to pick Soho up, but the ref waved him off and wouldn't start a count until Vince found a neutral corner. He tried three of them before he found one that seemed to satisfy everybody, and by that time Soho was on his feet and Vince realized what an awful thing he had just almost done.

"So he jumped Soho up and down and danced him around the rest of the round to bring him around as Soho was still suffering since Vince had fractured his jaw in two places.

"When he came back to his corner Vince said, 'This guy is going to faint on me.' 'Hold him up,' the bucket-man told Vince, so Vince did, and in the fourth round Soho was his old self again and threw a hook like he was playing pin-the-tail-on-the-donkey, and Vince went down as if the donkey had fallen on him.

"It was purely awful. I never saw anything so raw in all my life. What a *ham*. He made them carry him to his corner and he wasn't through then. He decided to milk the situation, and the bucket-man and the manager had to lift him back to the dressing room before he would admit he was conscious. Vince was a *terrible* ham."

The letter I had been holding was written by a man with large hands not used to holding a pencil, so I figured it must be from a correspondent of *The Chicago Tribune*. But no, it really *was* from the fellow who liked to tear up money.

His boxing career had been interrupted three times by prison, and the burden of the letter was that it might turn out that it was only his prison career that had been interrupted by boxing, because one more offense could send him to the joint for keeps and he'd recently committed it.

He was working as a bartender on a transatlantic liner, and had crossed the Atlantic seventeen times without disembarking as he didn't wish to go back to the place where the warden puts the boys to bed early. Why this floating bartender felt he was better off on an ocean I don't know, as the Atlantic closes down at nine. I don't know about the Mediterranean, they may stay open all night there.

"Why," I asked the girl, "can't the New York Police Department dispatch a couple flics to climb the gangplank if the boat should make the Port of New York any time other than the Jewish holidays?"

"Because The Department doesn't know Vince is at sea," she explained; "they're looking for him on dry land."

The idea of anyone looking for Vince Loman on dry land struck me as slightly hilarious. "I have an idea how to get your friend loose of the law," I suggested; "have them pick up Archie Moore instead—he *never* goes into hiding."

The girl didn't laugh, possibly because nothing comical had been said. She wanted to finish her story.

"In fact, he wouldn't even get dressed until they had collected their twenty grand apiece. Then they had to get right out to the airport. If they had tried to get back to the hotel it would have been a pinch.

"I called the girls to bring the baggage out to the airport, and they were good kids, they really showed up with the stuff. It looked like the boys would make it. But somebody had tipped the customs people about all those pounds going out of the country. They couldn't make the plane till they came clean.

"'Give me the roll'—Vince told the manager right in front of a customs man—and handed 13,000 pounds over to the hookers and kissed them both goodbye. That was all there was to it. Vince *liked* getting rid of money, that's all there was to it."

"Hemingway wrote that one up," Zane kind of boggled up looking vague.

"No," I felt obliged to correct him, "Hemingway's was about a fighter who bet fifty grand against himself. Vince only had twenty going."

"Same story all the same," he insisted, "there're six basic stories, all the rest, made up from them six."

"Where's *my* drink?" the girl wanted to know, but he didn't hear. He was focusing on me: I was the one who kept hiding his ham.

"The best way to know the ins and outs of the boxing game," I informed everybody authoritatively, "is just you talk to an ex-fighter—any ex-fighter. Once I talked to Tony Zale about his fight in Chicago with Al Hostak, and when I got through he asked me if my hand had healed. He thought *I* was Hostak."

Zane eyed me steadily. He was digesting the news piece by piece. Putting his hands on both arms of the chair brought his chin up close. "You're not Hostak."

"No," I told him, "I've gained weight."

The girl poked him in the side.

"Where's my drink, buddy?" She was being jocular.

Zane wasn't to be jocularized. "You've had it," he told her without unfastening his eyes from mine.

"How long does it take *you* to get ham and eggs?" he demanded of me.

"I get them right away because I tip so heavy," I told him talking over my head as I haven't tipped a waiter in years and am not planning to begin now.

"You go for this serv*ees* compr*ee* thing?" He put it to me. It was a political question.

"I'm *very* strong against it," I assured him. After all, it isn't easy to stay on the good side of everybody when they are standing so close together.

"If everybody on our side keeps adding something extra, where is it all going to *end?*" I asked. "Before the summer is over *they'll* be eating the steaks. No, we have to draw the line," I painted the Federals' position darkly, "we can't let their side shove *our* side around."

Apparently it was something along these lines he had been waiting to hear.

"Buddy," he told me, "I was in the Service four years, four months, and eighteen days. How long were *you* in?"

"Long enough to be offered promotion," I assured him, "but I didn't feel I was ready for the responsibility of Pfc."

The girl poked him again. He didn't feel it.

"My grandmother was a Cherokee squaw," he told me, *"nobody* shoves this soldier around."

"Don't apologize for your folks," I suggested, "My people weren't exactly hipsters, either." I thought he'd said "Cherokee square."

"Honey," the girl told him, "look *out.* You're talking to Solly Levitt."

It sounded like she might be trying to set something up.

He studied me again. "You're not Solly Levitt," he decided.

"You're not exactly Hurricane Jackson yourself," I had to point out.

"I just wish you was heavyweight champ," he warned me, "'n I was the channelger! You never whipped nobody your whole life!"

I couldn't recall any recent triumphs. "No," I had to admit, "but at one time I could have whipped Chico Vejar. He was the channelger."

"Anybody *you* whipped went into a dive," he decided, and turned on the girl—"Vince Loman never fought a clean fight in his life," he accused her, "it's why he's in a fix now. He never made a nickel except when it was fixed. He was born in a fix."

"We're all born in a fix, baby," she told him gently, "but we're not all at sea."

That had the earmarks of a pointed observation, but she handed him her glass before he could catch up. "That last one was for Mother," she told him, "now get one for Baby." He moved off with one shoulder higher than the other. He couldn't whip Chico Vejar either. He couldn't even whip me.

"Do you know why Donoghue quit fighting?" I asked her, just to get things going again.

"Because the Mexican died their second fight is what you're going to tell me," she told me. "Schulberg wrote that one up. Go see what Verina is doing. I'm going to bed. "

"Any man who wears canvas suits can't be all bad," I defended Schulberg. But the girl was gone. She wasn't Ava Gardner. But she was a beauty all the same.

Verina, I judged, must be the girl wearing horn-rimmed glasses who was having trouble finding a husband for her boxer. I was sure that if she let her bitch off the leash for ten minutes on any side street the problem would resolve itself. All that remained was to choose a street. I decided to recommend the Rue Tiquetonne simply because I like the name.

Verina's glasses had fallen over her nose, which was pugged, lending her the aspect of female boxer wearing glasses.

"Why isn't the Grab-the-First-Thing-That-Comes-Your-Way System, employed by people in finding a soul mate, good enough for dogs?" I inquired courteously yet keeping my distance. You have to be careful about making jokes to Americans these days as they have more troubles than other people.

"Because *anything* is good enough for people," Verina told me, "but *anything* isn't good enough for dogs. Don't tell *me—I know.*"

"I didn't know," I went along. "Can I ask how you found it out? Or am I being personal?"

"Nothing personal at all. I found it out by marrying *two* of them, *that's* how *I* found out. O *God*, why did it have to be *me?*"

I waited politely to find out why it *had* to be her.

"Oh, why did I have to marry an Argentinian built like a *stallion?*" she grieved; *"no* woman could stand *that."*

"I begin to get the drift," I assured her, thinking of a Great Dane capturing Mimi's heart.

"You get the wrong drift," she assured me in turn. "Oh, why did I have to marry a Frenchman built like a *trout?* I was better off with Ramón! I couldn't even tell if we were in the same bed!" She tossed a lipstick into her handbag and shut it with a click. "O God," she strangely prayed, "where is the *Truth?*" And she left.

I put my back against the wall and thought about fighters who came up fast and couldn't be beat. Then went down slow and finally didn't fight anybody anymore. Satterfield and Vince Foster and Lew Jenkins and Booker Beckwith and Anton Radek and Johnny Colan and Altus Allen and Nick Castiglione and Carl Vinciquerra and Milt Aron and Willie Reddish and Billy Marquart and Pete Lello and Willie Joyce and Bratton.

Till the moon of the night-trees, at last set free, rose with a single leaf touching its tip.

Then I thought of the friends I had had a lifetime away, but one decade before.

The face of Juliette Greco was no longer memorable. I had seen her again. Waiting to take a train to Marseilles, we had gone to the station's dining room and sat next to a table that looked unusual. A dozen American men and one woman holding a huge doll. She was quite pale, rather fragile, with the appearance of an American starlet. The men, by their conversation, were plainly a film outfit going south, probably to Africa, for a film.

The woman looked familiar. I thought she was an American starlet who was trying to look like Juliette Greco.

When she passed, carting her doll, Castor greeted her as Greco.

"We were wondering who the beauty was, and weren't certain," she explained diplomatically.

"It's not all it seems to be," Greco answered, smiling wanly, and passed on.

What transformation a decade had made in Mouloudji I do not know. Having gone through his talent for writing, then painting, then for singing, I had seen him, the last time, in a bit part in an Italian film. I don't think I'll see Mouloudji again.

Cau I had also seen. Cau was a success. He had been assigned by *L' Express* to follow Hemingway on Hemingway's last tour of the bullrings. Hemingway, being sick and dying, would make good reading for a certain type of reader.

Hemingway had known of this particular danger in Africa.

"Highly humorous was the hyena," he had written in *Green Hills of Africa*, "obscenely loping, full belly dragging at daylight on the plain, who, shot from the stern, skittered on into speed to tumble end over end. Mirth provoking was the hyena that stopped out of range by an alkali lake to look back and, hit in the chest, went over on his back, his four feet and full belly in the air. Nothing could be more jolly than the hyena coming suddenly wedge-headed and stinking out of high grass by a *donga*, hit at ten yards, who raced his tail in three narrowing, scampering circles until he died.

"It was funny to M'Cola to see a hyena shot at close range. There was that comic slap of the bullet and the hyena's agitated surprise to find death inside him. It was funnier to see a hyena shot at a great distance, in the heat shimmer of the plain, to see him go over backwards, to see him start that frantic circle, to see that electric speed that meant that he was racing the little nick-elled death inside him. But the great joke of all, the thing M'Cola waved his hands across his face about, and turned away and shook his head and laughed, ashamed even of the hyena; the pin-nacle of hyenic humor, was the hyena, the classic hyena, that hit too far back while running, would circle madly, snapping and tearing at himself until he pulled his own intestines out, and then stood there, jerking them out and eating them with relish.

"'*Fisi*' M'Cola would say and shake his head in delighted sor-row at there being such an awful beast. *Fisi,* the hyena, hermaphroditic, self-eating devourer of the dead, trailer of calv-ing cows, ham-stringer, potential biter-off of your face at night while you slept, sad yowler, camp-follower, stinking, foul, with jaws that crack the bones the lion leaves, belly dragging, loping away on the brown plain, looking back, mongrel dog-smart in the face; whack from the little Mannlicher and then the horrid circle starting. '*Fisi,*' M'Cola laughed, ashamed of him, shaking his bald black head. '*Fisi.*' Eats himself. '*Fisi.*'"

Cau was the right man for the job.

Boris Vian was dead. He had come out of a movie house, where he had seen an American version of a book he had written, and collapsed of a heart attack on the walk.

The Golden Zazu had lost some of her sheen. But was still the Michele who cared for people.

Bost had both failed and succeeded. He had done no creative work since *The Last Profession,* and had had no commercial success. He had simply gone along doing odd-jobs in scenario writing and journalism. After ten years he had not aged or changed. He had not succeeded, yet had not failed. He seemed content to be a journalist, though he had begun more creatively. But he had kept respect for integrity and had sustained respect for himself in others. He remained Sartre's closest friend.

Of all, Castor alone seemed to have gained personal strength in the decade. Djamila Boupacha wrote to her in gratitude from prison in Algiers:

"My fate seems marvelous now."

The moon of the night-trees, at last set free, rose with a single leaf touching its tip.

I saw the river cruiser returning. The people behind the glass walls were still looking out at the couples walking the quai.

The people on the boat waved at the few lovers still strolling.

And not one lover waved back.

> *Within The Metro's fluorescent deep*
> *Are cries unheard on the busy street.*
> *One night I rode it all alone*
> *It never stopped. Nobody got on.*
> *That night was ferris-wheeled*
> *For one by one*
> *The darkened platforms passed like being swung.*
> *Dark against the white of the Metro wall*
> *I saw the girl with the black coiffure.*
>
> *For some girls clocks chime within the heart*
> *For others, each clock must strike apart.*
>
> *In a rain that lightly rains regret*
> *Upon the hour of the unbought whore*
> *I'll come in my turn to the final door*

To pay up my money.
To spit out the pit.

When I come to the dance on the bed of the whore
To marry my bride with the black Coiffure
Let bells marry bells, let no lamp burn apart
Let all clocks of Paris strike hard on the heart.
Let odor of peaches mix with that of perfume
Let the green of the moss break the heart of the stone
Let no clock strike singly
Let all jukes cry one song.
And above a bed on the Rue Tiquetonne
Keep two lamps burning each to each—
   Tique-DONG!
    Tique-DONG!
     Tique-DONG!
      Tique-DONG!

BARCELONA

THE BRIGHT ENORMOUS MORNING

The-Porter-Who-Almost-Has-It-Made never moves any farther from the elevator door than Yogi Berra does from home plate, but the thing is automatic and I don't need anyone to raise the handle of a door for me.

He blocks me off, raises the handle, smiles while I pass in review before him into the cage, holds the smile when he follows me in, presses the button that says *tercero*—and smiles. The three of us go up together—myself, the porter, and the smile.

"This thing is *automático*," I explained this morning, thinking he didn't know. He smiled: *automático*.

If he keeps on smiling like that I'll have to tell him frankly, I am promised to another.

No, I haven't tipped him. That would only be to encourage him.

I took a one-peseta ride down the Rambla de Las Floras on a streetcar called Ataranzas, but the conductor put me off for aiming my camera at something through his window. If you're the conductor of a streetcar anywhere you can't be too careful about who you take aboard.

The Rambla de Las Floras is a wide and prosperous ramble through arbors of flowers and arbors of books. Barcelona is a woman reading with mimosa in her hair. She is reading James Hadley Chase; there is no censorship of flowers.

The Rambla is made for strolling. Though at nine o'clock of a weekday morning the people on it are hurrying to get somewhere as fast as those on Fifth Avenue. I caught a glimpse of an American wearing a pith helmet. Now, what country did he think *he* was in? But the people I wanted to talk to were those who weren't going anywhere, if they were up yet. I took a turn into the Calle de San Pablo, and that was a good move because it brought me into the Barrio-Chino.

The Barrio-Chino is the bottom of Barcelona, a town that tries to go straight down as well as straight up instead of just slopping over at the sides like Los Angeles. This is because the Spaniard is a person who goes straight up or straight down without slopping over. What some of these straight-up-and-down types were up to was almost any thing they thought would get them over the wall; such as walking down the street with government lottery tickets promising winners to everybody the day after tomorrow.

I didn't see how they could tell which numbers were that sure to win because those who weren't blind in their reading eye had lost the sight of both. I hope nobody was lying as the totally blind aren't supposed to lie. It's alright for people who have lost sight in one, and nothing is any longer expected of people who can see out of both. But if the totally blind were telling the truth that morning in Barcelona, the Chief of State has begun robbing the rich to give to the poor.

To tell the truth myself, the things people do in The Barrio to get over the wall don't come to anything more than what the people who would just as soon stay inside it are doing. A boy of ten had deliberately put himself between the shafts of a two-wheeled cart and was hauling it uphill to the fish market. What made him think his future would be more secure if he got seventy-five pounds of shovelnosed garpike to the top of a hill I sometimes still wonder.

Another, a smaller boy, was putting in his time better by urinating from the curb to the street. Two girls, who looked like sisters, but not his, were watching him with flat-eyed curiosity. *"Qué práctico!"* the taller of the two observed. How practical! The littler one nodded in agreement: *Quite* practical. I was glad to see some people weren't losing ground.

A grown-up girl hurried up to me and stuck a pin in my neck. It was attached to a paper heart and it was my jacket she'd aimed at. I didn't feel entitled to contribute as I don't yet have heart disease, but I looked around to see who'd sent her, thinking it might be someone I knew. In France you're permitted to refuse a paper heart, but if you walk past a heart-tag pusher here you're insulting Franco. He's a fellow in politics here.

Somebody had chalked a cup of coffee, with red and green chalk, on the window of the coffeehouse and written below:

Café—El Café Verdadero
*Black Coffee—*THAT's *coffee*

But across the window of the coffeehouse directly opposite someone else had chalked a cup of coffee with a jug of milk beside it, and the milk was steaming. This had been done in black and white and under it was another promise:

Café con leche—El Único Verdadero
*Coffee with milk—*THAT's *coffee*

I'd known Spain was divided but had had no idea things had gone this far.

A woman with coffee-colored hair was standing in front of the *Café Verdadero* place. She gave me a black-coffee smile. She didn't use sugar either; that much was plain.

Another woman smiled from the coffee-with-milk capitol, and her smile was pure cream. Grade A.A smile like *that*—never ask if it's pasteurized, the smile is what matters. I crossed over to find out what she thought of Castro. I didn't intend to join *any*body. What I wanted was both sides of the argument.

When she saw me coming she held the smile and the smile stayed pure cream. Her hair was down on one side of her face and she had a plain, beseeching face.

She knew it was time to turn off the smile; yet she couldn't. She knew all she was doing was grinning like an embarrassed fool at being badly dressed in front of an American millionaire. When she accepted a cigarette I told her to keep the pack.

She handed the pack back.

"Gracias, señor."

She had shown me a little of what she was like. One cigarette was courtesy, a pack was charity. She didn't have to grin any longer.

This struck me as a distinct improvement in manners over those of Mrs. Alfred Paperfish, wife of the Footnote King, to whom I had once, in a moment of absent-mindedness, extended a pack of Chesterfields. She had taken one and handed the pack to her husband, who had put it in his pocket for later.

"Good for you, Alfred," she had congratulated him. Meaning he might amount to something yet.

Perhaps she was running low herself and sensed it was a good moment to change brands. But good for Alfred all the same. He doesn't smoke. That was how he got his start—by not smoking other people's cigarettes.

I was also struck by my own presumption that a hungry woman couldn't have manners up to those of a well-fed one. A presumption Americans often make. I am now working on the presumption that the closer to hunger anyone is, the better his manners get; and, conversely, the longer it has been since he lacked the price of a meal, the more of a boor he becomes. My reasoning may not be flawless, but it has at least as good a chance of being true as the Paperfish theory that good manners belong to the man who keeps saying I'm Getting Mine until he gets his.

Now, I may at any moment be able to figure out why the Spanish aren't as smart as we are, and the minute I do I'll report in to Clare Luce Tooth. It's plain to be seen that they aren't, because if they were they wouldn't be where they are and we wouldn't be where we are and I wouldn't be where I am, talking to a native whose name I don't know. But who looks farther from home than myself.

For though her eyes were warm and her smile was white, she was ashamed to be standing in a pair of used-to-be shoes and carrying no handbag at all. There was no brassiere behind her blouse, that was black with white buttons; and no stockings below her skirt, that was gray with black checks. One look was enough to tell she had no pimp. Maybe *that* was what she was feeling so self-conscious about.

She wanted to know where I had parked the *coche,* and I told her I didn't have a car. She said, Oh, she had taken me for Americano.

"*Sí, Americano,*" I assured her.

"Then where is *coche?*"

Honey, we can't stand here and do this all morning even though I do own two Chryslers and come from Grosse Pointe, I thought, but all I actually asked her was, "Why stand in the doorway when there are chairs?"

"*La cuenta y la puerta,*" she summed matters up—if you don't order something you don't sit in a chair.

She was a poor girl badly dressed but not ashamed to eat. She was a poor whore traveling light but she'd sure got down early for breakfast. She was a perfectly lousy whore but maybe she'd never been given a real chance to be a good one. She was a poor girl far from home and in fact she wasn't a whore at all.

She was just a woman who had to get downstairs early to have breakfast at all.

The glance the *café-con-leche* owner threw me when I brought *this* one in to his *café-con-leche* tables told me I'd come down in the world in practically no time at all. That look left me with nowhere to go but up. He was one of those people who won't rap to you unless you have recently been seen talking to Diana Dors. If his glance hadn't told me I was keeping bad company, the way he slopped my friend's coffee into her saucer would have.

I didn't look at the cup when he brought mine. I looked at *him.*

He didn't spill a drop. What I'm trying to say is that he put it down *carefully.* Everybody else has to take chances for this type because he never takes a chance for himself.

Then I looked at the woman. The reason she was wearing her hair down one side was that that side of her face was pocked. The darkness under her eyes wasn't eye shadow. She was about thirty-five, but hard times had added a decade to her mileage, so I took ten years off thirty-five. She showed me her *carte de seguridad* so I wouldn't think I was dating a security risk, and I showed her my certificate of membership in the Division Street Y.M.C.A., Men's Division. So she wouldn't think she was dating a child.

She was Loren Domingués, born at Torremolinos. I found this of interest, as Torremolinos is a resort town noted for the backwardness of its natives and the forwardness of its Americans. The men of Torremolinos don't understand why American men are more interested in the young fishermen of Torremolinos than in the young girls of the town. They think it is comical. Wait till they find out.

Loren Domingués, child of scorn, was three years old at the time of the massacre in the bullring at Badajoz. I was the same age at the time that Stanley Ketchel fought Philadelphia Jack O'Brien. I don't know what side Loren was on, but most three-year-olds lost. So has everyone born in Spain since except generals and bishops.

There is a fisherman in the port of Barcelona who can eat fire, and other fishermen say Franco taught him how: once you swallow Franco you can swallow anything.

I don't know how good Loren Domingués is at eating fire, but she was very good at swallowing milk. She drank her own and then she drank mine. I asked her if she wanted more and she said yes. When she finished that off I began to look at her a little closer. That's an awful lot of milk for a single woman.

After the fourth glass I began to look for milk coming out of her ears. "It is bad to be afraid and it is bad to grow old," she told me—"but to grow old being afraid—" She broke off, being afraid that talking of fear might be poor pay for milk. Having fear that if she spoke of age she might have no milk at all tomorrow.

Your body dark and delicious,

she began to sing loudly enough for me to hear, but not so loudly as to draw the owner's attention—

Your body dark and odorous,

and broke off again, smiling apologetically. Perhaps I did not like Spanish songs?

"You're feeling better," I answered.

Everybody was feeling better.

Encouraged, she sang more slowly, as women do when they are really feeling better:

Yours is a slim body the hue of sin
Your kiss is wet, such a kiss is a scandal—

The Barrio is a city where poor men try to make a living from the sea and poor girls work for whatever men have left over. Sometimes the sea gives a man enough for food and drink, sometimes not enough. When the sea is generous, it gives him a wife for an hour or a night. Lonely men looking to the sea for help; lonely girls looking to men for help. Poor girls of The Barrio looking for money from strangers.

Strangers in need of poor girls of The Barrio.

They have put the black tricorn on the head of the gypsy who once played the small guitar at saints' fairs: he will have no pesos for girls this year.

The side-street solitary drinks standing up in the violet neon's flare. The man who drinks wine standing up will have nothing left in his pocket for love—no matter. He is only a postman who never gets a letter himself.

> *Your kiss fell on my lips lightly*
> *Yet the touch of it stays and stays.*

False-promising vendors of the forenoon streets come in darker hours to the Calle San Pablo; to buy love that is all false promising. Has the one who sells the smuggled English cigarettes been past yet? Has the old cobbler come?

All day the old man bends over a last in a cave of leather, talking to shoes. At the hour when the last pimp has given up, he comes seeking the last unbought whore.

The old man buys shoes no one else will wear. Never speaks, but shows his money.

All the next day he will be telling the story of the night before to his shoes.

Has the pharmacist come? The one who wears the white intern's jacket to sell contraceptives that fit the tongue?

He lives in a hotel where water and light are turned off between nine and six and he comes looking for a wife between six and nine. He will never know the touch of warm water.

When Loren Domingués showed her *carte de seguridad* to the clerk who sits below the hotel stairs, he had to let her in, but the disappointment on his face was plain. A man who comes with Senorita Domingués is one who pays no more than the legal rate for *habitación*.

She was a poor girl traveling light who liked swallowing milk better than fire.

> *You have kissed my mouth that is the mouth*
> > *of the people*
> *In your kiss on my mouth*
> *Mouths you have not known know your kiss.*
> *My mouth that is the mouth of the people*
> *Cannot forget.*

The clerk-below-the-stairs would have shown more respect had the man shown up with some elegant mopsie like the small blonde from Córdoba, no more than eighteen, calling herself Encarnación.

"Bon soir, m'sieur," this girl who never saw France greets me. Causing me to wonder whether a new people might not be in process, one merging the virtues without the flaws of France and the U.S.A.: forming one noble race of which I will be a leading member. Stanley Ketchel fought Philadelphia Jack O'Brien the same week I was born. My father pedaled to work on a bicycle but O'Brien ran like a thief.

"C'est la vie, m'sieur, I kiss you *lov*-ing"—Encarnación pirouettes, wearing no underclothing at all. A single pirouette can sure carry a lot of meaning when it's done right. All the English she knows is "I kiss you *loving*." I was afraid she'd catch cold.

"Servez-vous, c'est ça, merci"—I understand: she has put the money that should go for underclothes into dresses. She owns fourteen dresses and six pairs of shoes. She told me so herself. That is very good for a girl working only two hours a night. Talent can spring up anywhere.

Encarnación has had proposals of marriage in every language of Europe. That isn't hard to believe, judging by the competition for her around the Café El Kosmo. Though I doubt marriage is the first thing the competitors have in mind.

She asked me to come to her room to help her count her clothes, as she had recently lost track. I went with her and, what do you know, that girl really *does* have fourteen dresses and six pairs of shoes! I counted twice to make sure. Then we went back to the café because I wanted to take her picture while there was still a good light. She seemed puzzled about something. My father was born in San Francisco and raised in Black Oak, Indiana, which was at that time hardly more than a village. Later a rich vein of silver tinfoil was discovered there, so the town has now entirely disappeared.

I took Encarnación's picture in front of Café El Kosmo with the streetcars called Ataranzas clanging past, and gave her a pencil and paper for her address so I could send her the picture. She handed both to another village child working at the same trade, who could write.

How did a thing like *that* happen—a village girl who can write her own language? The *Guardia Civil* must have slipped.

The chances of learning to write her own language, for a village child on the town here, are roughly the same as those against her becoming a whore. 8–5 and take your pick.

In a single bold move, Spain's fearless leader has abolished prostitution and emancipated women simply by herding the unwanted girls of the villages into the back streets of the cities, where nobody wants them either. A girl from the country now has as good a chance as a girl from the city to become a whore, so half the battle against vice has been won. When Franco has finished wiping out corruption in Spain he can come to work for us.

The war the Germans and Italians won here wasn't won against Communism after all. It was won against Loren Domingués and Encarnación Castell.

Meanwhile, it would be a nice idea if someone would buy chairs for the girls of Barcelona who have to stand up all day, in narrow doors as well as wide. Who also wait on the terraces or walk down the Rambla between the flowers.

Between Soho and the Rue Saint-Denis, Dublin to the Barrio-Chino, there is a vast wasteland that cannot be seen from any plane. A continent of young women abandoned more wantonly than sheep, than dogs, than cattle are ever abandoned.

A room of one's own doesn't sound like much, but to a poor girl of Spain who doesn't want to make her living on her back it sounds like the hope of those people in Hell who want ice water. There are many empty rooms in France, and Spanish girls are the best housekeepers in the world. The French say so, who keep house well themselves. The Spanish girl will work for little more than enough to eat and a place to stay. The trick is to get out of the country.

So the strong girls with big feet come to the Barrio-Chino from the villages of the barren south, because in such villages children go barefoot their whole childhood. Ash-blondes from Córdoba or doe-colored women with a touch of Moor, girls from the Balearics or the Canaries. By the time one gets to the Barrio she has shoes and knows how to say "I kiss you *lov*-ing."

All she needs now is a place to stand.

I have found the clue to the everlasting smile of The-Porter-Who-Never-Has-It-Made. The hotel's menu explains it:

> *In an Italian restaurant, a customer*
> *who asked to see the manager was told,*
> "You *are the Manager, sir."*

Below it is the boast:

Le Patron c'est vous, monsieur.

And, under the Spanish menu:

El Dueño es Ud., señor.

The Spanish have had to go to the French to learn the proper attitudes of service. But your average Spaniard can't learn service. I understood this when I saw the waiter *serving* me a napkin. He brought it held high between two forks and deposited it with care before me, that I might see for myself that its spotless purity was unstained. I didn't mind that it had the remains of someone else's *gaspacho* from the night before on it. A lot of people like a cold soup before they turn in.

What gets me is that the hotel takes such precautions for me against the germs on the waiter's hands, but won't spare me a bar of soap. I'll take my chances on the waiter's germs if someone will put a bar of Lifebuoy in the bathroom.

The porter is beginning to look like a piggybank to me. What *is* this everlasting smile? Was the man raised in Los Angeles?

In front of a cave called Club Java I heard a woman singing:

> *This is a great big city*
> *There's a million things to see*
> *But the one I love is missing*
> *'n there's no town big enough for me*

Everyone in The Club Java looked like he was raised in East St. Louis, including the bartender, but the paper on the bar wasn't the *Globe-Democrat,* it was *Arriba. Arriba,* as in *Arriba España!* meaning "Property Owners of Spain, Arise!" On the cover is the customary photograph of El Porko saluting other investors.

I myself was one of that happy number of Americans who once hoped somebody would defeat the Italians and Germans. I know I was thinking along those lines because I joined the local chapter of Rear-Echelon Radicals Against Fascism. There were at that time many American writers,

mostly in New York City, whose politics were left wing because of a shortage of business opportunities in the right wing. None of these could go to
Spain to do any actual fighting themselves because they had a magazine
called *Partisan Review* which the editors decided was indispensable to culture, the thing the Spanish people were then fighting to preserve. I didn't
go to Spain to fight either, but this was only because I didn't want to die
young. A flimsy excuse. I didn't want to give up listening to Bessie Smith.

> *It's mighty strange beyond a doubt,*
> *No man can use you when you're down and out.*

I saluted the photograph to amuse the bartender, but he wasn't about to
be amused. He fought on the winning side in the Civil War but they didn't
give him a prize. So he merely looked glum and pushed down one thumb.

He was a little late in turning down a thumb. While Americans who
were turning down their thumbs on El Porko twenty-five years ago are
now putting them up. Chiefly rear-echelon liberals against Fascism who
may earnestly point out that the bartender of The Java isn't as badly off
as he would have been under Hitler. I've never cared for this Reader's
Digest type of Richard Rovere-ish product, however marketable. To bring
the record up to date, I still don't.

In the women's prison at Alcalá de Henares there are ten Christian
Democrats serving from ten to thirty years. One, who was a student of
twenty when she was arrested in 1941, has contracted tuberculosis.
Another, a woman of fifty-five who has now done eighteen years, is paralyzed. Two days after Eisenhower's visit to Madrid in 1959, seventeen
Christian Democrat Catholics were put on trial for distributing leaflets at
a football game. One received a sentence of eight years at hard labor. The
other sixteen got terms of from six months to six years. Records on 1,900
political prisoners belie the insistence of El Porko that there are no political prisoners in Spain.

An American wearing a white pullover on which the name HANK had
been sewn with red thread came into The Java and sat beside me. Hank
was looking for someone to tell how hard it is to get ham and eggs in this
country. He looked at me steadily but I wouldn't rap to him. Finally he
asked me the time, so I had to give him an opening.

He told me he was from Milford Junction, Ohio, and had been walking all over Barcelona. "I heerd there was hoo-ers in this town but I could of done better in Columbus. Ain't seen nare *one*."

What country did HANK think *he* was in?

The bartender says when a country is at war everybody ought to go. But that if there *is* another in his own, he will give up his turn for once to somebody who has never had a chance to go before.

He doesn't believe that the Spanish people are going to war against each other in his lifetime.

So if you were the editor of a magazine the Spanish people were giving their lives to preserve in the mid-thirties but are now shopping around for a chance to dynamite an indispensable bridge across the Ebro twenty-six seconds ahead of the Italian cavalry so that you can crawl into a sleeping bag containing Ingrid Bergman with her head shaved, it looks like you'll have to shop around for somebody else's river and somebody else with her head shaved. In somebody else's sleeping bag. Personally, the one I liked best was the one about the great white shark, Over The River And Into The Ocean. Although I have never dynamited a bridge I'll call it off if the cavalry will give up their horses.

The Bartender-Who-Knows-the-Answer-to-Everything says Spain would be a happier nation if it only had a king. Those were good times, simpler times, he says, when Spain was a kingdom. Now what country does he think *he* is in?

I didn't trouble to tell him that what he is living in *is* a kingdom. But, so long as it is, perhaps they ought to go all the way and pick one and now is a good time because there are three candidates who have a legal claim: Don Jaime, Dona Beatriz, and Don Juan. The first is a deaf mute, Dona Beatriz is blind, and Don Juan is an idiot. *Arriba, España!*

The bartender's wife asked me if I were English and I felt I was losing altitude. "*Americano*," I told her. But when she answered that it came to the same thing because both peoples spoke the same language, I felt my seat belt snap. I informed her that what the woman on the juke was singing was *Americano* and if she wanted to hear *Inglés* she should catch Reinald Werrenrath doing *The Road to Mandalay.* So much for The Boxer Rebellion.

The Bartender-Who-Is-an-Authority-on-Everything taxied in with the news that the greatest American singer of all time was Johnny Ray and the greatest song ever sung was *The Little White Cloud That Cried.* As I hadn't seen an American newspaper for a week this came as a complete surprise. "You don't hear so much about Johnny Ray since Sal Mineo came along," I told him.

> *When a woman get weary,*
> *No tellin' what she'll do—*

Another *Americano* wandered in. This one was wearing a coat so I couldn't tell what his name was. He sat beside me but I didn't ask him where he was from. Finally I got tired of that and told him the time without his having to ask it.

"They don't know how to make a hamburger in this country," he replied immediately; "they don't know what butter is. I waited an hour and a half this morning to get two poached eggs!"

"You can get a *good* hamburger on the *Champs-Élysées*," I told him. "Why don't you try there?" After a minute he left too. That left me the only American in Barcelona who liked The Club Java.

The reason there are so many crippled dogs along this street is because the new cars are so wide and come on so fast that the brutes don't have a chance to get out of the way. The biggest cars, the blackest, that make everything moving leap for the wall, are the ones with liveried chauffeurs.

I have a sightline from here on the ancient street fountain where women of the waterless tenements come, kettle and pitcher, pan and pot, for water for drinking and bathing and washing. Whether you live in village or city in Spain, it's an uphill grind and a downhill slide for water. In rooms of dreamers, city or town, sleepers go forever uphill then go forever down: winding up a stairwell's steep abyss or slowly down the spiraling cliff. Hope means hope for soap and water to last the day and saving the suds for tomorrow. Those big black cars that make you leap for the wall are Portuguese. The passenger in the back seat of one was a bishop.

Two Barcelona men are on trial here before a military court charged with "insults to the chief of state." If Franco is going to try everyone who insults him here I'd like to have a peseta a head for turning people in. I'd come before El Porko wearing a black tricorn and a monkey suit, give him that nutty-looking salute and say respectfully, "El Caudillo, Spain insults you," and he'd owe me thirty million pesetas. But I'd say it respectfully so he wouldn't put me in jail too. They called it a Civil War, but if that one was civil I would as soon not be around when they lose their manners. The big problem to me is the Portuguese. If it's true that their power has declined, where do they get those cars? Is everyone in Portugal a bishop?

The bartender asked me if I'd like to taste a *carraquillo* and I said I'd bite anything that wouldn't bite me back. He said No, it was just a little drink that would warm me up. I said I wasn't cold just to see if he could think of another reason. I kept putting obstacles in his path like that. I didn't want to make things easy for someone who wanted a king. He insisted on making me warm enough even though I wasn't cold. By this time it was plain that what he had in mind was to knock me out and steal my camera. Well, I know a trick or two myself, one being to fall backward off a barstool and lie on the floor pretending I am unconscious. When he took down an unlabeled bottle, I demanded that he give me *only a small glass*, thus reducing his chances of knocking me out by 50 per cent.

He and his wife then began laughing at something together—a pair of operators if I ever saw a pair—they even contended a little over the bottle for the honor of being the one to pour the dirty drink. It must have been her turn, because she served me and stepped back, waiting. I drank it and looked around. They make coffee cups in Spain too small.

Actually, all you have to do is pour a spot of cognac into a cup of Spanish coffee to have the drink called *carraquillo*. Unless you prefer to do it with anise, in which case it is called Death in the Afternoon. In France they say red wine is the communion of the poor and in Ireland they say Guinness is the communion of the poor. But if they call cognac-coffee a hard drink, then in Spain the communion of the poor must be Communion.

The good wine is the *Bueno,* the cheap wine is the *Ordinario,* but there is no bad wine as there is no bad dancing; and the *Ordinario* is *bueno* enough for anybody.

Except, of course, for Portuguese bishops who live on wood alcohol strained through a bandanna.

Below the great gaiety of the Spanish heart is a stern, ancestral passion for control. To be *loosely* gay will not do. As one does not drink or dance or face the death on the horns of the bull loosely. Like the Irish, the Spanish are infatuated with death, but with an infatuation as different as midnight from noon. The Irishman goes by degrees, half willingly, into that good night. Goes too gently into that good night. The Spaniard stays death's stern hand with his own. No man gives so little to death and no man dies so hard. As the Irishman leaves lightly, he drinks hard. As the Spaniard goes hard, he drinks lightly.

Penalties for public drunkenness here seem inordinately severe. An offense that would get an incorrigible lush thirty days on a state farm in the States will get him years at hard labor here. Dignity is more important to the Spaniard.

Man's first triumph, in the Spanish view, is over the great bull of passion within every man. The bull of lust and the bull of fear, that must be faced with no outward show. Personal dignity is the communion of the poor.

There is also big money to be made here in robbing the blind. My own personal control was remarkable, inasmuch as the bartender kept pouring the great bull of *carraquillo*. For I concealed my inner excitement that the stuff was being poured on the house, and he kept pouring it. He even poured one for himself. So I knew the man realized he wasn't dealing with some fool who would turn down a free drink just because it might zonk him onto his skull. He kept pouring.

My assumption that everything was free was gradually earning me his respect. My strategy was to keep him pouring out of respect until he would realize that it would be cheaper to quit pouring free cognac and offer me *keef.*

I stood up and drew on a cigarette until my eyes crossed. Then I uncrossed them and looked at him inquiringly. *Keef* is a mild hypnotic combining the finest virtues of hashish and marijuana into a single noble blend. Humanitarian seamen bring it into Barcelona from Africa. I don't know what they call the name of the stuff from Greece. You might call *keef* the communion of the poor, too, because that is what the poor here really do call it, except that it costs more than the poor can afford.

The bartender shook his head. Either he didn't have any or he didn't trust me. All he did was turn Bessie Smith over.

> *Gimme a pigfoot and bottle of*
> *beer,*
> *And I don't care.*

Past times, simpler times, when we went to a bar to drink whiskey instead of staying home to smoke pot. Past days, gone days, when every saloon had a print of Custer's Last Stand donated by the Budweiser Brewery. Old times, Budweiser times, when we called for a boilermaker when we wanted a shot and a beer. Gone times, Schlitz times, when a man would say "I'm taking a count" when he wanted to know how much money he had instead of "I'm reviewing my holdings." Lost times when nothing was easier than to forget an army serial number. Times that had transpired upon some first-person person's planet before third-person times came along. Times when there had been nothing to get grim about except crapping out three rolls running or having to go to a war. How was it then that the campus fellows, arrived with their blueprints to which the arts must henceforward conform at peril of getting bad grades, felt grim about everything?

Had the big crapout to them been simply in being born? Or had it begun later, and all Daddy's fault too, when he'd forbidden his boy to ride a bicycle for fear of a skinned knee? Had the fathers, out of love, built a picture-window world wherein well-behaved sons could watch others ride no-hands with no risk to themselves? Was Junior so grim about everything because his true self had been left looking out of a picture window?

While campus fellows, authentic paperfish authorities, began seeking ways and means of bringing the arts into a picture-window world where the artist would be both safer and richer, certain prebeatnik cats went searching Chicago's South Side for ways and means of passing for black.

Through Richard Wright we had become aware that those who ran the white world had lost the will to act honestly. We had learned from Wright that it is those who have nothing to lose by speaking out who become the ones to speak the truth. And to these, all the horrors of poverty—schizophrenia, homosexuality, drug addiction, prostitution, disease, and sudden death on the gamblers' stairs—were no more remarkable than the sight of a man with a fresh haircut. In the midst of life, where there are nothing but horrors, there is no horror.

Crafty madams and ancient midwives, tenor-sax players and policy-runners, con men, quacks, pimps and tarts, poolroom sharks and intellectuals, all were citizens of a country whose capital was Forty-seventh and Indiana. But only the latter had divorced themselves, intellectually, from Negro life. Talking in phrases picked up in evening courses at the University of Chicago or at Northwestern, we knew that the phrases, so high-sounding to their own ears, were as artificial as hair-straighteners and skin-lighteners. We had been made suspicious of the values of the white world by Wright. Our suspicions had been confirmed in war.

Wright had made us aware that the Christianity of the white American middle class had lost it nerve: now we saw it to be a coast-to-coast fraud. And the fraud lay in this: that property was more valuable than people. The Negro had come up in America, putting the value of people above that of property simply because he had no property to evaluate.

This fraud, as essential to successful merchandising as making a profit, had by 1948 so pervaded the American white middle class that its ancient image of Jesus Christ had become that of The Young Man On His Way Up whose total purpose was accumulation of securities; and whose morality was confined by the warning: "Don't Get Caught."

By 1948 everything went, in the race through the supermart of publishing, advertising, television, and bond-selling; and Christianity had lent its blessing to the Supermart. The image of America reflected in editorials in *Life,* on TV, in movies and on the stage, was a painted image that had nothing to do with the real life of these States.

"The horror, gentlemen, lies precisely in this: that there is no horror."

But in Negro music we heard voices of men and women whose connection with life was still real.

Still heard—and yet were already being overwhelmed by Negro voices in praise of hair that was no longer nappy. They became so cool that they surpassed themselves; causing whites to imitate their coolness.

Under the impetus of a new American affluence, a new Negro elite, as eager as the white middle class ever had been to put aside feeling for ownership, began to emerge. Taking its cue from the enormous circulations of *Time, Life, Look,* and *Reader's Digest,* the Negro press now began presenting an image of the Negro bourgeoisie, as flattering to that class as the white journals to theirs. In it we saw the same disconnection between the life of the States and its representation that marked the white bourgeoisie.

This saddening change was never demonstrated more inadvertently than in a soap opera so corny that it would scarcely have been tolerated on afternoon TV. *Raisin in the Sun* gained instant acclaim by white critics because it presented the identical aspirations, among Negroes, as had led the white American middle class to founder in a world of gadgets. *Raisin in the Sun,* enacted by Negro players, was not a play about Negro life at all. It came straight out of the turn-of-the-century Yiddish theater by way of Clifford Odets.

Its characters, like those of *The Motor Boys in Mexico,* were immediately identifiable. The only dimension was that which faced the audience. The story moved flatfootedly about an investment in real estate; and, indeed, it was nothing more than a play about investing in real estate. For its reality was the make-believe reality in which the white merchandising class had invested. And had never been able to understand how life, lived for acquisition, rather than for living, leaves the liver dead long before he dies.

The new Negro elite, in adapting the hypocrisy of the white ruling class, had now made their adaption theatrical.

This elite found its apologist in the expatriate novelist James Baldwin.

"All I can do," Baldwin wrote, "is attempt to prove, by hard precept and harder example, that people can be better than they are."

This admirable sentiment would have rung less hollowly had it not been composed in Corsica.

And had the writer not been sporting a papier-mâché fez.

The hypocrisy, having become theatrical, had now become hilarious.

The Bartender-Who-Didn't-Get-a-Prize began a long rigmarole about how he used to run a café but didn't get a prize for that either. He didn't want to serve coffee with milk because once you started something like that it led to serving ham and eggs, and there was no end to *that* but bankruptcy. Why he thought bankruptcy was worse than the condition he was in he didn't explain.

He appeared to have suffered some more recent loss, because he kept peeking inside my camera to see if he could find it in there. Then he would hand it to his wife and she would peek in, but she couldn't see anything either. Finally I took a peek myself and what do you know: I'd forgotten to load it.

This was a shock, because I have been trying to get a start in life since 1929 and if it isn't one damned thing, then it's another. One decade it's a nationwide depression, so that if you make a living you're a fink; the next decade it's a war, if you don't go you're 4-F; and the next decade if you don't get your picture on the cover of *Time,* your relatives are ashamed of you, especially your mother.

*It's mighty strange beyond a
doubt,
Nobody knows you when
you're down and out.*

What I ought to do right now to start getting a start, is to load this camera with color film and do a photograph book called *Poor People of Barcelona* and follow it up with *Poor People of Andalusia*. When I finish with the poor people of Spain I'll do the poor people of Italy. I'll do *Poor People of Naples, Poor People of Sicily, Poor People of Rome*—any place where they have a good hotel. Great journals like *Playboy* will hire me to make their subscribers even more self-satisfied. I will cater slavishly to the utterly complacent; I will be the poor man's Cecil Beaton. In my work, children bitten by dock rats in Istanbul will come to serve a social purpose by helping subscribers to *Heritage* who read in bed to feel that much the more contented. What was it that brush salesman wrote in *Saturday Review*— "There is no *true* compassion in these modern works. The degraded and the criminal are identified with. One has to be a pervert or a savage to elicit sympathy." Al*right*, I'll work along *these* lines—compassion is for the healthy and the well-to-do and by the time I hit Budapest we'll *all* feel more secure.

Perhaps the Innerspring Mattress people will send me to India. Benares, or Indore. I'll get to photograph the Maharajah of Indore outdoors and the Maharanee indoors. In no time at all my picture will be on the cover of *Time* and Clare Luce Tooth will be on the phone telling me there is a little party at Fleur Scheisskopf's place and *I* am invited!

What shall I say *then?* Why, that I'm not able to leave my typewriter, thank you all the same, until my masterwork, *Inside the Inside of Europe* is completed.

"I can't wait to read it," Clare will tell me, "I'm *terribly* interested in Europe."

"The book has nothing to do with Europe," I'll have to forewarn Clare; "it deals only with what it is like on the inside of the inside. What it's *really* like."

This touristic fantasy left me faint, and I came around only because someone kept tugging at the loose piece of my jacket. It's that clown of a porter again, I realized. But it wasn't. It was the bartender returning my camera. What was I doing leaning against somebody's wall? I hadn't noticed at the time but it sure looked like I'd left the bar.

"That was pretty good *carraquillo*," I congratulated him.

No, I didn't tip him either. "Honesty is its own reward," I let him know and, pushing him gently yet firmly to one side, went on my way contentedly.

Well, how would *you* feel if *you* had been Zane Grey when James Jones came along?

Not only that, but how would you feel hauling a stupid camera by a stupid strap and feeling stupider by the minute? It's true nobody asked me to start a thing like this, but looking at it another way, I'd like to know who is going to stop me.

Tomorrow I go up on the roofs. There must be *something* up there.

The Porter-Who-Has-It-Almost-Made knocked this morning when I came out of the bathroom. The reason I came out was that there was no soap in there. The reason there is no soap, of course, is that the clown steals it and sells it on the black market. Sure enough, when I opened the door there he was, bearing a tray on which there rested a token of affection: a bar of Palmolive. I didn't miss the point of the tray. But all I did was take the soap and slam the door. Later, I realized I hadn't heard him walk away, and opened the door again. There he still stood, tray, smile, and all.

"*Arriba, España!*" I told him, and shut it again.

You'll never reach a rooftop in Barcelona by going up a well-lighted stair, because buildings that take good care of themselves don't let people climb onto their roofs. The stair you want is one in a building that don't give a damn, lights or no lights, the hell with the broom and all like that, because that's exactly the kind of house that leaves a little door, at the very top of its creaking rickety stair, open just enough so you can force it the rest of the way and there you are: On top of Barcelona.

The first door I made was held by a wire from the outside, that I could have made sooner but for a dog who stuck his nose in the crack of light and pretended he was guarding Darryl Zanuck. A woman lifted the wire from the outside and took the pooch off. It was some roof. It was one hell of a roof.

People had built shacks up there and on the roofs all around that made me wonder whether Hoover was running again. They had made them out of wine-barrel staves, orange crates, paper, iron and tar, and all the litter of the Barrio-Chino. A few pesetas to the *concierja* and what the landlord don't know won't hurt him was the idea.

They even kept chickens up there. I didn't see any hens but a rooster came out who looked married.

The woman looked young but haggard, the way mountain women often look in the States. Well, we were pretty high up at that; maybe it's altitude does it. Her husband came out and stood beside her and I offered him a pack of cigarettes. He took one and handed the pack back.

"*Gracias, señor.*"

They weren't from New York, either.

He asked me did I *sprechen Deutsch* and I said if I did it would come as a pure surprise as I wasn't *Deutsch,* I wasn't even German. It developed that if he had a choice of who should be on his roof, he would prefer a German; but if he couldn't get one an American was better than nothing. The reason for this is that the Germans have a better record than we have here for fighting Communism. That is the thing you say you are doing here when you want to get cheap labor. It covers a surprising number of holds, all of which are unbreakable.

The man didn't want a photograph of himself and I hardly blame him. Besides, they were in the way of my sky and so was their damned rooster. I sent them all back to the shack, but told the rooster he could stay outside and peck at things. I wanted to see if he'd hit a worm. I hadn't had breakfast myself and I couldn't remember anyone saying Stay for lunch. Were they planning to surprise me? If they just had coffee and a spot of flour, I know how to make poor-do gravy. But I didn't come to Barcelona for a good time, I came here to get a start in life.

The reason I am a little late in getting a start is that just when I got my Pfc stripe, that war was over. One more week and I would have been an acting corporal!

It goes that way for me for days at a time. Then it gets worse. The time it got *really* worse was when I left the dog tags on the bedpost and didn't miss them until the M.P. asked me where they were. He was just a fellow who enjoyed making a bet on something now and then and had nobody to bet with, so he'd made a bet with himself that the next fellow coming out would have left his tags on a bedpost. He was as surprised as I was.

Both of us were even more surprised when it turned out I didn't have a pass either.

In fact, I had no evidence, outside of a uniform, that I was in anybody's army at all. Speaking English didn't prove I was an American, as the English had an army around somewhere that was making a good thing out of singing *Lili Marlene* and smoking American cigarettes. (Nevertheless it had been recognized by Truman Capote.) What I demanded to know of the M.P. was whether he was for us or Churchill. Just because he spoke English didn't make *him* an American either. He kept getting in deeper and deeper until he started feeling suspicious of himself. He felt he was either trying to arrest somebody from another army or was being a big fink for pinching an American.

If I wasn't in the right army, I wanted to know, what would I be doing carrying six cartons of Pall Malls around?

He apologized, so I let him go. They never had any right to send me overseas in the first place, as I had contributed to democracy by writing book reviews for liberal periodicals.

A woman one roof away was hanging clothes to dry. She had her back turned to me. Way, way up, very high, a couple of black oversized birds were wheeling. They were Portuguese buzzards looking for dead Africans.

I never saw a sky so blue, so high. Across roof, tower, steeple and stack, the white light of old Greece came blowing. I looked below. And in every room the enormous hours had begun.

No end to the blue overhead and no end to the anguish below.

Below lay humanity's own Barrio-Chino, the pit where the light barely filters down. Down there was where the millions who had come to life before time began, then had worked blindly so long to give time eyes. There, for untold Chinese ages, untold millions had sweated and suffered with no light to tell them why. Now in fishermen's ships moving at night across the Mediterranean, waking at daybreak in the huts of Africa or in the rooms below, millions unknowingly yet make the truths of our own time. While wise men search the best hotels for news of Heaven.

Never knowing that, every man being his own Barrio-Chino, true news of Man never comes but from below.

No end to the everlasting light. No end to the dark below.

The woman one roof away began singing something, but all I could catch was the one word *paloma*—only this was a lonelier song.

My love is a dove with a broken wing
My love has lost her way far out at sea
The waves warn that the storm is coming
My love has lost her way.

The rooster came over, pecking at pebbles, and the dog came out and ran him off for me. The pooch wanted to show me he was sorry he had raised such a storm over nothing. He wanted to see how things were going, if I'd let him stick around. I told him Go back to bed you bum. He went back. He didn't mind being called a bum. He knew.

I figured if I could get over to the next roof *that* woman would ask me for dinner. I got one leg over the narrow abyss between buildings, so it was just a matter of getting the other leg over. The only trouble with that was that I have this thing about height. I should have remembered before I got one leg over. The position I was in, I couldn't move either. It was a question of whether to advance or retreat, so I retreated. I got back on my own roof.

For me it is easier to go down six flights and come up by the next stair-case. What is even easier is to put my back up against a chimney and sun myself, so that was what I did. It was the chance I have always wanted, to think about getting a start in life.

The way to begin, I realized, is to show yourself willing to work for nothing, as nobody ever got to be a millionaire by asking for one raise after another. The more work you're willing to do for nothing, the surer you are to be able to retire at forty to lovely Miami and watch the moon rise over the ryebread trees until you die at forty-one. Having reached the age of fifty deeper in debt than I was when I was merely flat broke, I now find myself faced with gathering doubt. My friends who took the risk of begin-ning at the very top are now so wealthy that they never travel with more than four dollars in pocket. When I say I liked that book about the big white shark I mean I *really* liked it. Now, how did *that* fellow get *his* start?

God, how that Assyrian could write. I really wouldn't want to write that good myself. The responsibility must be terrible.

If I could just write as good as Orville Prescott I'd be content. If I could turn out one paragraph such as, "This novel is a distillation of a perfumed youth remembered in age. In reading it, the air about one is pervaded by the essence of the *Ancien Régime*. It brings the exquisite to the level of the excruciating."

If I could turn out a bit like *that,* by the time it hit the streets Dorothy Kilgallen would be on the phone inviting me to "a little after-theater dinner party," where someone would say, "I would like to have you meet Mr. John Mason Nothing," and there *he'd* be. I'd drop something. casual like "I hear Noel Coward is getting braver," or "De Gaulle can kiss my Montparnasse." After that there would be nothing to do but wait for the morning papers.

I must in all modesty point out that the quarter of a century that I've been writing I've learned a few tricks of the trade myself; such as making a dot over the 'i' and adding an 's' when you want to show there is more than one of something. I was born in the same week that Stanley Ketchel fought Philadelphia Jack O'Brien and to this very day nobody knows which one won.

I stood up and looked over at the next roof to see why the woman over there had stopped singing but she had just gone inside to cook something. It smelled like chicken with rice. I looked around for the rooster and he was gone. He should have stayed on his own roof.

I got one leg over again and you know what happened. That was the position I was in when this definition of literature hit me out of the blue. I am always in that position, figuratively straddling the abyss, when a definition of literature hits me. But this was the first time it had happened to me literally. "Any challenge to laws made by people on top, in the interest of people below," I decided, "is literature." Then I got the other leg back.

What the hell, I thought, I'll buy my own dinner.

Once you start horsing around with American literature there is simply no telling in what position you may find yourself.

There is also simply no telling when you may meet Frank Sinatra. When I do I'm not going to forget myself and holler: "Spit on me, Frankie! I'm in the very front row!" Like we used to do when we were kids.

I decided to think about Spanish literature, as that may be the coming thing when the present run on Buddhism peters out. I figured it shouldn't take long, as I am no better informed on Spanish literature than on American, my entire library consisting of the works of Max Shulman.

Yet I can assure you that, at one time, I was well read. But that was before I consciously set forth on a course of knowing less and less, especially about literature. I had always before me the example of Paperfish

The Footnote King, whose course had been to know more and more about literature and who succeeded so well he finally got steady work as a ventriloquist. I saw then that erudition may lead to nothing more than becoming an authority; so I settled for knowing less about books and more about people.

Well, what would *you* have done if *you* had been Arch Oboler when Rod Serling came along?

There is a fellow around Spain who fought as a mercenary for Franco, and he didn't get a prize either. But after the war something happened to him and he began to write novels that are banned in Spain before they are even begun. The Chief of State is having some trouble trying to figure this out, as the man has a good war record from the present government's point of view. So he has become the most important novelist in the world now writing in Spanish. His name is Camilo Cela.

Cela's novels are published, as is all the work of Spain's best writers, in Argentina. But the censorship that weighs heaviest in Spain today is not upon its writers but upon those who have simply been censored out of any life at all except that lived out between the shafts of a two-wheeled cart. Or on the back between bedposts.

I asked Camilo Cela how it happened that his work, like that of Hemingway, Sartre, and the Goytisolos, is banned in Spain, while that of Albert Camus is acceptable and, indeed, popular. Cela's explanation is that there is nothing in the work of Camus that cannot be presented as a little lecture in how to be well behaved in a world where there would be less violence if there were only less protest.

This conversation occurred in the same week that Chessman was executed in California. As the man had been reprieved two months before, for political reasons, the execution struck me as an act of complete cynicism. Cela, however, felt that the execution was in a realm beyond that of the merely cynical. A cynical act, Cela felt, was one which is made in awareness of moral values, but refutes them. The act involving Chessman, however, seemed to him to be one carried out without an awareness of any values. It was not an act of cynicism, an act of vengeance, or an act of sadism, but simply the disposal of a man because he was in the way of a legal decision. He was killed simply because there was *nothing better to do.* There was no longer a way of justifying his execution, Cela felt, so Chessman was simply put out of the way to put an end to the matter.

But the smell of death hung over that California execution chamber as though the executioners had died there. For the smell came over the ocean and pervaded Spain.

Cela smelled it, for he knows the odor.

The lives going uphill here to nowhere and downhill without hope, the odor of death, begins in that great glassy showcase named Madrid.

The odor of death, the smell of lifelessness that flavors all Spanish life down to La Paloma Blanco, that great barnlike brothel of Barcelona where women sit knitting, naked upon a platform, and men stand against the walls watching them knit. Once in a while, in the bar of the Paloma Blanco, one snaps his fingers toward one of the women; she puts down her knitting and walks before him past a cashier's window, where the man pays one of two prices, depending on how many minutes he wishes to purchase, and is handed a towel.

No word need be spoken, love is not required. Here at last life has been reduced to its barest needs. As it has been reduced everywhere in Spain:

> "Two little boys, five to six years old, are playing at trains between the tables, wearily and without any enthusiasm. When they're going toward the back of the café, one is the engine and the other the carriages. On the way back to the entrance they change places. Nobody ever takes any notice of them, but they go on stolidly, joylessly, running backward and forward with immense seriousness. They are a pair of thoroughly logical disciplinarians, two small boys who play at trains though it bores them stiff because they have decided to have fun, and, to have fun, they have decided that come what may they are going to play at trains the whole afternoon. If they don't get any fun out of it is not their fault. They are doing their best.
>
> ". . . playing at trains without faith, without hope, and even without charity, as though carrying a painful duty."*

I asked Cela, hypothetically, what he would do if his worst political enemy were to be pursued by police and come to Cela's house for refuge. "I would hide him," Cela replied without hesitation.

---

* Camilo Cela, *The Hive.*

This is, of course, the wrong answer for Rear-Echelon Liberals Against Fascism. It is the wrong answer for literary mercenaries with shaky Garands and New York sub-critics who know one can't be too careful. But it is the right answer for people who care about people.

There is but one crime in modern society, to Cela, and that is to cooperate with the contemptuous waste our Western civilization makes of the lives of ordinary men and women.

When the sun was straight up, I had had enough of literature and got off the chimney.

I looked over to the woman one roof away whom I'd never see again. When she came closer to where I was standing, I pointed to the camera, meaning, could I come over and take pictures?

She shrugged, meaning she didn't share my enthusiasm but wouldn't pull a knife if I insisted. Then she turned her face to me and spoke gravely:

"Subir y bajar como Ud. con una camera fotográfica puede ser divertido. Pero, para nosotros, que subimos y bajamos todo el santo día, es el infierno."

(For you it is amusing to climb up and down with a camera, but for us, for whom there is no end of climbing up and going down, it is sheer hell.)

I took the streetcar called Atarazanas back down the Rambla, but I didn't take pictures. When the car passed the Café El Kosmo I saw that Encarnación had come to work early. She was sitting out front waiting for someone to buy her a beer. When the car stopped I called her name, and waved. She looked up and saw me but she didn't wave back. I knew they would like me in Barcelona.

The impression of bigness, out of all proportion to its size, that Spain leaves upon visitors is due, I believe, not only to its great variation of climate and scene. It is due also to an awareness that everything that happens in Spain happens to men everywhere.

Spain is the spiritual center of humanity, affecting all other parts. When Ireland bleeds only Ireland grows weak. But when Spain loses, Mankind loses. When the Spanish people were forced back into the Middle Ages in the 1930's, they pulled the world back with them. Anyone who tells you we're out of the Middle Ages today is somebody whose mind has snapped.

The corruption of the legalized tyranny at present holding the Spanish people under its cold control begins with the big-business brass. The generalship of any fascism does not begin with generals, but with men in business clothes who never handled a gun and never will. Generals can always be found.

Here its corruption extends to its officer caste, and has reduced its bishops to mere defenders of gold-inlaid entities, edifices built upon usury called cathedrals; that tacitly bless the degradation of Spain's young womanhood.

This is not the work of Franco, but of France, that cut off the guns. The waste of women like Loren Domingués is not the work of the generals who gave the orders, but of England; that preferred a fascist state to a democracy. It is the work of the United States' distrust of the idea of a people governing itself.

Nor has the work in the bullring at Badajoz by Franco's "Blond Moors" lent wisdom to the democracies twenty-three years after. Precisely as the democrats of Spain asked Western help, Portuguese democrats are asking it today—and are denied as was Spain. And again the Eastern bloc offers the arms needed by antifascists.

Spain today is not the work of a piece of activated pork in a tasseled hat named Francisco Franco. It is our Spain.

Yet now in the bright enormous morning twenty-three years after the fall of the city (making Barcelona forever new) I remain curiously proud of belonging to the curious, tragic, preposterous people once called "The Americans."

You may remember: we began by saying "We are bound where no mariner has yet dared to sail. We risk the ship, ourselves and all," and then we got rich. And wound up saying You can't be too careful. You remember.

You remember we began by saying No man is an island, but thought better of that toward the end; so changed it to I'm getting mine. You remember. We began in the search for the great white whale, yet dragged up nothing but Norman Manlifellow; that had to be tossed back for being under six inches.

We occupied a continent to the west and for a while there were quite a few of us. You remember.

You remember we began asking Are those really Congressmen? Are those the great Judges? Is that the President? Then I will sleep awhile yet. For I see that these States sleep.

I decided that fifty pesetas to the chambermaid, fifty to the kid who takes the bags down to the desk, and a hundred to the *concierja* would get me out of the Hotel El Kosmo. It meant walking downstairs to slip by The-Porter-Who'll-Never-Make-It.

The first part of THE PLAN worked fine. He was looking out the front door, his back turned, while I paid off at the desk. I got by him, with both bags, onto the street just as the cab pulled to the curb. *Now* who has it made? was my thought.

There was a rush behind me and a tug at my collar—he had hold of the piece of cloth that flops out of my jacket. I had to stand helplessly in the street while he tucked it in and brushed me down. He could have measured me for a new suit for the time he took.

All right, I was caught, and all I had was a hundred-peseta note and a half a pack of cigarettes. I broke down and handed him both.

He took one cigarette and handed me back the pack. With the hundred pesetas.

"*Gracias, señor.*"

And stepped back with his hands in his pockets.

Farewell, lovely Barcelona, city of contrasts, where the old contrasts with the new. Farewell, quaint city of Old Iberia where the healthy contrasts with the sick and the rich contrasts with the poor and the poor contrasts with the very poor. Farewell, striving metropolis, city of flowers and Portuguese automobiles. Farewell, Rambla de Las Floras, where the dark-eyed señorita smiles at her faithful caballero after being out all night with an American marine. Farewell, busy capital where the tourists gets to be the manager of the restaurant—*Adieu! Adieu! Adieu!*

ALMERÍA

SHOW ME A GYPSY AND
I'LL SHOW YOU A NUT

When I saw that little two-motored orphan waiting for me out there on the windless Spanish grass, it looked like a plane without a mother. As I had not brought my own mother along, I felt sympathetic.

Once inside it I felt pure pity for the little brute. A plane without a stewardess doesn't care whether it *ever* gets off the ground.

The only other passenger was an American Air Force fellow in civvies who told me he makes the run to Almería twice a week, but I couldn't imagine why. My own reason was so preposterous as not to bear admission. I simply clicked the shutter of my camera once or twice to show I had film and didn't care how fast I used it, and let it go at that.

"Where's the runway?" I wanted to know, glancing out the window, "Where do they take off from?"

"Right here off the grass, Dad. There ain't no runway."

"They'll have to warm this thing up half an hour to do *that.*"

"They don't warm nothing up in this country. They just take off, Dad."

"I think I'll just watch from the ground," I decided.

"Sit down, Unk," he urged me, "Ozark has a very good safety record."

"OZARK? *Ozark?* Are they going to try to bring this mousetrap into *St. Louis?* For God's sake, we'll never make Cincinnati. Let me get out of this here."

"We just call it Ozark because it barely clears those big hills, Dad"— pointing to the majestic heights of the Sierra Nevadas. A gesture that surprised me as the Sierra Nevadas are in another part of the country altogether.

The two-motored orphan began bumping about like a baby buffalo snouting for corn, got its wheels off the grass, ran into a storm a hundred feet off the ground though there wasn't a breath of wind inside or outside the plane, and finally got a tentative sort of grip on the air. By the time I had regained my composure I was in a damp sweat. I am never a man to be easily frightened by danger. But imminent peril really gets me.

All the way to Almería the pilot killed time by banking into a climb just to see what was going on up there, then shutting off the motors to slip into a plummeting glide. I'd never seen anything like it.

"Exactly what do you think he has in mind," I couldn't help wondering. "Is he trying to discover something?"

"Saving gas," Air Force Jack informed me.

Recalling an occasion when a Spanish pilot took it upon himself to discover Seville while I was in the plane, I steeled myself against the moment when this one, upon some wild surmise, would discover Almería. Ever since Columbus had his little success, the Spanish pilot has an *idée fixe* about getting to places before anyone else. Though it will take him the better part of a morning to fix you up with a cup of coffee, the reason is that he is bemused by the marvels of space travel in the kitchen. That's how it *is* in Spain, Man, that's what it's actually *like*.

The people below looked like ants. As we came down and raced toward the airport I looked out and saw they really *were* ants. There was nobody else around the airport at all.

"How much gas do you figure we saved *that* trip?" I asked Air Force Jack, who handed me a pack of Air Force cigarettes for reply. This kid must be loaded.

I offered to buy a drink provided it was on the ground, and he accepted at the little airport bar. He really seemed a deserving sort, so I regaled him with an account of the crossing of the Remagen Bridgehead.

I've told the story of how we crossed at Remagen so often and so well that if I ever run into somebody who actually crossed it I can only hope he'll have the simple decency to doubt himself so I don't have to bother. I have come to embrace this fantasy so wholeheartedly, in fact, that I can now recall quite clearly how I tricked two SS officers into chasing me until one dropped dead and the other died laughing; but before I reached this climax I looked up to see that Air Force Jack had gone.

Gone with Goth and Byzantine; gone with Scythian and Moor. Gone, like the Brooklyn Robins, taking his PX cigarettes.

The reason I had come to Almería was to photograph *The People from God Knows Where,* the cave-dwelling race who live in the immemorial rocks in the heights above the city. The title, inclusive of italics, was my own device, as one most likely to captivate the editor of any magazine that can afford to buy photographic plates.

Almería is a provincial town of streets as narrow as its people, a kind of Indianapolis without smoke. Having seen Indianapolis, I didn't bother with the town. The townspeople will tell you there is nobody living up there, because the idea of Spanish people living in caves touches their pride. But I knew better. I took a cab to the end of town and told the driver to wait as I was coming down on the other side. As that is a sheer drop of five hundred feet he said he would be pleased to catch me. I told him I'd take my own chances.

The road keeps going up into a toyless sun until there is no road, but merely loose gravel, and I went slip-sliding on all fours, camera dangling, from rock to rock wondering how Herman Wouk got *his* start. It occurred to me that the Abominable Snowman might turn out to be no more than another American trying to get pictures of people nobody had taken before. Frankly I don't even know how the Abominable Snowman got *his* start.

Nobody knows where these people came from, though there is conjecture that they might have come from caves along the Red Sea, a conjecture I made just this minute. At any rate, whoever they were, they found the rock of Greece too hard to carve. Why they didn't want to live in houses I have no idea. But in southern Italy they found rock soft enough to carve, and in Africa northeast of Ksar-es-Souk, they dug into the ground, where whole towns, large enough to hold ten thousand people, thrive today. I saw two blond, stocky little blue-eyed fellows perched on a rock, and they didn't run and hide when I came up, as the Bedouins northeast of Ksar-es-Souk do. They run and hide in Ksar-es-Souk. I never chased one into Ksar-es-Souk myself. but if I had a Diners' Club card I'd go in and bring one back. It might turn out to be Martin Bormann. Well, how would *you* feel if *you* were Bobby Breen when Tony Curtis came along?

I was pleased the kids didn't run from me and even more pleased they didn't start posturing when they saw the camera in hope of pay—asking *"Foto gitano? Foto gitano?"* even though they weren't gypsies. They had a ten-foot bamboo pole lying between them, across their knees. It looked suspiciously like a fishing pole, but I didn't want to ask them if they'd caught anything, not being in a hurry to make a fool of myself.

Other than their bamboo pole, there is no sign of a plaything in these toyless heights. No doll, ball, or bicycle. Just the beating heat on the gravel and the shade of the silence-colored rock. It's too hot for dogs; goats can't make it. Only men, women, and children, the hardiest brute that still roams free, can survive. If you ask me what they live on, I'll tell you that they must work as servants in the town below. That's only a guess, but it's as good as yours.

Some of the caves are natural wonders; others have been dug out and a window carved in one side, toward the morning sun, and the front whitewashed. One had palms across its doorway to remember the coming of Christ to Jerusalem. I *told* you they've been here a long time.

I stopped before one labyrinth that looked as if it had been old when the moon was new. A man's turtle-neck sweatshirt was hanging on a line to dry beside the opening, so I looked in thinking I might find James Jones at work. Nobody was in, so I judged he was downtown taking notes. A heavy-set young woman came along carrying a bucket of water in either hand. I stepped aside to let her by, but she didn't wish me good day. I waited to give her time to set the table for lunch, then put my head in and asked her if I could come inside.

She didn't say I couldn't, so I did. Some fellow who looked like he might be boarding with her sat in a corner, but I couldn't see him clearly because there wasn't enough light. But he didn't have anything to say either. Well, if the Troglodytes aren't a race of grouches, at least I'd found two who were.

He took a cigarette from me, sparing the pack, and when I offered her one she didn't know what to do. He said it was alright, take one, so she did and handed it to him. If he had handed it back to me I would have figured they were both in need of analysis, but they weren't. They just wanted to know what the hell I wanted. They were sure they hadn't sent for me.

I told them I had a hard time understanding Spanish, so they both began talking so loud, both at once, with gestures, that I realized they had misunderstood me—they thought I was hard of hearing. I put my fingers in my ears and shook my head, to show there was no need of hollering.

Finally I understood that not being able to understand Spanish words well meant I did not understand any words well. They could not conceive of another language because they had never been faced with the concept of another country. "Spain" and "world" meant the same thing. A Spaniard was a man and a man was a Spaniard. If a man did not understand Spanish it was because his hearing was bad.

I did not tell them there were other countries. Had one of the pair found out, he could have told the other. But as nobody has told either and both were now past middle age, neither would be able to believe it anyhow. Yet both man and wife were in good shape physically.

When I came back into the sun, toyless boys with bamboo poles were perched on a rock with their lines out over a sheer drop of rock. They were fishing for birds. A starling dived at the bait of bread, got hooked, and was hauled in. One of the bird-fishers had half a dozen birds beside him and the other had two. Wait till the sailors searching for sailfish off Palm Beach hear of *this!*

I asked where I could find the gypsies and they pointed downhill and up again, to see the *gitanos*.

The road up was solid and easy, so I made it upright. At the top of the road a mob of them were waiting, for they had spotted the camera. Five-year-olds to ancestral hags in bandanas, all crowding, hollering, and posturing, *"Foto gitano? Foto gitano?"* I didn't see one good-looking girl in the crowd.

This race, if it is a race and not a roadshow, has but one cultural distinction—that of holding out the hand for you to put something in. If you do there is, immediately, a whole host of cousins, brothers, sisters, babies, youths, grandparents, all hollering *"Foto gitano!" "Foto gitano!"*

One entrepreneur, a boy of about fourteen, was working along different lines. He was standing in the shadow of a door and, as I passed, exposed himself.

My single hope was to get out of town with the camera. There was no use of trying to take a picture. Darryl Zanuck couldn't have afforded it.

From the barrooms of Barcelona to the gravel heights above Almería I saw a tough and vigorous race. A monarchy of hungry peasants controlled, yet scarcely governed, by a military establishment shot through with corruption and sustained by a contented American State Department. The stink in the herring begins in the head.

Should this writer's convictions trouble his reader, please bear in mind that the writer paid his own way. That he remains, today, not a bought journalist (although working in a corrupted estate) only by the chance that there have been no offers, in no wise alters his honor. The virgin who retains her virginity by the happenstance of being overlooked is no less the virgin for that. The writer is therefore resolved to cherish his unstained condition so assiduously in the future as to provoke the passions of parties who might be interested in soiling it simply to amuse themselves.

The point here is not to gain riches, but only to be able to attend a writers' conference somewhere and not have to feel, when seated on a panel facing an audience, that he is different than the other members.

"Foto gitano? Foto gitano?"

Show me a gypsy and I'll show you a nut.

Back at the airport I picked up a week-old *Herald Tribune,* Paris edition. Frank Lary of Detroit had beaten Pedro Ramos of the Senators in their second pitching duel within the week, retiring the last twelve men in order.

Another American wearing a pith helmet and Bermuda shorts was standing at the bar. I was going to ask him if he'd checked his Mannlicher, but it's best not to start anything with an American.

Yet I kept wondering what country *he* thought *he* was in.

SEVILLE

THE PESETA WITH THE
HOLE IN THE MIDDLE

The plane's enormous shadow keeps wandering above The Land of Visible Silence: to these vast rock-colored wastes no bird ever comes. No grass grows, no tree can flower. I'm the pilot's only passenger, and the cabin door is closed. If I open it and he isn't in there I'll have to learn to fly real fast.

A plane without a stewardess is home without a mother, and on Lineas Aéreas España it's home without a Spanish mother. If I could see somebody down there, just *anybody,* it would be less lonesome up here. Nothing could be more lonesome than the silence-colored wastes below.

Until a savannah green with hope takes the plane's shadow by surprise—here the Moors brought water long ago. Then the wastes once more. If the Catholic kings couldn't irrigate themselves, the least they could have done was not to bother the Moors when they were gardening.

Besides being great gardeners, the Moors took great strides toward going to seed themselves. Nobody in Spain would have had to bother getting decadent today had the Spaniards let them alone. The work would have all been done. This means that the modern Spaniard has lost the opportunity of becoming decadent through satiation. He has to find some other means. Such as hunger.

I'm told Spanish power is no longer what it was, and in that event I'm tickled that I wasn't around when it was really cranked up. Unless I could have been a Spaniard too. In which event I would have gone to Mexico and made life a living hell for Montezuma. Then I'd buy Goa with the profits and give it back to the Portuguese.

I found the copy of *The Ring* magazine with Carmen Basilio on the cover, and turned to. "Harry Greb King of the Alley Fighters." I'll have to remember to ask the pilot what ever became of Paolino Uzcudun.

If I *have* a pilot. If he isn't in there I'll grab the most likely looking stick and taxi into Seville as gracefully as though I'd been expected. When the reporters start throwing questions at me I'll say, No, I've never flown before; it's just that an American adapts himself to danger by disposing of it. Yes, I'm single at the moment but if I'd stayed in Marseilles at the end of the war I would now be the father of six.

How I'd support a family like that on one PX card gave my sense of security such a jolt that I decided to settle every doubt I'd gathered since 1946 simply by knocking on the cabin door and shouting, "Are you *in* there, in there?" At that moment I knew there really was somebody in there, because he and I both spotted the city below at the same moment. I judged it to be Seville, but he thought he had discovered something, because he pointed the nose of the plane straight down and shut off both motors.

We didn't descend. Men, we *plummeted.*

He straightened me out at the last possible second for the headlong race down the runaway with every loose rivet in the plane rattling barely loud enough to cover the rattling of my own; which aren't any too tight, anyhow.

That's how it is in Spain, men. That's how it *really* is. When you see something you never saw before, get there first.

You may have discovered something.

As the bulls were not being fought on the day of my arrival, several Europeans had driven to the airport in hope of seeing a plane come down in flames. Among these sophisticates I spotted a novelist, Juan Goytisolo, whose brother, Luis, was being held incommunicado by Franco in Barcelona; and Mme. Simone de Beauvoir, who is never incommunicado under any circumstances.

They put on a poorly rehearsed business about having come to meet me, but I was *on*. One brief nod covered both *voyeurs*.

Between them stood a moustachioed brigand for whom they hastily invented the pseudonym of "Vicente Andarra" and introduced him as "our translator."

Some translator. What was he doing with a German camera dangling from his neck and his pockets bulging, apparently with film? One photographer on this safari would serve our purposes, was *my* thinking. I pressed my own small Kodak to my side, for I felt her trembling under the Prussian aristocrat's arrogant glare.

"Nothing will come of the camera," Mme. de Beauvoir, a French philosopher, philosophized, to assure her Spanish companions that my Kodak was nothing more than a prop.

"Something *will* come of it," I corrected her. We were off to a good start.

"Our translator" had maneuvered a small rented car to the airport upon the assumption that all Americans love to drive. He had never seen one who had never driven. I had to climb into the back seat to establish this move: this not only prevented a terrible crash on the highway, but, as it left no one but Andarra to handle the wheel, cast me as the expedition's official photographer; a post richly deserved.

"*Now* let's see you take pictures," I challenged him silently when he took the wheel.

"Nothing will come of *either* camera," Goytisolo observed—the first occasion he had had to slander somebody in English. I was going to have trouble with him too. That was plain enough.

Out of the corner of my eye, on both sides of the road, I saw a crowd of dust-green dwarfs racing us to Seville; but when I turned my head they stiffened into attitudes of trees.

Like people, olive trees become stagestruck early and seldom recover, spending their whole lives twisting themselves into unnatural attitudes in trying to be something they are not. One old paunchy rogue was trying to give some dusky girl-trees the impression that he was Harry Belafonte by doing a calypso bit. Although they were laughing at him to themselves, he thought he was making it and making it big.

An austere, imperious sort, a very De Gaulle of olive trees, directed the entire grove, holding his branches like olive whips while reminding all of the ancestral grandeur of his grove; which, I had the impression, he had planted himself. He was telling them that he was different than most trees because he thought in terms of decades, and I guess he was right, because half of the grove kept marching the other way as if thinking in terms of what was going to happen tomorrow. Personally I felt they should all go home; including their commander.

Yet all—rogues, girls, reluctant conscripts—in whatever direction they strove, struggled hard against the Spanish wind.

The wind off the Sierra Nevadas of which peasants say, "It will not blow a candle out, but will kill a man in a night."

One widowed olive, draped in a silvered shawl, her other arm shielding her eyes, was cradling a dead infant at her breast.

A grief wholly Spanish.

A contented-looking teen-age tree stood looking on, feeling cocky about being so much smarter than anybody else; but I think he gave himself too much credit. He reminded me, in fact, of myself on an occasion when I outsmarted both the owner of the corner poolroom and my mother in an early westside coup. The owner wouldn't let me shoot pool in short pants and my mother wouldn't let me put on long ones until I was fourteen.

I was the only sport on Kedzie Avenue still in short pants, and I had three months to go before I could shoot pool with my colleagues of the Kedzie Avenue Arrows. That was a lifetime to wait.

So I bought a pair with money I'd earned myself, and put them on in the poolroom washroom. At the clack of the cue ball breaking up the triangle, the fifteen ball raced to the corner pocket and dropped in. When I touched the tip of the cue to the wooden markers by which we kept score on the wire overhead, to rack up my first point, I had become a man at last.

I don't know how many points it *really* takes; but racking up the fifteen ball did it for *that* day.

"It's not as easy as you think, punk," I told him as we passed.

One seed, one soil, and one wind had formed them all. Yet each felt certain he was unique.

"Olive trees act like people," I therefore informed the French philosopher, confident that she would translate this nifty notion and in no time at all we'd all be laughing.

"People act more like olive trees," was her fast rejoinder.

Next time I'd keep my mouth shut.

Goytisolo reported that he had not succeeded in seeing his brother, but had learned that Luis had been in solitary confinement forty-three days and was sick as a dog. No reason had been offered for his arrest.

At the time of his arrest, Señor Fernando Castiella, Minister of Foreign Affairs for Spain, was in the United States, having been invited by the Eisenhower Administration (presumably on the advice of the C.I.A.) to speak at Georgetown University. In this address Señor Castiella neglected to mention "the passionate permanent unity between Spanish Fascism and German Nazism" that he had declared in his own book; in which he asserts with pride that World War II was planned and rehearsed in the

Spanish Civil War. His invitation followed his private discussion with
Eisenhower in London in 1959. Since that secret occasion, Señor Castiella
has echoed Franco's declaration of solidarity with Portugal.

"I estimate we have killed 30,000 of these animals already," a Portuguese major has informed a correspondent of *Time;* "there are perhaps
100,000 of them in revolt, and we intend to kill every one of them when
the dry season starts late in May."

Nobody in Spain knows when the dry season starts for the C.I.A.

Goytisolo was five when Mussolini and Hitler invaded Spain, and now
lives in Paris because it's hard to get a lawyer when you're locked up in
Barcelona. But being inordinately fond of Spanish dancing, Spanish food,
Spanish wine, the Spanish guitar, Spanish girls, the Spanish language,
toros, fiestas, mantillas, gaspacho, carraquillo, and all the rest of that crazy
stuff they have over there, he ducks back to Barcelona now and again to
see who else he knows is being held incommunicado.

The melancholy information that Luis Goytisolo was being held in
solitary confinement was as close as Juan had been able to come to seeing
his brother. The information had been conveyed to Juan through the good
offices of the prison physician, who had let him have this news for a hundred dollars, as he was an idealist. Had he not been, the information
would have cost less.

It isn't in despite of their Catholicism that these Catalans resist Franco,
but because of it. These are the people whose priests were put to the wall
by Franco's "blond Moors"—as he called his German brigades.

All Goytisolos, being Catalans, speak at once, and I doubt that any
member of the family stops talking even in solitary. Mme. de Beauvoir
speaks a broken English more fluently than I can speak it unbroken. This
left me only my Kodak as a means of asserting my presence, so I kept aiming it at the olive groves and snapping the shutter whether I had film in it
or not. This revealed me as an American tourist of the most unbearable
variety; an identity I was trying to establish so that nobody could say I was
going out of my way just to endear myself to everyone. Well, how would
you feel if *you* had been Richard Widmark when Rip Torn came along?

Goytisolo and Andarra began brushing up on their English by asking
me the English name of objects along the road. Goytisolo would point at
a grove and I would explain: "Tree. Olive. Martini." And Andarra would
disagree—"No Martini. Wicky"—"wicky" being the closest people south

of Madrid can come to saying "whiskey." They have as much difficulty with our "s" as we do with their double "r."

The olive-tree people kept trailing us, some waving us on, some calling us back.

The last one I saw, as we rounded a curve into Seville, was a youthful relay runner straining toward some everlasting finishing line with a hard wind against him.

The wind off the Sierra Nevadas that prevails against men as well as against trees.

Seville is the place where the harsh Saturday-night clamor of old Barcelona, jesting cries of sellers and jesting answers of buyers, the big free laughter of fishermen, whores, and bartenders, flower women and lottery vendors, fades to a churchly Sunday-morning hymnal. It is always Sunday morning in churchly Sevilla, where well-behaved girls with self-important behinds and big feet leave their embroidering to hurry to Mass but take their time coming back to embroidering.

It is a city of women watching the street from small barred windows, because the Moors not only built delicately, but strongly as well: it takes strong walls to keep women indoors, and the Moors never did devise a wall strong enough.

Yet their strategy was an improvement over the Byzantine school, that bricked the girls in solid. As this hadn't worked in Byzantium, the Moors let their women have windows—with bars if the windows were on the ground floor. When the window was too high to leap out of without breaking a leg, the Moors were progressive enough to leave the bars off. These left high arching apertures in which the great day, or the night thronged by stars, were framed.

But by high window or low, the common lot of the woman of Spain south, yet today, is a life sentence of doing embroidery while watching a street owned by men.

"Needle and thread for the woman, mule and lash for the man," is the saying.

Neither the good girl nor the bad frequents the streets of Seville except to go to church or on a shopping errand. A respectable woman doesn't take a walk when she feels like taking a walk. She does her walking with her fingers, across a bit of fabric.

The good girl embroiders for her hope chest and the brothel woman works for the Virgin of Macarena above her bed: to give thanks for last night's favors and in hope of men who are young and rich in the night to come.

Sons of officers and breeders of bulls who sit all day over long-stemmed glasses of manzanilla on the Calle de Sierpe speaking of bulls, horses, and women in one breath: of women of good family as of those protected by none but the Virgin. Young men who feel it is as right to be Spanish as confidently as the Englishman feels it is right to be English.

It is therefore unnecessary for the Spaniard to identify himself as Spanish, in the Italian and American manner. "Me Italiano!" the man you meet for a moment assures you. Or, "Ah'm from Tayxus" another shouts across a dining room.

Well, good, but why be so shaky about it, Dad? We aren't going to throw you out of the old Union. We need your oil.

At the Plaza de Toros of Seville we met Goytisolo and Andarra. Goytisolo had learned that his brother had been released in Barcelona, with no more reason given for releasing him than had been given for his arrest.

We saw the first bull, The Foolish Bull of Seville, storm out into the arena in a smoking fury, and a strong yellow smell mixed of urine and rage blew off his furious hide. Ladies coughed into handkerchiefs and men stood up to get a better look at this passionate brute who didn't know that, if he wanted to win, he was certainly going about matters the wrong way. Perhaps his wife had just told him she was leaving him—"Honey, you've supported me all these years; now go out and get a job for yourself."

The animal did have one good idea, and that was to wipe out the other side. He got one good horn under the horse, and horse goes upsy, rider and all, rider comes downsy, and Goytisolo began reciting "At Five in the Afternoon." I stood up and hollered, "Finish them both off!"

The bull didn't hear me because he had so much stuff sticking in him he looked like a fruitcake and it hurt. He had had enough of the picador and the picador had had enough of him. The point I'm trying to make is that they had had enough of each other.

The matador came out but he came out too soon, because the bull caught him with the flat of the horn, and up the matador went too. That was a great day for going up in Seville.

Torero came down kneeling with the bull's nose in his face; the preliminary boys ran out. *Torero* waved them away to indicate he now had the bull transfixed. I wondered what he was going to transfix him with, as his sword was yards away. His left pant leg had been ripped to the waist, and if it hadn't been padded he'd be riding that horn yet. Yet he boldly turned his backside directly on the bull and recovered his sword—there was one moment of truth as he stooped to recover it, but the bull hadn't read *Death in the Afternoon.*

He was over at the fence, looking up at the judges, thinking he had won. The next move was to give him the matador's ear and half his pants, was his thinking. This seemed to me to be the right moment for some-one to mount the fence with a sledgehammer, finish the bull off and jump down, as the animal was streaming blood.

Nobody had a sledgehammer in Seville, and with or without a ham-mer, nobody wanted to get that near to *Toro.* The thinking was that the longer everyone stayed out of his way, the better for everybody. So the pre-liminary boys merely trotted cautiously after *Toro* as he trotted till the very air stank of blood.

By this time even Goytisolo no longer liked it. Andarra didn't like it. I doubted even the bull enjoyed it. Personally I felt I could do without it. The whole team followed him till his legs gave way at last and one of the valiant clowns gave him the dagger. *Arriba España!*

"I want Scotch," Mme. de Beauvoir said.

"I want wicky," Andarra said.

"Who's going to wipe up the blood?" I inquired.

The horns resounded and who should trot out but The Wise Bull of Seville looking for a friend. That The Wise Bull of Seville had been well brought up was immediately apparent, for he was a bull who remembered his promise to Mother. How she had planted her gentle hoof on the back of his neck and warned him, "Once you make a run at one of these fools, you've answered the first question, so you'll have to answer all the rest and the horses will drag you off like they dragged off your poor daddy."

"Why did Daddy answer the fools, Mother?"

"He was a proud bull, Son. Too proud to take the fifth."

The Wise Bull of Seville had been a mere calf when he'd promised his widowed mother to take the fifth. He had never had anything against peo-ple as such—some of his best friends had been people—but he had never seen so many at once as he saw now. Then he caught a whiff of Chanel that brought him to a dead stop nose up, for the woman who was giving off something that smelled like *that* must be a beauty. He saw her, down front, a red-haired Andalusian, and lowered his horns toward her by way of indicating that he was a gentleman who had no intention of goring anybody.

Mother had been right, he saw then for sure. For out of the corner of his eye he saw people in yellow pants prancing and dancing toward him: they were surely up to something.

The Wise Bull of Seville got the feeling he better get the hell out of there; so he nodded a "Pleased to have met you, Baby," at the lovely redhead and trotted quietly away.

After that it was touch and go, because some came running and some came sneaking, and one caught him a couple sharp shots with something in the back of his neck. He pretended not to notice. The Wise Bull didn't even snort, not wishing to be held in contempt.

They began to applaud his good manners—he would have been hurt had he understood they were clapping because he was boring everyone stiff.

When he finally realized they were clapping out of displeasure, he thought it must be the people who kept chasing him on the horse who was wearing everyone down. He resented the fellow for being so imperceptive.

Yet, he supposed, the fellow must be a steady employee with some seniority, while he himself was a newcomer; so he might as well be gracious about it, and trotted out through the same gate by which he came.

Well, what would *you* have done if *you* had been Potash and Perlmutter when Morris Fishbein came along?

And though he was proud of himself for having kept his word to Mother so well, at the same time he couldn't help feeling sad, for in his heart he knew he could whip anyone of those little peoples in the fancy pants. As a matter of fact he wouldn't mind taking a shot at that finkylooking horse.

Next time he wouldn't tell Mother—but oh, how proud she was going to be when she read in the papers that he had *won!*

The penalty for engaging young bulls in mock bullfights while they are being raised for the arena is extremely severe, in order to discourage such sport among Spanish teenagers. The boys are fond of slipping over a fence after dark and teasing a young bull with a stick in lieu of a sword, and then hitting out for the fence when he charges. The peril is not to the boy, but to the matador the bull will one day meet, for *Toro* learns fast and remembers well. A year later, in the arena, assuming it is the bull's first time out, a torero may pay with his life for not knowing it is the bull's second time out.

The bulls that followed were all foolish bulls. All answered the fifth and all wound up as bloody carcasses being dragged out by finky-looking horses.

We went to a coffee joint on the Calle de Sierpe to have a final *carraquillo* with Andarra and Goytisolo, who were leaving that evening for Barcelona. I realized then that my antagonism toward Andarra was really only toward his camera. And as he was leaving the whole south of Spain to me to photograph, I relented long enough to shake his hand and tell him I was looking forward to seeing the pictures he had taken.

"Yes," Mme. de Beauvoir agreed, "that would be fortunate, as nothing will come of our own efforts."

We would see about that: we decided to climb the Giralda, Seville's ancient tower; then to have dinner.

The hand of the Christian can be seen above the hand of the Moor, in the most famous belfry tower of Christendom erected in Praise of Allah: The Giralda.

The Moors turned a warlike, masculine, invulnerable mask to the world. But within the mask they were as vulnerable as flowers. They built with a feminine grace. The smile of a woman and the flow of water were their delights. They made light to fall like water and water to fall like light.

They built slowly, never working ahead of their feelings, and their feeling had delicacy. After they had left, leaving The Giralda unfinished, the Catholic kings plastered a heap of brickwork above it, thinking to complete what the Moors had begun.

But the Moorish hand can be followed to a clear and precise line. Above it, one is left with the same impression one might obtain had the last chapter of *Moby-Dick* been written by Dwight MacDonald. It has no significance. The Catholic kings assumed that energy was enough, but the Moors knew that it isn't how much stone you can accumulate into a pile, but how much heart you can get into the stone.

For my own taste the Moors built quite high enough. The Giralda is a long, slow climb up cobbled ramps similar to the upgrade journey to the upper stands one takes at Comiskey Park if the Yankees are in town for a doubleheader.

Why the Moors were so fond of walking uphill so much puzzled me, as the landscape provided them with mountains. But when we reached the highest tower and saw Seville, river, rooftop and tower under an African sky, I understood why.

El Suspiro del Moro—the sigh of the Moor—still breathes across this land. A nation without a country, a remote wave of the great Arabian inundation, they held the land for a thousand years yet never made it their true home. Cut off from Islam by desert and sea, separated from the Christians by custom, faith, and language, they could have kept their hold only by pushing up into France and making Europe theirs. There is no reason to believe Europe would have been worse off today had they succeeded. Or better. Had they not been defeated at Tours, their civilization would not have become the light of the world for a thousand years.

After Tours they ceased to be a conquering race, and developed a civilization wherein the arts of antiquity shone with new light. Their universities welcomed the youth of dark Europe into an intelligent, graceful, tolerant land. But, as their towers, even today, present an implacable masculine face to the world yet are softly feminized within, behind their terrible armor they too became feminized. Their final annihilation was complete, some bare few escaping down Africa's vast maw. The green land was left bleak by their departure.

Leaving, for their thousand years, nothing but empty towers showing like masts of sunken ships in a receding sea.

And that strange ancestral wail, full of longing and full of loss, one hears behind the Spanish singing.

The Moors aren't playing here anymore. They aren't playing anywhere anymore. Gone with Goth and Byzantine; gone with Assyrian and Greek. Gone with the Scythians and the Boston Red Stockings.

On the way to his exile the last Moorish sultan turned in his saddle on a height above Granada and looked for the last time at the city.

And wept for the thousand years.

          ❀   ❀   ❀

She must have been almost ten, and wore a castoff black rag for a dress. I saw her face, the mouth of innocence and the large dark eyes pressed to the bars. A face so young yet so old; that had come so far. Just to see an American eat. And she laid her hands lightly, palms up, between the narrow bars. I had never seen hands look so empty.

A child of one of those small whitewashed hovels behind the fish market of the Guadalquivir. A daughter of one of those men who come bearing life-sized sculptured images of Christ and the twelve disciples at The Last Supper, through the streets of Holy Week, with real food set out before them. But the Christ of Seville is a bejeweled colossus in the service of a medieval real-estate chain. A churchly syndicate which has changed the meaning of The Last Supper to: The Less Bread for the Children, the More for Us.

And this one wasn't invited to ours, either. A bit of fish on a clothless board makes a meal behind the fish market on the Guadalquivir, but what she saw before her, between the bars of the restaurant window, was fish soup *and* fish. *And* meat. *And* fruit. *And* flowers. And forks of silver and wine of two colors, all arranged, under a soft electric glow, on damask white as snow.

"We have a spectator," I informed Mme. de Beauvoir on the other side of our table.

"Disregard the sight," she told me, "I can't see it."

I shifted in my chair, not to shut the child out of my sightline so much as to shut myself out of hers. But when the waiter refilled the wineglasses I felt her eyes. She was waiting for me to drink.

"Of all the people drinking manzanilla in Sevilla," I complained, "she has eyes just for me."

"Try giving her something."

I put an open pack of cigarettes beween the bars. It touched her hand but her fingers didn't take it. In fact, she didn't even look at it. Yet her lips said, *"No, gracias."*

I took the pack back.

"She doesn't smoke," I reported.

"Give her money."

I found a peseta with a hole in the middle. Before I had it out her lips whispered again:

"No, gracias."

"She doesn't use money."

Although Spain is an underdeveloped country, they know how to pour *kirsch* over pineapple in a way that is a distinct improvement over canned heat strained through a bandanna onto a piece of rye bread two days old. I thought of offering the girl a spoonful in the hope she'd get zonked and stagger home. But my hand was unsteady. I had to eat the stuff myself just to keep it from spilling.

"What *exactly* are you trying to do?"

"I was trying to give this girl something to eat."

"Try sugar."

I succeeded in getting two lumps of sugar onto the windowsill. As they were wrapped in paper I didn't spill a drop. But the waiter's shadow passed across my hand. He took the sugar back and replaced it on my saucer.

"No, señor," he spoke firmly.

"I *offered* her money," I explained.

"A Spanish child is not a beggar, señor."

"I offered her cigarettes."

"A Spanish child is not a gypsy, señor."

"She isn't a beggar and she isn't a gypsy but she likes to eat, so I gave her sugar."

"A Spanish child is not a donkey, señor."

I took a flower out of the vase, handed it through the window; and still unsmiling, the little girl stuck the stem in her hair and said, *"Gracias, señor"*—and backed off, still unsmiling; her small face melting into the solemn darkness of the Calle de Sierpe. Where young men speak of bulls over thin-stemmed glasses.

We finished the meal with no further word. But the restaurant was not lit as brightly as it had been when we had entered. The eternal bells of The Cathedral rang, inviting all good children to Mass. Yet Seville itself was no longer smiling.

"Is everything alright, señor?" the waiter returned to ask.

A Frenchman can play a waiter's part flawlessly, an Italian may actually enjoy *service,* but your Spaniard isn't built for waiting on others, and when he pretends to humility it is worse than when he is his own arrogant self.

"Everything is *not* alright," I assured him, regaining my own arrogant self; "there were feathers in the duck, the coffee was cold, and the wine had cork."

"Why don't you have him fired," my sarcastic friend suggested in English, "as you did the waiter in Paris who would not bring you an American soda?"

"I did *not* have him fired," I was forced to correct her.

"You *wanted* to, and that is the same thing. For shame, a big man ordering a strawberry soda. I did not blame the man for refusing."

"It was not strawberry—I *despise* strawberry, it was *chocolate,* and he brought the people at the next table four of them."

"They were Americans; they had the right to have American sodas."

"What am I—a Persian, for God's sake?"

"When you are with a Frenchwoman on Champs Élysées, you are French."

"I'm not French even if I'm in a tepee on top of the Eiffel Tower and I'm not a Spaniard and there *was* a feather in that damned duck."

"I'll bring you fresh wine, señor," the Falangist disguised as a waiter offered.

"Don't bother," I told him.

"But *I* did not *send* for you, señor," was what his shrug conveyed. "*Buenas noches,*" he told Mme. de Beauvoir.

"Let's get out of this peseta with the hole in the middle," I decided.

It took four shots of wicky before I felt myself beginning to forgive the children and its restaurants, the waiters and the wine of churchly Seville.

Walking downhill we saw a small man coming up. He was bending under a load of firewood heavier than himself and kept his eyes, perforce, to the ground. He held to the middle of the street. As he did not see us, we parted to let him pass.

"When you see people doing the work of animals, that indicates you are in an undeveloped country," the French philosopher pointed out.

"Oh, I thought that was Aristotle Onassis," I thanked my companion, grateful for any shred of enlightenment.

I wonder whether I could have gotten a reaction by saying, "Oh, I thought that was Brigitte Bardot."

But no, I realized sadly, Bardot wouldn't have worked either.

Once the dancing began, however, in some offstreet, gypsified dim-lit trap, it began to look to me as if that waspwaisted lightweight on the tiny stage, built into his suit and boots like a black knife into its sheath, was a serious waste of fighting talent. If someone could get a kid like that away from the girl with the castanets and the dunce with the guitar, the American lightweight division would pick up class.

The whole trouble with all these Europeans, excepting the English, however, is that their power is in their legs instead of their arms where power rightly ought to be. They forget about their arms. They don't jab or hook or cross. They just let them hang.

The lighter races—French and Italian and Spanish—think that the way to win a fight is to kick the opponent in the stomach. The heavy races—Greek, Turkish, and Russian—think the main idea is to lean all your weight on him and when he goes down, stay on top and keep leaning. I don't know about the Germans, but my hunch is that their idea is to avoid physical contact altogether: just press a button or pull a lever and find out who won by phone. The more impersonal, the better, seems to be their thinking. But the Spanish idea is to do everything as personally as possible.

This is plain in the dancing, that is more than dancing: it is pride personified. The great insistence on dignity, the courage and the grace that, I had been told, I would see in the fighting of the bulls, was in the dancing. Well, I must have hit the bullring on the wrong day, because I failed to catch anything but the spectacle of some overdressed gypsies butchering several head of cattle to the sounding of horns blowing out of tune.

In the dancing I caught it, immediately, in the magical speed of the lightweight's foot moving faster than the eye could follow, that comes to a dead stop without perceptible pause. I saw a dance meaning: Let there be no folly.

Dancing that gave coherence to passion and emotion to form, where all feeling was wild yet sternly controlled.

And when the dancer was a girl in a red-and-black skirt doing an Aragonese village dance, I saw as though for the first time what true gayety can be. As well as what a girl can be.

Then, behind a massive gypsy woman as light on her feet as a fawn in the morning, the chorus mounted a slow clapping of hands, increasing in intensity till a single singer's voice broke through in some old lost Asiatic blues—then broke off on an upbeat wail as the dancer's feet came to that dead-still stop.

I'd been somewhere. A place to which I could go back.

Is it because such dancing, asserting that ancestral struggle of every

race, Bushman to Britisher, to give dignity to the phenomenon of finding oneself a human being, is more vivid in Spain than in any other land
because the struggle has been fought here against such tragic odds so long?

Because whether the Spanish dancing is good dancing or bad dancing,
it is always good dancing. For it says man is unconquerable.

They tell me the Greeks gave us the concept of beauty and the Romans
sound rules for keeping order.

To me, the Spanish gift is the most precious.

The next morning we drank a goodbye *carraquillo* to Seville.

So farewell, sunny Soho, glamorous metropolis of hospitable Spain,
where the dark-eyed señorita smiles down on her faithful caballero after
being out all night with an American ensign. Farewell, busy capital of
modern Iberia where the new contrasts with the old and the rich contrasts
with the poor. Farewell, historic Seattle.

And farewell, child of the fish market behind the Guadalquivir, who
declined my peseta with the hole in the middle.

CRETE

THERE'S LOTS OF CRAZY
STUFF IN THE OCEAN

CRETA TRAVEL BUREAU—"Opposite city air terminal"—the folder informed me, offered "excursion with experienced guide speaking English, French and German in luxurious motor coach."

As I had never heard anyone speaking three languages in a luxurious coach, I hurried to the terminal and paid 180 drachmas to get the whole deal.

I could have gotten by for 150, but that was without lunch and I wanted to be among the ones who would be eating while the others stood around and watched.

The only luxurious appointment of the coach was the driver, a Greek millionaire affecting raggedy pants, a rained-on cap, a windworn face and careworn eyes so he would look like a peasant driving a bus. He had a good act and he might have gotten by with it if he had shaved. The three-day stubble was a dead giveaway.

Although there were thirty seats for eight passengers and the bus wasn't due to leave for half an hour, everybody raced to get a seat the second the driver opened the door; with the result that I got wedged fast with an American girl of good family who had been dispatched to Greece to pick up Hellenic culture and a husband of any old culture at all.

When we got unwedged she claimed that her name was Milly, that she was studying the history of art, and that this was the first time she'd been wedged. I assured her it was the first time I'd wedged a historian, and we were off and winging. I offered her the window seat and, by sliding into it in front of her, discovered Milly was a slow-breaker. Once she broke, however, Milly made up ground. She talked so fast it sounded like she'd taken a course in advanced chattering.

She had just come from Athens and was put out with a French utility magnate, name of Malraux, who'd obtained the lighting and sound rights to The Acropolis. All I could make of it was that Milly felt the rights should have been retained by the Greeks. I comforted her by assuring her that the Greeks would be getting a kickback from Mister Malraux and what we really had to watch out for was Englishmen sifting the rubble.

Milly was dead serious about The Glory That Was Greece, and wanted me to be serious about it too. The moment she chose was on a narrow, climbing run, growing steeper, narrower, and more winding by the moment.

The morning papers had carried a front-page story about a coachload of people going over a sheer drop of 3,455 kilometers straight down without a pause, somewhere in Turkey. I couldn't for the life of me see how The Glory That Was Byzantium had been of any more use to them then than The Glory That Was Greece would be to me if the millionaire in the driver's seat dozed off.

Even on a three-lane highway, I can't get serious about The Glory That Was Greece because at the time they were being glorious, the Greeks themselves didn't know it. All they were doing was trying to please their wives and stay out of jail. The glory thing wasn't put down until after their scene had been blacked out for a millennium. The claim of the present occupants of the peninsula has no more to do with ancestral Greece than with The Old Ashmolean Marching Society and Single Ladies Band. If not less.

But Milly was so sure of herself I had to take the side of the Turks, in war or peace, even to the point of insisting that Turks are better drivers than Greeks. She didn't believe this as she had seen the morning papers too, and as it was the fifth time, since the first of the year, that a Turkish bus had gone over a cliff, while the Greeks have a perfect safety record since Venus rose from the waves.

The Greeks might have a perfect safety record, I conceded, but to anyone, such as myself, who has had the experience of asking an Athenian cab driver to take him to The Parthenon and then having the man ask where it was, a good safety record doesn't cut butter. Milly replied that when the Turks could produce anyone who could sing like Maria Callas she'd buy a ticket. I didn't tell her about Eartha Kitt, but I did happen to recall an East St. Louis chick by name of Marie Kallas who used to sing *If I Can't Sell It I'll Keep Settin' on It I Just Won't Give It Away*, at the Rock

Garden Club on the river, who married a Greek, and I wondered if it could be the same chick stepping up. Milly said she had heard Mme. Callas *was* engaged to a Greek fellow at that.

The fellow the East St. Louis girl married was in the shipping business too, I told Milly, and it struck her that Callas' friend was in that field also. The whole thing struck me as such a coincidence that, when Milly told me she had only put out 150 drachmas, I invited her to share my lunch: the coincidence must have stunned me. I got a promise out of her that she'd take me to dinner.

We had to get out of the bus in order to see Gortynia, but there was nobody home. Candidly, all I could see was a hill with a lot of good stonework gone to hell. Milly told me what I was looking at was really something, so we had to climb it.

She told me these people had been far ahead of the Greeks, and I told her I never knew anybody who was far ahead of a Greek unless it was an Armenian, but the joke had gone to pieces too.

Anyhow, the Cretans used to give bright Greek boys and girls fellowships to come to study here and, on the other hand, the Cretans had learned a lot from the Egyptians, so in what the Greeks later picked up from Crete there was a lot of Egypt.

Nobody knows anything about the Cretans except that they had things their own way around the Mediterranean for some time and were remarkable athletes.

The particular fresco revealing this shows an acrobat somersaulting over a bull's back. That any human could have grasped a bull by the horns and somersaulted over its back is for somebody else to believe.

We had lunch on a restaurant overlooking the plain where the palace of Phaestos once stood. Behind it rose the mountain where Zeus was born. Above us someone had put two stupid canaries in a glass cage.

Not that canaries are ever particularly bright—but these two were the *pit*. The cage had been fitted with an electric bulb, and every time the waiter switched it on, this pair would start to chirp because the sun was coming up. That's what I call *stupid*.

The waiter had a different attitude.

"Greek television," he explained, and walked off.

Later the same waiter put a dish of black olives on the table. They looked sad. An olive that has at least an outside chance of being the beginning of a Martini is an olive that has hope. But, even as olives, this plateful were plainly second-class citizens. The waiter helped himself to one.

"Greek mutton chop," he explained, popped it into his mouth and walked away again.

"They know how to laugh without laughing," Milly had to point out.

"That's because they belong to us now," I assured Milly.

And wondered, looking out at the sun slanting across the ruins of the palace of Phaestos above the plain of Messara, whether the Phaecians, in their time, had been a people who knew how to laugh without laughing. From what the poet of another people wrote of them it would seem so:

> "But the things in which we take perennial delight are the feast, the lyre, the dance, clean linen in plenty, a hot bath and our beds. So forward now, my champion dancers, and show us your steps, so that when he gets home our guest may be able to tell his friends how far we leave all other folk behind in seamanship, in speed of foot, in dancing and in song."

Then we rode back to old Herakleion where sellers of sponges walk the parks.

I bought Milly a sponge as a token of my esteem. And her confusion.

King Minos of Crete lived in Egyptian luxury among gardens perfumed by the jasmine flower. His merchant marine kept his seas in hand while the Greeks were barely making it on dry land. The Greeks couldn't resist feeling sorry for themselves, a tradition maintained to the present day.

Paul of Ephesus got around to telling the Cretans off—*The Cretans, ever cheats, brute beasts and idle windbags*—a bad rap he had picked up from one of the Cretan's own philosophers.

As the Greeks saw it, the reason King Minos had it so good was that Zeus had been born there and apparently hadn't yet left. The Greeks not only had no gods, but didn't even have a boat in which to row to Crete and steal the plans for one.

Eventually a Greek infiltrated King Minos' shipyard and stole the plans for a ship. As soon as the Greeks had a boat of their own, things began to change. By rowing steadily for six weeks they were able to bring King Minos his annual tribute instead of him having to send somebody to pick it up.

We know that Athens paid tribute to Minos because the Minoans have left pictures all over Crete showing the Athenians coming to King Minos bearing wooden bracelets they had gilded to resemble gold. It wasn't too hard to can King Minos in an operation such as this, as he thought wood was a precious metal. He would scrape off the gold, throw it away, and make wooden crowns for himself.

At this time the Greek C.I.A. reported that Minos was running short of wood, so they decided to bring him down a peg.

Instead of bringing him the annual tribute, they sent an emissary who said, "Here, King, call *this* a tribute," and pitched him a herring.

Minos, who would eat anything, pushed the whole deal into his face, gills and all, swallowed once and spat out the bones. Some king.

"Fry me a pan full of tributes," he commanded his mess sergeant, "but this time leave out the bones."

Minos really *liked* that fish.

Ever since that day the fishermen of old Herakleion have been going out to sea toward evening and returning just after the break of day with a boatload of herring for the morning market.

I hung around the dock of the blue Aegean watching the men of the *Anna* prepare their nets. Every time the *Anna* went to sea I felt left behind. I would wave them off but nobody would wave back. I got up before day to see the *Anna* return.

During the day I watched local boys, stripped to the. waist, fishing for octopus with their hands.

The first thing you do, when an octopus comes at you, I saw, is to realize he doesn't see well or he'd go the other way. The surest method of holding him at bay is to beat his brains out.

Don't wait till his screams grow faint before throwing him into the pot. Pity has no part in preparing octopus soup. His shrieks of agony as he hits the boiling water add a special poignancy. There's all kinds of crazy stuff in the ocean.

If you're the kind of person who goes for a second helping simply because it tastes as though the brute died bitterly, that's a lot more than anyone can say for Australian corned mutton, who die like sheep.

Your best bet when going after devilfish is to hire a boat, as he isn't likely to knock on your hotel door and turn himself in. By the time you're so far out to sea that you can't tell helm from portside, just stand leeside and watch for white water. When that happens you know a devilfish is surfacing. Your job is to leap overboard with a sardine in your teeth. The purpose of this is to get in good with the Captain. If you don't care what the Captain thinks of you, stay aboard and eat the sardine yourself.

Always carry a master key while aboard, as European canners of anything don't put a key on the can. This bemuses the American who keeps turning the can around thinking the key is lost; but it saves a lot of key making.

On the other hand, the Medusa is a changeable creature, as he looks dirt-brown near bottom but turns a sickly violet as he surfaces. It makes him sick to turn violet and it makes me sick to see him do it. He will never look another medusa in the eye—they're both afraid somebody is going to get turned to stone. As a matter of fact, medusae are much less enthusiastic about living in the ocean than herring, and are forever trying to get ashore.

I sat on the prow of a small boat and watched them just below. The water was so clear that I could even see which couples were going steady. There were so many that it looked like they were going on a convention where both parties would be represented. I hope they elected somebody who didn't take a threat, by some other medusa, to bury every other medusa, as a sign that all loyal medusae should start living underground to save expense on both sides.

These useless monsters raise pure hell with people who have just put up their life savings to buy a small hotel, and advertised it as having a beach perfect for swimming in hope of accommodating vacationers touring the Aegean. It may also turn out to be perfect swimming for medusae who are touring the Aegean too. All the denials then about medusae haunting your waters won't bring one screaming American back to your hotel.

All you see of him at first is one of him—a brownish blob near the bottom that may be anything till you see that it is moving and that there is another brownish blob, and another and another and the whole fool sea is full of the varmints and if the sight of him don't make you queasy it ought to, as he'll make you wish you were in a hospital with your back broke.

The boy medusa hates his mother secretly because she turns such a beautiful violet when she surfaces, while all the old man does is make a brown blob of himself and won't get off the bottom. He senses that nobody wants him, not even people, because if he crawls into a net with some herring, people keep the herring and throw *him* back.

"People expect so much of me and I have so little to give," the medusa realizes that he has disappointed everybody. That makes him want to burn people just for the pure meanness of it. So it's better to fish for sunfish and better for the sunfish too. A sunfish gets ecstatic at the prospect of being caught. The medusa has the stronger mind but the sunfish has all the fun and that's all there is to it.

I found a Cretan fisherman who understood English, as he studies it two evenings a week in Herakleion. His name is Ionnis Romanos, and he looked uneasy when I offered to pay for a night's passage on the *Anna*.

"We are poor men, we do not take money," was his answer. Meaning these men earn their few piastres as fishermen, not as guides. Could I bring a few bottles of wine aboard, then? No, when Greek fishermen go to work they go to work, not to drink. The prospect of facing the Aegean with nothing to drink was frightening, but I decided I'd live till morning.

We left Herakleion aboard the smack *Anna*, towing half a dozen lighters in our wake, on the afternoon of August 6th. Outside the fact that the men didn't have to row it, and it had a single light bulb strung onto the mast, it was essentially the same craft as that in which the Minoan fishermen went to sea six thousand years ago.

Although they have held their own with King Minos in methods of catching herring, they have gained not at all in the comfort department. Men of Herakleion put out to sea barefoot, without life preservers, to risk their lives for the sake of a few boxes of fish; yet they make light of their very hard lot.

"Biggest net in Herakleion," Romanos boasted of the *Anna's* net.

And as their lives are balanced to the rocky soil of Crete, so is the *Anna* balanced to their sea. The *Anna* that looked stodgy in dock, turned into a spare, ascetic creature when the waters moved about her. Yielding as deceptively to the sea as a wrestler who gives ground, hoarding her strength secretly against an infinitely more powerful opponent, she awaited the moment that the opponent would let his strength lapse, then would right her self lightly.

All that afternoon, through an amber mist, the sea tried the *Anna* with wave upon wave. Sometimes it tossed the light green waves lightly as if in contempt; then threw a darker sea against her like a threat. It grew seduc-

tive, sucking us into deeper waters. So far out that the rim of the mountains behind Herakleion was lost, the huge mute waters took a firmer
hold, pressing the *Anna* from stem to stern.

The *Anna* would yield, push on in a lifting movement, then slide
down-wave with a few yards gained.

Romanos was feeding the depth line off a rude spool to a fisherman
who passed it overboard as it was fed. Neither man wore gloves.

"It do cold," Romanos said.

The line sank fast, and the sea held still as though watching like an
aging animal that has seen the same thing done time out of memory, and
yet cannot understand.

And the moon of King Minos rose seven-eighths full. Four hours out
of the Port of Herakleion.

"We find out how deep same way King Minos do," Romanos laughed
at himself while half-blaming old Minos—"*Ah,* it *do* do cold."

"We do like King Minos do," he repeated, fearing I had not understood.

"Then you haven't lost any ground," I encouraged everybody.

The bulb between the masts blinked out as the moon's full light came
on. Now the waters were strangely renewed. Now they came like hunt-
ing-waves, unafraid. Now was the hour when all things, sea and
cloud-wrack and moon, are against men. Now was the hour when sleep is
man's hiding-cave.

I heard the silver-lit sea seeking, I heard it moving all about. How old,
I thought, how very old, is the ceaselessly-seeking sea. And fell asleep to its
seeking.

When I wakened, the men in the lighters encircling the *Anna* were calling over the water and the men of the *Anna* were hauling the net. They
were closing in on the herring as farmers do on rabbits in a field, by starting on the circumference of the net—"the biggest net in
Herakleion"—and gradually cutting the field down.

By the time the net came in it was filled with leaping herring and a
fewer larger fish. Including a squid who didn't like me any more than I
liked him.

The herring were boxed for market aboard ship. We started back,
through the first break of dawn, for Herakleion. Now it was the sea's turn
to sleep; the hour when men are the victors.

Romanos insisted on depriving himself, by sharing his morning meal with me, that I could have foregone as easily as I could have given up eating cat on a rainy night. His breakfast consisted of cold okra in oil, and black olives and Spam canned in France. This particular delicacy never had an appeal for me before World War II, and my experience with it in that interval left me with greater revulsion than I ever felt toward land mines. I had to share it or hurt his feelings; so I shared it, as well as the cold okra.

Greek coffee is the best in the world, but there was no Greek coffee. There was no coffee, period. But Romanos broke a loaf of bread with his hands, handed me half, and apologized—"Greek bread knife."

When he whistled to a man on the other end of the boat, he added, "Greek telephone."

I don't know what would happen to Ionnis' mind if he ever sat down to *bifteck poivre* and a bottle of Beaujolais. It would snap, that's all.

A dusty South Italian light was beginning to fall aslant the walls of the Venetian fortress that guards old Herakleion. Behind us the sun came up Egyptian gold.

Romanos strung a dozen herring together and tied on the squid who didn't care for me. It was money out of the pockets of the men, yet nobody grumbled. It was a gift. I took it.

"Send me postcard, Eiffel Tower," Ionnis Romanos asked me.

Behind the desk at the hotel the clerk was still sleeping. I tied the line of fish to his chair and laid the squid on his desk.

Maybe it would like the clerk better than me was my thinking.

ISTANBUL

WHEN A MUSLIM MAKES HIS VIOLIN CRY, HEAD FOR THE DOOR

The singular plan the management of the Conrad-Istangump had devised for non-Muslims consisted of placing a non-Muslim sporting a bow tie, namely myself, upon a veranda overlooking the Sea of Marmara. Here I was forced to strain my eyes to make out the small print of my guidebook because the batteries of the tie had gone dead that same morning.

Encyclopedic Istanbul, Including a Dictionary of Prominent Persons was by one Monim Eser, and one was enough.

"Turks are members of the White Race," Monim lost no time in cheering me up, for that's how I got my own start and I'm not going to turn on society now by asking Under What Circumstances Did You Leave Your Last Employer, Kemal? If someone wants to wait till the last possible minute to join a losing organization, that's nobody's business but some other Turk's. The moment for a fresh extension of the White Western world had come and, speaking personally, I was pleased to look upon these simple folk with new eyes; this being the color that bears closest watching.

Whether my waiter or the Sea of Marmara would be the first to make a funny move was 6–5, and take your pick. Sure enough, it turned out to be our new member. He put something down on me that tasted like a cross between English grog and the hair of a hyena that has been out all night. One glance at the sneak who'd served me this deathly potion and my worst suspicions about hyenas were confirmed. They'll date *anybody*.

He stopped beaming idiotically long enough to make a circular movement with his dial finger while inquiring, "You wish to do shoppings?"

For reply I pitched the contents of his hyenafied grog over the veranda rail—not so much out of disgust with the stuff as in hope of hitting somebody below.

Should my mood appear foul, bear in mind that it was one imposed upon me, like all that sea water, by a management that had promptly disclaimed its responsibility.

And also considering that the most cheerful note of my childhood was my father's Saturday-night pealing of

> *O sweet Dardanella*
> *I love your hair 'n' eyes*

my mood was about as light as anyone has a right to expect.

Pa's lifelong confusion about Turkish women was only an extension of his confusion about all women. When Black Oak, Indiana, lost him to Chicago in 1893, my own difficulties began. He came to see the World's Columbian Exposition, but all he recalled of it later was Little Egypt. His reminiscing eventually led me to haunt the burlesque houses of South State Street in search of some Little Egypt of my own.

The closest I came was my discovery, in 1929, of Miss June St. Clair. Had it not been for her I might well have completed a four-year high-school course in four and a half years. Because of Miss St. Clair, it took me only five.

So in expecting someone either to take me off the veranda or to remove the Sea of Marmara, I was hardly asking more than I richly deserved.

I resolved, nonetheless, that any personal disappointment I felt in the Near East would not be taken out upon this innocent countryman unless an opportunity presented itself.

"Turks are fine-looking people, something like North Italians of medium size," Monim filled me in, "with light-blond or dark-colored hair and brown to dark-colored eyes, many having green and blue eyes and small feet." I glanced at my waiter's shoes and saw he had been obtained in a cultural exchange with the Harlem Globetrotters. Who they'd be playing in Turkey is an issue that still gives me wakeful nights.

"U.S. tourists know to tip," Monim had to concede, "but for their information there is no limit to generosity. Tip an additional 5 to 10 per cent at restaurants, bellboy, maid, porter and suitable sum to doorman and elevator but never involve friendship with sightseeing."

Not only have I never been involved in friendly fashion with a sightseer but I haven't yet tipped a waiter and don't plan to begin. Not after once having suffered entrapment at the hands of one in The Oak Room. Had he cleared that table instead of nattering away with the chef, the half-dollar under the saucer would never have come to the attention of my hand just as the sneak padfooted up.

That is all part of the past, of course, as there are four waiters to every American diner in comradely Istangump and all four see very clearly out of brown to dark-colored eyes. Many having green and blue eyes and small feet.

"Turks are members of the Celtic race," Monim resumed his interminable nagging, "which through intermarriage with Circassian, European and Greek women have lost their Asiatic features." —Why do the males of any clan you care to name inevitably take it for granted that while they are balling the daughters of the nearest unfriendly tribe, Circassian studs are playing unnatural games? A pure curiosity as we say in Black Oak; yet one which explains the lush crop of Asiatic features among us Circassians, Europeans, Greeks, and Black Oakians.

Monim having just read Greek women out of Europe, I couldn't help wondering where they would go now. After a while I discovered I didn't care. Assuming they would take their husbands with them, the idea had its appeal.

"What do you think those Greek heroes were doing while you were horsing around on the wrong side of the Bosporus, Izmet?" I'd put the issue straight to our New Member—"playing unnatural games?" (You have to let these people know you have the upper hand or they'll take advantage every time. It once took me an hour and a half to get ham and eggs in the Alhambra, and for a Turkish waiter to hold himself the equal of a Spanish one is sheer nonsense, Spanish waiters having belonged to us so much longer.)

Not to deny Turkey's just claim to civil treatment, both countries being great democracies because if they know what's good for them they'd better be. Otherwise they can't belong to *us*.

"Whose features do you figure those Persian studs were taking over while you were singing *A Good Man Is Hard to Find,* Akbar?" was how I'd put it—"Or did you think they were *playing unnatural games?"*

Somehow that didn't ring as well as it had the first time I'd rung. It might even be I was in a rut. Perhaps I ought simply to punish him with historical objectivity, like Churchill.

"Slaughtered any Armenian babies this morning, Fireball?" I'd say, "Where were you when Dienbienphu fell, Firefell?"

I'd grind him into powder, I'd historically objectivize him. "A big help you were when we took Balaclava, brave guy—What do you think those Bulgarian studs were up to when you singing *I'm a Dingdong Daddy from the Dardanelles?—Playing unnatural games?*" (If the Globetrotters actually were playing a Turkish team they'd have to find somebody else to keep score.)

An involuntary movement of the lips, which I make while talking to myself voluntarily, brought Selim to my side of his own volition. If ever I've set eye on an agent of a foreign power, such as the C.I.A., it was this triple-dyed dimwit from Usküdar repeating the circular movement of the index finger while asking *"Shoppings?"* This was by now so plainly a ruse to get me into the Covered Bazaar that I'm certain it would have worked with Joseph Cotten but it didn't work with me. I wasn't even about to be trapped in a sewer with Orson Welles.

Yet if someone would whip me up something with gin in it I'd meet someone halfway. He could whip it and I'd drink it. Hair and all.

Abdul returned with a pot of raki, a development signifying that the management was now putting me on the Native, or Islamic, Plan; assuming they had one. A safe assumption, as the Harlem Globetrotters really *were* in town. One swig of the stuff and I decided I might as well get trapped in a Covered Bazaar.

I repeated the mystic circular movement with the curious result that the waiter removed the Sea of Marmara from my sightline simply by turning me right about, chair and all. What a *nerve*.

All I had to contend with now was the *Bosporus*. At last we were face to face. "Don't just *lie* there, Bosporus," I instructed it; "*Do* something."

Bosporus splashed around in a helpless kind of way. Some Bosporus. "Stop putting on the helpless act," I told it, "you're a *big* ocean now."

Bos just lay there looking simpler by the second. "I won't even look you up in *Encyclopedic Istanbul* by one Monim Eser and one is enough," I threatened it. As good as my word, I handed Monim's book to the waiter and signed the tab "Hugh Hefner." In an absurd society all men are absurd except the absurd man.

Then I rose unassisted.

Leaving the New Member as tipless as he had been before he joined *us*.

For a sight of pure dumb suffering there's nothing so great as a muzzled bear up on its hind legs seven foot high; a frothing brute lifting one leg then the other to the beat of a drum. In the hope he's earning his dinner.

The only spectator beside myself is a ten-year-old Mongol waif, a boy in charge of a shine-box the size of himself. The bottles lining the box's sides lend it a resemblance to a crude portable operating table. He has decorated it with Elvis Presley's face—clipped from an American magazine—under the caption *Will This Yearning Never Cease?*

One tug of the leash on the bear's forepaw lets him know he may rest now, and he lowers himself on all fours to go nosing in the gutter like a dog. A small girl holds an empty tambourine blindly toward the noonday windows, and a few coins tinkle onto the cobbles. She follows a rolling coin and retrieves it from under the bear's very nose. Bear don't care. He's doing enough for these people, he knows, without counting the house for them too.

The drummer gives a single beat, toneless as the beat of rain, then hauls the bear back onto its hunkers: now the left foot, now the right. Even for a bear he isn't a good dancer. But a drummer who can't get more tone out of an instrument than this bird can hardly complain about not getting Agnes de Mille to dance for him.

Let's not expect too much of Turkish bears. In a place where two-leggers consider that sticking pins in themselves and whirling about is as far as you can go in the art of the dance, how can we expect a four-legger who isn't getting enough to eat to interpret *Swan Lake?* A bear at least has the excuse of being a bear.

A hungry one at that. But what's a dervish's excuse? Exactly what does *he* have in mind? If he weren't some kind of nut right off the frosting of the fruitcake, he'd realize he could do better than to go whirling around Turkey. He'd go to the American Embassy and get himself exchanged for something, maybe Barry Goldwater. I delivered milk at twelve myself, but still can't figure out how that nullifies the right of somebody else under that age to a pint a day in or out of wedlock. Another solution to the dervish problem might be simply to appoint himself a New Frontier for Cultural Backwash so we could trade off Jack Paar to the Bushmen. Every nation should take advantage of *somebody.*

I hope I don't appear to be carping at the administration here. For the sake of the record, I have never seen a dervish whirl. To make a clean breast of matters, I'd rather see a dervish whirl than watch Morris Fishbein treat a hangnail.

The girl came to me with one beggar-hand extended, showing she knew an American when she saw one but would rather see than be one. I put the tip I had so justifiably withheld from the waiter because he had dated a hyena, on her.

She toted that buck like a flag to the drummer, who put down the happiest rat-a-tat-tat to send the message straight through to the bear—*We eat!* The bear began lifting his knees to his chin, trying to show me what it felt like to have a yearning really cease. He was so happy he didn't care if it hurt. And neither did the shine-kid—he raced up with his portable operating table and I began catching the spirit of the thing myself. I started to lie down to let him operate.

I had never had my shoes shined to a drum roll before. It was my first time. And to a dancing bear at that! Talk about your happy times! But when the bear put his paws on his hips I felt he was going too far. Although this was exactly the development the drummer had had in mind when he'd bought the big fag, I feared for its effect upon a small girl. She was already confused at being liberated by the Amurikuns. It was *her* first time. It was the first time for something for everybody. By the time the shine-kid had finished the second shoe he had so much momentum left he began crawling around looking for my third. Either that or one of us had been counting wrong. I held his payment down to two. I was firm about it too.

Then drummer, beggar girl, beggar boy, and bear—and a second small girl—now, where had *that* one come from?—the whole stupid troupe trooped off with the bear still trying to kick himself in the chin. He still wasn't sure they were going to put his name in the pot. I waved goodbye to him but he didn't wave back.

Nobody waves back in Istanbul.

I boarded a trolley and began proceeding in the general direction of Inner Soho. My thinking was that we might pass a seraglio that really *was* a seraglio, but all we got to was a car barn that really *was* a car barn.

It was set among high wooden tenements with windows so small that Raskolnikov would have gotten his head wedged if he'd stuck it out to see what I was doing.

What I was doing was helping two solemn-looking boys—the only kind there are in Turkey—to hunt for small hard-rubber squares, of the kind used in window jambs of trolleys, to fit their slings. This ammunition was easy to find, and I contributed a handful on the condition it would be used against Armenians. Then I put them both up against the side of the barn, where they stood very straight, hands to their sides and looking straight ahead, proud that they were to be shot without a trial. When all I did was level a camera and snap the shutter, both were disappointed. Turkey is a nation of martyrs in the worst sense of the word.

Consequently it has only one martyr today in the best sense of the word: the poet Nazim Hikmet. Understandably, he is in hiding for having committed what Brendan Behan has observed is the writer's first responsibility—to bring his country down.

Turks are less tolerant of this sort of carryings-on than the Irish. To the Irishmen a uniform indicates subservience; to the Turk it signifies righteousness. Therefore the Turks, a righteous people, respect only action conducted in a military fashion, even though it may consist of no more than dominoes in a coffeehouse. Spectators to the contest don't just sit around; they observe in a military manner.

I asked my carbarn heroes the direction to The Seraglio, and both pointed, in a military manner, to the center of town. I gave them some paper-wrapped pieces of sugar I'd been hoarding, as a reward for service beyond the call of duty. When I looked back both were still at attention. Some martyrs.

Though the airless warehouse, through whose rooms stood fixtures uncalled for from another day, was entitled The Seraglio, it looked more like a tourist trap to me. I joined a gaggle of stupefied American schoolgirls, being led by a guide, past a collection of cumbrous armor, into the *Bab-i-Sa'adet,* where once Ottoman emperors were proclaimed. I stared, with other starers, upon the very couch whereon a sultan was once used to accepting congratulations by permitting admirers to kiss the tip of his ten-foot staff.

"Official dignity tends to increase," Aldous Huxley has observed, "in inverse ratio to the importance of the country in which his office is held."

This was the Holy of Holies whose sanctified threshold all who once entered had had to kiss. The throne room had then been barred, by thirty white eunuchs, to all save those whom the sultan bade enter. With other starers I stared upon a gold-and-beryl throne that had once accommodated the huge hunkers of Ahmet I. Then we all stared upon the ebony throne, inlaid with precious stones, that had accommodated the bestial behind of Murat IV; then we stood stunned by the very divan whereon the great Khan Ismail had placed his delicate Persian can. The guide neglected to point out where Otto Preminger had sat, so I assumed he just lay on the floor. The official importance of the individual also tends to enhance itself in inverse proportion to its talent.

The sultan who kept his admirers ten feet off may not have been quite so vain as all that. It could just have been that he was aware that Turks were people with brown to dark-colored hair with a fondness for slipping an up-the-sleeve shiv into the high brass, and the man preferred having his staff kissed to having a lung punctured. A disappointed admirer would then be inconsolable until the sultan permitted him to climb into the harem nursery and stick needles and pins into the little ones. Through chambers where this sultan was garroted and that one poisoned, my father's tune returned—

> *O sweet Dardanella*
> *I love your hair 'n' eyes*

Through chambers where one was done in with his whole family and that one alone by a silken cord, we came at last to the chamber that had once held the women. The air here was close, though all doors were open. The climate of deadly boredom in which the creatures had lived out their lives clung yet to the walls that had enclosed them.

One Sultan Ibraham, along toward the middle of the seventeenth century, looked over his stable of a thousand vessels and grew even more bored than they. So he turned the whole lot over to his Chief Gardener, who placed each in a sack, ostensibly upon the promise to each that she was going on a blind date.

She was. A diver, who went down off Seraglio Point many years later, saw innumerable sacks, still upright for having been weighted, dancing gently in the undersea currents.

The present danger in Turkey, the guide assured me, is of a Communist dictatorship, and produced a leaflet showing a hand grasping a Communist by the throat. The leaflet didn't indicate to whom the hand belonged.

But I decided the hell with your bloodstained, staff-kissing Seraglio, and walked out into the inarticulate city.

Istanbul is a town with no special style of its own, as Turkey has no particular style. Unlike the Morisco Spaniards, who modified the arts of Arabia with those of Christendom to forge a style distinct from either, the Turks simply brought down everything that looked like Allah might not care to have it left standing.

The Turkish claim to civilizations that once flowered between Europe and Asia, when The Golden Gate was the center of the world, is simply no good. Turkish soldiery brought down the ancestral temples of Greece pillar by pillar and marble by marble, then sold the rubble shard by shard. Had an Englishman not come along to do some salvaging, the Turk would have disposed of the lot in the nearest bazaar.

A humorless, soldierly people whose arts are courage, honor, and bloodletting—stuff of which we have already contrived so many Christian heroes as to have no present need of new heroes from Islam. What Turkey needs today isn't heroes but good old rogues, sporty-O poets and downright cowards. I see no reason why some lucky country might not one day get all three.

Remembering the poor of those lion-colored villages along the Sahara's blowing rim, of the Barrio-Chino and Naples' incensed slums, bright Crete and shadowed Dublin, these of Istanbul were the first I had ever seen who did not make sport of their poverty. The common consolations of homemade wine, homemade music, and homemade love appear to be missing here. There is no joy, there is no juice, there is no jazz in Istangump. A city without Negroes doesn't jump, and smiles in Turkey are not for free. If you're fond of athletics, it's a good town to watch someone lift a thousand-pound barbell in a single pull or a conduit where human heads were thrown after a mass decapitation. Istanbul may be the town for you—but it isn't the town for me.

And what makes the Turk think he will be better off looking at the world through a Caucasoid eye instead of an epicanthic one is just one of those things people get to believing after they've tried everything else.

At the Mosque of Saint Sophia I ran into a little foot trouble. The Sacred Guardian of a crummy rattan mat pointed menacingly at my infidel's shoes. So I stood on one leg alternately to scrape the mud off each and then proceeded toward the door. I'm nothing if not dainty.

That didn't get it. He was just a doorman but he believed in his work. My Christian shoes were stepping on The Prophet's untouchable floor. Mohammed himself wouldn't, I'm sure, have particularly cared.

I tried to explain that no offense had been intended. That I had simply gone into the only shoestore in Black Oak and bought a pair of shoes, completely forgetting that the place was run by Christians.

The issue was solved when he handed me a pair of holy shower slippers. They weren't any cleaner than my Black Oak pair but they got me into his mosque.

This curious edifice was constructed, after a couple of false starts, by a Roman emperor who got his own start the same way I got mine: as a Christian. When the Turks took it over they beheaded so many of us that only a first-class Christian could get his head on a Mohammedan pike. Second-class Christians had to be content with getting their ears pinned up. There were more than enough Christians to go around, but there was a serious lack of pikes.

The Turks then put a crescent on top of the cross and let it be known that they wanted to be brothers to all the Christians they hadn't yet caught. This worked out pretty well until the uncaught Christians began feeling brotherly too. They impaled all the Turkish women and children and put the cross on top of the crescent, to show survivors that their own idea was to turn the other cheek.

The Turks agreed that this was what *they* had in mind, and would like to redecorate.

So they pulled the Christians apart with wild horses and put up minarets. This is why you can scarcely blame us Christians, when we took the place back, for plastering our Muslim brothers up into the walls in the name of the Holy Trinity and to save cement. Struck by the infinite wonder of this holy place, I simply stood looking up. What I was wondering was who had been the construction foreman.

Nobody has to tell *me* that Turkey is an undeveloped country. I found that out for myself by peeking under old melon rinds every time I heard something meow. Istanbul is the Mecca of Mohammedan cats, and it's about time them cats changed Meccas. After a kitten has used up its last strength to get its eyes open, it sees that the effort wasn't worthwhile. Mother has left for the Covered Bazaar, where she is practicing cover and concealment under a café table in hope that if somebody doesn't drop a piece of shish on her accidentally, someone might slug her deliberately with a kebab. If you showed a Mohammedan cat a saucer of cream he'd scratch you for trying to poison him, an attitude adopted early by the

Turks toward the world in general. It goes to show that a nation that can't feed its cats and won't bother to drown its kittens lacks both milk and sentience.

Personally, I'd rather be a Mohammedan mouse any day than an Islamic cat, because if anybody put me down for never purring, I'd have a damned good excuse.

The one who gained my attention by meowing, "Take this *thing* off me, Dad," from under half a grapefruit, wasn't even thankful when I obliged her. She was a cat caught in the worldwide struggle between Democracy and Communism, so it was my duty as an American to liberate her because we invented milk. Now we have a surplus we want to donate to undernourished peoples unconditionally in return for airbases and affection. If you don't love *us* more than *them,* you can't have *our* nice milk. But this was a Commie cat; she told me Keep Your Goddamned Milk, I'm a cheese-eating left-wing Radical Red and I subsist on blood and yogurt. Even her yowl was curdled.

I asked her where Mother was, and she said that was none of my business; but Father, she was happy to report, had been eaten by wild dogs under the veranda of the Conrad-Istangump. I could verify this, as it was under my window they'd gotten him, and the next day the menu featured *koftë.* Somebody is going to catch hell from Allah.

If you're now feeling superior to Asia because you've never eaten kitten, don't take too much for granted. You wouldn't be the first tourist who'd gone into a French restaurant and had the *surprise-du-chef* without knowing it. I once saw a Frenchwoman in pursuit of game down the *Rue Bûcherie* before the horsemeat restaurants had opened, and if that was a horse she was after it was the smallest lead-pony I've yet seen—the only one in Paris bearing fur. The point is that if you're planning to open a restaurant in Paris, you had better make it of the *classe premiére,* as cat under *Sauce Béarnaise* can easily be mistaken for rabbit—but you'll never get away with this in a *classe-quatre* joint. I'd like to invent a sauce that would make cat taste like horse. In three weeks we'd all be rich.

I found myself walking along a ruined wall, and ducked into one of the gaps to see whatever it was they had built a wall around to keep me from seeing.

I stood among the grass and bones of old Turkey dead and gone, carven fez and fallen headstone, stone turbans cracked by time and a real hard fall. The unkept, unkempt Muslim dead; under cypresses leaning with grief that so many had gone. The Mohammedan dead are buried shallow and return aboveground soon; as though they had left the living yet not found oblivion.

A stonecutter was sitting crosslegged chipping away at a stone while another stonecutter stood watching. When one got tired chipping he would stand up; then the other would sit crosslegged and chip. For the manhours the two were putting in, they could have been chipping out two stones.

On the other hand, they themselves didn't yet know for whom the stone was being fitted. It was a cinch *he* wasn't in a hurry, so why should they be? Isn't life just chock-full of little surprises? If I wanted to stand around minding *their* business they didn't mind, it appeared, so long as I didn't try to tell them mine.

"I'm from Black Oak, Indiana," I explained my concern in Mohammedan headstone-hewing; "I'm looking for a girl named Dardanella."

The one standing up pointed, with his chisel, in the general direction of the Dardanelles.

I had a distinct impression I could leave now anytime without causing any parting pangs. So I left. When I got to the break in the wall I had come through, I turned and waved goodbye.

But nobody waves goodbye in Istangump.

I'm fully as fond of a mad cab driver as the next fare, but I had no more chance of getting a coherent thought out of Osman Israhar than I would had Jack Kerouac been driving, and I'm still not sure it wasn't. Dizzy Israhar came whipping crosstown in a jalopy with a smashed headlight, one hand on the wheel and the other on a bottle of Pepsi-Cola. Had he been chewing a steak I wouldn't have thought it was Kerouac.

Dizzy came from Üsküdar, the town that made an Asiatic out of Eartha Kitt, but how he perceived I wasn't a French aristocrat I haven't yet figured. When he told me in what small regard he held the French, I knew he didn't think I was on *their* side.

His grudge burned so deep I felt it must be because the French have become fond of giving Mohammedans electrified baths; but no—what-

ever happens to an Arab in a bathtub, he has it coming, was the thinking
of Osman Israhar. In fact, the chief trouble in the Arab world wasn't in
Algeria at all. It was the Jews God was *really* mad at. They *really* had it
coming.

Had God wanted Jews to have a flag, he explained, He would have
given them a flag instead of dispersing them. When God disperses somebody, he doesn't intend they should get an army together. God doesn't like
people to *begin* things; that is all there is to it. *Beginning* things is God's
business. He, Osman Israhar, was on God's side. Had been all his life, and
wasn't going to switch sides now.

"I wonder what He had in mind in letting Jews win a war," I marveled
aloud.

"*They* win no war," Osman corrected me, "only a battle. Allah willing,
the *real* war is yet to begin."

"Well, I be dog," I explained, "then why not let God begin it?"

For reply Osman pulled up his left trouser to reveal shrapnel scars. A
sight upon which, I assume, I was supposed to shriek. I decided to con-
gratulate him instead.

"You got off light," I assured him. "An Indian in my outfit stepped on a
land mine at Château-Regnault and it blew both legs and half his head off."
Actually, that fool Indian lost only two feet and a part of a hand. I threw in
the rest purely to make this Asiatic feel he was one of the lucky ones.

There are some people you can't do anything for. Osman didn't feel
luckier than anybody. A fellow like this could be in a hospital with his
back broke and he'd still complain. "Oh," he assured me, "a wound is
nothing. All Turks have wounds. We are a wounded people."

"If you'd stop hollering 'Fix Bayonets!' for a generation, you'd catch up
with us more able-bodied groups," was my merry rejoinder.

Osman didn't grasp that concept. He didn't grasp anything, not even
the wheel. He was just a wounded Asiatic heading for a general smashup,
in which event we would both be wounded people. As nobody in my family has ever yet suffered so much as a black-and-blue mark, I don't intend
to start a trend.

All I wanted was to find a bartender who would begin a Martini which,
Allah willing, I would finish without Allah's help.

Osman's beef was that, after all, he had fought for France, and won.
But the French had not let him go to fight the Jews.

"I'm sure you would have turned the tide," I assured him.

That almost brought us head on into a mosque with our shoes on. When he straightened us out I told him that if he could find a dance hall for infidels I'd brag about him all over Athens.

All that funny stuff being wasted on a skinny Asiatic, an undeveloped Muslim with his right headlight smashed. Just a shiftless Mohammedan caught in the worldwide struggle between Democracy and a world without a key club.

"How about some Egyptian belly dancers?" I asked as though he had a stable in every watering hole. "How about them Bulgarian chicks? I hear there's an awful lot of Chinese living out of China now—or is that just another rumor?"

"We keep women *inside,*" Osman told me.

"I know you keep them inside," I assured him; "so do we when the weather is bad." The truth was I not only had the wrong country, I didn't even have the right century. Strong drink, good music, and women are out of bounds to Turks even if their shoes are size 14. But this was the first time I'd been up against sexual apartheid, and felt I ought to do something about it before the idea spread to Johannesburg and we'd all be in trouble.

"In old days," grieved Osman Israhar, "was forbidden to *look* by woman. Then was better."

I immediately fell into a funk at thought of all the good times I had missed.

"We don't even let them in The Oak Room," I agreed happily, thinking to cheer him up. But this cross between a crow and a barbed-wire fence didn't even catch the reference.

"It's the men's bar of a hotel I happen to own in New York," I felt obliged to explain. "I used to own The Downstairs at The Upstairs too, but I traded it for St. Nick's Arena. Then the boxing game went to hell and I bartered my holdings for 50 per cent of Hurricane Jackson. I was ruined."

They would have laughed in Black Oak. But on this provincial it was pure waste of good material. I had to talk to *somebody*—but why couldn't it be Barry Goldwater instead of a ragged Turk driving a jalopy with a spring coming through the seat? Why did it have to be a skinny Asiatic instead of Ramfis Trujillo? Why did it have to be somebody who couldn't drive better than Jack Kerouac? All I had to sharpen my wits on was an undeveloped Mongol caught between Khrushchev and David Susskind, and if I had a ten-foot strap I'd flog him out of the studio. "Raped any Circassian school kids today, Abdul?" I'd put it to him. "How many Christian ears did you pin up this morning—or were you too busy *playing unnatural games?*" Honest to God, isn't it bad enough to have a crowd of Uruguayans tossing tomatoes at James C. Hagerty without my being trapped in Istanbul with a cab driver who can't find his way to the Bosporus? The more I thought about it, the more certain I felt that the French ought to have let Osman take his own chances. He plainly didn't know where he was going, and I was spiteful enough not to tell him, purely to see what his own plans might be.

It did cross my mind to have him take me to a Turkish bath. I once went to one in Chicago, and the man at the window gave me two bars of soap and said, "Have fun and come out clean." *Fun?* I was there three days, and when I came out I still had both bars! On the other hand, a Turkish bath on Division Street is one thing, but one full of Mohammedans is a different proposition; one I decided to forego lest they get the idea I had come around to gather material instead of taking a bath.

Osman's plan, as it is that of every cab driver in Istanbul, was to ignore all requests of the infidel in the rear seat and drive straight to the hill where someone named Pierre Loti once lived. Not that interest in this forgotten littérateur is that lively among Turkish cabbies, but merely because it is the longest drive in town.

I have never been moved by the writing of this French maritime officer, but when Osman assured me that where we were going was to *Piyer* Loti I submitted, thinking that, even if he had not been much of a writer, it might be a good idea to look at the scene where he had such a success that his name still gives a big assist to the tourist racket around the Dardanelles. I'd see how he got his start without bothering with how he finished.

He had gotten his start by dwelling at great length on "the mysterious heart of the Turkish woman." The question thereafter arising that, if Turkish women were *that* mysterious, how was it that *Piyer* was more interested in the mysterious heart of the Turkish boy? A sense of responsibility toward his literary reputation subsequently beguiled him into an affair with three veiled women at once just to save time. When the three turned out to be Frenchwomen who were putting him on, it was about time.

At the foot of the height upon which *Piyer's* cottage still stood, I abandoned Osman Israhar without a parting song.

The way up was narrow, steep, and overgrown by weeds. I would not have minded getting out of breath to see how a good writer of the past had gotten his start, but making it uphill to see how this *Tümmler* had put it over was somewhat discouraging. It was like getting out of breath to see the typewriter of Max Shulman.

Once I'd made it, however, I was glad I had. It offered a view of the Dardanelles truly startling. Who was more startled, myself or the Dardanelles, is a question only posterity will answer. Yet there below me lay The Golden Gate, Galata Bridge, Ataturk Bridge, Ataboy Bay, The Sea of Marmara, The Vale of Tralee, and my old buddy, Bosporus.

I could see Besikatas, Domabahçe Beyoglu, and somebody cooking shish kebab in Kabatas Iskelesi. I could even make out the umlauts in Üsküdar standing up like tiny minarets but I couldn't see what Eartha Kitt was up to. It was a commanding view but it wasn't *that* commanding. I could make out the Florence Nightingale Hospital, the German Hospital, the Belgian Consulate, and five Laotians led by a landing party of C.I.A. marines. A battalion of SS troops was practicing the Marseillaise and a Portuguese bishop was telling Pandit Nehru that he'd give India Angola if Nehru would let the Portuguese keep Goa. It looked like Nehru was shaking his head, No. I could see the Harlem Globetrotters too. But I couldn't make out who that was they were still playing.

So leave us bid farewell to fashionable Asia where the new contrasts with the old and the old contrasts with the prehistoric and the prehistoric just mills around because *it* doesn't have a damn thing to which to contrast itself. A fond adieu to bonny Dundee where kittens live under melon rinds and June St. Clair once captured my schoolboy's heart. *Auf wiedersehen*, old Asiatic squatters on cobbles turned rust-red with blood of Scythian and Khan; thanks for turning a color that matched my shoes. *À votre santé* to all French wenches between Rue Saint-Denis and Ataboy Bridge. Hip-hip-hooray for Osman Israhar who couldn't find his way to the Bosporus. Thank God for Greek cab drivers who would rather go to Piraeus than the Parthenon because it is farther. May Allah send alms to sellers of water and sellers of weight, beggar and bootblack both alike—and if Allah don't care then God help you, privates of all Turkish barracks paying for your American fatigues by eating American pork and beans: May your dog tags never return to Beyoglu without you.

And one lingering Continental-type kiss to the Turkish woman whose heart is mysterious so long as she stays indoors. Goodbye and good luck to all small men at desks with English dictionaries writing "Americans know to tip but there is no limit to generosity."

Farewell to ancestral Byzantium where ancient and modern world meet and both are that much worse for meeting. Goodbye and goodbye, great bear of the noonday street; may you stay out of jail forever. For I loved your hair and eyes. *Au revoir* to all covered bazaars, may none of you be uncovered. I wish adieu and fresh milk to milkless kittens—better luck next time around.

Goodbye to bear and shine-boy alike and to all who must dance in the noonday street. May your yearnings never cease.

Goodbye for keeps and a single day, forgotten farm boy who came to town in 1893, who came to hear music and see the dancing.

And heard, in all the years that followed, no music save the beat of one toneless drum.

CHICAGO I

THE NIGHT-COLORED RIDER

A winter of a single wind has tattered the El-station ad that once promised lessons in the waltz by the Waltz-King of the Merry Gardens. Its tatters seem less merry now: Waltz-King and waltzers alike are gone.

Gone with the Twelfth Street dandy with cap tipped for love in Garfield Park, who stepped off here beside the Monday-morning salesgirl, her lashes still tinted by Sunday's mascara. Gone with the Mogen David wino and Virginia Dare drunky, wearing Happy-New-Year snow over their shoulders, who once sought summertime in a bottle below these ties. Rain has stained the gum machine that gave strangers a choice of Spearmint, Doublemint, or Juicy Fruit. It has rusted the rounded guardrail that now has nothing left to guard save a peanut machine; whose peanuts are long vended now.

Up the banked snow to tattery ads in a blood-red glare, shadows race like snow-children tonight; then toboggan down. Two railroad lamps, at either end of the platform, tip and dip when the midnight B-train passes, like flares left burning on a raft abandoned in a rising sea. Till a fog shot with neon shuts out all sound.

All sound save that of some carefree summer's couldn't-care-less piano, honkytonking a midnight out of times long gone—

> If it wasn't for powder
> 'n for store-bought hair—

a midnight when saloon doors kept swinging all night for the first summer night of the year.

For the blue-and-white legend that once named this platform, its ads that once wheedled, its legends that bragged, all have passed in the wash of this last of blue snows. Leaving nothing but lovers' kisses, given while pigeons made summer strut, in its evening corners.

Forgotten fixers and finders who climbed these steps one step a year, menders of machinery in nameless garages whose footfalls keep coming up: all have passed in the B-train's echo that trails the B-train, when the long cars lean toward the land where old Els wait for winter to pass.

> *Then a fog shot with neon closes down*
> *Waltz-King and waltzers alike are gone.*

He was a fixer of tools, a mender of machinery in basements and garages. He used electrical tape as a physician uses a tourniquet. He was a geneticist of lathes, for he prolonged the lives of brushes stiff with sclerosis of paint. He was one who had no life except while fixing:

The plaster that had cracked, the rainpipe that had clogged, the hinge that had rusted, the saw that had blunted, the glass that had shattered, the beam that had split.

Other men wished to be forever drunken. He wished to be forever fixing:

The step that had rotted, the fence wind had bent, the clock that lost time, the light fixture gone dark.

He ministered to bolts whose threading was worn; he had an understanding with cement. He moved among pistons and vises and cylinders carrying an oilcan and a rag. His ear was less attuned to human speech than to the delicate play of gears: in dreams of ball bearings he sensed that one dream-bearing was less rounded than others.

He was a solderer, a welder, a tool-and-dye maker, a carpenter who could handle electricity.

My father was a fixer of machinery in basements and garages.

He could get a piece of machinery to work for him that would work for nobody else. But when he was put in charge of men their gears meshed to a stop; until somebody who knew how to get work out of men was sent.

"You're so damned smart, how come you don't get to be foreman?" was my mother's ceaseless accusation. Until it seemed to me that the highest condition of Man was being "Foreman." I would hear her going at him when the bulb that lit our kitchen and the lamp that lit our door were the only lights foretelling the beginning of the winer workday.

"*Some* men *make* theirselves Foreman"—a rattle of kettles was his reply, made in serving himself breakfast to show her how little kindness remained in the world.

"If you're so damned smart"—the slam of the kitchen door would cut her challenge off and send his footsteps hurrying down the stone toward the place where *some* men became Foremen.

And others never became much of anything.

The gas lamp burned above our door once more before his steps returned along the stone.

"If you're so damned smart"—she would be at him again before the kitchen door shut.

There were no foremen on my father's side. All the foremen and fore-women, all the heroes and heroines, belonged to my mother's family. Of whom the most foremanlike was Uncle-Theodore-The-Great-Lakes-Sailor.

He had had a fistfight with the ship's cook along the deck of the steamer *Chicora,* but the captain had stopped it just when Uncle Teddy was getting ready to knock the cook overboard. Which one of the brawlers had begun the battle the captain didn't care to hear: one of them would have to pack his gear and get off the *Chicora,* and that would be an end of the matter.

Uncle Theodore packed and walked ashore at Benton Harbor; after shaking hands all around with everyone but the captain.

He should have said goodbye to the captain too. On her next trip the *Chicora* went down with all hands, somewhere off South Haven.

Down with all hands to leave not a trace on the unshaken waters. Not an overturned lifeboat nor a seaman's blue cap. Not a cork, a clay pipe, a smudge of oil, or a dead cigar. Cutters scoured the waters for days, yet found no sign. Then the wind blew the memory of their names into winter; waves that freeze in midspill became their headstones.

Till spring began and the waters flowed as though the *Chicora* had never moved upon them.

But, a son of the *Chicora's* fireman built a glass-bottomed boat in his backyard, determined to find the wreck on the lake's shifting floor or go down himself, and named it the *Chicago.* Five days after he had put out, the *Chicago* capsized.

Down went the brave son of the brave fireman to join the brave crew below the cowardly waves. Down went the *Chicago,* that determined vessel, determined to go *all* the way down.

My mother spoke of these seafaring upsets as if that of the glass-bottomed craft were the greater disaster. But my father insisted that the youth who had followed his father had simply been one more glass-bottomed damned fool.

"Not all the damned fools are at the bottom of the lake," my mother observed. That sounded like a pointed remark to me.

How having a relative who didn't happen to go down with the *Chicora* made anyone an authority on shipping disasters my father said he failed to perceive.

How a man could work six years for the Yellow Cab Company and not get to be Foreman was what my mother failed to perceive.

How a man could get to be a Foreman when he had a woman who never let him rest was another thing my father said he himself failed to catch.

If a man didn't have a woman to inspire him he could never be a millionaire was how things looked to my mother.

If a man had to be nagged into being a millionaire, he'd just as soon stay poor was my father's decision.

Some men couldn't even be nagged into being a foreman, my mother implied.

In a case like that she might as well save her breath, my father concluded, threw the cat off the davenport, and drew the *Saturday Evening Blade* across his face.

"Don't blame the cat," my mother warned him.

"What good is a cat that won't hunt mice?" my father wanted to know.

"You can't blame a dumb animal for being handicapped," she instructed him.

"*Handicapped?*" my father wanted to know, throwing the *Blade* off his face and sitting upright—"since when is the cat handicapped?"

"He can't smell," my mother reported smugly. "A cat can hardly be expected to hunt mice he can't smell. How can he tell where they're at?"

"He could hunt a handicapped mouse," my father resolved the issue. He always was one for fair play.

My mother overlooked his solution. "The cat can't smell because his whiskers were snipped when he was a kitten," she persisted. "A cat whose whiskers are snipped can't smell *anything.*"

"How does he tell the difference between liver and mush?" my father asked quietly. For by now he understood that unless the cat were shortly found guilty of *something* he himself would be found guilty of *everything.* It was himself or the cat.

"If the cat can't smell because his whiskers are snipped," he added thoughtfully, "he might try using his nose."

And drew the *Saturday Evening Blade* back across his face.

My mother took it off, because she didn't like instructing a person whose face she couldn't see.

"A cat don't hunt purely by sense of smell," she explained, as if the matter were urgent. "He measures a mouse hole by his whiskers, and if he doesn't have anything to use as a measure, he's helpless."

"That cat don't look helpless to me," my father observed. "I think he don't hunt mice because he doesn't care to take unnecessary chances, that's all. Stop feeding him cream and he'll hunt the milkman." Then he put the *Blade* back across his face and pretended to snore.

"Punishment is *never* the answer to *anything,*" my mother instructed both him and myself. The way she put me in front of her broom as well as the old man made me wonder whether she knew I was the one who'd snipped off the cat's whiskers the winter before.

For although this was all long before we knew that some creatures are more accident-prone than others, yet my mother, in her intuitive way, sensed that the cat's real handicap was that it *was* accident-prone—when I was in reaching distance of it.

But when the brute limped into the kitchen licking red paint off its hide, *that* was no doing of mine. Dipping a cat into a bucket of red paint was just something that hadn't occurred to me. The stuff stuck pretty good, too. That cat was licking its forepaws all winter.

My mother and father agreed this far: nobody could have done anything so idiotic as painting a cat except John Sheeley, a retarded kid who delivered our milk. He had already distinguished himself by locking himself into a bathroom with a six-year-old boy and shaving the kid's head. It followed, by an iron logic, that nobody but John Sheeley would paint a cat. Not *red,* anyhow.

I knew better, but I didn't say anything. I was afraid to say anything. The kid who'd done it, the only kid who *could* have done it, the only kid *mean* enough to have done it wasn't John Sheeley. It was Baldy Costello.

Baldy was *really* mean and *really* bald. And *really* accident-prone. So much so that the Seventy-first Street trolley, that had never harmed a soul in all its endless runs between Halsted Street and Cottage Grove, suddenly ran this sprout down and chomped off two of his toes. Up to that moment the kid had not been a particular threat to society. But when the Seventy-first Street trolley singled him out like that, he became one. Doctors said shock had caused his hair to fall out. I think he never really wanted hair in the first place.

No sooner would the word go from back porch to back porch that Mrs. O'Connor's kitchen-money had been stolen than Baldy would be showing off in front of John the Greek's with the front of his skull plastered with purple and green designs. He invested every penny he stole in "cockomanies"-decal papers. Either he was trying to divert attention from his baldness or was defiantly calling attention to a skull as naked as that of a man on his way to the electric chair.

I never laughed at Baldy. I didn't dare. Nobody laughed at Baldy. Nobody dared. Yet he must have felt that everybody was laughing at him.

I was nailing a pushmobile together upon the promise of neighbor Kooglin, the local newspaper agent, that he would give me a paper route if I had a wagon or a pushmobile to make deliveries. On my first run with it, Baldy pushed me off and raced it down to the Seventy-first Street tracks and left it lying in the trolley's path. I recovered it. On the next evening he waylaid me making my first evening-paper route, grabbed all my *Abendposts,* and scattered them down the alley. I ran after them in desperation, for the wind was on his side. It blew them apart faster than I could gather them, and when I went back to my pushmobile the wind had reached into it and blown half my *Evening Posts* after the *Abendposts.* I chased up and down the alley, crying in the wind, and finally, in a fright, abandoned paper, pushmobile, and all. When my father heard the story, at the supper table, his only word was for me to finish my supper.

Then he took me back down the alley, picked up the pushmobile with one hand and, holding my hand with the other, assured me that Mr. Kooglin wouldn't fire me, and Mr. Kooglin didn't.

A few years later Baldy Costello became one of the first men to go to the electric chair in Cook County. The conviction was for murder and rape.

I *told* you that kid was accident-prone.

Out of odd lore and remnants of old rains, memory ties rainbows of forgetfulness about the old lost years.

Out of old rains, new rainbows.

One such rainbow, for me, is a winter remembrance of two children, a seven-year-old boy and an eight-year-old girl at a South Park Avenue window watching the winter sun go down. We saw the church across the prairie lifting its cross like a command; till daylight and cloudlight broke the sky wide, pouring an orange-red light. Triumph and doom shone down: The End and the Beginning.

"Gawd's blood is burning," the girl instructed me in an awed whisper, genuflecting, and pulled me down beside her—"*Pray!*"

"*Why?*" I wanted to know.

"*So you'll see the face of Gawd.*"

"Is that the same as 'God'?"

I just wanted to know.

"*Don't say 'God,*'" she warned me, "say '*Gawd*'—or you'll *never* see His face."

If I missed His face tonight I'd catch tomorrow's performance was my secret thinking. And though, in the winter evenings that followed, Ethel's faith encouraged me to wait by the window to see His colors rage the sunset sky, yet I did not feel I had as much in common with Him as I had with the lamplighter who came after.

Came riding a dark bike softly; softly as the snow came riding. God's colors would begin to die on walk and tree and street when he would prop his ladder against the night to defend us all till day. The torch he touched to the filament, that came up hard as a green gem, then softly fanned to a blue flutter, gave me a greater sense of personal protection than Gawd's incomprehensible raging.

I followed the lamplighter with my eyes to see a line of light come on like many tethered fireflies. God's colors passed, but the night flares burned steadily on.

> *For we are very lucky*
> *With a lamp before the door—*
> *And Leerie stops to light it—*

I read in a book my sister had gotten for me at a library—

> *As he lights so many more.*

My memory of that Chicago winter is made of blue-green gas flares across a shining sheet, ice so black and snow so white, it became a marvel to me to recall that, under that ice sheet, tomatoes had lately flowered.

St. Columbanus kids stood around the ice pond's rim with skates under their arms, for an inch of water was already spreading to the pond's edges. When they tested the ice it squeaked the first squeak of spring.

In March came the true thaw, running waters in running weather, when we raced the sky to school and raced it home once more. The St. Columbanus kids began lingering on the steps of their church—then the light, that had closed each night like a door behind their cross, began to linger too. To see what they would be up to next.

Then the fly-a-kite spring came on, and I fled through the ruins of Victory Gardens pulling a great orange grin of a kite higher than the cross of St. Columbanus, with Ethel behind me.

When it soared so high it no longer grinned, I anchored it and Ethel sent a message up *I Love My Savior.* I don't know yet what had frightened that kid so.

Yet that whole blue forenoon she stayed in continuous touch with the Virgin Mary, assisted by an unlikely assortment of angels, dead uncles, saints, martyrs, erring friends and, of course, *Gawd.* The kite went to work for the church. It became a Jesuit kite scouring Heaven for proselytes. Ethel ran home and came back with a cup of holy water to help it. I made no protest when she sprinkled me. She was older and infinitely wiser than myself.

"I'm a Catholic now," I announced that night at supper.

"Eat your soup," my mother instructed me.

"Ethel baptized me."

"That takes a priest. Eat your soup."

"I want to see the face of Gawd."

"Eat your soup."

I ate the soup, yet I brooded.

Nobody knew I was brooding until I looked at the bread pudding with distaste. Then it was plain something had gone wrong.

So my sister ate it for me and helped my mother with the dishes while I sat on, bread-puddingless, till the last dish was stacked.

Ethel burst into our kitchen. She was weeping with anger or disappointment—"I'm running away from home! I'm going to live with you!"

My father looked at my mother for an explanation. My mother looked at Ethel.

Her father had died without last rites and her mother had paid a priest a hundred dollars to keep her late husband from spending eternity in Purgatory. Now the priest, Ethel told us between sobs, had returned to tell the family that all the hundred dollars had done was to get the old man to his knees. It would take another hundred to get him out. But Ethel's mother had answered, "If the old man is on his knees, let him jump the rest of the way," and had sent the priest on his way. Her mother's blasphemy had provoked Ethel's decision to run away from home.

Ethel's mother opened the kitchen door, tossed in an armful of the girl's clothing onto the floor—"And don't come home!" she announced, and slammed the door on her pious daughter.

The castout girl stood silently. Then her features began working.

"He'll never see the face of Gawd!" she howled her grief and love. "He'll never see *His* face!"

"Then let him look at His ass," my father decided firmly.

On weekdays I got a penny for candy and blew my nose into a rag. But on Sundays I got a dime and a clean handkerchief.

Weekdays afforded only such mean choices as that between two yellow jawbreakers or a piece of chewing wax shaped like a wine bottle, containing a few drops of sugar water. But Sundays one chose between a chocolate, vanilla, or strawberry sundae.

Sunday was for sundaes, and Ethel was my girl because I was the one with the dime. Ethel gave me orders on weekdays because she was closer to Gawd. Sunday was my day because I was closer to John The Greek.

John The Greek's was the place where ice cream came true. In John The Greek's country, maraschino cherries lived atop vanilla ice-cream cones. There strawberries loved whipped cream and whipped cream loved pineapple and pineapple must have loved banana, for it ran down both sides of banana splits.

It was all butter-cream frosting, there where caramels lived in candy pans and Green River fizzed beside marzipan. It was always root-beer and ginger-ale time at John The Greek's; there it was always time for lemonade with a cherry in it. There where butterscotch and maple embraced as one.

Ethel's church was St. Columbanus. Mine was The Store Where Ice Cream Came True.

Even there Ethel couldn't forget Gawd. That kid was dotty on Jesus. As soon as John brought us ice water she'd start sprinkling me. As the day was warm I didn't mind the wetting. But as she'd already used Holy Water without doing any good, I couldn't see how a couple of glasses of soda-fountain water would do any better.

And as though that weren't superstition enough for Sunday, she warned me not to step on a crack dividing the sidewalk. Gawd would strike me dead if I did.

"*Dare* me."

"I *dare* you."

"*Double*-dare me."

"Double-dare and *triple*-dare you."

Wow.

I came down with both feet flat on a crack and didn't miss one all the way home.

I had dared, double-, and triple-dared Gawd, and He hadn't done a thing.

My mother never entertained notions. With her, every notion immediately became a conviction. And, once she had one, there was no way either of prying her off it or of prying the conviction off her.

I began addressing valentines, as our winter life began addressing spring, to bring to my second-grade teacher. There were forty-eight kids in that class, and Miss Burke was to call out the names on every valentine in a kind of election to determine who was the most popular girl and the most popular boy in the class.

"Are you sending one to Mildred Ford?" my mother asked.

That I had a valentine for every other kid in the class but none for Mildred, wasn't because I had anything *against* her. It was just that I felt it would be better for *her* if I didn't send any. Mildred Ford was the only colored kid in the Park Manor school, and *I* hadn't sent for her I was sure. It was only that I felt it would be best for everybody if we proceeded more gradually toward integration. On a different holiday, in another school. Promotion to second-class citizenship, coming too suddenly, can leave a person unbalanced for the rest of his life.

"*Are* you sending Mildred Ford a valentine?" my mother repeated.

It ought to have been plain enough to her that, when there are forty-seven people on one side and one on the other, it isn't going to help anybody to change the ratio to forty-six to two. Yet I sensed that this wouldn't convince her, so I ignored the question a second time.

She scooped up my tableful of heart-shaped greetings, arrows with bows, tears with vows.

"If you don't send a valentine to everyone you can't send *any* to *anybody.*"

"Nobody sent Mildred any last year, Ma," I fell back on precedent.

"Then *this* is the year to start."

"But *nobody* sends a valentine to a *nigger,* Ma."

As Governor Faubus was to express it in later years, the situation had become untenable.

"*You* do," was the decision.

From that verdict there was no appeal.

The valentine that Mildred received from me possessed as much wit as one penny could buy. It showed a tearful puppy pleading: "Don't Treat Me Like a Dog. Be My Valentine."

That was about as far as *anybody* could go and still stay segregated in 1918.

All I could see of her, from where I sat, was a pair of nappy pigtails tied with blue-ribbon bows, bent above a reluctant valentine.

I never spoke to Mildred Ford; she never spoke to me. Yet by one shuttered glance, passing through a door while I stood to one side to let her pass, she acknowledged my gift.

"You're on the other side, *Stay* there," that glance plainly told me.

A few weeks after, in Sunday weather, Ethel and her mother, my mother and myself, put swimming suits in a basket lunch and went picnicking in Jackson Park.

A replica of Columbus' flagship had been rotting on the Jackson Park lagoon since 1893. We took our lunch on the sunny grass in view of the *Santa Maria's* bulging hulk.

I was too big to change to a swimming suit in front of women, my mother felt. If I wanted to go swimming I had to go to the men's bathhouse. Fair enough—but I had to keep my winter underwear on! Those were *orders.*

I didn't realize what a skinny kid wearing a man's trunks looks like in public when he is wearing them over long flannels, but when Ethel's mother began to laugh I began to get the idea. When my mother laughed I knew: I was a pitiful sight. But when Ethel laughed I slugged her. My mother promptly slugged me.

First she had caused my public humiliation, then she'd hit me—I began to bawl.

Ethel's mother promptly slugged Ethel simply to make matters even. Ethel began to bawl. Matters were evened, so I quit bawling. When I quit, Ethel quit.

Nobody was mad at anybody—until her mother and mine left us alone a little later. Ethel took one more look at the longies—but she didn't laugh. She knew better now. All she did was express a kind of overall disdain.

"*You* send valentines to niggers," she observed.

I didn't crack her.

"*I* send valentines to *everybody,*" I answered with a disdain quite as derisive as her own.

Mildred Ford had been wrong. If I didn't send valentines to everybody, I couldn't send them to anybody. I needed her to send a valentine to as much as she needed me to receive one.

No, she didn't want me on *her* side. I didn't want to be on her side.

Yet I was there all the same.

My mother's idea of making things up to me for the battle of the *Santa Maria* was a promise to cut down my Uncle Harry's Spanish-American naval uniform. Uncle Harry had died of yellow fever in Cuba in 1898, but, twenty years afterward, his uniform still hung in our clothes closet awaiting the final trump. The promise was that I could wear it to school on the anniversary of the sinking of the battleship *Maine.*

To be the only kid in the school with a colored sweetheart was tough, but the prospect now offered was too much. I believe that it was the first time I stood my mother off successfully.

Yet in pauses in our play Ethel would now survey me gravely—then give me a smile of thinnest mockery as she saw me once more in a swimming suit drawn over a suit of long underwear. Ground lost by such experience is never regained.

As the roll-a-hoop spring came on as blue as peace. By the light that now lingered, the light that held, I stood bowed against the gas-lamp crying warning—"eight—nine—ten—*redlight!*" As the roll-a-hoop spring raced to a summer of redlit pursuit.

And our Edison Vic hit a crack—the same crack every time—

> *America I love you*
> *You're like an old sweetheart of mine*
> *From ocean to ocean*
> *A nation's devotion—devotion—devotion—*

I also worked up a bit on Uncle-Theodore-The-Great-Lakes-Sailor coming home drunk which my mother said she could live without.

A terrier got hit in the street by a car that kept going. We heard its yelp and watched it drag itself to the curb. Ethel gave it last rites.

The next morning she got me out of bed to give it a Catholic burial. I hadn't even known the brute was a Christian.

We took turns digging with a toy shovel. When it was deep enough Ethel began crossing herself, and I stepped back until she should tell me to throw in the deceased.

Crazy Johnny Sheely came up, put his container of six quarts of milk down, and took the shovel from me. The grave wasn't deep enough, it looked to Johnny.

At his first stroke, the shovel bent and Johnny looked humiliated.

"Wait for me," he asked us. We stood around until he came back bearing a man-sized shovel.

Johnny dug until we grew tired of watching him and wandered off to find four-leaf clovers. When we came back he had dug himself down to his waist.

The dead terrier lay beside the milk. Ethel threw in a prayer for Crazy Johnny and I practiced crossing myself until it was time for lunch.

From our front window, I watched Johnny digging for his life. He had, it was plain, forgotten both dog and milk, dirty home and dirty mother. In the early afternoon Ethel came down to fetch me, and we went out to watch Johnny for lack of anything else to do. A crowd had gathered.

"You're going to catch it if you don't get home," Ethel shouted down into the hole from which we could see Johnny's dark, sweat-tousled

head. Her answer was a shovelful of dirt from which we both jumped
back.

Johnny dug until we saw his mother coming—somebody had snitched!
This was a formidable harridan who supported half-a-dozen nutty sons
and nuttier daughters by her backyard dairy, doing more herself than her
whole nutty brood combined. Johnny tried to scramble out but couldn't
get a hold. His mother had to get two of his nutty brothers out of bed to
pull him up.

When they got him up, without a word they both began punching
him, while his mother slapped him with the broad of her hand. Johnny
ducked into a running crouch and all three followed, punching and slap-
ping, the old woman carrying the soured milk in her left hand while she
slapped at his ears with her right. The battle went across South Park
Avenue, with Ethel and I following, drawn by flying joy, through a narrow
way between buildings and up the alley between South Park and Vernon
Avenue, when Ethel's mother and mine both hollered us back into our
own yards. I don't remember whether the terrier ever got buried.

I know the great hole remained there until my father filled it, with the
shovel Johnny had left, and Ethel and I had to return the shovel as some
sort of punishment. Nobody knew what we had to be punished for, but
my punishment now was always the same: "You're excommunicated," my
father told me. I don't see how my father was qualified to excommunicate
anybody, but he did it all the same.

Somebody was always excommunicating me.

This time it was my mother who thought the action was comical and
my father who went around growling that somebody ought to have that
milk-delivery kid locked up before he started thinking about girls.

So far as I know, Johnny never got any ideas about girls that were any
funnier than anybody else's.

In the late sunflowered summer of nineteen-and-eighteen nobody
played Cops and Robbers any more. Some of us had to be Allies and some
of us had to be Huns. Those who were Huns had to die or run when stuck
by a sunflower stalk-bayonet. Most Huns chose to die, as that was not
only more dramatic but much braver. Some died face-down, some leaped
as though blown—if we had a few yards of barbed wire I'm sure we would
have had volunteers for impalement.

Then the Huns rose as Allies, Brave American Boys, Heroic Frenchmen, and Noble English, and it was the turn of those who had so recently been victorious to decide which was better, retreat or death.

But on Sundays there was no war. That was the day I escorted Ethel to John The Greek's at Seventy-first and Vernon. Ethel would order a strawberry sundae and I would order chocolate and John would put a roll in the player-piano and, pumping away, no hands on the keys, would sing—

> *I'm floating down the old Green River*
> *On the good ship Rock and Rye*

or—

> *If you don't like your Uncle Sammy,*
> *If you don't like the red, white, and blue—*

In the cornstalked autumn of nineteen-and-eighteen my father bought me a new pair of roller skates, so I could use one for a new pushmobile. He helped me screw the front wheels on so that it would swing a corner. He bought me a bell for the handlebars, and then I punched holes in an old tomato can, hung it by a wire below the bell, and stuck a candle in the can.

When my father got off the Seventy-first Street trolley with his lunch box under his arm, he saw me flickering, he heard me ringing toward him in the dark. And I carried his lunchbox for him all the way home.

I did not know, then, how much this meant to him. I know now. It meant more than a father's pride in having a son. It meant he had a son to whom *he* had given a home. His own father had been an Indiana squatter who had deserted wife and sons on unclaimed land near Black Oak. Now he knew he was doing better for his own than his father had done for him.

He had come off the farm, with a brother, to see the World's Fair of 1893. They had seen Little Egypt dance, but neither had done any dancing since. One to the steel mills and one to the garages—their fun times had been few and now were fewer.

But before his marriage my father had gone, once or twice or perhaps oftener, to the Columbia Dance Hall on North Clark where musicians, calling themselves "McGuire's Ice-Cream Kings," had worn white pants.

And a "Special Introducer" had stood by to introduce backward youths to up-to-date ladies who knew The Speedy Three-Step.

He had also been to Heinie Kabibbler's saloon, where he'd been given a slit mug of beer. When he'd lifted it to his mouth, the beer had spilled down the front of his shirt.

He remembered Patrick Prendergast, a thirty-year-old newsboy who had handed a revolver to Sergeant McDonnell of the Desplaines Street Station, one October evening of 1893, and explained, "I've just killed the mayor."

He had shot Carter Harrison in the mayor's home out of a fantasy that Harrison had promised to make him Corporation Counsel. For his poor judgment and accurate aim, Prendergast The Newsboy had been hanged.

Both my mother and father had been scandalized by Bad-News Tillie, who had told a grocer that she'd like to do her Daddy in—and she didn't mean her father—a couple of hours before Tillie's Daddy slipped on a bar of soap while bathing and broke his neck. It looked like more bad news for Bad-News Tillie until her lawyer pointed out that the bar Daddy had slipped on was a different brand than the one Tillie had bought from the grocer. That had been good news for Bad-News Tillie.

Both my parents had been to the Electrified Fountain in Lincoln Park and had gone together to the Bismarck Gardens; that once stood where the Marigold Gardens now stand.

My father was a workingman in a day when the working hour was from 6:00 A.M. to 6:00 P.M. He left the house before daylight six days a week and returned home after dark six days a week, year in and year out.

He worked for McCormick Reaper and Otis Elevator and Packard and The Yellow Cab Company in a time when there were no sick leave, no vacations, no seniority, and no social security. There was nothing for him to do but to get a hold as a machinist and to hold on as hard as he could for as long as he could.

He was a good holder, but he was unable to hold on to any one job because he was as unable to give orders as he was to take them. He was a tenacious holder; but, after four or five years he would hit a foreman. This would happen so suddenly, so blindly, that he would be as stunned by it as the man he had hit. There was never an understandable provocation.

When he walked into the kitchen at noon with his tool chest under his arm, my mother knew it had happened again. The first time this happened I was frightened, because I had never seen him in the middle of a weekday. My mother was going to go for him now like never before, I felt.

That was one time she didn't go for him at all.

Yet for days we lived under an oppression of which none but the tool chest in the kitchen spoke. On the morning I rose to find the tool chest and the old man gone to work together, life began once more.

He was a fixer of machinery in basements and garages who had seen the Electrified Fountain in Lincoln Park.

My father was a farm youth who had come to the city to see Little Egypt dance, and had stayed on to work. For many great plants that offered him twice the wages that others were getting for doing the same work.

My father liked getting double wages, and would stay on the job loyally until some picket would take him aside and ask him how he would like to have his head blown off his shoulders.

My father would say that he would like to wait until after lunch if he wasn't asking too much.

He had witnessed the fight between police and anarchists on the Black Road near the McCormick works. He had heard Samuel Fielden speak on the lakefront. Yet his most vivid memory was of Honeythroat Regan singing *If He Can Fight Like He Can Love / Goodby Germany.*

My father avoided being killed in situations simmering with violence only because he didn't know anything was cooking.

That autumn my mother took me to see my grandmother and grandfather. We walked together below the Lake Street El, and a grandfatherly light fell through the Lake Street ties, all the way to The Westside House.

The Westside House was where my grandfather sat sealing cigars of his own making with a lick of his tongue. The red band with which he bound each cigar said each was a Father & Son Cigar.

And the old man had promised that, one day, he would tell me a secret he had never told any of his other grandchildren.

Neither of us knew that it was his last autumn.

And the secret that I was never to tell was that he himself, personally, my own grandfather, had thought up the name of the Father & Son Cigar! That he was therefore the *inventor* of the Father & Son Cigar! And that he had applied for a patent on the name: *Father & Son Cigar.*

And that it was a *good* cigar.

I was proud to have the man who had invented the Father & Son Cigar for a grandfather.

Then he made the wooden half-figure of a clown on his worktable blow real smoke at me, and we went upstairs to dinner.

Behind my grandfather's Westside House stood the *Sommerhaus,* a little old-world cottage with blinds.

It was always summer in the *Sommerhaus.*

The old man sat at dinner with his wife at his right hand and all his married daughters, and all his married sons, and his grandchildren running in and out of The Westside House. He was proud of being a Civil War veteran and that all his grandchildren had been born in The States. But I was the only one in that whole tribe for whom he made a wooden clown that blew real smoke.

I was the only one the old man ever told *who* thought up the name of the Father & Son Cigar.

And it was a *good* cigar.

After dinner Uncle Bill sat at the player piano and played *The Faded Coat of Blue* and Aunt Toby sang the words. Aunt Toby didn't look exactly faint and hungry the way it said in the song—

> *He sank faint and hungry*
> *Among the vanquished brave,*
> *And they laid him sad and lonely*
> *In a grave unknown.*
> *O no more the bugle*
> *Calls the lonely one,*
> *Rest, noble spirit*
> *In thy grave unknown—*

but I figured it must be because she'd just had dinner.

Then in no time at all it was time to go home, and I walked back with my mother below the Lake Street El, listening to her humming cheerfully—

> *Take me out for a joy ride*
> *A girl-ride, a boy-ride,*

I'm as reckless as I can be,
I don't care what becomes of me—

it had been a good day.

And a grandfatherly light like yellow cigar smoke drifted down between the Lake Street ties.

All the way home.

That Halloween Ethel and I put on false-faces and went up and down Seventy-first Street chalking windows of laundry, undertaker, delicatessen and butcher shop. Dotty as ever, Ethel chalked a cross on John The Greek's, and I wrote below the cross—*Everything inside is a penny!* and we ran off screaming. On my way home from the Park Manor School the next noon, all the store windows had been washed clean except John The Greek's.

John's window stayed chalked. On Sunday morning police broke the lock and found John hanging by his belt above his candy tins.

Now I knew what I had sensed in that rage behind the evening cross: there *was* a fury padfooting the world.

"Gawd called him home," Ethel explained contentedly.

I began to skip cracks in the sidewalk. I skipped the cracks with particular care when passing The Hanged Man's Place. Frost froze the cracks over and The Hanged Man's windows went white.

I rubbed off the frost with my mitten and peered in: Dust and cold had laid their gray hands across Green River and Coca-Cola. The great jar of fresh strawberry syrup had fermented, then split the bowl and bubbled over the counter: it hung in a long frozen drip, like a string of raw meat.

The magic of strawberry had been hung. The magic of its smell and the magic of its color.

Hanged.

In a freezing dust.

That night I said the German prayer my mother had taught me out of her own childhood:

Ich bin klein
Mein Herz ist rein

Kinder dehrfen reinvonen
Blos Gott und der angels allein—

Yet somewhere between St. Valentine's Day and The Place Where Ice Cream Came True I had realized that where God's colors raged behind a lifted cross was no business of mine. His colors were for people who lived upstairs. Not for people who lived down.

CHICAGO II

IF YOU GOT THE BREAD YOU WALK

"The people of these parts address each other as Mulai (Lord) and Sayyid (Sir), and use the expressions 'Your Servant' and 'Your Excellency.' When one meets another, instead of giving the ordinary greeting he says respectfully, 'Here is your slave,' or 'Here is your servant at your service.' They make presents of honorifics to each other. Gravity with them is a fabulous affair.

"Their style of salutation is either a deep bow or prostration, and you will see their necks in play, lifting and lowering, stretching and contracting. Sometimes they will go on like this for a long time, one going down as the other rises, their turbans tumbling between them. This style of greeting, inclining as in prayer, we have observed in female slaves, or when handmaids make some request.

"They apply themselves with assiduity to things that proud souls disdain. What odd people! The tail is equal to the head with them. Glory to God who created men of all kinds. He has no partner. There is no God but He."

> —Notes on the condition of the city of Damascus from the tenth of August to the eighth of September in the year 1184, from the chronicle of the Spanish Moor Abu 'l-Husayn Muhammad ibn Ahmad ibn Jubayr.

Chicago is fond of the image of itself as a row-de-dow young peasant with a healthy stink going straight to his pigs ticking after brawling on bar whisky all night—Ho! Ho! Ho!—hog butcher to the world and all of that—but actually Row-De-Dow pulled off his sweatshirt and sat down to a glass-topped desk about the time we got electricity in City Hall.

It used to be a ball-every-night town, but now it's a Friday-and-Saturday-night town, and not much doing on Fridays. Time was when you couldn't walk down West Division without seeing five people being bounced for creating a disturbance in a bar, but now it's a rarity if a customer raises his voice to a bartender. It's nice, of course, that we're so much nicer than we used to be—but are we? Isn't it even nicer to punch somebody in the nose instead of merely smiling politely and finding out where he works so he'll never know who had him fired? The good thing about arguing with a hog butcher is that you know where you're at. Nobody knows what a businessman is thinking.

There are no painted women waiting under gas lamps here any more. Chicago is a middleman in business-blues who has one daiquiri before dinner and the filet better be just as he ordered it or somebody is going to catch hell. In his gardened and glass-walled nest high above the light-filled boulevard, the hog butcher's grandson can feel he has done pretty well for himself. And he has.

Other than being asphyxiated, struck mute, deaf, and staring blind by boredom, he has life by the tail.

"We have a feeling which has persisted for some time," a *Chicago Sun-Times* hand tries to place a persistent feeling, "that squalor is going out of fashion in Chicago. Perhaps it's been largely due to our mayor's efforts in brightening up and tidying our streets, the popularity of cheering colors and the Schenley advertising display of modern masterpieces in the subway concourse—a step in dispelling the sordid gloom of our subway décor that adds a touch of brightness to the day for the weary homeward bound."

That all depends upon which way you're bound home, Mr. Homeward. Chicago's streets were never so lawless and corruption never so common. Whenever is someone going to come along who'll say right out, "We *like* it this way?"

And yet what complacency a ribbon salesman can achieve when you give him a posture chair on which to put his behind down! The smugness begins coming out of his ears—if he can just keep it up he'll be a *Daily News* columnist advocating a return to old-fashioned spanking as a cure-all for juvenile delinquency.

Offer him a chunk of a Cicero whorehouse and he'll snap it up like a bass snapping a fly, and bank the bills in his wall safe without feeling a riffle in his morality.

Dying cries of outraged innocence, with which our local press was lately ringing, commonly follow disclosure that cops have been stripping stores of electric appliances again. They are in reality simply cries of middlemen protesting a retail operation being conducted wholesale. It isn't the thefts, but the audacity of officers in raising their percentage from 50 percent to 100 at the cost of middlemen who have invested in trucks and crowbars which incense us.

Using their own vehicles, supplying their own labor and their own crowbars, the police were guilty on two counts—first, of jobbing professional movers of electric appliances who have served district stations faithfully, and second, of getting caught. When this occurs a shudder goes through the middle of Chicago's middle class.

During the following confusion as to who was the least crooked, crooks or cops (the cops offering the impregnable defense that the crooks had gotten as much as *they* had), an officer of the Patrolmen's Union was entrapped, by fellow officers, taking a bribe on the South Side. The union immediately went to bat for him, pleading the illegality of entrapment. Which it is and so he was.

But why does no one mention the use of entrapment by police when the entrapped party is a penniless whore trying to make her rent at the same time that an officer needs to meet his monthly quota of arrests?

Yet one can scarcely find the police culpable of entrapment when they see it practiced by the columnist crusading against B-girls. If it's a criminal offense for an officer to entrap a suspect, why not a criminal offense for a columnist?

And how can one decry police for being primitive while a columnist can come to his desk on the hawks for impaling somebody? Providing, of course, that she can't hit back.

The crusades conducted by Chicago columnists in the past two years against children born out of wedlock, B-girls, panhandlers, drag-car racers, and drug addicts probably broke every local record for unadulterated cowardice. In which a high standard among columnists had already been set by that patriot, who, caught selling cars on the black market in Detroit, volunteered for army service without mentioning what war. Presumably he wanted to fight the Blackhawks.

If our cops have gotten a bad name for bribe taking, columnists who take payola preserve an air of innocence.

Our corruption doesn't rise from stews below, but descends like a pall from air-conditioned offices above. Not with the girl waiting in the dim-lit cocktail lounge with a false-bottomed glass before her; but with the newspaper owner whose one reality is his circulation department.

Our corruption begins with the assumption that a newspaper owner, being a private enterpriser, has as much right to decide what will increase circulation as a delicatessen owner has to decide whether he will push pastrami or liverwurst.

When a member of an American medical commission in Mexico, who was earning six hundred a month and expenses, was asked, "How long will the epidemic last?" he answered, "As long as we can keep it going— maybe it will break out in South America."

Pointing the finger of accusation at a crooked police department or calling in a convenient spectre called "The Syndicate" is simply no good. If the hand that holds the poison pen is what you're looking for, take a peek at your *Tribune* cartoons.

To believe that a newspaper's sole purpose is to reach as many readers as possible leads to the replacing of vital news by a mindless stackpiling of the names of "celebs." The *Tribune* circumvents this problem by rewriting news to fit the views of the late Colonel McCormick, a man of such severe limitations that he once ordered a star cut out of the American flag in the *Tribune* lobby by way of reading Rhode Island out of the Union for not voting his way.

This point, at which pettiness verges on the idiotic, is also practiced by our courts. As was recently demonstrated by a judge of the Criminal Court who quashed an indictment, against detectives accused of thefts, because a semicolon was used where a common was more appropriate. It is not yet certain whether the judge was even correct grammatically.

The man who had obtained the indictment was a professional burglar, a stripling named Richard Morrison. When instructed by another judge that he was free to leave the courtroom, the youth held tight to the safety of the witness chair: he had been semicoloned into being a moving target, and he knew it.

"The way I feel now," he confessed to reporters, "is that if what I did doesn't help, this city will never be cleaned up. Everything blew up in my face, as usual. No, I wouldn't do it again. Here I've spent seventeen months in custody, and that's time that won't be counted if I'm ever sentenced. And when I get out I'll be looking over my shoulder the rest of my life, even if I can go straight as I want to do. There are always going to be people who will want to look me up."

They will, son. They will. When you wind up in an alley with the cats looking at you, it will be one more step in dispelling the sordid gloom of our subway décor.

To add a touch of brightness to the day for the weary homeward bound.

POLICE STRATEGISTS HUDDLE ON RASH OF GANG SLAYINGS

"Police strategists Thursday huddled behind closed doors, pondering ways to deal with the recent rash of Gangland-style killings. Its participants conceded that liaison between unit detectives and the Organized Crime Division left something to be desired and may have hampered investigation of Gangland-style murders. It was suggested that officers of both groups might have information which furnished investigative leads but which was not exchanged because of a breakdown in communication. Participants agreed that some officers, hoping to make a score, had withheld information from fellow investigators. The passing around of stool pigeons from policeman to policeman was suggested."*

In what other city can I become a rotating fink?

And should not a fink, having been rotating faithfully for twenty years, be eligible for a fink's pension? Hasn't he done as much as anyone else to brighten our subway décor?

Thus, as above a widening universe, nuclear death draws nearer, I pick up the *Chicago Daily News* and find the front page divided by a reprint of Horatio Alger's *Luke Walton,* an exposure of the American League by an ex-manager, and a recipe for drawn butter.

Not to be surpassed in public service, the *Evening American* offers a new crusade by Chicago's most heavily decorated fink; one whose honors are all self-awarded. While keeping an eagle eye on the broken brutes of Skid Row's broken walks, he also finds time to expose mothers of illegitimate children found in movie houses while receiving state aid. This Malthusian revisionist's cry is, "They're multiplying like guinea pigs out there!" Implying that *his* kind of people have hit upon a method of reproducing themselves different from that of guinea pigs.

This is a nasty reversal of the morality of earlier Chicago newspapermen, such as Lloyd Lewis and Finley Peter Dunne, who felt that the job

---

* *Chicago Sun-Times*

was to get the judge down out of the dock to get a look at *his* hands. The job today, as Ross, Mabley, Malloy, and Smith see it, is to see what his honor's fee is for the privilege of sitting beside him. They're multiplying like guinea pigs out there.

"But do you know it is impossible," Dostoevsky inquired, "to charge man with sin, to burden him with debts and turning the other cheek, when society is organized so meanly that he cannot help but perpetrate villainies—when economically he is brought to villainy and that it is silly and cruel to demand of him that which he is impotent to perform?"

Our contemporary columnists here are more demanding than Dostoevsky. Not enough people, as they see it, are turning the other cheek. "If you're not guilty of something what do you think we're doing here questioning you?" is their assumption. "Don't think you can scare *us* by bleeding. If you're not guilty of something you must be innocent of something, and that's far worse." Trying to understand one's society by reading pietists like Malloy and Mabley is like trying to get perspective through the eyes of guards in a maximum-security penitentiary.

Since clocks first ticked, the captains and the kings have been demanding that writers uphold their authority; and, since the first tick, writers have been trying to bring that authority down. Yet today in Chicago it is the writers who most praise the captains and the kings—and Chicago runs from coast to coast.

Thus Europe's century-old fear of the American businessman, that he would level Western Europe's ancestral culture, takes this surprising turn: that the American businessman is not quite so busy at leveling as is the American writer.

The artist's usefulness has always been to stand in an ironic affiliation to his society, and every society needs him standing so. Though it gags, disdains, and dishonors him, it needs him to know truth from falsehood. The businessman is of no use whatsoever in this: his truth is always false.

Poets, philosophers, scientists, men of the cloth and court jesters are the people upon whom any society must depend for its survival. For these, if true to themselves, lend the perspective that the business and military mind, in its eagerness for profit and victory, loses.

Yet here we have no such poet to teach us. Our leading philosopher has no larger claim to distinction, by packaging and distributing other men's ideas, than if he were packaging Ma's Home-Made Noodles.

John Justin Smith and the Reverend Father Dussman are representative, respectively, of the press and the right-wing clergy. The former informs us, for example, that a cartoonist showing an American climbing into a bomb shelter shaped like a coffin, must be sick. Yet, if a fallout shelter *is* anything else *but* a coffin, that wasn't a firestorm that hit Hiroshima. It was a brush fire started by a careless motorist. Fortunately, nobody got hurt.

Smith feels people to whom nothing is sacred are sick. But as *everything* is sacred to Smith, I think Smith is far sicker. A cartoonist showing an American spaceman making a pass at another spaceman's wife while hubby is in orbit seems to me no more than an extension of an old human custom—one also indulged in by columnists when an other columnist is in orbit—yet here comes John Justin demanding a stop to satirizing of the Air Force. This eye-rolling ass has picked up a conviction that fallout shelters, spacemen, and a carnie-talking revivalist named Graham are beyond criticism.

This dour demand to stop spoofing, in a country that never needed spoofing more, is companioned by the urge to punish. What the Chicago press wants, basically, is a world where everyone has been printed and mugged. "If you aren't planning to steal for a living, why not let us have your prints just in the event you change your mind?" bespeaks the world of Ross, Mabley, Malloy, and Smith.

It isn't that these people believe in anything, one way or another. Whichever way the wind blows is the way *they'll* blow. Whoever is running things is right—a complete shift in the American dream. The fink, once disdained, becomes a heroic figure.

Nor are men of conscience lacking only in the press. Here is the Reverend Father Dussman addressing us:

"Should we forewarn Russia of its doom? We have no moral obligation to do so, since they may get the jump on us, if what they boast they have is true. Now you might say, What about all the lives of the innocent people of Russia, non-card-carrying citizens who may be as disgusted with their warmongering as we are? If our intelligence is as good as it should be in these perilous times, we should know the location of every last launching pad in Russia and its satellite countries. Those are areas that should be bombed without further ado, and without forewarning under the circumstances. You might say that would mean the demise of some

Americans, as the Russians would retaliate from submarines and the like. That is a calculated risk. Far better that a few of us pass into God's Eternal City a bit prematurely than that half or more of the human race perish a few years hence."*

Now, some people are going to say that if it's so much better to pass a bit prematurely into God's Eternal City, what is keeping the Reverend Father back? Just natural courtesy, I'm sure—it wouldn't look right for a man to be elbowing ahead of people who deserve to go as much as himself.

One thing strikes me curiously: I recently heard the Reverend Father's thought expressed by a man in a Division Street bar, and the owner of the place threw him out. "I've heard enough, you poisonous nut," the owner told this fellow, and threw him out.

I feel we should give a man wearing a cassock the benefit of the doubt: he may be poisonous without being a nut.

"I am standing on the threshold of a literary career," a girl writes me. "What is my next move?"

Your next move is take one step back, honey, turn slowly and *run like hell*. That isn't a threshold you're standing on. It's a precipice. And what you're standing above isn't Literature.

It's a termitary.

A certain man was once standing at the head of a long line of men and women, like the line that forms in front of a bleacher box office the first morning of a world series. Only, these people already had their tickets, and their tickets were stones. Each held one stone.

But the man at the head held a housebrick in either hand. He was *loaded*.

A little Jew from out of town happened to be passing and wanted to know what was going on.

"We're stoning a broad today," First-In-Line informed him, "Get to the end of the line."

"How come you have two tickets while the other sports have only one?" the little Jew inquired, being strong for fair play.

"Because I am a columnist, and society therefore owes me twice as much of everything," First-Every-Time explained.

---

* Interview by Joseph Haas in the *Chicago Daily News.*

"How is it that a columnist such as yourself has so much coming?"

"Because I take people's minds off their troubles. I show them it's *good* to be alive. Who do you think dreamed up the idea of a local stoning anyhow?"

"It's not a coincidence that you're at the head of the line," the Jew suddenly made up his mind. "Wait for me here."

He went into a lumber yard across the street and returned carrying two two-by-fours nailed crosswise.

"Are you still the Head Of The Line?" he inquired, keeping his invention behind his back out of modesty.

"Nobody has got ahead of me yet and nobody's getting ahead of me today," the columnist let the Jew know. "I'm from Rome and I'm getting mine."

"I'm from East Jesus, Kansas," the Jew informed him, "and you *are* getting yours"—whereupon he brought his two two-by-fours nailed crosswise dead center on the columnist's skull with surprising power.

First-In-Line-Every-Time zonked out for the first time. He lay stone cold in the middle of the street.

Still, he was still first in line.

He was holding a house brick in either hand. Yet he wouldn't be laying brick for some time.

Nobody, it looked like, was going to get to do any brick laying for some time.

"No rainchecks," the Jew announced to those still standing hopefully in line.

So some dropped their stones and turned for home without rainchecks. Others turned for home still holding their stones but threw them at birds on the way. Only one woman held on to hers and didn't turn for home. She came up to the Jew and asked him to sign it.

"What for?" the Jew wanted to know.

"Because I didn't come to town to rock anybody in the first place," the woman explained. "I just came because I'm dying to have a celebrity's autograph."

"In that event," the Jew assured her, "you can give me yours. You're the only celebrity around here."

So the woman signed the stone and handed it to the Jew, pleased no end to find how easy it had been to be come a celebrity. Then the Jew threw the stone away and told her to go home and sign no more.

"I won't go home without *somebody's* autograph," the disappointed woman insisted, producing a scroll she had picked up on the Dead Sea. So the Jew signed his name by drawing a large *X* on the back of the scroll, and the woman went home, to find nobody there had noticed that she had left.

But the Jew had observed that those who had dropped their stones when informed that there was to be no stoning, and those who had used them only to aim at birds, had thrown them or dropped them in the manner of persons who had never wanted to rock anybody else in the first place.

That evening the Governor of the province called in his Chief Scorekeeper.

"How did the stoning go today, Chief Scorekeeper?" he asked.

"Called off," The C.S. had to break the bad news, "a Jew from East Jesus broke it up with two two-by-fours nailed crosswise."

The Governor stroked his beard, studying the Chief Scorekeeper.

"Keep an eye on that fellow," he decided at last. "If the sonofabitch ever learns to write, he'll be dangerous."

CHICAGO III

Old Chicago, that seesaw town, when one end of its teeter-tawter goes up its other end goes down.

The White Sox once stayed thirty-odd games out of first place (some were *very* odd), so long that someone started calling Shields Avenue Seventh Place. South Side fans, in our seasons of sorrow, had to sift the ashes of defeat to find victories. Ted Lyons was our consolation because he led both leagues in handling pitchers' chances. Luke Appling had broken all existing records for consecutive games played by a shortstop—and he was on *our* side! Di Maggio had hit consecutively for over fifty straight games—and he was on *their* side!

Trampled by the Yankees, we pointed out that it had taken them eleven innings to whip us. To lose by only one run was a good day in those years.

One season a pitcher called Bullfrog Bill Dietrich won seven games while losing only thirteen. The next season he won four while losing only six—it became plain that if he had been allowed to pitch twice as often he would have won eight while losing only twelve. Such improvement encouraged Dietrich to hold out for an increase in salary—and he got it.

He got it and he earned it. On June 1, 1937, he shut out the St. Louis Browns, 8-0, thus keeping the White Sox in seventh place and the Browns in eighth. Bullfrog Bill Dietrich had pitched the most useless no-hitter in history! He was on *our* side!

These were the years of hitless wonders who couldn't field, either. Our heroes were Banana-Nose Bonura, who never lost a ball in the sun because his nose would get in the way instead; of Moe Berg, the only backstop in the majors with a Ph.D.; and of Great-Man Shires, whose biggest asset was a right hook to the jaw. Nobody called them the Go-Sox then because every time they started to go, they went.

Yet if we lacked first-division athletes through the twenties and thirties, we were still the city that made the big music, wrote the big books, and brought up the unbeatable fighters. It became the place where the song was first felt, in a South Side cave or West Side honkytonk, that would be cut into a million recordings after the singer was dead. It was the city where the play, lived out by men and women unknowingly behind shadowed doors, would later become box office in Hollywood and New York. It was the city that made the singers who never made New York; the place where the fighters came up who never got to Madison Square.

New York is the place of casual acquaintances who become your Great-and-Good-Friends in *Time*. It is the glasswalled place where the junior editor whose editorship began in the howling chair of infancy evolves to the high-chair of senior editorship—still behind glass doors. It is where the real thing is turned to the unreal thing yet everyone gets his cut: the place of sharp lawyers, quick girls, and agile cats; where culture is conducted by Great-and-Good-Friends.

Chicago is the place that Louis Armstrong and Lil Green came to from New Orleans a few years before Banana-Nose Bonura came from there too.

Up from New Orleans, up from Springfield, up from Galesburg and Terre Haute, downriver singers and trumpet players, fighters who carried their own shoes, and poets without fellowships—Vachel Lindsay and Bessie Smith, King Oliver and Tony Zale, Dreiser and Anderson and Carl Sandburg—each had his go-go day.

Then each went.

Down into the lamplit yesterday, into the go-gone dark, the best who came up swiftly with the least who came up slow.

Who changed the city of ceaseless change.

That stays changeless for keeps.

Old seesaw Chicago town where you start going up, then feel yourself going down.

No city ever owed its poets more. No poet could owe any city less. A city that will honor the South Side cop because he killed more people in one year than all the rest of the officers of his district combined, yet has not yet understood the simple truth told by a poet during the South Side race riots: "The slums take their revenge."

Chicago today is a massive brute that, like that dog devised by the Russians, has two heads. The head of a feisty poodle is yapping out of the neck of an inarticulate, bearlike dog—and the poodle does the talking for both heads. Chicago's press never ceases yapping. Yet the city itself is no yapper. Its heart is that of the dark slow brute below; for the city has a somber heart.

Pay no heed to the upper pup: its yip has no meaning, its bark has no bite.

For in times of our deepest corruption, we have heard the city's dark conscience cry out.

Culturally, our southernmost outpost (bounded on the north by Comiskey Park), is presently supervised by a passionless pedagog named Adler; while the spiritual life of the North Side is guarded by a cheerful Shakespearean buff named Bradley. The West Side has to fend for itself.

Chicago is justly proud of both these philosophers, since both are readily distinguishable from sixteen-fingered pickpockets. Although Doc A. has the most degrees, Doc B. is nearer to God. He got in on the ground floor by learning the customers' first names some time ago.

Doc B. possesses a leonine head adjustable to any microphone five and a half feet off a platform. He so combines the figure and self-assurance of Stephen A. Douglas with a jolly St. Nick's air that he doesn't lend the impression of being fat so much as of having been constructed along these lines deliberately. He is an orator of the William Jennings Bryan school whose resonance gets him ashore when his logic breaks up in the shallows. He prefers the personal popularity of a flesh-and-blood flock to the ghostly multitudes available to TV prophets. He is a Christian businessman and a businessman's Christian speaking for a Kiwanis-Club Christ that lost its nerve before World War I.

Doc A., on the other hand, is the fellow for a fast turnover, a saintly distributor and a distributor's saint. Every time a new saint appears on his sightline he leaps like a jackrabbit goosed by a porcupine. Perpetually seeking to get closer to God, he once made a panicky dash from Minyan to Mass without getting appreciably nearer. Eyewitnesses to this remarkable event say they never saw anything like it until Sherman Lollar was caught flatfooted in the 1959 series. If you want to blame St. Thomas (who was coaching Doc A. at the time), bear in mind that it was Tony Cuccinello who waved Lollar home. Both Tony and St. Thomas should have known they were working with heavy men.

I don't know what Cuccinello's excuse was, but Doc A. explained himself in a radio interview—"I now know so much about everything that I can no longer express myself simply."

In short, Doc A. has not only forgotten how to slide: he has forgotten how to move.

Yet one must give the philosopher his due. Dr. Adler, it has to be conceded, has broadened American thought. His application of the principle of All-The-Chicken-You-Can-Eat to All-The-Ideas-You-Can-Repeat for a flat $1.50 has not only broadened thought, but has led to better packaging of drumsticks from coast to coast.

Safaris leave Doc's Institute for Philosophical Research just before dawn, to trek waterless wastes through burning noons and return, having found no oasis, but bearing a hard-won wisdom. That might have been obtained without all that trekking at Ann Landers' less pretentious bazaar in the same newspaper. For the ambiguities the Doc peddles there is no need to go out of the house.

"Women have traditionally let men dominate them," Mrs. H. De Pree addresses Doc's Institute, "but today she has advanced to the position of equality. Would the great thinkers of the past have welcomed this change, or would they have insisted that the little woman stay home?" Ann Landers here might have pointed out that no little woman to date has ever stayed home because a great thinker has insisted on it. But for ambiguity, Mrs. De Pree came to the right place.

"While St. Paul enjoins women to be submissive," Doc replies, "Don Quixote felt that she should be treated as a relic to be adored but not touched"—an answer reminiscent of Ring Lardner's report of a rookie shortstop that "although he doesn't move well to his right he can't hit a lick."

"We are about to become parents," Mr. and Mrs. M. A. Ossey announce as if resolved not to be taken by surprise; "naturally, we are concerned with the development of our expected child's character. We are curious to learn what virtues should be instilled in our offspring."

"Understanding, knowledge and wisdom are the basic intellectual virtues," Doc assures Mr. and Mrs. Ossey, and the baby is ready to be born.

The hard necessity of bringing the judge on the bench down into the dock has been the peculiar responsibility of the writer in all ages of man. In Chicago, in our own curious span, we have seesawed between blind assault and blind counterassault, hanging men in one decade for beliefs which, in another, we honor others.

And that there has hardly been an American writer of stature who has not come up through the Chicago Palatinate, was an observation which, when somebody first made it, was still true. God help the poor joker who comes up through the Chicago Palatinate today. Between TV poseurs, key-club operators, and retarded Kilgallens in charge of columns, any writer whose thought is simply to report the sounds and sights of the city is unlikely to create interest. It isn't a matter of whether he has anything to say as it is whether he can give a performance. Anyone who doesn't own a key with a bunny on it must be Some-Kind-Of-Nut.

And let the word get around here that some kind of nut has been taking films of the ordinary streets of day, rather than of the interiors of salons not one Chicagoan in ten thousand has ever seen, and some fantasist from Balaban & Katz will put it down sight unseen—"Art? *Nuts.*" Someone else who admittedly hasn't seen the film will write an editorial protesting that "it presents an imbalanced picture," and the mayor, who hasn't seen it either, will then ban it because it would not serve public interest in a city of pleasures so chaste as those of Chicago.

"What do you want? A bloody travelogue?" one of Europe's top filmmakers asked when informed that the documentary he had made of Chicago could not be shown because art is nuts.

But that, of course, is precisely what is wanted. Because that's how things are in the sodden old Palatinate, men. That's what it's really like in Chicago.

There are a number of answers to the old query about why writers so often take a one-way flight from Midway or O'Hare and never come back here. One answer becomes self-evident to anyone who has witnessed a henyard full of hipless biddies entitling themselves "Friends of Literature" in the act of honoring Shakespeare and Lincoln. It looks more like they had Frank Harris in mind but I'm sure they don't eat that way at home. Another reason is that the medieval nonentities of City Hall who have outlawed the work of Rossellini, Sartre, and Denis Mitchell here don't care for the local talent either. Any bookkeeper speaking in the name of Balaban & Katz Forever can make it plain enough that the town isn't all it's cracked up to be *Town and Country.*

San Francisco is more daring. It has listeners wanting to hear somebody saying something not said before. Who will be better than anybody up till now.

Yet Chicago is the same city where a literature bred by hard times on the river, hard times on the range, and hard times in town became a world literature.

It's the same town that once carried a literature emanating from large feelings to all men in all tongues.

It was here that those arrangements more convenient to owners of property than to the propertyless were most persistently contested by the American conscience.

Chicago has progressed, culturally, from being The Second City to being The Secondhand City. The vital cog in our culture now is not the artist, but the middleman whose commercial status lends art the aura of status when he acquires a collection of originals. The word "culture" now means nothing more here than "approved." It isn't what is exhibited so much that matters as where: that being where one meets the people who matter.

Of concern for the city's night colors, its special sounds like those of no other city, for the ceaseless drama of its lives lived out behind blind doors; for the special language of Chicagoese as spoken in its Saturday night dance halls or in its shops and bars, these have no approval. Yet it is of these that the warp and woof of true poetry is woven.

Chicago is an El-rider without remembrance.

As one Colonel Riley, speaking for the mayor, put it when a BBC documentary on the city was banned, "People in Chicago don't know about these things, so why bother them?"

Thus the Chicago of the 1940's is forgotten and unrecorded and that of the fifties is gone for keeps. A thousand dollars' worth of film and sound equipment could salvage a remembrance of the city of the sixties beyond a view of the Prudential Building. The colonel is right—we don't want to bother. We don't even care enough for the city to want remembrance of it. So why stick around just for a kick in the Palatinate?

You don't have to leave Chicago just to be gone.

If America's Richard Morrisons have gained the concern of her novelists, so have her novelists gained stature by concern for America's losers.

The search for the great white whale by the foredoomed hero Ahab across dangerous seas was extended across the deeps of the American conscience by Dreiser's equally foredoomed youth, Clyde Griffiths, pursuing Success.

Emerging into a ripjaw-and-tearclaw civilization disguised by signs reading "If-You-Can't-Stop-Smile-As-You-Pass-By," he tried smiling his defenselessness away by assuring his superiors, "Yes, sir, I will do just as you say, sir. Yes, sir, I understand, sir," until he had smiled his way into a courtroom on trial for his life, listening to a prosecuting attorney describe one Clyde Griffiths—

"Seduction! Seduction! The secret and intended and immoral and illegal and socially unwarranted use of her body outside the regenerative and ennobling pale of matrimony! *That* was his purpose, gentlemen!"

It was then too late for the youth to learn that the images along the chamber of mirages were false. That the signs saying "Smile-Darn-You-Smile" camouflaged a struggle for survival as ferocious as that between bulldogs in a bulldog pit.

Yes, sir, I understand, sir; I will do just as you say, sir.

"I didn't know I was alive until I killed," another youth who walked through mirages explains himself in the final chapter of Wright's *Native Son*. But Bigger Thomas was one who smashed mirrors rather than accept his own reflection in them.

Yet each, although pictured by the prosecution as men who had sought victims, were themselves society's victims. Dreiser's method of challenging the legal apparatus and Wright's method were different, but the purpose of both was to demand that those economically empowered disprove their complicity in the crimes for which Clyde Griffiths and Bigger Thomas stood accused. Both writers made literature by demanding that the prosecuting attorney show his hands.

The outcast Ahab's pursuit of the great white whale was followed by other strange innocents more alive in their fictional lives than were the men and women who were reading about them: heroes and heroines, each foredoomed.

For these were not innocents in the sense of being untouched by the world but rather of having been caught by it. There is no accomplishment in being innocent of rain when one has lived in a windowless room. The only true innocent is one who has withstood the test of evil. Which is why the protected woman is never so innocent as your real true eleven-times-through-the-mill-and-one-more-time-around whore who has seen every breed and color of male with his pants flung over the bedpost.

These were the heroes and heroines the best of American writers sought, and the search led from New York's Bowery down Main Street to the edge of Winesburg, where the town's last gas lamp made the last wagon road look haggard. And in town or out, on either hand, both sides of the highway, past backland farm and railroad yards, faces of men and women living without alternatives stood revealed.

A search past country ball parks under a moon that said Repose. Repose. To where the 3:00 A.M. arc lamps of Chicago start, down streets that Sister Carrie knew. Everywhere men and women, awake or sleeping, trapped with no repose.

The city of no repose that Dreiser found; that Richard Wright reached and Sandburg celebrated.

Today its arc lamps light a city whose back streets are more dangerous than a backtrack of the Kalahari Desert. Where every 3:00 A.M. corner looks hired.

Where a street-corner nineteen-year-old once replied to a judge who had just handed down a verdict of death in the electric chair, "I knew I'd never get to be twenty-one anyhow," and snapped his bubble gum.

A novel written around this same bubble-gum snapper, in the early 1940's, by the present writer, sustained the antilegalistic tradition toward society which had distinguished Chicago writers since the early years of the century.

Another novel, told more forcefully at the close of that decade, was lost to this tradition through a film presentation which confused it, in the public mind, with a biography of Frank Sinatra.

Yet the literary spirit of "I belong to these convicts and prostitutes myself," from which these novels derived, were written for a reader who was no longer around.

That reader and that spirit had been overwhelmed by the newly affluent cat asking querulously, "What are they doing to me?" because he had just charged off ten thousand dollars in entertainment of friends to the government and was having trouble making it stick. What this new reader wanted was not to feel there shall be no difference between him and the rest but that the difference between himself and the rest be officially recognized by the federal government.

Whitman's offer, bred by hard times on the Middle Border, "If you tire, give me both burdens," holds no interest for the boy who came unburdened into his own the day Daddy had his name painted beside his own on the frost-glass office door. To say "Each man's death diminishes me" today only rouses interest in Blue Cross.

Well, we're all born equal. Anyone in Chicago can now become an expatriate without leaving town.

Town and Country reports that "anyone who knows Chicago today will admit it is a beautiful place to live." Now, it isn't too difficult for an editor in New York to put a man on a plane to O'Hare Field and helicopter him onto Michigan Boulevard long enough to take a snapshot of a chewing-gum heir stuck up against the side of Papa's building and distribute the Juicy-Fruit mess as a "Chicago" edition—but *Town and Country* is putting us on. Because anyone who lives *inside* Chicago today has to admit it is a gray subcivilization surrounded by suburbs.

Or are these loveless castaways watching Clark Kent battling the forces of evil in the shadowed lobby of the stag hotel merely awaiting the wave of the future the easy way?

Otherwise, what did the fifteen-year-old mean when he answered the judge who had asked him what he did all day, "I just find a hallway 'n' take a shot 'n' lean. Just lean 'n' dream"?

And what did another teen-ager mean when he told the arresting officers, "Put me in the electric chair; my mother can watch me burn"?

From the bleak inhumanity of our forests of furnished rooms, stretching doorway after anonymous doorway block after block, guarding stairways leading only to numbered doors, out of hallways shadowed by fixtures of another day, emerge the dangerous boys who are not professional burglars or professional car thieves or pete men or mobsters (who never fly blind), but are those who go on the prowl without knowing what they're after. Their needs crisscross, they're on the hawks, and will take whatever comes along first-a woman, money, or just the cold pleasure of kicking a queer's teeth down his neck. Whatever wants to happen, the dangerous boys let the damn thing happen—and we'll all read about it in the papers tomorrow.

Town and Country's congratulations to us for having "an old-shoe guy" for mayor (one of the best kinds that there are) because he once took a walk to the corner drugstore to bring back an armful of milkshakes (instead of having a detail from Central Police deliver them), seems almost too good to be true. Yet watching the ceaseless allnight traffic moving without a stoplight down the proud new perfect thruway to O'Hare, headlight pursuing taillight, taillight fleeing headlight, it is as if each dark unseen driver were not driving, but were driven.

So the city itself moves across the thruway of the years, a city in both flight and pursuit. And surely more driven than driving.

Love is by remembrance, and, unlike the people of Paris or London or New York or San Francisco, who prove their love by recording their times in painting and plays and books and films and poetry, the lack of love of Chicagoans for Chicago stands self-evident by the fact that we make no living record of it here, and are, in fact, opposed to first-hand creativity. All we have today of the past is the poetry of Sandburg, now as remote from the Chicago of today as Wordsworth's.

"Late at night, and alone, I am touched by an apprehension that we no longer live in America, that we no longer love her. We merely occupy her," Dalton Trumbo writes, reflecting a disconnection, on a national scale, transpiring locally.

For at the very moment when a national effort is being made to extend the great American beginning—"not one shall be slighted"—to grass huts of the Congo, Hoovervilles of Caracas and to the terribly deprived peoples of India, our press is preoccupied with the pursuit of barroom drudges sitting in front of whiskey glasses with false bottoms, poor girls trying for their rent money from week to week; or with a woman drawing state aid in support of an illegitimate child who has been entrapped drinking a beer.

The presumption that immorality derives largely from acceptance of welfare assistance is a Hearstian concept. So that, although there are no Hearst-owned papers here, whatever paper you buy you still read Hearst.

This disregard of human dignity in the interests of circulation makes it more appropriate to regard the men who run the Chicago newspapers as auditors rather than editors. Of what newspaper owner here cannot the same thing be said as the American poet once said of the Supreme Court of Massachusetts—"These people made you nervous."

Nor can I see in what fashion depriving a woman of her personal dignity, no matter how demeaning her trade, can be justified. If an Eichmann is to be held responsible for lacking a conscience, is not a newspaper owner to be held responsible for employing a columnist who has parlayed an urge to punish into a press pass?

That entrapment, as practiced by an aforementioned columnist here, is illegal even when used by the Police Department is not the point. The point is that construction of a thruway running without a stoplight from state to state doesn't make any city "a beautiful place to live in" so long as no restraint is put on men armed by the power of the press to hunt down anybody if the hunt will help circulation.

And should you say such a woman cannot go unpunished, I must ask in what fashion has she harmed anyone? She has assaulted nobody, robbed nobody, done nothing criminal, yet her chance of staying out of jail is nowhere near so good as that of a utility executive who has made a fortune by price fixing. Still, everyone feels entitled to punish her.

She is not the huntress, but the prey. She does not send for men: they seek her out. And the simple irrefutable fact is that she has been essential to every society, has outlasted every society, is essential to our own and will outlast our own.

So long as the institution of marriage exists she remains essential, for she is not supported by single men, but by married ones.

"Prostitutes everywhere report that their trade is in large measure financed by married men who are weary of the indifference or antagonism of their wives and turn to public women for gratification," Houghton Hooker reports in *Laws of Sex*.

Another thing I intend asking Mother about is whether the papers aren't leaving something out. Every time a girl is made in a raid we get a full description of her: name, age, address, and place of employment. What I can't figure out is: What was she doing in that room that was so awful if there wasn't somebody just as awful helping her to do something awful? If there was a pair of pants on the bedpost, where is the spendthrift who walked into the room inside them? Why isn't *he* entitled to get his name in the paper and a ride downtown? Why doesn't somebody give *him* a chance to stand up in front of a judge and get fined a hundred dollars or fifty days in County? If everybody is born free and equal, as they say, when does *he* get a chance to go to the Chicago Intensive Treatment Hospital for a free checkup? If this is a true democracy, why doesn't he have the same right as any other second-class citizen? It looks like a businessman don't stand a chance in this country anymore.

I've seen the people who keep the shops
Merchant or lawyer, whatever you got
And I wouldn't swap you the lowliest wench
For the most high thief on the most high bench
Merchant or lawyer, whatever you got—
God send them mercy—
Then job the whole lot.

Crusades from pulpit, court, or column against prostitution can have no effect except to divert it to another part of town or from brothel to escort service, because the basic cause isn't with the women who practice it, but in our own concept of sex. The conviction that sex is basically evil is a perversion out of which prostitution develops. So long as we remain punitive toward sex, we are going to have crimes of sex. Until we recognize sex as a natural urge, pleasant, beautiful, interesting, and useful, to be treated, like any other important faculty, such as work or learning, by welcoming it, enjoying it without reverence, and permitting discussion of it to be as open as that about art or play or science, we will have crimes of sex.

Sandburg's Chicago, Dreiser's Chicago, Farrell's and Wright's and my own Chicago, that was somebody else's Chicago. That was a play with a different plot. Today the curtain rises on—
Act I: Scene One—Annual Meeting of The Chicago Greater Hollerers Association.
On Stage: Chicago's leaders as selected by *Town and Country.*
Sitting in an aisle seat, seeing on stage my city's suntanned elders just back from the Fontainebleau with their armpits tanned from long days under the rye-bread trees, I too applaud the brave flash of their costume jewelry and high credit ratings.
Yet I feel a pang of secret regret that I played the black market in soap and cigarettes in Marseilles instead of staying home and playing it in automobiles in Detroit; to wait until the war was over to volunteer for overseas duty. I realize now that one must begin young to become a leader of one's city in middle age.
Oh, if there *really* is a little somebody for every boy in the world, why doesn't some little somebody phone *me?* And ask in a voice ever-so-refined, if *I* would conduct a purple-heart cruise for my city? I too wish to stand at

the helm of a water-borne scow and cry *"Now, Voyager!"* while peeling Eskimo pies for handless vets. I'll peel *anything* to get a fringe benefit.

And if I can't earn a fringe benefit myself, won't somebody let me be somebody else's little fringe benefit? Won't somebody send *me* a ten-year-old epileptic to froth for me on a TV marathon? Can't I get to froth on somebody else's marathon for myself? Why won't *anybody* let *me* find prizes in crackerjack boxes for retarded kids? Is somebody in City Hall afraid I'll steal the prizes? The only prize I want is a deduction for entertaining the stupid brats—or am I asking too much? All *I* want is to tie little Fourth-of-July flags in the wheels of paraplegic's chairs. *I'll tie, I'll peel, I'll froth, I'll wheel, I'll lope and double-back*—but how am *I* ever to be an old-shoe guy who goes down to the drugstore and brings back milkshakes for his family when nobody will let me get a start in life?

I too wish to defend my city from people who keep saying it is crooked. In what other city can you be so sure a judge will keep his word for five hundred dollars? What's so crooked about that? I'm tired of hearing detractors of my city say it is br*oo*-tul. In what other city, head held high, sweating, laughing, all of that, can you get homicide reduced to manslaughter and manslaughter to a felony and felony to a misdemeanor? What do you want, for God's sake—to get your gun back?

"We have to keep Chicago strong and America mighty!" I heard His Honor proclaim before sentencing the girl with a record for addiction, "A year and a day! Take her away!"

Blinking out of the window of an Ogden Avenue trolley at the sunlight she hadn't seen for almost a year, "I guess it was lucky I done that time," the girl philosophized later, "Chicago still looks pretty strong and America looks mighty mighty."

Still, nobody seems to be laughing.

Perhaps the reason our thinking has shifted from the informal attitude of a society that makes allowances, to the "he brought it all on himself" position, derives from the isolation of so many Americans, bubble-gum snappers and key-club cats alike; for the isolated man is a loveless man. Although his children may call him Papa and go through the gestures of love, they yet can't reach him. An isolation common enough to justify calling it The American Disease; and that is directly related to the lack of creativity in this city that was once America's creative center.

Is it that the fraudulence essential to successful merchandising becomes pervasive, leaving the class which is economically empowered to become emotionally hollowed?

This would account for the fact that every enduring portrait in American fiction is that of a man or woman outside the upper middle-class. From Ahab to Ethan Frome and Willie Loman, Hawthorne's branded woman to Blanche du Bois, all are people who, living without alternatives, are thus forced to feel life all the way. While the attempts at middle-class portraiture, such as Marjorie Morningstar, fade as fast as last year's best seller.

No use to call out the hook-and-ladders. So long as Jerry Lewis is doing such a good job of handling children's diseases for us, and Sammy Davis, Jr., has integration in hand, I see no reason why our city should not take pride in giving America Hugh Hefner to handle sex.

As I once heard a thoughtful young woman put it during a matinee at the Chicago theater where Sinatra was appearing in person—

"Spit on me, Frankie! I'm in the very front row!"

As the girl was in the second balcony, I thought the idea a little unusual.

Mediocrity is never a passive lack: it avenges its deprivation. Like furnishing a toothless man with artificial teeth, it wishes to bite something that won't bite back.

Between the majestic drumroll of Chicago's newspaper presses one hears the tiny intermittent clicking of false teeth.

Banana-Nose Bonura once made three errors on a single play. Tony Weitzel of the *Chicago Daily News* once made six in a single sentence.

"Carlson McCullough," he wrote, "will appear here next week in his own play, 'Remember Our Wedding.'" After that it didn't much matter whether he got the name of the theater right or not.

Weitzel's façade is that of a sage who lives in a house by the side of the road, flintlock over the fireplace, being a friend to man. The tone he lends his column is that of a gentle uncle full of years and wisdom. I don't know his age, but years is not what he is full of.

Irv Kupcinet is about the height of Jack Eigen standing on Marty Faye's shoulders, and once startled his readers by adding, after reporting the death of the late Jimmy Dean—"a tough break for the kid."

Kup handles language with elephantine care, one "celeb" at a time, with the result that his column always is arranged, at the end of a day, in an orderly heap with the names of the day's favorite people in heavy type so everybody can see them without bothering to read the words between. People compete to see their names there. All in all, there is no more harm done at a game of "pin the tail on the donkey."

Kup's Saturday-evening TV program, *At Random,* really is at random, yet is of service in showing us who our bright boys are and who are our boobies. The beautiful and terrible thing about the TV screen is that it reveals the inner man like an X-ray when the man doesn't know he's under it. They sit together, the sound and the phoney, equally naked to thousands. Despite Kup's panic when a controversial subject jumps up, it has been the moments of controversy that have kept the program consistently interesting. Kup himself is usually behind his guests, particularly the politically developed men and women from Africa, Cuba, and Europe, who often make generous allowances for Kup's obvious limitations.

Nevertheless, it is to his credit that he does get them, that he is aware of who has something to say, and thus gives a link to the outer world which our press has severed. Moreover, since he has learned to keep his own big beak out of discussions when he himself has nothing to offer, the program has improved immensely.

The Beatnik invasion here now seems as remote as Johnny Ray, the sinking of the *Lusitania* or the early work of Lorraine Hansberry. Three youths appeared, as night was falling fast, who looked to be falling even faster. They bore a banner with a strange device: a pair of shoes rampant on a field of flame, and were billed as "The Holy Barbarians."

When asked by a puzzled interviewer what they stood for, the leader stepped out and replied, "Death is a letter that was never sent." The second stepped forth and explained, "Chicago is a rose!" The third stole the show by declaiming:

"FRIED SHOES!"

They then recited poetry to a jazz background. The jazz was all right, but the poetry was just typing.

It became plain that they were neither holy nor barbaric. They were nihilism's organization men giving demonstrations of how to be a non-conformist without risking one's personal security: "Classes in nonconformism every Wednesday at 8:00 P.M. Please be on time."

It never got to be anything beyond typing because it never asserted itself in terms of an individual, but always in terms of "We" and "Us." And art can never be asserted except in terms of "I."

So they passed on to their next booking. I hope that all three have found steady work by now. But surely no investigating committee is ever going to ask anybody, "Were you ever, or are you now, a Beatnik?" And it fell as far short of life artistically as it did politically. As Chicago today falls short in men and women of living vision. To have such men and women there must be believers. We have no great poet here because there is no real belief in poetry. And in this lack of belief our true corruption lies: not in the hearts of heroin pushers or prostitutes, but in a consciencelessness bred by affluence.

Yet we have had prophets, we have had companions. We have had a man to say, "While there is a soul in prison I am not free." We have had men and women who knew that a city of a hundred tents, owning the voice of single man speaking for the conscience of those hundred tents, is a city more enduring than that which we are now building.

For the only city that endures is the city of the heart.

Mr. Frank Lloyd Wright was a saint of architecture. Mr. Wright liked stone buildings, steel buildings, tall buildings and low buildings. He liked round buildings and square buildings. He even liked wet buildings and dry buildings. He liked expensive buildings better than he liked cheap buildings, but if there wasn't any expensive building near at hand to like, Mr. Wright would just go ahead and like any old building. Nobody could stop him from liking buildings. It seemed as if there were some thing about buildings that just *got* Mr. Wright.

What Mr. Wright thought made a city great was its buildings. How the people inside a building were feeling wasn't as important to him as how the building was feeling. He thought that what was most important was how the whole scene looked when you took a sightline on it and saw all the stone buildings and all the steel buildings and all the tall buidings and all the low buildings and all the round buildings and all the square buildings and all the wet buildings and all the dry buildings.

What I always thought was most important was the names on the doorbell in the hall.

Therefore my own name, on the day that Mr. Wright's skyscraper rises a mile hope-high into the air out of a foundation a mile dream-deep in stone, shall not be among those carved on its cornerstone. On the day that the double-tiered causeway is merged with the expressway that merges with the coast-to-coast thruway making right-hand turns every mile into a hundred solid miles of mile-high skyscrapers, each rising a mile hope-high to the sky out of a mile dream-deep in earth, my own name will not be brought up.

But just in case anyone asks how I spelled it, look on the doorbell in the hall.

I'll be alright on that great day if only, in some woman's court, a judge who is about to pass sentence on a girl with needlemarks on her arm without giving her legal defense, is told he can't do that, it isn't legal anymore.

I'll be all right if somewhere a narcotics detail puts a drug addict on the witness stand to testify against another addict and is then told to take her down, they can't do that, it isn't legal anymore.

I'll be all right if somewhere a prosecuting attorney changes a charge of using drugs to a charge of selling and finds he can't do that, it isn't legal anymore.

City that walks with her shoulder-bag banging her hip, you gave me your gutters and I gave you back gold. City I never pretended to love for something you were not, I never told you you smelled of anything but cheap cologne. I never told you you were anything but a loud old bag. Yet you're still the doll of the world and I'm proud to have slept in your tireless arms.

I'll be alright on that great day though you look on the doorbell in the hall and find my name isn't there anymore. I'll be alright so long as it has been written on some cornerstone of a human heart.

On the heart it don't matter how you spell it.

CHICAGO IV

THE IRISHMAN IN THE GROTTO, THE MAN IN
THE IRON SUIT, AND THE GIRL IN GRAVITY-Z:
THE PLAYBOY MAGAZINE STORY
or MR. PEEPERS AS DON JUAN

Of all my childhood dreams, the one I most cherished was that of some-day getting to spurn somebody with less money—and now my chance had come! There would, I felt certain, be only our own select circle taking turns hawking spit graciously over an elegant ironwork balustrade upon a rabble eager to bear any indignity in exchange for the privilege of being spurned.

They would, of course, be kept under control by our Boys in Blue, any one of whom can handle a dozen of these street-corner subhumans; provided he has a good mount under him and eleven colleagues equally well mounted.

But when the guardians of the Victorian mansion on North State failed to ask either my name or unique qualifications, but merely indicated a red-carpeted stairway I could climb or not, whichever I wished, my dream went *pfft*. If this was the kind of place *I* could get into, I thought resentfully, who the hell *were* they keeping out?

I can tell you right off that though not *everybody* in town gets invited to house parties thrown by the editor and publisher of *Playboy* Magazine, everybody comes all the same. The only people not invited are those employed by *Esquire,* who don't want to come anyhow. They're waiting for an invitation from Huntington-Hartford.

The great baronial hall was serving as a guest room for a gaggle of humans wearing all the clothes anyone could possibly need to break into society once they found a society to break into.

This plainly wasn't it. This was high shlockhouse—employing the term in its Milwaukee Avenue sense to indicate a furniture store using colored lighting to lend an expensive glow to its sofas and chairs, and deducting the light bill from the markup later. I began stepping off a twenty-speaker stereophonic hi-fi which ran the length of four divans, or two inches shorter than the SS *United States,* while a young woman was coming down the other side pricing the stuff, unaware that the rosy glow didn't go with the dream. Wait till she owned that orange divan for her very own and turned up the kerosene lamp—"Get your leather jacket and meet me down at the chicken-run," she'd cry, "I've been *had!*" I hadn't seen anything like it since Joan Crawford threw the lingerie party in *Dance, Fools, Dance.* There just isn't enough of that sort of thing today.

If what was going on here was high society, Caroline Kennedy is president of the Veteran Boxers' Association.

A three-piece band, each member six degrees cooler than the next, began playing cool chords in a nook strangely dominated by a suit of medieval armor. How a suit of armor had gotten in here I couldn't begin to fancy, unless the musicians had rented it to throw a protective shadow across themselves in event people showed up who'd been present at the last place they'd played.

I walked over to get a closer look. I couldn't climb up to look inside as it was on a pedestal. Even if it were in a hole I wouldn't have been able to tell who was in there.

The ratio of males to females was roughly five to three, I'm sure I don't know why. Unless it was because male employees are requested to bring wives and girl friends while female employees are instructed to come alone.

Even with the odds so heavy in their favor, the males still looked as if they were attending only because they hadn't risen high enough in the *Playboy* hierarchy to risk going to bed nights. Because when you work for *Playboy* you have to keep in touch with the arts, and when you feel you're getting out of touch you'll do well to catch up in your employer's parlor, as a chance to slip two pounds of sugar into a colleague's gas tank may present itself.

I wheedled the bartender, implying that if he'd let me have a glass of champagne for fifteen cents I'd leave some in the glass for him, pretending to be joshing but letting him know I meant it.

"Champagne is on the house," he cut me short.

"Make that a double, boy, and keep your fingers out of the glass," I let him know who was boss now.

I toted the glass, which he'd filled to brimming out of sheer spite, to the cool nook to have another look at that cool suit. I walked around it to see whether I could see light coming through the chinks. Something told me there was somebody in there—otherwise why was he keeping his helmet down?

Then the cool people struck up The Peppermint Twist—

> *It's alright all night*
> *It's okay all day—*

the same beat that was so abhorred, a couple years ago, when accompanied by Elvis Presley, that TV cameras were forbidden to pick him up below his waist. Every cad in the room was now working his hips wildly toward the nearest girl, and if the nearest party wasn't a girl, another cad seemed to do. The girl-cads were equally unselective. There was nothing wrong in any of this because everybody took great care not to touch or be touched by any other cad.

I stood trying to keep my champagne from spilling because of the shaking the floor was taking. I didn't want to resort to standard barroom procedure for trembling glasses—that of using one's cravat as a pulley by which to heist the glass to the lips, as I lacked a cravat. I didn't even have a tie. All I could do was to hope that, in the heat of The Twist, one of the young women might fling off her bra and I could use *that* for a pulley. I was paying the price of being badly groomed.

> *You gotta twist, you gotta turn*
> *You gotta dance to learn*
> *You gotta move right in the groove—*

Most of the girls looked like their bras had been wired on in puberty—well fitted but unreleased. In no time at all now they'd be using the wire cutters but then it would be too late. The panic would be on.

> *You gotta rock, you gotta reel*
> *You gotta get that certain feel—*

Although most of the girls appeared to have been snatched from behind a receptionist's desk in the august chambers of the Greater Michigan Avenue Marching Society And Single Gentlemen's Band and given a bouffant hairdo for the present occasion, they also looked as if they had been told to keep their pretty mouths shut. Or maybe silence was their own idea. At any rate they didn't seem to communicate even when twisting violently.

> *You gotta slide you gotta drive*
> *You got to make your fingers pop*
> *You got to join the social hop—*

Everyone seemed to be trying to join herself as though she'd been away too long. And the men were trying just as hard to twist themselves into finding out who *they* really were—

> *My baby wrote me a letter*
> *Just got it in the mail*
> *Told me that she'd marry me—*
> *I'm so happy that I got to wail—*
>> *one more time!*
>> *one more time!*
>> *one more time!*

I studied the competition but all I could see was editors who would have been floorwalkers had it not been for the paperback boom. The 5-3 odds in my favor rose to 16-10, still in my favor. This realization made me so light headed that I drained the champagne in a single movement without spilling a drop-isn't it wonderful what confidence can do? The second the stuff hit I began to twist myself—

> *When I see my baby*
> *Gonna take her in my arms*
> *Just the thrill of one more kiss—*
>> *one more time!*
>> *one more time!*
>> *one more time!*

and the moment the music quit I steered up to a dark-haired child with a full-blown figure in a bikini and said, "You look like you came out of some water still I don't see no pool," intending this as a sharp comment. Without losing one twist she pointed to a stairway and said, "The pool is downstairs, Pops."

I passed three bars where other guests were freeloading, spiraled down a spiral stair and into a swimming suit and with the cry, "Me John A. McCone! You Jane!" I struck out for the waterfall which divides the pool from the Woo Grotto.

I have no grudge against waterfalls even when they splash me. The resentment I took to this one was because the water it splashed me with was warm pink. Nonetheless I completed the course.

In the grotto, a cream-colored girl in a salmon-colored bikini and a bouffant hairdo with strands that went wandering like those of a girl's hair underwater, was lolling on air cushions the hue of an evening sea. Whether she was bucking a strong headwind in a Mercedes-Benz or was a plate of creamed salmon I couldn't be certain. Since I couldn't see any-one driving I settled for salmon.

Any man who puts up fifty dollars for a tin key with a rabbit's head on it has an obligation to society to be choosy about air cushions, so I picked one of smoking chartreuse with a vermilion stripe and another of smol-dering chartreuse with a urine-colored stripe. If this girl challenged me by asking, "Let's see your key," my defense would be that there have been no pockets in my trunks since I began wearing them while playing guard for the Kedzie Avenue Arrows, *circa* 1926. I made a very strong impression at that time.

Yet how had this cream-and-salmon child come through a cataract without getting damp? Anybody who can emerge from a waterfall with-out getting wet shows that talent can spring up anywhere. The only other explanation I could entertain was that I was in a panel joint and she'd come through a wall.

I listened to hear if I could detect breathing on the other side, but all that came to my ears was that ceaseless beat—

One more time!
One more time!

That's not from *Kismet.*

I looked at the girl implacably just to see how long she could bear it without breaking. "I am J. M. Anslinger," I informed her; "I own all the heroin in the United States."

"Seeing is believing," she apprised me. "Let's see some."

"I don't carry it on me."

"Cheating proves."

"I don't have to *prove* it," I assured her. "I wrote a biography of Frank Sinatra, so you have to take my word."

"That might mean something to somebody who is *here,*" she told me.

"You give an impression of being present," I encouraged the child.

"You don't dig," she assured me, dreamily uncoiling.

"I have a shovel but I don't know where to start," I offered.

"I know right from wrong but I can't get foot on the ground either way. I'm like in orbit without a pressure suit. Nothing can happen to me because everything that happens to me is really happening to somebody else."

"How did you get into Gravity-Z without a runway, honey?" I employed my solicitous tone.

"All I know is that on my better days it seems like it wouldn't be bad to be half alive, but I can't find a reason for making the effort."

"For somebody in a vacuum," I observed, "your sense of self-preservation seems to be functioning well. On top of that, you have a very good built. Shall we try the steam room?"

My languid logician turned with no word and jack-knifed into the woo. The cataract gleamed in the flow and the splash, and as she came up on the other side, shone rose upon her flippers. She flipped me one rose-colored farewell and was gone wherever they go: good gravity-zero girls, midair babies built like jaguars and checkered like cheetahs yet who can't get a paw on the ground either way.

For they rise from all waters dry as bone.

Having no further reason for getting wet myself, I decided to hold the grotto against all comers till the next playmate of any month came along. If I could keep my mouth shut perhaps one would de-orbit.

"I *do* talk too much," I had to admit ruefully to myself. I've always wondered what admitting things ruefully to oneself was like. Now I knew.

"I *do* talk too much," the grotto's low echo agreed with me, sounding even more ruefully-admitting than myself.

"You're a little slow on the pickup," I reproached the echo; "stay on your toes there, Grotto."

"A little slow on the pickup, stay on your toes, Otto," it replied.

"My name isn't Otto," I explained.

"*My* name isn't Otto either."

"I *know* your name isn't Otto, Grotto." I was losing patience.

"And it isn't Grotto either. It's O'Connor."

"I never heard of a grotto named O'Connor."

"We changed the family name in honor of Tay Pay O'Connor. Before that it was O'Connaught. Tommy's the first name."

"Not *terrible* Tommy?"

"None other. Been here ever since I broke out of the old County Jail. Only had to walk three blocks. Took the first job I found open."

"Don't give *me* that. There wasn't anything like *Playboy* around in 1920."

"No. But there *was* a grotto. There always was a grotto, Otto. The *Playboy* plant was built around a grotto, and the PR department was built around *me*. The whole *Playboy* thing developed around the concept of an Irishman in a grotto."

"Being Irish ain't *that* great, O'Connor."

"Not a matter of being Irish—I just knew that if I kept on being myself, Terrible Tommy, sooner or later Terrible Tommy was sure to be caught. Didn't the signs in all the post offices say TOMMY (Terrible) O'CONNOR WANTED DEAD OR ALIVE? They didn't say DEAD OR MERELY EXISTING, did they? You see? A loophole! How can you pin a dead-or-alive fugitive warrant upon a man who isn't alive yet neither is he dead? You dig?"

"No, man, I *don't* dig."

"Like simple, cat. All I had to do was to stop walking in the first person and start walking in the third. When I got the hang of that, I found myself *thinking* in the third person instead of the first. I found I could get as much kick out of watching somebody else fall in love than fall in love myself—and look how much safer! It was like doing the twist spiritually— you go through the motions like you're *very* excited—but the real point of all the motion is that, while you're moving you can't get caught. The only trouble is—"

"I know," I cut him off, "the trouble is you can't get foot on the ground either way. I've been getting that from too many people around here lately."

"Yes—but who started it? Didn't I *tell* you they built the system around *me?*"

"I'll take your word. Now would you mind de-echoizing? Like stop haunting yourself? Or simply go into the fourth person? Like disappear altogether?"

"I *live* here, buddy."

"You live nowhere. You said so yourself. Don't give me a hard time because you work for *Playboy.*"

"You don't know what it's like," he pleaded for sympathy.

"Stop whining," I stopped his act, "go out and get a steady job, O'Connor."

"If you'd get a steady job yourself," he continued to sniffle around, "and settle down, you could have your *own* grotto,"—and a low faint whistling went along the walls like a wind out of times long gone.

I was alone.

I returned to my reading and came upon a typewritten memo planted, it became plain, by a West Coast counteragent between the pages of *Playboy.* For it bore a black M pendant on a field of gold, that I guessed stood for "Money," which revealed itself as the seal of THE MILLIONAIRE CLUB:

"The nation's first penta-cabaret" addressed itself to TOP EXECUTIVES without qualifying what it was they had to be atop of. The way they were going about getting members, any farmer who did his own milking could get in and I hoped he would.

"You don't have to be a millionaire, just *think* like one," the invitation explained. Now they'd gone and let in everybody in the country except the millionaires.

"The fact that you have been selected for charter membership will indicate without further elaboration the type and caliber of the gentlemen to whom this invitation is being made."

As you are a well-known overstuffed ass, in short, you are entitled to bray with us other asses *if* you come well dressed.

"In a very special sense this is a very special sort of club. The reason is presaged in the name of the club itself—The Millionaire Club.

"The point is, this is more than just a gentleman's club. It goes considerably beyond being a first-rate restaurant and entertainment palace (with perhaps the finest bouquet of luscious mamsells in all the world to serve you).

"It's a club where you will meet the most outstanding group of successful, creative, accomplished, and forward-moving executives in the West. You will rub elbows with The New Millionaires . . . participate in the excitement of Million Dollar ideas . . . catch the tempo of Million Dollar deals.

"It's because of the very special character of our membership that you will receive the title MEMBER OF THE BOARD ROOM of the Millionaire Club."

"O'Connor!" I hollered, leaping in fright to my feet. "Come back, Terrible Tommy! I want to join *you!* It's you or Billy Sol Estes!"

No echo returned. O'Connor was gone.

Gone with the light of Chicago past, when I earned seven cents every Sunday morning by going to the cigar store for a package of Ploughboy snuff for Mr. Kooglin, the newspaper agent who had never made me account for ten copies of the *Abendpost,* undelivered yet. Gone with the days, a little later, when if someone asked you for a cigarette, you had to give it to him and say, "How are you for spit?" Gone with noons when we made sun pictures of Blanche Sweet and streetcars had green trolly shades. When Ada Leonard danced at the Rialto and Kenny Brenna sang, *O Why Did I Pick a Lemon in the Garden of Love Where Only Peaches Grow?*

And Billy Marquart looked like he could whip anybody in the world, and Milt Aron knocked out Fritzie Zivic, and Altus Allen put up the best fight of his career against Johnny Colan, and Lem Franklin kayoed Willie Reddish, and Davey Day knocked out Nick Castiglione, and a kid named Johnny Rock used to get knocked out, week in and week out, at the Marigold. And everybody went to see Johnny Rock get knocked out.

They had come up and gone down, some fast and some slower, those who got too good too soon and those who came along slower and got less. But had made it last longer.

When had this great change taken place? When had we suddenly come into a time when nobody said, "I'm counting my money," but said instead, "I'm reviewing my holdings," though it seemed he was still doing the same thing? When had it come about that it was said of someone, "He swings," when all that was meant was that he consumed much more than he needed?

The reduction of the American dream to a race whose purpose, apparently, was to see who would become a member of a make-believe board had not begun, I knew, with Hugh Hefner. What Hefner had done, consciously or not, was to effect a transition of the hope of an American aristocracy qualified only by capacity to consume, that had been proffered by *Time* in the 1930's.

"The *Time* community is an upstanding, right-thinking group," its editors had addressed potential subscribers then, "shrewd as they are able. So far only one of you has insured himself for $7,000,000 and only one of you has become King of England. Most of you are just alert, intelligent Americans, quietly successful in your own fields or headed for success. Among you, for example, are thirty percent of the officers and directors of practically every well-known U.S. corporation. All told, you entertain 1,640,000 dinner guests each week. *Time* is more proud of its subscribers than of anything else—that is why we like to think of our subscribers as a unique *community*—the most alert group of men and women in America. And now speaking for the community, we invite you to join us."

Time walking streets she walked when young like an old whore in the rain, boggles blindly out from under her torn umbrella at that flashy new hooker working the other side of the street, yet sticks stubbornly to her own pitch—"one of you is the King of England, thirty percent of you entertain 1,640,000 dinner guests" (she's grown a little confused of late), while the new hooker is pulling in hundred-dollar tricks by giving each a tin key with the story: "Fulfill your dream world! Make money on everything! Become a member of the board and get into the tempo of million-dollar deals!"

The price I had paid for doubting the Divine Rightship of Business in 1937 had left me stuck in a woo grotto in 1962, I perceived, contending with the spiritual heirs of those who had believed. Yet I felt no sense of loss.

Where were they? What had they won, the young men and women of the thirties who had gained membership in the same community as that of the fantasist who had had himself insured for $7,000,000? Like myself in the narrowing years, by now they had either had it or they had missed it: neither those who had accepted the invitation of *Time* nor those who had declined it would be invited anywhere again. Yet among those who had sought the profferred success, I could not recall one to whom it had brought more than physical comforts accompanied by persistent anxieties. Of whose achievement was no more than that of having a bottle of one's own upon a stool of one's own among other quietly successful Americans, each drinking a defeat of his own, I do not speak—yet by such failures as have had to be buried fast and forgotten faster, one may now surmise the casualties to be incurred and left unattended in order to keep bright the colors of *Playboy's* promise of an exclusive community built upon consciencelessness.

"Police said the body of Connie Petrie, 26, was found in her bed. In the room were four empty prescription bottles and a bottle half full of a powerful stimulant.

"'We offer our girls lie tests,' Victor Lownes III, Playboy Club vice-president explained, 'we try to protect ourselves and the girls if we hear any bad rumors about them. She had a delightful personality. Very sweet. She wasn't the prettiest bunny in the place, but she had such a nice personality that sort of made up for it. When she refused to take a lie test, that was no indication she was guilty of anything. But it was an indication that we could not afford to keep her in our employ. We don't necessarily believe every rumor, but we do feel an obligation to protect ourselves.'"*

"The man with whom she was living told police she came in drunk at 5:30 A.M. He slapped her, and she went out for a walk. When she returned at 7:30 she went to bed, where she was found dead by her lover at 10:30 A.M."†

"'What we have going is a cult,' adds Victor Lownes III. 'The rabbit is a father symbol. We could tell them to go right out the window and they would follow our advice.'"

"'I'm in the happy position of becoming a living legend in my own time,' Hefner said, 'I have everything I ever wanted—success in business and identity as an individual.'"‡

Chicago's Playboy Key Club, its owners claim, is the most profitable bar, per square foot, in the world, and employs more talent than any other employer of talent in the city.

The Key Club waitress with a bunny tail pinned on her behind pays two dollars a night for rental of her bunny suit, contributes two dollars a

---

* *Chicago Sun-Times*
† *Saturday Evening Post*
‡ *Wall Street Journal*

night to a bartenders' pool, and earns no straight salary herself. She is dependent upon tips, which average around two hundred dollars a week. Her foundation garments, of which she has two, cost fourteen dollars apiece. If she is one of the more fortunate girls, she may get to model as the Playmate of the Month.

This monthly nude featured by *Playboy* is never modeled by a professional. The girl is recruited from the offices of *Playboy* or the tables of the Key Club, and is by contract bound not to model elsewhere for two years after *Playboy's* use of her. She receives three thousand dollars upon signing a release and two more at later dates.

Although it is understood that key holders are forbidden to touch the girls, and that the girls are forbidden to date key holders, *Playboy's* public relations people have projected the image that these constitute Hugh Hefner's private harem.

This is purely for public consumption. What the bunny is to Hefner is what it is to his *Playboy* community: an object of temptation to be resisted. The psychology is that of the man who derives his morality by *not* drinking, by *not* gambling. by *not* making love: one whose conception of the successful man is he in whom all passions, all temptations have been diverted into a single devotion to *business, business, business.* The restrictive walls of which Hefner complains are those which he himself has raised to keep life away. The success of the key clubs is due to the fact that millions of young American males cannot function except within this same restricted existence. Although the projected image of Hefner is that of a man living spaciously, he is actually a man in a broom closet. The importance of this being that his success speaks for broom-closeted multitudes.

"My girl and I are having fairly frequent flareups about dating others," one *Playboy* reader writes to the *Playboy* Adviser for help. "I agree with her completely that if I do, she should be allowed to also. I agree intellectually, but not emotionally. My feelings are, bluntly, that I don't like it a bit. She says this is unfair and I say, 'How right you are. I'm selfish and illogical. But I don't feel guilty when I'm dating other girls and I do feel unhappy when you're out with other guys, and you've told me you want me to be totally honest in our relationship.' Then she cries or rants and I clam up and the evening is ruined. Last time it happened I got mad enough to say, calmly, that she could take it or leave it, we weren't married and had no obligation to each other. My point is that if I can't have a relationship on my own terms I'd rather do without it, though I'd far prefer to sustain it. Her point is that any third party would see things her way. As a third party do you think she is right?—A.B. New York City."

"No."

You made a good move in not asking Ann Landers, A.B.

A third-person view of the Woo Grotto is made by a trapdoor in its roof, some busybody reported in *Time*. I glanced up uneasily to see if Victor Lownes III were looking down in the third person. Another window, offering an underwater view of swimmers, has been built for Victor or anyone else who enjoys watching other people swim underwater, in a bar which can be reached either by a rockified spiral stair or a fireman's pole. I didn't think I was ever going to be in that much of a hurry.

My host's earliest ambition, I learned, was to be a cartoonist, and that, of a sixty-nine volume scrapbook detailing his life, the first several volumes are of cartoons. "I remember the early embarrassment of putting my arm around a girl . . . this became one of the most difficult periods of my life. So I withdrew into fantasies by writing and drawing," Hefner explains.

The cartoons are not about Hugh Hefner, but about a youth named Goo Heffer, attending a school called Stink-much High. There are no girls in these cartoons.

Causing me to wonder whether the girls who were twisting now, the girls wearing bunny tails and the girls who were modeling, all the girls who were becoming professional girls, were girls any more at all. Hefner had moved into his present arrangement, he says, "to live the life we were writing about," just as the waitresses in the key Playboy Club are images projected from the foldout nude offered monthly by *Playboy*. The *Playboy* complex had not begun, as Hefner himself appears to believe, with the loan he had made to start a magazine, but with the projection of his teen-age fantasies into teen-age cartoons. Hugh Hefner, Playboy of the Midwestern World, non-conformist *bon vivant,* was nothing more than a public-relations image. My host, I now knew, though he himself did not know it, was Goo Heffer. I put down *Time* and picked up the *Wall Street Journal* to see how Goo's impostor had managed to make his fantasy come true.

"Mr. Hefner's image of success is not without some tarnish. Recently he decided to fold *Show Business Illustrated,* a magazine he started last August. The magazine's backlog of manuscripts and advertising will be turned over to its chief rival for $250,000, hardly enough to lighten the loss of 1.5 million incurred in its brief life.

"If SBI has been a flop that Mr. Hefner would like to forget, there is no disputing the success nor the important role Mr. Hefner has played in attaining it for *Playboy* . . . its advertising income in the 1961 calendar year was up 74% from 1960 and its circulation was up 15%.

"'*Playboy* is the bible of the upbeat generation,' Mr. Hefner explains, 'it promotes good material things—status, growth, individualism, the idea that you can't get ahead unless you get off your backside and get moving.'

"Readership surveys made by *Playboy* show that most of its readers are males between 18 and 35 years of age.

"Most other magazine publishers say that *Playboy's* penchant for nudes is what sells the magazine, a suggestion which is deeply resented by Mr. Hefner. Each issue of *Playboy* has a fold-out picture of a Playmate of the Month, who for her near-nude modeling is paid $3,000, the same amount received by the writer of *Playboy's* lead story.

"Few magazines are so closely identified with their creators as *Playboy*. Mr. Hefner vigorously promotes himself as a suave playboy constantly in the company of comely females.

"The 'carefree playboy' image can be deceiving. It is studiously promoted as part of the magazine's success formula, and hides a serious, business-like approach to profit-making. . . . Despite the image built up by his magazine, Mr. Hefner's associates say his greatest interest is work, not girls.

"Nearly every week-end Mr. Hefner throws open his house for midnight-to-dawn parties attended by 'my bunnies,' entertainers, advertising executives and others. Despite this apparent gregariousness, Mr. Hefner has few intimate friends. He considers himself a non-conformist with a cause. He says he was born into a strict, somewhat puritanical family—'an earth fertile and ripe for the blossoming of a rebel. . . .'

"32,000 keys (at $100.00 per key) have been purchased for a seven-storey Playboy Club to open on New York's East Side in late summer or fall. Clubs are also due to open this year in St. Louis and Baltimore and in at least six other cities in 1963, including one to be built in conjunction with a 200-room Playboy luxury hotel on Los Angeles's Sunset Boulevard. 'If the hotel bit is successful we may try it in other cities, particularly in Chicago.'

"Mr. Frank Gibney, formerly editorial director of *Show Business Illus-*

trated and now publisher of *Show,* explains the failure of the former: 'I wanted to intellectualise SBI. Hefner wanted to use his *Playboy* techniques and make everything breathless. The two concepts just didn't go together.'

"Hefner insists he sold SBI 'Not because it wasn't doing well, but because it wasn't doing well enough, by my standards.'

"On his office wall hangs a framed share of *Esquire, Inc.* common stock. Beneath it is a sign bearing these instructions: 'In case of emergency, Break Glass.'"

I put aside the attitude assumed by the *Wall Street Journal* toward Hefner as being envious toward my host simply because he had become a multimillionaire without going to New York. I returned to the *Post* story, confident that it would be fairer.

"My father and mother gave us intellectual freedom . . . but they imposed rigid Protestant fundamentalist ethics on us. There was no drinking, no smoking, no swearing, no going to movies on Sunday. Worst of all was their attitude toward sex, which they considered a horrid thing never to be mentioned. . . . What we're selling is good, healthy, upbeat revolt against the things that have been ruining America. The nudity is the revolt against the Puritanism that overtook us in those grim days after the 1920s and stifled creative expression."

Well, I be dawg, I told myself, putting the *Post* down carefully and saying it again to myself, this time aloud, just to be sure I was still in my own skin, "I just be purely *dawg.*"

I was in the predicament of the bettor who has seen his animal finish plainly a head ahead of the bettor who has seen *his* animal finish a half-length in front. For my own recollection of the days that had followed the 1920s had been the days of the 1930s. And that in those days Hemingway had returned to write his greatest book, while Steinbeck and Richard Wright and Tennessee Williams and James Agee were making their discovery of America too. It had been a decade of bold discoverers in all the arts; a time when beauties appeared of whom men still speak with wonder: Garbo and Hedy Lamarr and Katharine Hepburn and Elisabeth Bergner. *Anna Christie, Ecstasy, The Glass Menagerie, The Maltese Falcon, The Petrified Forest, The Grapes of Wrath,* and *The Ox-Bow Incident* all broke with Puritan thinking, I knew. It had been a first-person time because the inhibitions that make people act in the third had been broken by the plain economic need of acting in the first-person. Hunger is never resolved in the third person. We could not *afford* inhibitions.

When you're drinking another man's booze and yet you feel his success is a hollow fraud, your obvious move, as a gentleman, is to say good night.

Lucky for me, I'm no gentleman. Even when asked to leave, if the booze is free I stay on in the event that some one may start frying eggs. After that I *may* say good night, but only when force is resorted to and not always then. What I wanted to get straight, before leaving here, was which generation, the Beat or the Upbeat, was the most revolutionary. I wanted to stick around long enough to see whether Allen Howlberg or Gregory Corset would drop in. Their poetry, like Hefner's cartoons, had always spoken as the voice of a group. Of "We" but never of "I." I felt they would be at home among people who preferred dances in which nobody touched another.

One eye on the entrance to the grotto in event next month's Playmate of the Month should swim in, and the other squirrel-eyeing Vic Lownes's door in the ceiling, I had a hard time reading Mr. Davidson's piece in the *Post*.

"The emphasis on hi-fi, sports cars, good food and drink," Hefner kept explaining to Mr. Davidson, who seemed to be getting bored, "good entertainment, good literature and good music"—

> *One more time!*
> *One more time!*

"is to stimulate our young men to educate themselves so they can make enough money to enjoy these benefits. In this way we can help overcome the educational gap between ourselves and the Russians. Our mission is to make this the Upbeat Generation instead of the Beat Generation and thus perform a service for America."

Meaning, I took it, that "we'll eat so well and dress so well and drive so many sports models that the Russians will break at last. 'We can't stand the pace,' they'd have to admit. 'Please take us over.'"

And overnight the conquering symbol of the Upbeat Generation, a pair of bunny ears, would be flying over the Kremlin!

For it wasn't, as Marx had thought, hunger that led to revolution. It was affluent rebels buying Hollywood beds and nylon carpeting, rotating sunlamps and Playboy party kits who were overthrowing the old regime. I glanced apprehensively about me: these people were *dangerous*.

Which was the *real* Hefner, the *Post* inquired; the playboy or the businessman? And promptly plumped for the businessman who was selling "mail-order sophistication" to middle-aged American sophomores who think they can buy good taste "for a six-dollar magazine subscription."

The *Post's* Mr. Davidson had just scored a near miss. He was right in pointing out that Hefner is a businessman and no closer to being a playboy than Pepsi Cola is to being a Martini, but the product Hefner is selling is more than mail-order sophistication. Hefner himself provides the lead:

"My whole early life was a telescoping of the Puritanical, unproductive years that the entire country went through. Maybe I have become a symbol of revolt because of that, because I was never really free until the day my magazine was born. Before then I had lived through one series of restrictions after another. We had three unhappy years," he adds of his marriage, "and the walls around me grew higher."

In recalling his early embarrassment at putting an arm around a girl, the interviewer had given his subject the benefit of the doubt that he no longer suffers such embarrassment. But the bosomy girls blooming in the pages of *Playboy* or serving the key holders of the Playboy Club are not blooming in order to gain a lover's caress; but, rather, to serve as an object of temptation that the righteous man (read "business" for "righteous") will resist.

The weakness in our society that the *Post* accredits Hefner with discovering is not a weakness so much as it is a falsification, and one of which H. L. Mencken made much. It is the puritan falsification that damns the act of love as evil because it leads to birth, and birth brings original sin.

No matter that the maddened fathers of Salem dressed their women in black instead of bunny suits: the feeling toward women was the same, and they sang it:

> *O lovely appearance of death,*
> *No sight upon earth is so fair*
> *As the flesh when the spirit hath fled—*

and as life that comes from women is evil, so women are evil. The force behind Hefner's image of a woman is one of contempt born of deepest fear. What he is selling is Cotton Mather Puritanism in a bunny outfit.

These were young men and women who saw that the promise of

America lay in what the country could do for them. It kept them doing the Twist to all hours.

Hefner's salary, as editor and publisher of *Playboy,* is $100,000 a year. He also receives $300 a week from International Playboy Clubs, Inc.

"These are material things," he explains, "but awfully fundamental and what made this country prosper. It was losing sight of them in the thirties and forties that placed this country in jeopardy."

Upstairs I could hear them getting the country out of jeopardy.

One more time!
One more time!

O'Daddyland was a secret country that rose on West Congress Street a decade ago, flourished secretly, then ceased to be when His Imperial Majesty, Our Lord High Sovereign Dingdong Daddy, ceased to be. Just as the first jackhammers of the new expressway began breaking stone a mile away.

Nobody came to the bare wood door of O'Daddyland but Daddy's old cellmate: some shambling piece of psychotic refuse who had his own knock late in each brown afternoon. And left after dark with several brown boxes, bound with brown twine and marked *First Class,* for depositing in out-of-town postal stations.

For there flowed behind O'Daddyland's door a ceaseless Niagara, a true rushing cataract, a winding Blue Nile of girls, girls, girls.

Don't-Care girls and Won't-Care girls and Can't-Care girls. Girls from the country looking flattered, girls from the brothels looking wronged. And some, it seemed, who were strangely praying.

All in attitudes of carnal passion. Blue films, stag films, stills, postcards, and comic strips that would have caused the mind of the creator of Daisy Mae Hawkins to snap instantly—all left like brown ships topheavy with obscenity for ports where love-making is never thought of as anything but a game.

So all day long the half-crazed king went slipper-slopping through the dark old flat, coughing, hawking, sneezing, sleezing, one shoulder higher than the other from sleeping forty years on federal iron, now and then spitting against the wall.

How young had he been when he'd gone up? So young, for certain, that he had never had a woman. And a leadpipe cinch he'd not had one since.

Why, the judge had wanted to know of the boy forty years before, had he not backed off from the man and gone his way? The boy had not known then, and the man still did not know now. Time and the goat had had Dingdong Daddy, and he still did not know why. The charge had been murder in the second degree.

It had turned out to be murder in the first.

"Not a can in the joint but wasn't there on a woman's account," Daddy would tell his old mate, and the old mate would nod on, nod off: he had heard all this before.

In a dream, a week before he died, Daddy saw himself binding a box marked *First Class* with brown twine. Just as he drew the twine taut, it went slack in his hands, and he wakened feeling there was barely time, just time. All day, in waking, he drew brown twine taut. And at night, the whole day's work unraveled in dreams.

He slept. And had bad dreams.

He died on a day when the birch beneath his window had just put on her first spring greenery. The old mate knocked once, knocked again; then let himself in.

Dingdong Daddy had the glaze on his eyes. But he sat up, when he sensed someone near, and began to sing—

> I'm a *Dingdong Daddy from Dumas*
> 'n' you oughta see me do my stuff.

He died on the first day of spring greenery, when jackhammers of the new expressway were breaking stone a mile away.

The old mate covered him. and went through the flat to see what he could pick up. He found nothing—yet he paused when the kitchen light went on. To see what Daddy had drawn on the wall above the sink.

It was a crude caricature of a naked woman, knock-kneed, bald, buttocks sagging, breasts hanging to her navel, and the whole stippled by a disfiguring hair. Below it he had scrawled:

WOMIN DRAW FLIES

That was Dingdong Daddy's message to the world.

✼   ✼   ✼

"Hef is the playboy of the western world who, at 34, has built a sixteen-million dollar empire by doing exactly what he wants, surrounding himself with more beauty than a pasha of the past, not as a sultan with a harem but because he seeks brains in bright packages."*

I reread that, and it came out the same: "Hef" employed good-looking women just in order to surround himself, and I had had no idea that there could be that much in merely being surrounded. Could there be something wrong with the interviewer?

"Hef had no idea of founding a successful magazine enterprise," I read on, "it was just that he wanted to publish a magazine in which he could do the things he wanted to do. He wanted to write and draw and crack jokes. He was champing at the bit, ready to break with whatever security he had—if only he could make a bare living at what *he* wanted to do. His is the wondrous tale of a Chicago boy who became the Midas of the Midwest."

It *was* the interviewer. Who, in the first rush of his excitement at finding himself in the living room of a pasha of the past, had nipped Hef unintentionally by naming him a Midas. Croesus was whom he had in mind, for the reputation that operator acquired for having amassed incredible wealth. Midas was merely a Greek scapegoat afflicted by Apollo with ass's ears for preferring the music of Pan to that of the gods.

Yet Midas succeeded in keeping the ears hidden from everyone but the town barber. The barber promised not to snitch, and kept his word. All he did was whisper a certain state secret to a hole in the ground.

And out of the hole grew a reed purely bursting with information. That tipped the wink to a passing breeze, and the breeze carried the shame of Midas to every Woo Grotto in Greece! That's how it is in mythology, men. That's how it *really* is.

It didn't necessarily follow, I took cognizance, that Hef Pasha was wearing ass's ears. They not only better befitted the interviewer but constituted a step upward, from kennel to stable, for him.

Thus absently dreaming on brains in bright packages, I folded the interview back into its nest and shuffled through other treasures of American journalism until one flipped open to an article entitled "Playboy's Number One Playboy."†

---

* *Chicago Evening American*, April 21, 1961
† *Pageant* magazine, July 1961

This was more like it. Now I was going to get the real lowdown on how fifty dollars for a key with a bunny engraved on it would put me back into circulation. I could get a Division Street locksmith to scratch a bunny's ears on a tin key, and who'd know the difference, if it unlocked the door to making me a key-club Rubirosa with the fast international set? In no time at all I'd be exchanging continental reminiscences with Porfirio and Ramfis. I'd be saying "How's Kim and how's Maria and how's Aristotle and guess what we had for breakfast with Mr. Wonderful—hog snout 'n' fried chitlin's! Yuk! Yuk! Yuk!"

Although the air of the grotto remained untroubled by pleas of maidens weary of being unmolested, the curious phrase "brains in bright packages" kept buzzing about inside my skull like a bee without wings. I tried to rid myself of the creature by flipping through the demands of *Playboy* advertisers.

WHAT SORT OF MAN READS PLAYBOY? was the first full-page challenge.

"A young man, both urban and urbane, who lights up a cigarette or a young lady's eyes with equal ease, the *Playboy* reader is as quick on the draw with his favorite smoke as in drawing admiring feminine attention. Facts: According to the latest *Starch Report,* 77.1% of *Playboy* male readers smoke some form of tobacco—the percentage reported for *any* leading magazine. Each month 6,893,000 men (plus a bonus of 4,319,000 women) read *Playboy* —enough to kindle a new demand for any brand. And *Playboy* has more *male* smokers per 100 copies than *any* other magazine reported by *Starch*—69.9% of them smoke cigarettes, 29.9% enjoy cigars and 27.8% pack their smoking pleasure in a pipe."*

"You drive *it,* it doesn't drive you," was the sporty-O warning an automobile manufacturer gave me—then went to pieces like a fourth-hand Maxwell and plainly begged—"*Is it a date?*"

"I don't double-date, Dad," I had to explain, and read on.

"Real men demand this masculine smoke," a tobacco king told me in hopes I'd buy one of his de-Cubanized Havanas. Instead of appealing to my craving for tobacco, he was playing on hope of my having doubts of my virility. Although I was dying for a smoke I had to turn him down to keep my self-respect. He didn't care *what* he rolled into that cigar.

A fur-lined canvas jacket was next offered me because it was "the most

* 1961 *Starch Consumer Magazine Report* and *Sindlinger Audience Action Study*

masculine thing since the cave-man." I hadn't apparently been giving sufficient attention to the question of how masculine I wished to be. Was it possible that I really didn't want to be the most masculine object since the cave-man? And how do we know that Neolithic man wasn't as careless as ourselves in distinguishing between sexes?

The overall idea by now seemed fairly plain: this was a magazine that showed me what to be, how to be it, and when to show up with the evidence. The evidence being a line of accessories I had already lived without for half a century.

No real distinction was made between the primary uses of convertibles, canvas jackets, cigars, or girls: all were now required to fill an inner vacuum caused by the question, "Am I flagrant queer or a latent heterosexual?" My own psychology has always been that of the cop who once told me, "I don't want to frisk you—I'm afraid of what I'd find." I don't believe in frisking my innards simply because that would entail loss of time that can better be put to gaining the interest of a woman. And if I don't want *her* interest, or *any* woman's interest—why, then, there is the whole great world whose interest I want. And the world won't give it to me unless I grab it and say: "Look here what *I* got for *you,* World. And it won't do me any good to say "look here" unless I *got* it.

Thus we came to a parting of the roads, the *Playboy* reader and myself. The party who believes that the world is an endless department-store counter enclosing accessories, leaving him with no obligation in life except to choose what best lends him the appearance of being a man in the world of men—and myself as a party who happened to come up at a time when there was no way to become a man in the world of men except by identifying oneself with those who grab good hold well dressed or no, and do their very damnedest to change it.

"Life," Peer Gynt felt, means "passing safe and dryshod down the rushing stream of time."

"Man is Man," Mme. de Beauvoir disagrees with Herr Gynt, "only by his refusal to be passive; by the urge which thrusts him toward things with the aim of dominating and shaping them; for him, to exist is to remake existence. To live is to will to live."

PLAYBOY HEFNER REALLY A REBEL, I read: "His whole life has been a revolt against authority. His strict Methodist upbringing led him, while in his teens, to draw bosomy nudes."

So it's been the Methodists marking up those washroom walls. I thought so all along.

Three Playboy Clubs are presently operating in Chicago, Miami, and New Orleans. By the close of 1963 there will be fourteen (in order of opening: in New York, Los Angeles, San Francisco, Detroit, Baltimore, St. Louis, Pittsburgh, Boston, Dallas, Washington, D.C., and San Juan). Most elaborate of these will be the Los Angeles club, where, in addition to the usual Playboy Club playrooms—"The Playroom," "The Penthouse," and "The Library"—there will also be a 200-room hotel with a heliport.

"It will be a regular Disneyland for adults," Hefner promises.

It seems too good to be true.

Twenty thousand memberships to the Chicago Playboy Club, symbolized by a key bearing a rabbit's ears, have been bought at twenty-five dollars per ear. LP jazz albums, jet-propelled bachelor tours to Europe, Playboy party kits, Playboy cufflinks, and a Playboy jazz festival also operate profitably under the sign of the available bunny. A TV show called "Playboy Penthouse," and a magazine, *Show Business Illustrated,* were unsuccessful.

A Playboy sports car and a Playboy building, housing a museum of modern art, are contemplated. A biographical film of Hugh Hefner's life, produced by Columbia Pictures, will star Tony Curtis. I always knew there was lots of salt air on the ocean but I never guessed there was that much crazy stuff in the sea.

The reader who buys the magazine to get a leer at prostitution without danger of infection, or a fireside guffaw at homosexuality, must be disappointed. Nowhere does the magazine offer mechanical sadism mixed with mechanical sex for fans of Mike Hammer. Its nudes do not strip garment by lacy garment. They are simply businesswomen who have removed their clothing.

The playmate of the month is a businessman's beauty. She folds out into an image of total accessibility, saying, "Take all of me," while requiring of him no output in passion or cash.

The young woman whose trade it has become to sustain this image of a surrender devoid of sexual content is herself a business-child recruited from a filing cabinet or a desk. She has learned that Man's highest law is the sanctity of a business contract, and she folds out under contract only.

She knows there is no higher bliss, here below, than to be seen on the arm of an executive high in the *Playboy* hierarchy.

"To be seen putting a hand on his [Hefner's] shoulder or be spotted in quiet conversation with him carries as much prestige for a status-hungry member as a spanking new Jaguar."*

The key with the bunny's head that makes living worthwhile would never have succeeded had the figure been the head of a cat. It would mean the girl might bite or scratch. But a bunny tail pinned above a girl's behind verifies the promise of something that can be run down without retaliating. The girl herself makes cocktail lights burn brighter when introducing herself: "I'm your bunny for tonight."

Caveat and don't run your *emptor*—she isn't your bunny: the field is fenced off and her night is not yours. Like the trade of the foldout nude, hers is that of being a paper doll: a third-person person for third-person people who earns between two hundred and three hundred dollars a week in tips. She gets no first-person salary.

Hefner has perceived that the American businessman's most erotic zone is the skin of his wallet. That the excitement engendered by the proximity of the baby-faced girl waiting upon him derives from the customer's awareness that the proximity is tax-deductible. He'd run into trouble on his tax report if he tried deducting for a strip-tease act.

The key holder need not be apprehensive that she is going to invite him to sleep with her. Floor detectives (not wearing bunny tails) turn in any waitress who extends her relationship, on or off the premises, beyond serving him a view of her breasts with the shish kebab. Hefner knows that our carte blanche bourgeois is content with shish kebab.

The basic appeal of Playboy ideology, whether conveyed by the playmate or the bunny tail is not sexuality, but simply that one is getting something for nothing.

A philosophy leaving these young women abandoned in the Land-of-Something-for-Nothing—a weightless nation suspended between earth and sky wherein they subsist by living on tips, appear well dressed, and are carefully taught how to walk self-consciously. And each, while waiting in ultimate hope of a carte blanche boy with whom to make the American dream come true, gets her beauty work done free.

---

* *Pageant* magazine, July 1961

But the rainbow above the split-level home is of paper. As she knows when hubby gives her a carte blanche card all her own to show he truly loves her. As she senses that he is an expressway gypsy who cannot feel at home except when alone in his car. As she herself realizes that her country is *her* car. What was that the gravity-zero girl assured me of in the Woo Grotto—"I can't get foot on the ground either way"? He wanted a girl who was a third-person person and she wanted a man who was a third-person man and they both got what they wanted—where's the beef?

So live on in midair, pressureless baby. All you need to learn now is how to be weightless.

To the personal history, the social philosophy, the personality at play and the personality at work ascribed to Hugh Hefner by daily and weekly press, financial journals, and the retarded Kilgallens of our gossip columns, psychologists rented by evening or day or flunkies from Hollywood Alley going anxiously in and coming out loaded with goodies, the present journalist can add nothing except that a plate of last week's spinach has greater value than the total coverage to date on *Playboy* now stacked from basement to roof.

The coverage has been incredibly docile. It has all been upon an awestruck assumption that the editor and publisher of *Playboy* is a phenom, something that just happened, like a summer lightning bolt or Kim Novak.

Yet the diary that our host began in the third person in high school, his current preference in Scotch, attitudes toward women and recollections of teachers, his early ambition as a department-store clerk, and his subsequent dismissal from *Esquire,* what he said by long distance to Tony Curtis and what Tony said by long distance to him, whether his divorce was amicable or hostile, exactly what does it mean that he slides down a fireman's pole from his bedroom to his swimming pool? Why should his convertible be cream-colored rather than mauve? Was it all luck or did chance play a part? Will success spoil Hef Pash or leave him unspoiled? And if I didn't have an iron inside I'd purely spew.

Because all this has no more relevance than has the history of any other half-finished postgraduate product of no particular gift, no particular charm and less promise, nothing even remotely approaching wit and whose highest hope is to see Tony Curtis playing himself. Hefner is no more a phenom in heart, spirit, or mind than was Mr. Peepers, Wally Cox's representation of the totally unprepossessing man.

Countless Hefner-Peepers have come and gone, but this particular Peepers-Hefner materializes at his mirror at the precise point upon which the American middle class attains such a moral and economic self-content that its sense of relationship to the rest of the world is severed in a torpor akin to funk. It vegetates in a hothouse made of reflecting windows, a chamber of mirages so self-sufficing that it mistakes its own strange growths for the reflected image of mankind.

The novelist James Baldwin depicts this blinded state (of what he terms "The Well-Meaning Square") in one bitter glimpse: "To be a Negro in this country is really never to be looked at. What white people see when they look at you is not visible. What they do see when they do look at you is . . . all the agony, and pain, and the danger, and the passion, and the torment, sin, death and hell of which everyone in this country is terrified."

Although Baldwin, a professional Negro, excludes any aspect of human anguish not endured primarily by Negroes, his perceptions remain of value. Because once Baldwin's challenge is extended to include all those multitudes who live in America while sharing its horrors but not its hopes, all those whose whole lives are spent like expatriates who never left town, his phrase "If you don't know my name you don't know your own," gains significance: if you don't know your own you can't know your own country's name.

The American bourgeois lives in a dream world wherein he sees the representation of himself pictured in *Time,* film, and so on, as his actual self. Then when people pitch tomatoes at Eisenhower it seems they are throwing at him; he is hurt whether he's hit or not.

The colossal self-deception of naming a throng of armed pyschotics out of the bars of Miami "Cuban counterrevolutionaries," and shipping the bums into the MG fire of people quite as determined to conduct their own affairs on their own soil as we are upon ours, again leaves the middle-class American thinking he is being attacked.

Action so divorced from other people's condition can derive only from a class whose affluence has formed into a jelly-like mass of complacency quivering with injured feelings. And is comparable to the stupefied state of the French bourgeois toward the close of the past century.

Hefner has sensed that the middle-class American he is pitching to is a frightened race more at ease with the appearance of passion than with passion itself.

A local executive recently attempted to avenge his wife's promiscuity by offering his checkbook and pen to a friend, an attractive but unattached woman. Not to purchase the actual privilege of her bed, but for the more degrading purpose of buying the *reputation* of having shared it. He was willing to pay her merely for cooperation in creating an *impression* that he had betrayed his wife. Thus at a single stroke to redeem honor and exculpate guilt.

This is a bourgeois product who really prefers going to bed nights to staying up to play. Yet who fears he may become dated just as business takes a fresh upturn. So goes on the nod below the lights about the same time that his woman friend takes an upturn.

The PR image of an ideal *Playboy* is of a college-educated bachelor of twenty-eight from a suburban background. What the PR department doesn't emphasize is that its ideal is attracted to the take-all-of-me nude because he doesn't have to do anything about her. Since he cannot identify himself with a living woman without anxiety, identifying himself with one who lends him a sense of relief is a real bargain.

This deep-set fear of the act of love propelling him pellmell away from desire may derive from a father's lifelong fear of economic disaster. Which is only to say that fear is pervasive.

Pervading the American sanctuary in which the child is safe from beetles and sleet and such small sudden explosions as that of a match scratched on a rough surface, he comes to young manhood with a dependence upon mechanical lighters.

Until he is at last housed independently where there are no sudden flares either outward or inward, having gained the immunity afforded by a checkbook with his own name on it in gilt and a single emotion working toward women: "If you'll let me stay a little boy I'll let you stay a little girl."

Yet he stays in good shape physically.

This headlong flight from living, toward make-believing that one is alive, has its fringe benefits, most of which are picked up by psychoanalysts. They know that a patient can be schooled so well against exposing himself to others that a marriage may be eventually arranged with another person just as self-contained. This can work out well for both parties so long as neither strikes a match.

Marking a progress over dreams of our hero's bachelorhood, where he would find himself embracing a Negro girl and waken already flying to the phone to have his afternoon appointment moved to the forenoon. When life closes in, it closes in so fast one barely has time to doublelock the door.

While the analyst has to rearrange his own appointment with *his* analyst, as he has been having a recurrent dream of finding himself in amen's washroom in Mexico City with the strange knowledge upon him that the sign on the door reads *Señoras*. That's how it goes in analysis, Men.

That's how it *really* goes.

Kedzie Avenue men were divided from Kedzie Avenue boys on the basis of who wore long pants and who wore shorties. Though half a head taller than any other kid on the block, I was condemned to an everlasting six-foot childhood.

My mother was convinced that, since her brothers had not worn long pants till they were sixteen, her son had to wait two more years. There was no use complaining, "Times have changed, Ma." I had to play junior to kids two grades behind me. In my old age men half my age would still be telling me, "Run along home and come back when your face clears up." I was doomed to old age in shorties.

In John's pool parlor the "No Minors Permitted" legend meant that short-pantsers could stand by, but had to step back when a long-pantser was lining up his cue. It was to here that the elders of the Kedzie Avenue Arrows retired as soon as classes let out at three o'clock. I was eld as any, yet was ungraded. I had to keep out of the way of kids younger than myself. I was a goof.

I ungoofed by buying a pair of longies with money I'd earned myself, and hanging them in the back of the joint.

I changed, in John's washroom, into longies, selected a cue on which I'd set my heart months before, broke the triangle, and saw the fourteen ball scoot into the corner pocket. When I notched the point up on the wire overhead, with the tip of my cue, I was a man at last.

After that, all I had to do was keep my head when all about me were losing theirs and blaming it on me. And send away for a pair of dumb-bells offered by Charles Atlas in *Ring Magazine* with the guarantee "You Can Have Muscles Like Mine in 60 Days."

Maybe it wasn't as easy as all that. Even Kedzie Avenue pool players who could spot you five points and still beat you had to solve the problem of what to do about girls.

But it was easier than now, when the boy who once sent for dumbbells can't make it until he gets financing for a sports car.

I once knew a Kedzie Avenue girl who wanted to get to be a swell, so I took her to where swells used to hang, at Guyon's Paradise Ballroom, and she thought she'd made it for certain.

To be perfectly frank I thought she had too.

Now it's easier for a girl to go to the places where swells go today—and tougher too. A girl with the looks and the figure qualifying her for a Playmateship or a degree in bunny-tailing need now have only the figure and the looks to be a swell herself.

The tough part is that she's only permitted entrée, through the door that opens without a touch, on the condition that she does not involve her key-holder companion emotionally. She must understand that sex is for kicks only. When it's done, she is not to put in one of these oldfashioned claims such as "What are we going to do about us?"

There is no *us* to it, honey. If you want an *us* thing, go back to Guyon's Paradise. An executive who would risk his emotions is as old-fashioned now as the man who would risk his life savings in starting a new business. You operate on other people's emotions as you operate on other people's money. Business is Business, and love is Business too.

"'Bachelor Hefner . . . is no detached artificer,'" I read on, "surveying the plebeians at their games. A 'true-believer,' the host boyishly bunny-hops from pool to bar to buffet table, reforming laggards by personal example."*

Does the energy behind this gigantic intellect never flag? I marveled. How *ever* does he do it? Plays all night, changes his shirt, and then bunnyhops boyishly to the job of expanding a sixteen-million-dollar empire into a sixteen-million-and-twelve-fifty one—oh, the sheer *romance* of it all! A saga of American business at long last! Nothing like this has happened in America since the New York police were called out to control crowds trying to buy a forty-nine-cent fountain pen for seventeen dollars because it could write under water.

I picked up another journal, and read, "An Impolite Interview with Hugh Hefner."†

Q. "As the publisher of *Playboy Magazine,* what would you say is your purpose?"

* *Pageant* magazine, July 1961
† *The Realist,* May 1961

A. "We edit *Playboy* to please, entertain and inform a literate, urban, male audience. We try to edit the magazine with honesty, insight, taste and integrity, for we very much believe in what we are doing and enjoy it. Now if you set out to edit, with honesty, any magazine for adult males, you aren't going to come up with *McCall's* or the *Reader's Digest.*

"If you begin listing the subjects of special interest to a male readership, you've got to come up with beautiful women and a rather broadminded attitude on sex fairly high on your list, or you're figuring the list upside down. As an editorially honest book, *Playboy* reflects the sex attitudes of its readership—and these attitudes shock a few people for whom sex has become something either sacred or obscene.

"*Playboy,* of course, is not really a very sexy or shocking magazine, and the fact that some few people consider it so is a sad commentary on the sexual mores of a portion of our population. Unhappily, this rather limited segment has been often the most vocal, and it is their view of life that we find most often depicted in the family magazines, on TV and radio and, until quite recently, in most books and movies. It is really a castrated, female view of life—one example out of many of the growing womanization of America.

"But we don't ever expect a specialized magazine like *Playboy* to appeal to everyone—if it did, it would no longer be especially urban or male in viewpoint—and we don't worry about those who don't dig us (no one is forced to buy the magazine—it costs 60¢ to get your hands on a copy) as long as they don't attempt to stop others from enjoying it who do understand and approve.

"Of course, it is the nature of the beast to find the prude and the bigot most anxious to *force* his or her opinion of what is right on the rest of us. They often seem to have nothing better to do with themselves than worry about the affairs of their neighbors. So occasionally, more often in the past and only rarely now, a small group of local citizens, a P.T.A., a police chief, a district attorney with political aspirations, puts on the mantle of the censor in hia community and starts banning books, magazines and movies.

"Whenever *Playboy* is involved in such attempted extralegal censorship, we take the matter into court; and whenever this is necessary, we win. *Playboy* has never been adjudged objectionable by any court anywhere in the U.S. and is never apt to be."

Hefner has also perceived that he is selling to a class, outwardly self-content but betrayed by inner fright, that is beating a blind retreat upon itself, declining even those risks by which it might save itself. Thus more at ease with a depiction of passion than with passion itself, it wishes to look longer upon pictures of passion, hear more songs about passion, and read more comments upon passion—anything to avoid *feeling* passion.

The businessman who keeps a mistress for prestige's sake rather than desire's may spend fifty dollars for a key as a prop to a personality he feels is unfinished. The spiritual void in which he encloses himself may be so lacking in person-to-person feeling that, in order to feel he is living at all, he has to feel that whatever it is he is getting, it's costing him less than it's worth.

Playboy is often reported to be lapping the field of men's magazines: *Cavalcade, Duke, Escapade, Gent, Gentleman's, Male, Mr., Nugget, Rogue, Sir, Swank,* and *Stud* (assuming there *must* be one to cover ridgelings and geldings alike)—but in reality *Playboy* is running its own racecourse with no other entry in the field.

Because while others are peddling material as close to blue as will get through the mails, *Playboy,* behind its foldout nude, is applying department-store technology to the most basic human relationship.

"Ever since I gave my girl a duplicate key to my apartment," another bemused heart asks The Adviser, "she has been gradually killing me with kindness . . . she has never mentioned the subject of marriage, although it is implied in her every action. She is a beautiful, intelligent, passionate girl and highly sensitive. What can I do to curtail her activities in my behalf and still not do anything to hurt her?"

"Hire a houseman who pre-empts the duties your girl is presently undertaking," is *Playboy's* advice; "you can explain it to her as a thoughtful move on your part to take mean tasks off her hands for more uplifting pursuits." The Adviser grows stern: "Don't ever again give anyone but a domestic worker a duplicate of your key to your digs. For when you do, as you may already suspect, you sacrifice the freedom of bachelorhood without gaining the benefits of connubiality. And things can only get stickier, more marital, as time goes on."

Another way of doing it might be to have the houseman tell the girl that his master doesn't want to marry her.

The success of Playboy Enterprises demonstrates that the question of how to be recognized as a man by the world of men is not so easily solved now as when it could be achieved by dropping a fourteen ball into the corner pocket. The problem then was not what to do about girls but how to get into long pants. We knew what to do about girls.

The mystery of sex outweighed its fears; its perils were outweighed by its joys. We pursued a rumor of a Chinese whorehouse around Twenty-second and Wentworth but never found it. Later, Kitty Davis used to advertise EVERY GIRL A COLLEGE GRADUATE. We didn't know we'd ever see the day when the appeal would be that the girl was a businesswoman. It would now appear, running through these ads, that for the young American today, love's terrors often far outweigh its joys. By allocating sex to "those areas where sex is important," the mystery of sex is taken away for mere safety's sake. When one does not commit himself to the world, the retreat continues through love.

Yet it is not possible to live without developing an attitude toward women. However paradoxical it may appear, the young male who assumes early that physical relationships with women are part of life is more likely to develop respect toward women than is the young male who abstains from such relationships.

Abstinence makes the heart contemptuous, and *Playboy* combines both by pinning a tail on a girl's behind. This is not to make her cute, but to encourage contempt of her. *Playboy* laps the magazines-for-men field because contempt is more needful to our middle class than suggestiveness.

Nothing conceals fear so well as contempt, but the Playboy Man is never fearful. If it seems that the young man who is fretting because a beautiful, passionate girl has a key to his apartment is not precisely Richard the Lion Heart, be assured that in his own orbit the Playboy Man is a tiger—and a relentless one.

A lyricist employed by *Playboy* to write a lyric descriptive of the magazine came up with one depicting the *Playboy* reader as exactly that—a tiger. His afterthought, however, was that it was a tiger that was "sometimes gentle and sometimes square." Lyric and lyricist were dismissed: the *Playboy* image is that of a tiger by day, by night, never restless and never relenting. Women have no choice but to surrender. And once the tiger has enjoyed them, they have no choice but to get out of the way so as not to impede his next leap.

This stance of male superiority possesses an aristocratic tradition asserted with confidence by the French essayist Montherlant:

"The wreaths we bestow upon ourselves are the only ones worth wearing," Montherlant repudiates dependent love; yet is drawn to that woman he meets on a train who had "so besotted an air that I began to desire her." As if he withdraws from an unbesotted woman. "I do not love in equality," he explains, "because I seek in woman the child." A besotted child would, of course, be even safer.

"The lion with good reason fears the mosquito," Montherlant excuses a fear that his leonine dignity may be too easily compromised. French lions and American tigers alike are aware that any of these girls can feint any forty-year-old businessman out of position and abandon him standing on his head with his socks falling. Strapping her into a contract, thus reducing her to an ornament upon peril of being out of work, is his one chance with her-tigers and lions both alike.

The scene which revolves around an iron suit to the tunes of a shadowy orchestra has been reported variously as the realization of the American dream, as a perversion of that dream, and as a semimonthly orgy. It is neither this nor that nor the other.

Neither the realization nor the perversion of a dream because it is not a dream at all. It is the extension of a PR image as empty of sex as that of the Borden cow. If it were real *somebody* would get drunk.

Nor is this American scene comparable to that representation of contemporary Rome we witnessed in Fellini's *La Dolce Vita*. The film derived tragedy from its depiction of a sensitive man degraded into a purchasable commodity. But when it is assumed that life's highest purpose is to proceed through it boyishly bunnyhopping, the only tragedy can be loss of money. As the only triumph can be that of being richer than anybody.

The heroic American, to *Playboy*, is a twenty-eight-year-old college-educated bachelor whose reason for driving a car is that he needs *something* that doesn't drive him.

The world is a threatening place to a young man who has been abruptly blessed with money and leisure.

In our teens we obtained a spurious maturity from comic books that we obtained from ads in *Ring*:

"FEAR NO MAN"

"Now for the first time, through my amazing course, learn how to use centuries-old methods of combat taken from the archives of the Indian and Japanese killercult temples, the ferocious Aztecs, Nazi and Communist Secret Police, all yours for the asking! You will immediately see and learn how a small weak man or woman can overpower and even cripple a 200 lb. brute—*in a flash!*"

BECOME A TERRIFYING SELF-DEFENSE FIGHTING MACHINE IN JUST 30 DAYS!

Playboy is presently fulfilling the same need by saying, "Don't hesitate—This assertive, self-assured weskit is what every man wants for the fall season."

Who would want an assertive, self-assured weskit except a hesitant man? *Playboy* speaks to those who wish desperately to know what it means to be male. It speaks to the reader whose masculinity depends upon his choice of deodorant or cigar, one who can maintain respect for a woman only so long as she abides by a tacit assurance not to arouse him sexually. It does not sell sex. It sells a way out of sex.

Sex that—in Karl Barth's meaning when he names the basic relationship of man's life—*Mitmensch*—co-humanity—is out of bounds to the *Playboy* believer. For him sex can be indulged in only as a recreation—"virtue in those areas where virtue is important." Virtue, like an assertive weskit, may be put on for an evening or for the fall season; but is not something to which one is to commit oneself.

Because one is not to commit oneself at any time, anywhere: not to a weskit, not to another human being nor to an issue alive in the world.

"We hold that man is free," Simone de Beauvoir writes, "but his freedom is real and concrete only to the degree that it is committed to something, only if it pursues some end and strives to effect some changes in the world. Man is free only if he sets himself concrete ends and strives to realize these: but an end can be called such only if it is chosen freely. The cult of money which one encounters here does not spring from avarice or meanness: it expresses the fact that the individual is unable to commit his freedom in any concrete realm; making money is the only aim one can set oneself in a world in which all aims have been reduced to this common denominator."

To seek to be free by avoiding involvement with the world, which is the commodity *Playboy* pitches, cannot be achieved. There never was a world—or a woman—who could be turned on and off like a faucet. The woman may run hot and she may run cold, but in all Man's time she has never been turned off.

The man who constitutes the backbone of *Playboy* readership by buying the magazine regularly from a newsstand for sixty cents is a man under thirty. After thirty, readership drops off abruptly: something happens to most of its readers between twenty-eight and thirty-one. You know what I think? I think he finds out you can't turn her off.

The reassurance that *Playboy* thinking offers the young American is that, by going into a blind retreat upon himself, arranging his own room comfortably and adopting those attitudes prescribed by the world of advertising, he has justified his existence; simply by protecting himself from disappointment, risked by falling in love with either the world or a woman, he has fulfilled himself.

"The reality of a man is not hidden in the mists of his own fancy," Mme. de Beauvoir wrote before these mists began to rise, "but lies beyond him, in the world, and can only be disclosed there . . . it is in economic success that the American finds a way of affirming his personal independence; but this independence remains wholly abstract, for it does not know on what to bestow itself."

Male failure is always attributable, with Montherlant, to mother, sister, or wife.

"The only place on his body where Achilles was vulnerable," he writes, "was where his mother had held him."

Woman, by the fact of being a woman, incarnates failure simply through lacking virility. She fails doubly by loving the man for his weakness instead of for the grandeur of his masculinity. Her justification for her existence is that she affords him pleasure.

This corresponds with Hefner's answer to an interviewer asking him, "What do you look for in a woman?"

"Virtue in those areas where virtue is important," Hefner replies as precisely, as politely, as a floorwalker saying, "Ladies' hosiery first aisle other side of the soda fountain, madam." Hefner's assertions are those of a small authority in a large department store, Montherlant's those of a poet.

Poet and floorwalker alike derive the total submission of woman from Oriental attitudes. Montherlant, finding his truth in Ecclesiastes—"the man who wishes you ill is better than the woman who wishes you well"— sees himself in an ancestral Hebraic light. *Playboy's* thinkers arrange Hefner as an American caliph surrounded by lounging beauties, his bed in the background and a pipe in his teeth, for *Time*.

There is no tobacco in the pipe. Like the bed strewn with beauties, the pipe is a prop.

Caliphs and pashas, khans of times long gone, herded their harems with the warlike dignity of bull walruses herding their cows. True voluptuaries, they peopled Heaven with women of whom one never wearied. On earth or in Heaven they had but one use for a woman, and in Heaven or earth they put her to it.

Yet no women walk the heavenly home of a key-club caliph. There are no bosomy nudes in that great key club in the sky. There is only a shadowy three-piece band playing cool music for executive-angels. There is no Scotch, there is no rye. There are only vending machines from which may flow Pepsi-Cola or Coca-Cola. But no booze.

There is only a spacious guest room that has no guests. Dominated by a suit of medieval armor wearing its helmet *affronté*.

On the fleshless intellectual Montherlant, the stance of an Eastern potentate looks weird enough. But in adapting it to Hugh Hefner it becomes a downright riot. The image of Dick Nixon being kind to a puppy is less preposterous, as Nixon may actually have liked the pup.

Hefner doesn't like his bunnies. Whenever a man perverts love to moneymaking, he builds resentment against the money-maker.

"What are you doing to me, Little Baby?" I once heard a procurer complain to his girl, "Why did you make a pimp out of a nice guy like me?"

I was brought to myself by the falling of a shadow. A dark-haired girl with a taut, wan look, was standing over me, fully dressed.

I did not have to ask who she was.

"Hello, Connie," I said.

"It wasn't five-thirty," she told me in a low voice; "it was a quarter to six. He slapped me at a quarter to six."

"I read something about it," I assured her. She didn't seem to hear.

"He didn't slap me because I was high. He slapped me because I lost my job."

"What did you do?"

"I walked along the lake up to North. It's where I used to go swimming when I was a kid. I started to walk back to my old neighborhood. Then I remembered everybody I knew was gone—what was the use? What was the use of anything? I didn't even belong to a neighborhood any more. Before I got back to the room I had it in mind—if he wasn't there, that was it."

"And?"

"He wasn't there."

That Hefner's entertainments pretend to taste but come no closer than a ludicrous vulgarity is merely a local circumstance. But, as a stage whereon young Americans are revealed as lacking any way of bestowing themselves upon the world, it is disturbing.

For those who cannot bestow themselves become severed not only from the world but from themselves. And in such severance, whether that of Connie Petrie or of Hugh Hefner, each takes his own: measures against his deprivation.

Each devises his own vengeance.

The winter day falls with a colder light today than the light that once fell between the blinds of a *Sommerhaus*.

It was always summer in the *Sommerhaus*. A grandfatherly light came down on the world that year and slanted between the blinds of the little old-world cottage; when many grandchildren ran in and out before dinner. But I was the only one of the many to whom my grandfather confided the name of the inventor of the Father & Son Cigar.

And the farm boy from Black Oak who worked for McCormick Reaper himself became a grandfather who had no *Sommerhaus*. He became an old man lying on a Westside bed with his wife and son looking down at him.

They saw his right hand take the fingers of his left, feeling something had gone wrong with the machinery of that hand; that had to be fixed with his right.

They saw him pass from life into death still trying to fix the machinery of everything. His old woman saw him go, and his son saw him go. Yet neither mother nor son wept for the father's death.

So it was that the son knew that, for all his fixing, the old man had not been able to fix anything after all.

EPILOGUE

Tricks Out of Times Long Gone

Again that hour when taxies are deadheading home
Before the trolley-buses start to run
And snow dreams in a lace of mist drift down
When from asylum, barrack, cell and cheap hotel
All those whose lives were lived by someone else
Who never had a choice but went on what was left
Return along old walks where thrusts of grass
By force of love have split the measured stone.

I think hep-people leave small ghosts behind
For haunting of winter ball parks and locked bars
That ghosts of old time hookers walk once more
That no ghost follows where a square has gone.

Tonight when chimneys race against the cold
Tricks out of times long gone, forgotten marks
Come seeking chances lost, and long-missed scores
Faces once dear now nameless and bereft
Hepghosts made of rain that softly try old doors
Forever trying to get down one last bet.

Tarts out of times long gone
Booth-broad, bluemoon cruiser, coneroo
Come once again, palms outstretched to claim
What never was their own.
Drifters of no trade whose voices, unremembered,
Speak in the city wires overhead—
Now is the victims' hour where they go
Where winoes used to drink themselves to death
Or merely slept away their 29c woes.
Upon the just-before-day bus I saw a woman,
The only one who rode

Look wanly out at streets she used to know—
"And here I went"—"and there I slept"—"and there I rose"—
Again by evening in a billboard's cold blue glow
She came forever toward me
Walking slow
Saying za za-za-zaza-za-zaza-za-zaza
Walking slow.

All day today old dreams like snowdreams drifting down
Faces once known now nameless in a mist
Return from hospital, prison and parole
Mouths that once the mouth of summer sweetly pressed
Saying zaza-za-zaza-za-zaza-za-zaza.

Within a rain that lightly rains regret.

Notes from a Sea Diary
Hemingway All the Way

For Max Geismar

Some of the anecdotes herein related have been told, here and there, before: in *Cavalier, Dial, Dude, Gent* and the *New York Herald Tribune*.

And to Miss Kamala Rao and Mr. S. D. Punekar, for their assistance, the author expresses his thanks.

An essay on Ernest Hemingway was a labor to which I felt compelled. Everyone else was acting so compulsively I had to do something compulsive too or I wouldn't get invited to any more parties. How is a writer to make The Hot Center unless he mills around where The Center is simmering?

Since Hemingway once announced to me that "it is now 0230 hours," I can make trouble for anyone who asks me to wait in the hall. I don't have to know what hour 0230 is to be on time for dinner.

But after dinner some stiff is certain to ask—in the tone of a bondsman recognizing a bail-jumper—"Well! What are you up to *now*? What's *next*?"

"Nothing, my key-shift is stuck," would serve as an answer but a short chop to the ear would serve better. Yet that would only confirm his suspicion that I must be dealing with half a deck—otherwise I'd be in a respectable field. Such as Criticism.

He assumes that the critic and the novelist are cats of the same litter though of various stripe; actually they are hostile breeds dammed in the same basket.

"We are oppressed at being men," Dostoevsky wrote, "and contrive to be some sort of impossible generalized Man."

The Impossible Generalized Man today is the critic who believes in loving those unworthy of love as well as those worthy—yet believes this only insofar as no personal risk is entailed. Meaning he loves no one, worthy or no. This is what makes him impossible.

He demands that perilous voyages be taken and storms be endured but himself stays on the dock. He reminds us that the proper study of mankind is man yet keeps his own distance from men and women. The goodness of his intention is 'lent expression, while his conscience is afforded ease, by the practice of Criticism. The risk of becoming identified with the objects of his compassion is obviated by his sagacity.

Yet the greater the creative man's sagacity, the less is his creativity. It is easy to replace art by profundity. Present examples of those whose harsh artistry has flattened into smooth profundity are Arthur Miller, John Hersey, Saul Bellow and Paul Goodman. (Although the latter had no art to start.) Their maps are drawn; their risks have been taken.

This is why nobody raps a critic's door unannounced after midnight: there's a Thinker in there but he's on a tight schedule. He drives a well-lighted route, strapped in by a safety-belt, and stops only at well-behaved motels. And there's nothing to drink in the house anyhow.

But if you're entertaining friends and the aquarium is closed, rap the novelist's disorderly lair—"You in there! What are you up to now? What's next?"

You-In-There doesn't know what he's up to at midnight, 0230 hours, nor upon the gong of noon. He drives a collision course, lights out, along an untraveled way. The risks he assumes are the kind for which he is wished failure by most; and particularly by those who never take any. Their most urgent need is to be able to say "We were right after all." Meaning that the man's failure will be all his own doing.

Yet the man's risks succeeding, he gains cheers from the same gallery. "We were right after all" now means that they have a claim on his triumph because they've been with him all along.

The practice of fiction involves the writer, personally, directly, and whether he would or no, with multitudes: that's the basket *he's* dammed in. The Practice of Criticism is a means of remaining personally uninvolved: that's *his* basket.

Benign critics there are. I know of at least one who would prefer to get the best from a living writer than to get the best of him. He makes allowances, in writers of the past, for those flaws which scar all human effort that has nobility.

But we are not concerned here with benignity. Our problem is the middle-aged youth, so convinced the world owes him a refund, he is too timid to damn and too stingy to applaud. Mediocrity is never passive; it avenges itself for its deprivation:

"All these reviewers inhabit much the same intellectual milieu, and what they have in common, apart from talent and intelligence, is an attitude toward books and an idea about the proper way to discuss them," one commentator promises proper subscribers to a new review—"a book is assumed to be guilty until it proves itself innocent. Books are too important to permit of charitable indulgence. A book for them [The *Milieu* People] is, quite simply, an occasion to do some writing of their own."

Such injunction against charitable indulgence of creative work, combined with a concession of dependence upon the work of others for something to write about, is not only to demand damages where no injury has been inflicted, but to demand them arrogantly. Talent can spring up anywhere; but it is never dependent. Unsolicited opinions should not be telephoned collect.

The injunction also illustrates the ancestral conflict between the artist's view of the world and that of the Establishment. To the artist, the landscape of commercial enterprise has always been a chamber of mirages by which the true world is perverted; and the *Milieu-Man*, the critic, has, traditionally, been the artist's apologist.

But to Business, Government, Church, Military, TV, Press and Hollywood, the world which feeds, clothes, arms and amuses men is the one real world; the artist is the distorter.

The *Milieu-Man* has now, by and large, become the Establishment's apologist. Whose proof, that the Establishment's reality *is* real, is that the Establishment *works*: that nowhere before has the artist been so widely benefacted. In no other age, no other land nor other season than our own, has the artist been more generously patronized.

Yet he must remain hostile or be untrue. For the Establishment lives in the third-person; the artist in the first. The devastation we have seen, and the dehumanization threatening, prove that the Establishment not only works but that it works too well.

In such a world the writer's single usefulness has come to be the man who lives by no image, let his flaws show naked as they may. For, however disastrous to human values a civilization geared to technology may seem to him, he's in it all the same. And the best he can do, by strength, luck or sheer stubbornness, is to stand in ironic affiliation to it.

The Impossible Generalized Man, The Sagacious Impossibility, either at the levers of a commercial publishing house or a chair of English Literature, cannot risk such irony.

Nor is this to quarrel with the just and necessary function of criticism:

how many times Hemingway might have pressed the trigger before releasing it is just what is needed for a fuller understanding of *Farewell to Arms.* Dedicating oneself to a chronological breakdown of the accidents Hemingway sustained, from the time he skinned a knee in 1904 to the time a chandelier fell on him in 1938, shows us that the proper study of mankind *is* man. Anybody who can merge criticism with autopsy is the boy for me. And *Harper's* will pay for it if you type it neatly.

Publish or perish is now the cry of the Ph.D., running head-and-head with another Ph.D. for the widest desk in the Department of Humanities. He'd *better* get attention in print. So; by adapting the attention-getting devices of television to criticism, he can entrench himself in a hard-bought chairmanship.* We understand, when *Time* anoints some persevering wheel as "a dedicated critic," the meaning is that the man has devised a literary image that keeps the paperback stock moving in The Village bookstores as well as hard-cover stock in the suburbs.

So much for Man's inhumanity to Man. Obsequiousness in one critic helps us all; for it puts money in circulation. Theses which establish the respective failures of Mark Twain, Jack London, Scott Fitzgerald, John Steinbeck, Sherwood Anderson, William Faulkner, Thomas Wolfe, Richard Wright and Ernest Hemingway are relieving unemployment of graduate students from coast to coast. For what would any head-on-a-stick marvel do for a livelihood were it not for having inherited a body of flawed art? Back to managing a Nedick's and telling the cook to hold back on the butter, no doubt.

Well, everybody has something he needs to throw up: instant erudition soundly based on servility will turn the trick every time. Articles like these restore criticism to its democratic purpose of nauseating everyone who can afford ninety-five cents per copy.†

        ✿   ✿   ✿

I was encouraged to give a boggling world yet another Hemingway paperback, by the realization that it would be a fresh contribution to write the same old things at sea. I would be the inventor of the very first essay on

---

* See "Come Back to the Raft, Huck Honey," an essay by Professor Leslie Fiedler.
† See *Man in Modern Fiction*, by Prof. Edmund Fuller, Vintage Press, 95¢.

Hemingway smelling of salt! What the other fellows had been getting into the mixture I couldn't identify; but it certainly was pervasive.

In fact, I'd always had the feeling that, one time or another, they'd planned to write as well as Hemingway but to be better paid. As things worked out, however, they had continued to write badly without growing wealthy; while Hemingway had gone on writing well without going broke. This had embittered everybody.

So I took a book of essays, by one Norman Podhoretz, to sea to remind me, should fire break out above or mutiny flare below, to be steadfastly magnanimous; so long as it didn't cost me anything.

Would my own efforts induce nausea? If retching was what it was going to take to get me to the docks of Singapore, was my thinking, everybody get set for a fast dash to the rail.

The Captain was on my side too.

His crew wanted to go to Japan, but he had a girl friend shelling copra for Proctor & Gamble and they don't grow coconuts in Japan; so they tossed for whether it should be Kyoto or Chittagong Charlie's in IIo-IIo. The Captain won the toss. "Make it two out of three, sir," the First Mate spoke up boldly in behalf of his men. The Captain proved himself a sport. "Make it three out of five," he offered—and won the next two tosses. Later I asked him to show me that half dollar and, sure enough, it had heads on both sides. "I didn't want to go out of my way," he apologized.

That's how it is in the Orient, men. That's how it *really* is.

And that's how it was that the *Malaysia Mail* made all of the small-pleasure docks and none of the sporty-O ports. Bound neither for Kyoto nor Saigon, neither would we see Macao nor Luzon. We would tie in only at places where copra bugs live in caves called *Bamboo Alley, Lion of Kowloon* and *472 Cho-Ryang-Dong*.

Happily, my Definitive Essay began with a ring so definitive that, by putting an ear to the page, I distinctly heard something inside *gong!* I'd hit it off! The thing *rang* with profundity! And yet it was so burdened by precepts that its chime rang leadenly and its tolling held no merriment. It was more of an elegy in a deserted delicatessen.

God! Had I but been able to sustain that I-Give-Unto-Thee-the-Keys-of-the-Kingdom-of-Heaven intonation, bookies would have been offering 6-5 and take your pick that it had been written by Podhoretz! "Well, we all have our good days.

That one bad night can ruin. Such as one when, through an ominous tenement on the quais of Calcutta, a schizoid seaman pursued me under the delusion that I was a salami requiring slicing and he had the knife. Though I remained unsliced, my grasp of the concept that the proper study of mankind is man was shaken.

Later, while trying to dispose of a watch engraved *77 Jewelries* (purchased in a free-trade port), my bowlines were severed and the Definitive Essay began drifting to sea. I bartered my Podhoretz essays for a pair of sandals to a boatman afflicted by elephantiasis—where else could I have picked up a pair so cheap?

Any reader assuming that memoirs of some moveable feast are offered here, should be advised that, by the time I got to Paris, nothing remained but empty napkin-rings on the grass.

I met Hemingway only once, and briefly. My only claim to his friendship is that nocturnal message: "it is now 0230 hours."

Yet, as he had once observed that all his life he had been peddling vitality, he surely would have understood my defection from critics peddling sterility.

NELSON ALGREN

TWO HOURS OUT OF THE PORT OF SEATTLE

Sooner or later, on her first trip out or her hundredth, every ship carries a doomed man.

For the *Malaysia Mail* this was the sixty-first time out of the barn and she labored like a mare too tightly reined; too old to whip, too mean to whinny. I watched her harbor-home going blind in a mist behind her.

There blue fogs kept bending red roses to rest; and girls, coming home from school, kept tossing their ponytails. No wonder the old scow kept grieving.

For doomful seas from the black edge of the world would come rolling through nights without a moon: no ocean had ever darkened so lonesomely. "Don't take things so hard, Pacific," I consoled the poor brute—"girls come home from school in Malaysia too." It wasn't my first time out of the barn either.

Lights of the rigging came on high and flickering. Then the big low lamps of the staterooms began burning too steadily. Was there somebody else aboard? I took a turn around the deck to a door marked PURSER, knocked, and got a direct command from the other side:

"Turn the handle!"

So *that* was how these things worked.

He was all officer. Under a cap so bound with braid I saw *it* had made the decision to go to sea and was only accompanied by the man below for his use as an interpreter. Why would a man be wearing such a self-important hat alone in his cabin unless he'd been practicing the hand salute in preparation for World War III?

There won't be time for that this time, sir, I wanted to assure him, as he introduced himself.

"*Mister* Manning," he let me know—and just by the way he told it I knew I need not fear mutiny on this trip.

"Algren," I identified myself, for he needed cheering up. The paperback he'd put down was *Japanese Simplified*.

Two Japanese lovelies stood framed on his desk. Neither looked simplified.

"How much time ashore will we have in Kyoto?" I inquired casually.

"We aren't going to Kyoto," he let me know, "but you'll get a good view of the coastline at Hokkadate."

The coastline at Hokkadate wasn't what I had in mind. "Will I be able to go ashore there?"

"We only stop at Hokkadate to refuel," *Mister* Manning told me, "but believe me when I tell you-you're better off staying aboard. The less you see of Asia the better off you'll be."

"Did you take these from the upper deck?" I inquired about the lovelies—one signed *With All My Love—Noriko* and the other *To Bill With All My Heart—Suzi*.

"They run a hotel for me in Kyoto," he assured me stiffly.

And throw the profits to you from the dock tied in a silk kimono, I assumed—but which one did the throwing? I concluded it must be Noriko because she had a chin like Whitey Ford's.

"These people aren't like us," Manning informed me, "they steal everything they can get their hands on."

I was pleased to learn Americans had given up stealing manually.

"All I had in mind was to take a few shots to prove to friends I've been out of town," I explained, "if the Captain is afraid I'll delay the ship I'll use a Polaroid."

He picked up the paperback that simplified Japanese lovelies.

"I hope you won't be disappointed in not getting ashore in Japan," Manning hoped; looking tickled pink.

If you went ashore you'd be trapped by enemies, seemed to be Manning's thinking; and if you stayed aboard friends might trap you. He hadn't gotten far enough in his plans to arrange entrapment by himself, yet seemed to be working toward some such arrangement.

"It's alright," I assured him. "Don't let me interfere with the ship's schedule: Just go ahead and refuel at any port you feel like."

Manning bestowed his Be-Kind-To-Our-Only-Passenger-He-May-Be-

Related-To-The-Front-Office smile upon me. He had a mug as round as a rhubarb pie and the smile seemed to *drip* through the juice.

I had no way of knowing that anyone with a face so self-satisfied could be doomed.

JUNE 22ND

This is one hell of a big ship. Wandering among freight cars in the fantail, I figured out that the reason they weren't rolling around the deck must be because somebody had had the foresight to button down their wheels. This would require very strong buttons in a monsoon, I realized, and went up to the point of the ship to see what other cargo I was being held responsible for.

The *point* of a ship is its front part. The reason for making a ship pointed is twofold: it makes the distance between ports shorter and prevents bumping when you run over a whale. Whales often sleep on top of the water because everybody goes to bed earlier in the Pacific than in the Atlantic. Unfortunately it wasn't yet my bedtime. I went to find the Captain to see where he needed me most.

I saw a fellow standing at a steering wheel and went into the cabin to see why he didn't sit down. The reason he wasn't sitting down was because he had to stand up to see over the wheel. He said he was a second mate and I told him I'd been married once myself. He asked me whether I'd like to try steering the ship but he didn't mention pay. Nevertheless I took over as he looked like he needed some rest.

I realized my responsibility: forty seamen and twelve officers, most of them with sweethearts or wives, were now depending on me not to hit anything. There was a clock that had lost one hand above the wheel and, whenever the wheel swung a bit, the clock's hand swung a little too. I put all my strength into holding our course steady as she goes.

"You don't have to bear down," the Second Mate let me know, "it's automatic"—and a fearsome blast just overhead nearly took off my ears, the wheel swung, the clock's hand boggled, the deck tilted.

"We're sinking, sir," I reported calmly.

"That was just the foghorn," the Second Mate informed me with the wannest of wan smiles, "it's automatic too."

I let him take the wheel back. I didn't yet know that Danielsen's smile, so thin, so faint, happened only in moments of his highest exuberance. The rest of the time he lived in some sunless world bereft of everything but memories out of years long gone. Though not yet forty, loneliness had aged him by twenty years more.

"How long have you been at sea?" I asked him.

"Since I've been born," he told me-and again that smile, so wan and wandering. If Danielsen wasn't the loneliest Second Mate on the Pacific they must be flying them in from Antarctica.

"Is there anything to drink aboard?" I asked him.

He whispered something (as he whispered almost everything) that sounded like "Communications Officer."

Communications Officer Concannon sat, earphones clamped to the perpetual *beep-bop-jot-jot*—then rose to six-foot-three to give me a big hand and grin, toss off the phones and begin pouring gin.

"I saw you come aboard," he told me. "'There's one in every crowd,' I thought, 'and two on every ship.'"

"One of *what?*"

"Why, one mark of course," he smiled, picked up a stained deck, shuffled and gave them to me to cut; then dealt seven hands of draw poker.

"Tell me what you need and I'll match it," he promised.

"Match my Jack."

He dealt around the board and a Jack fell on my hand. Not bad.

He placed my forefinger across the top of my cards—"You're signaling me for an Ace," and moved the finger down, between the top and the middle of the face-down card—"King." The finger dead-center was for a Queen. Beneath that indicated a Jack, and the finger at the card's bottom asked for a Ten. Moving back up, but using two fingers, defined every card down to a Deuce: for which the signal was a small sweeping motion of the card.

When I'd mastered the signals, Sparks gave me one admonishing word: "It all depends on the crimp I put in the deck. If the man beside me don't cut them at the crimp, it don't work. You sit opposite me so it don't look like cahoots. Now how about a couple hands of blackjack?"

I must have looked apprehensive because he grinned like a wolf.

"Don't you trust me, old buddy?"

"I trust everybody," I assured Concannon, "but I'll cut them twice just for luck."

❁   ❁   ❁

"I've sailed with Manning before," Concannon filled me in, "I'm ready to drop the subject when you are."

The subject dropped of its own dead weight.

Both Manning and Concannon are heavy boys, and each has naval service in World War II. There the resemblance ceases. No two men could be more American and no two men could be more different.

Concannon is "Sparks" or "Sparky" to the crew. Manning is "Acting Corporal." Manning conducts himself toward the men confident that he is both loved and feared by them. Yet their respect for him is perfunctory: as ship's storekeeper he can inconvenience them.

"You can run your poker game," Manning has told Able Seaman Gary ("Crooked-Neck") Smith, "so long as you run it just for the crew."

Smith had played it safe. "Yes, sir," he'd assured Manning. Then he'd gone to Sparks.

"You and Danielsen can't play any more," he'd reported to Concannon.

Concannon had gone directly to Manning.

"Let's go see the old man about this," he'd offered.

Manning, of course, had had to decline. The purser has neither responsibility for the crew nor authority over them; and that had put an end to the matter.

Sparks, on the other hand, with the most responsible job aboard, appears to have no concern other than, "Where's the deck? Who's got the gin?" He conceals a high competence by flaunting his flaws. While Manning pretends he's a seaborne executive, Concannon makes himself out as the ship's outstanding sadsack. Neither man, when they pass each other on deck, raps to the other.

"I tried to touch Manning for ten bucks," Muncie, a crew pantryman, complains with a speech impediment, "'n he asks me. Why don't I take advance. On my next draw. 'Had I a draw comin' I wouldn't. Be trying to borrow off you. Personally. Would I?' I asked him. 'N walk away."

"You should have gone to Sparky," Chief Crew-Pantryman Bridelove advises Muncie, "has Sparky got it, you can have it."

"Manning made forty thousand dollars one year," I filled both men in.

"How do *you* know?" Bridelove asked.

"He told me so."

"And he didn't spend. A dime of it. On me," Muncie mourned.

Concannon was brought up, after a manner of speaking, by relatives more or less distant, around Kingfisher, Oklahoma, in the dust-storm years; never had a home until somebody slipped a pair of headphones over his ears in 1941. Since then, while the hair has thinned, his home has been a radio shack.

And all the brothels, small and great, of the great East China Sea.

From Bugis Street in Singapore to Cebu of the blue-mist Philippines, Sparks has left enough empty gin-fifths behind him to capsize the *Malaysia Mail.*

Forever friendly, cheerful by the hour, dry, jocular, ready for anything, Concannon yet disclaims friendship. "The word 'friend' isn't in my book," he assured me, "the only things a seaman can depend upon are money and whiskey, because money and whiskey gets you the women—and what else is there besides women?"

"You don't want women because you're a seaman," I suggested, "you're a seaman because you want women."

"All I want," he skipped the suggestion, "is all the fun I can handle, and then go out at sea. I don't want to be buried on land. The last stitch through the nose and over the rail, *that's* the burial for me."

"You're putting me on," I told Concannon.

"Why? What have I got to lose? Pussy brought me here and pussy's going to take me away."

"I don't know what brought you here and I'm sure you're right about what will take you away. Only that wasn't what I meant. I meant the last stitch being through the nose."

Concannon gave me a look so cold I was startled. I'd never seen a man turn unfriendly so fast.

"Ask someone else," he instructed me, and clamped on his headphones. I was dismissed.

LIONS, LIONESSES, DEADBONE CRUNCHERS

In December of 1955, I bought a bag of unshelled peanuts in Miami and went into a strip-tease house, but I never saw the strip-tease. It was one of those places that show a film between stage shows, and the picture had just started when I came in. It was *The African Lion,* a Disney production.

It was the kind of house that always needs airing because it never closes long enough to open the doors. So many homeless men had slept here all night, to wake when the girls danced on, then had returned to sleep: to wake, to sleep, till sleep and waking were one. Now the stale death of their mingled breath hung waiting forever for girls to come dancing.

A bear-sized creature was hibernating in the seat in front of mine, with some kind of sun-helmet dangling off the back of his head. When his head lolled, the helmet rolled around the seat's curving back. It must be strapped to The Bear's neck, I decided, and dropped a handful of peanut shells into it.

On the screen, two lionesses were stalking some horned grass-chompers.

"What's *them,* honey?" a girl behind me asked her escort.

"Them is elks, Baby," I heard him tell her, in a voice so authoritative there was no use contradicting it.

One lioness cut off the escape-route: now the girls had the herd entrapped. As the other charged, The Bear sat up and hollered "Look out!"—but too late. Just as in Miami, the prey never escapes. The Bear jammed his helmet down over his ears and began to eat a banana. What country did he think he was in? I wondered. I tapped him on the shoulder. He swiveled about.

"What country you think you're in?" I asked.

"What country *you* think *you're* in?" he challenged me brilliantly.

"*Take off the lid, Dummy,*" the Elk Authority came to my support.

The Bear took the lid off and went back to sleep without finishing the banana. Some Bear.

Now on the screen a new prey appeared: a rhinoceros. Yet it wasn't a lioness that had gotten *him.* It was quicksand.

How Disney had induced that brute to lie down just there, when it had all the rest of Africa to rub its back in, is a trade secret I'm not free to disclose. In no time at all every hyena in Tanganyika was milling around, pleased as possible to be working as an extra again.

The hyena has two distinctions: he doesn't want to be first to try anything and he smells worse than everything. "You can't be *too* careful" is the essence of Hyena-Think. He feels his smell is a fringe benefit.

A buzzard is better. Every buzzard projects an image of himself as Top-Buzzard. He doesn't wait for the next buzzard to make the action. Where the hyena will settle for standing room only, the buzzard entitles himself to front-row center. When *they* came down, the hyenas didn't stop to ask to see their stubs. They hightailed for the back rows and began milling around.

"How come you birds always get seats front-row center?" they wanted to know from a safe distance, "when we're better looking?"

"We smell so nice we *deserve* front-row seats," the buzzards explained.

Which goes to show you that no matter how bad you may smell, someone always smells worse.

All of a sudden the rhino went all out to raise himself out of that bog. It looked, for a moment, as though he might make it; until his very power worked against him and he began sinking slowly onto his side. The Bear came to and saw what was happening. "Dig a hole!" he hollered—whether to the rhino, the buzzards or the hyenas I still don't know.

The-Biggest-Buzzard-Of-All hung one moment on the wing spreading air, watching his shadow enshroud the rhino—then plummeted with talons outspread and somebody popped me in the left ear with a piece of popcorn.

It didn't hurt.

The Bear jammed his helmet down over his ears.

"*Take off the lid, Dummy.*"

I didn't want to go through all that again. I got up and walked out.

The first thing I noticed, back on the street, was that the lionesses had begun wearing the manes. I had a chocolate phosphate under a rye bread tree and took the next ship to Havana.

Cuba was the first single-crop country I'd seen. I walked around Havana two days eating bananas before I realized bananas weren't the country's single crop.

Girls! *That* was Cuba's single crop. Girls waiting in taxis, girls waiting on corners, girls waiting in hotel lobbies; girls waiting in doorways, strolling the tables of the Tropicana or waiting in front of funeral parlors; girls in the shadows of the skyscrapers of Vedado; girls waiting in drugstores and meat markets; girls waiting in bars and girls with no places to wait: these were just walking around. Girls waiting for seamen and soldiers.

Girls to whom the sweet cane had brought only bitterness.

In stores that sold nothing they waited for anything.

One whose hair was platinum blond yet black as the devil at the roots, invited me to step into her Nothing-Anything door. An American was studying the jukebox, preparing to invest; but he wanted an American song for *his* investment. When he finished reading the Spanish numbers he finally found one on the American side. It was the very one *I* would have picked had it been *my* quarter:

> *I wouldn't trade the silver*
> *In my mother's hair*
> *For all the gold in the world—*

I've felt sentimental about that song ever since a so-long ago rainy afternoon when I skipped an algebra class to hear a baritone sing it at the Haymarket Burlesk and Miss June St. Clair came down the runway immediately after and shook all the Algebra out of my head for keeps:

> *God gave us mothers and tried to be fair*
> *When he gave me mine I got more than my share.*

I asked the young lady if she would care to go steady with me, but she nodded toward the investor: she was promised to another. Any man who could spend a quarter in a jukebox would make her a better provider than I would, I realized, and I left. I hope they found happiness.

I recalled then that I was supposed to visit the Hemingways.

Not that anyone had sent for me. But every American visitor to Havana who'd read a book was supposed to storm the Hemingways with the news. If you hadn't read one you were interviewing for the *Chicago Tribune.*

I phoned and told Mary Hemingway I'd seen a good movie in Havana, so she said come out right away—if I weren't interviewing for the *Chicago Tribune.*

Hemingway was sitting up in bed looking like John McGraw atoning from something; he wasn't atoning but he was abstaining, and invited me to help myself to the Scotch.

"How's the work going?" I asked him.

"I never turned the horse loose and let her run until this book," he told me—"but we are so far ahead now that it is pitiful. The next time they're going to give the money back in the mutuels."

He nodded toward the bottle beside his bed. Its label read: *Best Scotch Procurable.* "I can only have one an hour," he explained, "doctor's orders. You go ahead."

I went ahead.

A lion commanded one wall. Some sort of moose held an entire shelf of leatherbound Dickens at bay. On a wall all its own, like a sea all its own, a swordfish had room to zoom: or, if it would rather, just to sail around. A buffalo looked as if it had just thrust its head through the wall. Perhaps the rest of him was standing outside.

Every brute in the room seemed to proclaim its right to command, zoom, hold at bay or just sail around.

"You've got everything around here but a werewolf," I observed, trying to sound disappointed.

"Why go after small game?" Hemingway asked.

"I don't even run rabbits myself," I explained, "I go to movies instead. I just saw one where a rhinoceros got trapped in quicksand. Hyenas came around. You know what the worst thing about the hyena is?"

"I don't go to movies any more," he told me, "but I still go to fights."

"I'll tell you—it's the smell. Actually, of course, I couldn't smell a hyena in the movie, but you could tell, just by *looking* at him, how bad he smelled."

"The smartest fighter I ever saw was Leonard," Hemingway decided. "I never wrote a story about him."

Hemingway didn't want to talk about hyenas. He wanted to talk about fighters. I didn't want to talk about fighters. I wanted to talk about hyenas. It was *his* Scotch.

"A fellow named Nate Bolden whipped Zale twice one winter in the White City ring," I went along, "that was before the war. One night after the war, I caught a cab on the Southside and noticed that the driver was the same Bolden. 'I saw you beat Zale,' I told him.

"'Which one was he?' Bolden asked me. He wasn't punchy. He'd just never bothered learning the names of the men he'd fought. Some had been white; some black. At 160 pounds he'd whipped top-ranking light-heavies. Now he was driving a cab."

I'd thought that was a good story but it hadn't come off. Hemingway regarded me thoughtfully. Hemingway was a thoughtful-looking fellow.

"Go ahead," he said, "help yourself."

It was pretty good Scotch. In fact, it *was* the Best Procurable.

"Everybody thought Leonard would whip Britton," Hemingway recalled, "because Leonard was smarter than everybody and Britton wasn't smarter than anybody. But after Britton had whipped him, I asked him what he thought of Leonard. Britton said Leonard was the smartest fighter he'd ever been up against—'He was thinking all the time in there,' Britton told me, 'and all the time he was thinking, I was busting hell out of him.' I put *that* in a story," Hemingway added.

"A Lithuanian named Radek had Cerdan out on the ropes in Chicago, but the bell saved Cerdan," I remembered, "and Cerdan got the decision even though he didn't know who was holding up his hand. Later he said it was an improper way to win. That's the very word he used— 'improper.'"

"Carpentier liked to use words, too," Hemingway told me. "When he whipped Bombardier Billy Wells he said, 'Vice, as vice, is bad. But viciousness in the ring is essential.' What he meant was that Wens had had him the first round and let him go. So Carpentier knocked him out in the second."

The lion looked at the bison. The bison looked at the elk. All three were agreeing on something.

"Battling Siki was paid off to lose to Carpentier," Hemingway wanted me to know, "and the nigger knocked him cold."

I didn't know how to get back to my rhinoceros.

"Jack Delaney's real name was Ovila Chapdelaine," Hemingway went on, "he gave Oom-Paul Berlenbach the business. Do you know what the business is?"

I didn't know what the business was. I hadn't even known Oom-Paul was sick.

"Delaney was holding a druggist's pestle in the thumb of his glove," Hemingway explained. "He stood with his back to the ropes, waiting for the judge's decision and a second took the piece out of his glove, and he got the decision. That was 'the business.'"

"Well, it wouldn't have looked very good, when the ref was holding up Delaney's hand, for a hunk of iron to drop out of it, would it?" I inquired. I had to get off this boxing thing before the man confused me with George Plimpton.

But Hemingway only looked at me as though trying to decide something.

It was the Best Procurable alright. If it had been any better it wouldn't have been procurable at all. The distiller would have kept it all for himself.

Somebody behind me was eyeing me. I turned fast. That damned swordfish.

"You were saying something about somebody getting caught in quicksand," Hemingway reminded me. "How'd he get out?"

"It was a rhinoceros," I remembered. "Darryl Zanuck had dug this pit in Africa and pushed the brute into it. He must have had help. The hyenas came around. You know what the worst thing about a hyena is?"

"You told me. Its smell."

"No," I corrected him, "it's because when he laughs he giggles. I picked that up somewhere."

"Are you living in Paris?" he asked.

"No, I lost my passport."

"They'll issue you another."

"That wasn't how I lost it," I had to explain. "I meant they won't renew it."

"Why not?"

"They won't tell me why."

"The Shipley woman," Hemingway said, "she won't tell *anybody* why."

"I'd like to talk to her husband," I said.

"Help yourself," he suggested.

I did.

"Another big deal is the lioness," I reported, because I thought Hemingway ought to know. "The old man don't hunt. He has two old ladies in his stable he's pimping and just lays under a tree while they go out and run down an elk and drag it home. He won't even help drag. He just lays under that tree till his old lady comes back from the supermarket dragging the groceries. He don't even help drag. When dinner is over they move on so the hyenas can come up and crunch the bones."

There was a silence. Hemingway had run out of fighters and I'd nearly run out of hyenas.

"Another thing," I felt he ought to know, "if he catches you sleeping he'll bite off your face."

"Was *that* in the movie?" Hemingway asked quickly.

"No, I picked it up somewhere."

Hemingway got out of bed painfully. He was fully dressed. There were guests waiting.

He sat among them gravely serious. He carried an air of tranquility. He didn't throw a punch at anybody. He didn't stagger. He didn't brag. He listened, perceived, and he liked having company. What he brought to a table of many guests was the feeling that everyone understood one another. I remember hearing Spanish spoken, and French, and of understanding not a word of what was said; and of knowing, when I spoke English, that some of the guests didn't understand me. But because of Hemingway's presence everything seemed understood.

I spent that afternoon and the next day, which was Christmas, with the Hemingways. He was a big man who had had a big life; that had made those who had known him bigger.

But they weren't going to give the money back in the mutuels.

     ✿   ✿   ✿

Seven years later, cornered by death, a professor with a notebook came at him out of the shadows.

"He had read, or glanced at, I could soon see," the professor reported, "not only my essays, but practically everything any one had written on the modern novel in the United States. I fancied Hemingway flipping the pages, checking the indexes (or maybe he got it all out of the book reviews in *Time*), searching out the most obscure references to himself, trying to find the final word that would allay his fears about how he stood; and discovering instead, imbedded in the praise that could never quite appease his anguish, qualifications, slights, downright condemnations . . . 'A whole lifetime of achievement,' I wanted to shout at him, 'a whole lifetime of praise, a whole lifetime of reveling in both. What do you want?'"

For you to go away. Was that asking too much?

"Okay, so you've written those absurd and trivial pieces on Spain and published them in *Life*," the professor wrote, "okay, you've turned into the original old dog returning to his vomit. We've had to come to terms with your weaknesses as well as your even more disconcerting strengths—to know where we are and who, where we go from here and who we'll be when we get there."

("These damn students," Hemingway once complained, "call me up in the middle of the night to get something to hang on me so they can get a Ph.D.")

"Hemingway," the Ph.D. concluded, "sometimes puts down the closest thing to silence attainable in words, but often what he considers reticence is only the garrulousness of the inarticulate."

There is a corruption of prose which is jargon.

Gentlemen, I give you jargon: "Silence and platitude. Platitude and silence. This was the pattern of what never became a conversation. And I felt, not for the first time, how close Hemingway's prose style at its best was to both; how it lived in the meagre area of speech between inarticulateness and banality: a triumph wrung from the slenderest literary means ever employed to contrive a great style—that great decadent style in which a debased American speech somehow survives itself."

This is jargon: its "Yes" is not "Yes"; its "No" is not "No." It is jargon because it diffuses meaning in order to conceal, rather than reveal, the writer's thought. It is jargon because it conveys the impression that the writer is employing Elegant English at the same time that it enables him to falsify his thought. It is jargon because it seeks to make an idea, that is easily refutable, irrefutable. Put into prose, the writer's thought here is that Hemingway was uniquely fortunate in having devised a great style while he had nothing to write about. Put thus honestly, the writer would appear asinine. Jargon, therefore, is the corruption of prose deriving from the writer's own corruption.

"But what were we doing talking of 'next books,'" the professor continues, "when I could not stop the screaming inside my head—'How will anyone ever know? How will I ever know unless the critics, foolish, biased, bored, tell me, tell us?' I could foresee the pain of reading the reviews of my first novel, just as I could feel Hemingway's pain reading the reviews of his later work. And I wanted to protest in the name of pain itself that not separated but joined us."

Had the man driven from Montana to Idaho to interview Hemingway or to present himself as a victim? Hemingway hadn't sent for him.

"But all the while he [Hemingway] kept watching me warily, a little accusingly."

Hemingway knew about lions and he knew about lionesses. He had been the man lying with blue wounds from elbow to wrist; he had been the English girl dreaming herself dead in an Italian rain. He had felt the wind of buzzard wings; and knew what it felt like to be an ex-fighter driving a cab. He had seen the elephant, he had seen the owl. He had smelled the hyena:

> *Highly humorous was the hyena, obscenely loping, full belly dragging at daylight on the plain, who, shot from the stern, skittered on into speed to tumble end over end. Mirth-provoking was the hyena that stopped out of range by an alkali lake to look back and, hit in the chest, went over on his back, his four feet and full belly in the air. Nothing could be more jolly than the hyena coming suddenly wedge-headed and stinking out of the grass by a donga, hit at ten yards, who raced his tail in narrowing scampering circles until he died.*

Small wonder Hemingway kept watching warily.

> *The hyena, the classic hyena, that hit too far back while running circles madly, snapping and tearing at himself until he pulls his own intestines out, and then stands there jerking them out and eating them with relish.*

"I stood for a moment," the interview concludes at last, "watching Hemingway banging at the closed doors, rather feebly but obviously tickled to be able to feel. 'Shit,' he said finally to the dark interior and the empty street; and we headed for our car fast, fast, hoping to close the scene on the first authentic Hemingway line of the morning. But we did not move quite fast enough, had to hear over the slamming of our car door the voice of Mrs. Hemingway calling to her husband, 'Don't forget your vitamin tablets, Daddy.'"

Hemingway knew the action:

> —*Trailer of calving cows, ham-stringer, potential biter-off of your face at night while you slept, sad yowler, camp follower, stinking, foul with jaws that crack the bones the lion leaves—*

the trip had been worthwhile.

EAST CHINA SEA: WE DIDN'T COME TO GAMBLE.

"I came to gamble" is the land-gambler's brag and *Deal* is his one command. Don't tell us about your lovelife—*Deal.* While one deck is being dealt another is being shuffled so not a moment will be lost: all moments tonight are stolen from wife, children and home, we have to get in as much play as we can. And every deal seems slow.

Poker upon the roving deep isn't poker on dry land.

When goony-birds dip the deadly hours, pursuing, fleeing, again pursuing, the automatic foghorn mourns, the long deck tilts as the waters shift and the waters shift once more: then a rain-dashed fleck through an open port and the dealer lays down the deck.

Play stops. Talk stops. Even the engines below us wait; the port is closed.

Then like a great heart hauling hard, the engines begin to throb once more, the long deck tilts as the waters shift and the waters shift once more: the automatic foghorn mourns and the cards go around and around once more.

Seaman of The Republic, castoff care-nothing from suburb and slum, unschooled craftsman and long-schooled drunk, skilled mechanic sick of the land or drop-out dropping yet, under the moon of the East China Sea, with a pack of stained cards on a green-baize board, all are now gathered together:

1. Crooked-Neck Smith, age 38, ordinary seaman who runs this seaman's game.

2. Bridelove, about 35, squat and dark as a piece of heavy machinery beveled to a precision function.

3. Muncie, 22. Bridelove tells him what to do.

4. Quong, Officers' pantryman, an ageless, small, immaculate Chinese enormously skilled in minding his own business.

5. Chips, Ship's carpenter, about 50. Thirty years of exposure to the suns of Southeast Asia have left him as pale, from the folds of his neck to the folds of his belly to the folds of his mind, as though he'd been living in a sanitarium.

6. Carey "Sparks" Concannon. A seventeen-year tour of the gin-mills of Asia has not sufficed to wash the dust out of the throat of this dust-bowl refugee.

7. A free-lance journalist out of Chicago.

Lowball is the game with these seaborne stiffs who settle for low in everything. Concannon appears to be the only one of the lot deeply dissatisfied with a life of many big drunks and few small cares, a pint of cheap gin and a girl by the clock; of being expendable at sea and unwanted on the beach; and of coming at last to fear any woman not for sale or rent.

Call *that* a life on the roving deep.

If your wife can't stand your moods any more, your girl friend claims she's broke, if you can't dance and can't stay sober, then a mariner's life, a seaman's life, a jolly life on the rolling deep, *that's* the life for you.

The Negro seaman's story is something else, of course: a way out of a slum with equal pay and a tour of ports where color don't matter.

"What. Kind. Work. You. Do. Mister?" Munde asked me.

"I'm in iron and steel," I told him, "my wife irons and I steal."

Quong laughed. But, then, Quong laughs at everything.

"Quong," Concannon saw fit to put in, "here's a man *paying* to go to Calcutta—what do you think of *that?*"

"Oh-oh-oh-*Cay-O-Cutta*," Quong recalled, "*Cay-O-Cutta* gel, she treat *him* very nice. Very pretty gel, he *glad* he come *Cay-O-Cutta*."

"Wait," Bridelove tried to wise me up, "wait till you *see* Calcutta."

"Is it really that bad?"

"Wait," Bridelove reassured me.

"I. Don't. Like. Memphis," Muncie announced. Muncie didn't stutter. He just couldn't handle a whole sentence together.

"This boy ain't stupid," Bridelove assured me quickly, "just slightly retarded."

"Oh. No. I. Only. *Slow,*" Muncie explained.

Then the cards went around, the goony-birds dipped, the long deck tilted as the waters shifted.

"Seven-card stud," Concannon announced, "high-hand only," and gave the deck to Chips, beside me, to cut.

He dealt me two diamonds down and one up. I paid to stay in just to see what he had in mind. Two clubs fell. I would have dropped but for that interesting exhibition Sparks had given me. When the ten of diamonds fell I took another look at my hole cards: I lacked nothing but the queen of diamonds to have a straight flush, king high.

I centered my index finger dead-center on the back of my hole-cards. *O little queen dressed in faggoty pink—*

I waited until the cards had been dealt around, face-down, before I peeked—*fall my way and we'll all be rich.*

Six of clubs.

Ouch.

Smith won the hand. When Chips threw in his cards I saw that his last card had been the queen of diamonds. Missed by one. And it had cost me sixty dollars out of a traveler's check for a hundred.

"Let me have what you can spare," Chips asked me when Smith gave me forty dollars in change. I had three hundred more in traveler's checks when I pushed the forty to Chips.

In the next few hours I had a pat flush, a pat full-house, trips back to back three times and two straights. Sometimes the card I signaled Sparks for came; sometimes it didn't. When it did it made no difference. Smith topped me every time.

"Toward morning the farmer gets lucky," he encouraged me when my last hundred-dollar check went into a pot. I was holding two pair, aces up and deuces, and the game was draw. I signaled Sparks for a third ace. I didn't get it. I got the third deuce. As a full house it would have to do. I checked to Smith. He bet and I raised. I raised him back. He raised me.

I felt a sudden chill and merely called.

He had a full house with fours up.

"If you'd filled up with aces instead of deuces," he began to console me as he hauled in the pot—"If the rabbit had been carrying a gun he would have shot the ass off that hound," I reminded him.

"Yes," Sparks put in, looking too benign, "and if your ass was pointed—"

"*Deal, deal,*" I demanded irritably. Something had gone wrong on the *Malaysia Mail.*

Toward morning the farmer went broke.

"Deal me out," I told Smith, and went up to my stateroom to watch the goony-birds through the porthole.

I waited, when I heard Sparks come up, until he'd reached his shack. Then I followed him into it.

He already had his headphones on when I came in.

Beep-beep-jot-jot-beep-beep-beep.

I waited.

Jot-jit-beep-beep-jit-jot-beep.

I helped myself to his gin. He took the headphones off.

"How much did you go for?" he inquired.

"The roll."

"You can get it back."

"How?"

"Transistors. You can buy them for twenty apiece in Hong Kong and get sixty for them in Bombay. A hundred bucks will get you three hundred."

"I don't have a hundred left."

He pulled out his wallet and clamped on his headphones.

"Take two out of there," he told me.

I took it.

We were twenty-four hours from the Port of Pusan.

472 CHO-RYANG-DONG: A PARLOR ONCE PURPLE NOW FADED TO ROSE

It is evening in this fogbound warren above the East China Sea: that low-burning hour when the sourish-sweet tenement-supper smell of *kimchi* cooking upstairs and down, pervades harbor, hall and street. I'm waiting for Concannon in front of the American Club. The only sound is a lone hound's hunger-howl up the green mountain: then his echo begins sliding down. Chew your own echo, hound: call *that* supper.

"Man, do you think I'm going bamboo?" is all I've heard from Concannon for days. He's putting in so much time on this bamboo problem he's keeping *me* from going bamboo.

A woman naked to her waist and breast-feeding an infant comes slogging through the rutted mud toting a bucket of suds in her free hand. She's wearing a G.I. fatigue cap and sandals chopped out of a tire. Her features are ravaged so delicately it looks like hunger has used a thin chisel to form them. Four thousand years looks down, from that ancestral mountain, upon a race of hardluck aristocrats toting buckets of slopwater.

Slopwater is by courtesy of the American mess hall, *chapeau* by the Quartermaster Corps. Shod by Firestone, employed by nobody, impregnation courtesy of the American P.X. You can get anything at the P.X.

Homemade soap is stuffed into *Palmolive* wrappers here; something passing for candy is offered as *Baby Ruth;* and cigarette snipes are dressed in beat-up *Chesterfield* packs. Girls are permitted inside the Seamen's Club; but their pimps have to wait outside.

I'll only stand around pretending to be a spy fifteen minutes longer. If Concannon doesn't pick me up by then, he's finally gone bamboo.

Here comes an aging slicky-boy with a mug divided between a beetling scowl and a smile, sweet as apple pandowdy, under a frightwig of black-wire hair. How can a mug like this get himself a girl to work for him?

"Number-One Joe! Welcome Club Frisco!"

Pumping of my hand.

He looks like he's been creeping under a fence and part of the wire has stuck to his skull. One side of his face has been paralyzed and the other side survives only by that smile. Well, that's what comes of crawling under other people's barbed wire.

"Long time you gone, Number-One Joe!"

I feel like I've never been away.

"Make yourself home, Number-One Joe! What I got for *you!* A-One quality for Number-One Joe!"

The red, white and blue card he slipped into my hand framed an American sergeant embracing a slant-eyed girl under a palm. Slicky-Boy must have a Los Angeles Branch.

We have very nice girls and all kinds of drinks—try onece, the card informed me.

"Waiting for friend," I explained, returning the card.

"*What* frien' *Who* frien' *Where* frien'? *You* come by Club Frisco, *me* Number-One Joe's good old frien'." He took my arm—a move to which I have an aversion as it makes me feel I'm being pinched. I shook him loose and he looked dumbfounded. How could I walk out on him after he'd been waiting for me so long?

"You *Captain-Ship* now or something, Joe?"

"No," I had to admit, "not Captain. Only passenger."

"Pass-in-*Chair!* O God!" He struck the back of his hand to his forehead at the news. "*Now* you Pass-in-Chair! O, you come longside *me,* Number-One Joe. Pass-in-Chair! I got for *you* A-One Quality Eng-ilsh Pass-in-Chair-gel!" He took me into custody again.

Again I uncustodified myself; and again he didn't like it. He stepped in close and lowered his voice to a stoolie's whisper.

"*What* you like, Joe?"

Talent can spring up anywhere.

"I like you go," I guaranteed him.

"You give dollar, I go," was his counter-offer, "far."

"Give nothing."

"No go far."

His breath was formidable. But if he could stand it all day I could put up with it a few minutes.

Sparks was coming down the other side of the street with his specs in his hand, blind as an owl. I cut over to meet him.

Slicky-Boy Number One, Port of Pusan, came up on Sparks' other side. "Hi, Joe! Me your good old frien'!" Sparks adjusted his specs and looked down.

"Who's your buddy?" he asked me.

"I don't know," I replied, "but he's hard to shake."

Slicky-Boy followed us up to Kim's place, where Sparks blocked him and slammed the door in his face.

He hadn't been hard to shake after all.

Up a narrow stair through a cloud of *kimchi,* past a furlong of doors, all closed. Then an open one and a high, flat warning like a very old woman's cry—

"*Number four-seven-two Cho-Ryang-Dong! Ryang-Dong! Ryang-Dong!*"

It was a purple-black bird, no larger than a crow, perched in a cage big enough for a turkey. In a parlor from some age that was purple; that now had long faded to rose.

A great old-fashioned bed of the curtained kind, stood with its curtains drawn as though they'd been drawn for years. A portable record player and a few chairs: we were home.

"*Ryang-Dong! Ryang-Dong!*" the myna bird shrieked. "*Pay what you like!*"

A slant-eyed little fireship in a green kimono, her dark hair piled, came forward as softly as a Siamese cat. I saw why communications officers go bamboo.

"Him crazy," she nodded at the bird.

"Him not so crazy," I thought to myself.

"Meet Kim," Concannon decided to introduce me.

She gave me both hands so narrow, so firm; in her brief grip I felt a contained pride.

How many a midnight seaman, on leave or on the beach, had she locked fast between those slender thighs? And held till he'd fainted within her? Then had kicked him lightly in the small of the back with her child-like slipper—"Time up, Joe!"

And yet had kept her pride.

How many midnight passages with the robbed drunk sleeping it off and the desk clerk waiting below? How many madams? How many jails? How many slicky-boys? How many blows? Seamen on leave or on the beach, M.P., tourist, policeman and pimp, each had taken his measure of her flesh. Not one had let her go.

In bars where fists are what count most, chance had pitched her, small and weak. She'd made shore on her own strength alone.

"Me speak Eng-ilsh pretty good," Kim assured me, "but not read worth good damn"—she took a record off the player and put a finger on its title—"You tell, please."

The record was *Rock Love,* that I'd first heard in a Chicago bar nearly as old-fashioned as the parlor where I now stood, in 1953.

Kim stood over it as it played, guardedly. The machine was her most precious possession. Music that an American woman can buy for a dollar, she had had to pay for more dearly.

> *You got to have Rock Love*
> *Deep in your heart*

Concannon drew the bed-curtains aside and stretched out like a begoggled bear; the first low snore of Kingfisher (Oklahoma's) greatest lover, rumbled forth. Kim took my hand, led me to a window, raised the shade and pointed down.

"Port of Pusan," she explained.

A line of low roofs shimmered as though oiled; around a pond so stagnant that it gleamed. Thin trails of smoke rose from rooftops toward a moon so low it looked tethered.

"*Kimchi,*" she told me, "are *cook*-ing."

The women of the shacks were cooking *kimchi*. A dog head-down and dreaming of dinner came trotting between the pond and the moon.

Kim raised the window and called, in a silvery twitter, to someone below.

A girl, wearing a babushka, stepped out of a door that sagged on a single hinge. She turned her face up to us and waved; then went back into her sag-door house. Kim drew the shade.

472 CHO-RYANG-DONG **303**

"Port of Pusan," she repeated sorrowfully.

> So *when temptation rocks moves your soul*
> *The rock of love won't let you roll—*

And seamen's voices in the street took up her sorrow, like voices trying to feel happy far from home. I had heard that lonesome pining in voices of farm-boys singing no farther away from home than their town's last street-lamp.

Concannon murmured in sleep. Kim unlaced his boots and took them off without waking him. Concannon wriggled his toes as though dreaming he was walking barefoot in the sandhills again. Then turned on his side, cursing somebody—"*Ahr-ahr-your-ass-I'll take-ahr-ahr-arh-Ho-Phang Road—*" and into a dreaming triumph, I think, of pitching Manning over a rail into heavy seas.

Kim opened a brown paper bag and put it into the birdcage: the bird backed into it.

A light warning tap at the backstair door, and in walked a robust, smiling child, to fling off her babushka with a smile so white it lit the dimness. She was wearing dark bangs and looked as though she had been in town just long enough to shake the rice out of her sandals.

"Po-Tin," Kim introduced her.

"*Pass-in-Chair,*" she added.

Kim poured a shot of Scotch for me and another for Po-Tin. The country girl wrinkled her country nose: a mere nub of a nose as noses go.

"Wee-skee, no good," Po-Tin explained, "*Coca-cola, good.*" Her breasts were so full that their nipples indented the thin cloth of her sweater. All she wore, it appeared, was the sweater, a blue-belted skirt of dark red, and sandals. She drew a small fan out of the belt and came to me, smiling self-consciously while spreading the fan. I took it from her and put it aside. It didn't fit either the scene or herself. On my lap she cocked her head.

"*Pass-in-Chair?*"—and glanced at Kim for enlightenment.

"Him not work longside ship. Him pay money for just ride. Him sit in chair. Captain-Ship bring him *kimchi*," Kim explained authoritatively.

I finally got it: A passenger was one who passed over sea seated in a chair. Po-Tin studied me incredulously.

"You pay Captain-Ship for just *ride?*"

The American millionaire assented smugly.

She put an arm around my neck.

"You give Po-Tin much dollar?"

I held an American dime to the light, then put it between her breasts. Po-Tin giggled.

Then, lifting her arms above her head, she invited me to raise the sweater. It came off easily. The dime rolled onto the floor. Concannon's mug came through the curtains, his eyes filmed by sleep, struck out one paw and the dime rolled into it. It was like seeing an outfielder, blinded by sun, stick out his glove to let a line-drive smack into it.

The milky beauty on my lap felt no more self-consciousness about her breasts than she did about her ears. She poked a forefinger into my chest.

"Pass-in-Chair, you take Po-Tin longside ship? You take Po-Tin Ny-agara Fall by Cal-ifornia? Me cook for you. Me no make bad-business by Ny-agara Fall, Cal-ifornia."

Concannon reared, put on his specs, fixed his sightline and stared.

"Looks like we've *all* gone bamboo," he decided. And fell back to a snoring sleep with that dime still clutched in his paw.

> *When storm-winds blow and the waters shift*
> *The rock of love won't let you drift.*

From the depths of her green kimono, Kim brought up a narrow cigarette wrapped in brown paper and dragged on it deeply. Its odor, so poignant, flowered the dark and heavy air like a flurry of scented confetti. She passed it to Po-Tin.

Po-Tin put the stick to my lips; I closed my eyes and drew deep.

Nothing happened. Not a thing.

I turned it to Po-Tin's mouth and she dragged on it solemnly.

Her eyelids fluttered, as one viewing a more distant scene. Then a shutter fell across her vision. I took this phenomenal snipe from her lips and tried once again.

Nothing. Nothing *whatsoever.*

The girl against my chest let her arms drop loosely across my shoulders: my Smiling Child was stoned.

And her breath, that was sweet, fled across my cheek. And her breast swelled tight to the cup of my hand; like a small animal preparing itself for rest.

Girls, I thought, those with hair like light and those with hair darkly piled; girls, I thought, with smiles still expectant and those with no smile left at all; girls, I thought, whether in sleep or waking, lips parted in wonder or suddenly laughing: girls have a hard time of it everywhere.

The air grew weighted and all times felt troubled. For all ports with low-burning lights awaited a long ship low to the waters.

A long ship far out, moving without lights, through the fogs of the East China Sea: seeking its final dock. All voyages were now done.

All the lowball games at sea and all the poker hands had been played; at sea or on the beach. The gambler lay in the gambling-room. Cards were still scattered across the floor. The seaman slept beside his whore. The farm-child wakened beside its mother-and saw the lights of passing cars move across the ceiling.

Someone was standing on the other side of the door.

The room had gone cold, and the half-naked girl on my lap was pressing against me for warmth. Someone kept trying the latch.

Someone is always trying the other side of somebody's door, I thought, slipping back into darkness and fog. Someone is always trying somebody's latch.

When I came awake, later, it was because Kim was rocking Po-Tin awake. The girl's head was lolling like a child's.

"Ny-agara Fall by Cal-ifornia," she murmured.

I put her on her feet, snatched Concannon's bottle and held her against me down the dark backstairs, following Kim with a flashlight.

Kim held us back at the door while she went out into the warren of *kimchi* shacks and clotheslines stretched across the moon. Po-Tin put her hand on the back of my neck, while we waited in the darkness, and pressed my nape. Her fingers were strong.

"Come," Kim told us.

Po-Tin led me by the hand. She walked under a clothesline without stooping—it caught me across my forehead and I stumbled across a sleeping hog; that grunted and ran away. The girl laughed softly in the *kimchi* gloom.

She lived in a little *kimchi* house with an earthen floor, where *kimchi* mice ran in and out in the light of a *kimchi* moon. Incense cut the odor of *kimchi* while she undressed in the dark.

Po-Tin stood by the window a moment in the light of Asia's moon; a girl all smoky gold with hair like the sleeping sea.

Then she came toward me.

When I wakened the moon had set. What was I doing in Asia?

Upon other wakenings far from home, in a tent pitched on a German racetrack, in the bow of a Greek fishing boat or on a rooftop in Fez, I'd known what I was doing there. This time I could find no other reason than that I didn't want to be at home.

And what troubled Concannon so about going bamboo? What was wrong with bamboo-root for the man with no roots at all? I drew the sleeping girl to me. She pressed herself hard against me without waking. Her lips parted as her breath came harder, yet she didn't waken. Then took me in, so warm and so deep that I was glad I hadn't stayed at home.

I dreamt I was searching around a pond that was strangely still, for some flower that grows only under water. I was about to find it when I felt myself heaved bodily and wakened coming down on my face.

It was morning and Po-Tin was being playful. Naked as she had slept, she hurled herself like a small bear upon me. Despite a fifty-pound weight advantage, it was all I could do to keep from being pinned disgracefully. Yet, every time I squirmed out from under her, she butted me in the side.

Sensing my irritation at being unable to overpower her, she relaxed long enough to permit me to pin her. Then lay, smiling up, her long eyes glistening.

"What got into *you?*" I asked the little brute.

"I happy," she told me.

Well, what do you know.

Breakfast consisted of two cups of instant coffee, black. She was out of milk. She was out of sugar.

Orange juice: out. Cereal: out. Fried eggs with bacon curling: out. Toast, marmalade, wheatcakes, butter and cream: out.

Out like her checking account. Out like her social security. Out like her life insurance and her driver's license. Out like her electric lighting, her inside plumbing and running water; her morning paper and her diner's card. Out like her books, like her records; like her carpeting, curtains, music, and mail.

Lovely as she was by moonlight, I decided not to live with Po-Tin until the Westernization of Korea had gotten farther along.

The G.I. blanket under which we'd slept looked like it had been recaptured at Hill 29. A pair of G.I. combat boots, recently shined, stood in a corner. Somebody had been trying to reassemble a radio out of the parts of a half dozen shattered sets—and Po-Tin didn't seem to be mechanically inclined.

She clutched the ten-dollar bill I'd given her between her palms, in the manner of a child pleased at a gift yet secretly fearing it is going to be snatched away from her. I hoped Kim would catch her another trick before the tenner was gone.

"You come back, take me longside Ny-agara Fall, Cal-ifornia," she instructed me.

I poured a farewell shot of Concannon's Scotch.

"When I come back," I promised her.

I found my way across the slum where pigs slept below clotheslines and American tires, stripped of rubber, lay like ruined expatriates. Then, remembering I'd forgotten Concannon's bottle, cut back across the yard.

The door was shut. Po-Tin didn't answer my knock. I walked in all the same.

The bottle was on the table. Slicky-Boy sat on the edge of our bed smoothing my ten-spot across his knee. Po-Tin sat in a crashed-in heap at his feet, touching a dab of cotton to her mouth. Her lip had been split.

I snatched the ten-spot, wadded it, and flung it to a far corner of the room. Don't ask me why.

Slicky-Boy stared up with his jaw hanging. Then he looked down at his knee, where the bill had just been; and saw it wasn't there any more. Po-Tin scrambled across the floor on her hands and knees, snatched it and raced to Slicky-Boy with it; where she unwadded it across his knee.

There must be *some* way of getting out of this.

Slicky-Boy took the bottle from my hand, drank, and returned it to me.

"You got cigarette, Joe?" he asked.

He took the pack from my hand, extracted one; then pocketed the pack.

"Oh *man*," his heavy look warned me, "you *are* so *wrong*."

Kim came in looking for Concannon's bottle, saw Po-Tin on the floor, and began giving Slicky-Boy holy hell.

I didn't know what she was saying, but it was plain she was cussing him out. She took the bottle from me, poured a drop on her handkerchief, dabbed Po-Tin's broken lip with it. Po-Tin made small peeping noises.

Suddenly, Slicky-Boy began dissenting from Kim's condemnation and pointing toward me.

"What's he saying?" I asked.

"You *Captain-Ship?*" she asked me.

"No," I told her.

"Him say? *Yes,* you *Captain*-Ship, take Po-Tin longside you by Ny-agara Fall, Cal-ifornia. He say you no take Po-Tin without you take he too."

"Okay, I'm the captain, and I'm not going to take either one."

Kim translated.

Slicky-Boy looked at me sullenly.

"You no Number-One, Joe," was his verdict—"you Number Six! Number Nine! Fourteen!"

And on that deadly insult I left.

Yet all across the littered slum I heard him crying derisively behind me—"Number-Nineteen-Joe! Twenty-Eight! Hey! Number-Sixty-Joe!"

I felt like Number-One-Hundred-Joe.

EAST CHINA SEA

"My head may be on sidewise," Smith was acknowledging some jibe without anger, "but it's got the best nose on it on *this* ship. How do you think I got to be a smeller for Some People's Gas if I couldn't smell gas where nobody else could?"

"One day you're an ex-fighter, the next you're an ex-smeller," I professed to be skeptical. He let his neck out one notch.

"As a matter of fact, in my case the two trades were directly connected, sir," he assured me—"it so happened in the army that a certain First Sergeant took such a dislike to me I couldn't get off K.P. So I beefed to the Battery Commander I was being taken advantage of. 'Have you done any fighting?' he asked me. I sensed he had something in mind. 'Not professionally, sir,' I told him, 'but I never minded hitting somebody with my fists if it was alright with the other fellow.' 'Would you like to try your hand at inter-battalion fighting?' he asked me. 'I'll go where I'm needed most, sir,' I answered promptly."

"How'd you make out?" I encouraged him.

"I won my first two fights on knockouts as they were both with fellows from California. Which came to me as a complete surprise, as I'd never been in a fight where I didn't get hit myself before. It dawned on me that I'd hit on a way of staying off K.P. as long as they didn't match me with anybody from outside of Los Angeles. As luck would have it, my third match was with a fellow from West Virginia. 'If you can hold him to a draw I'll see you make Pfc,' the Second Lieutenant promised me. 'What do I get if I decision him, sir?' I asked. 'Acting Corporal,' the man came through. I didn't dare ask what would happen if I knocked the fellow out—I didn't feel I was ready for a responsibility like *that*."

"What happened, Smith?"

"What happened when?" he regarded me absently.

"When you fought the fellow from West Virginia."

"O, *that,*" he returned from whatever cloud he'd been on, "he broke my nose in the first round but I didn't know it till the bell rang for the last round. Then I sneezed and some fragments of bone blew out of my right ear. One hit the ref and he thought I'd done it a-purpose and give the West Virginia fellow the fight right there."

The story seemed to be over.

"What did that have to do with being a smeller for Some People's Gas?" I prodded him.

"O, that led directly *into* it. When I came up for discharge they told me I was entitled to a free operation so I would be able to breathe like a civilian, and the doc did such a good job, cleaning out my nose, that when I got back in civvies I found I could smell things I could never smell before—or that anybody else had ever smelled, for that matter. I could tell the smell of apples from the smell of pears from across the street of a vegetable store. I could smell the difference between a tomcat and his old lady. Put glue in a paste bottle and paste in a glue bottle and I could tell you you had those bottles mixed. I could smell things that you'd think didn't smell: Cardboard. Sawdust. Stamps. When I'd get on a street car— *Wow!* People smell strongest of all. In bars I got so I could tell whether it was Schlitz or Pabst in the schooner. Once a bartender bet me I couldn't tell bourbon from sour mash, and I won the bet—and one day—it was in the same bar—I told him he had a gas leak. Nobody else could smell it but me. I had to find it to prove myself, and I found it—his refrigerator. He called Some People's Gas and the guy they sent out couldn't smell it till I put his nose right *in* it. 'With a nose like that you ought to be on my job,' he told me. 'How much do you make?' I asked him. He got paid good. I went down there and they put me on as an apprentice smeller. But I rose through the ranks faster than I did in the army, and didn't have to get into a ring with anybody from West Virginia neither. I was there six months when I had my big success."

He was gone again, gazing at some far horizon through the open port.

"You were saying you had a big success with Some People's Gas," I reminded him when he looked ready to return.

"Why, the way it was with Some People's Gas was like this: sometimes I had to crawl around a roof and sometimes I had to crawl under the street. Sometimes I had to make a hole in a floor and hang upside-down. Sometimes I had to scale a wall and sometimes I had to fight off dogs. One night, toward closing time, I was under a filling station looking for a screwdriver I'd put down and couldn't locate, when I smelled gas. It was a new station, using bottled gas, and the bottles weren't leaking. I couldn't find the leak, but I reported it.

"Now, they got *Historians* at Some People's Gas that can't smell bananas from noodle-soup, but they know every inch of pipe ever laid down in Seattle, and they gave the report to one of these Gasified Historians. He looked at his histories, he studied all the maps, and the report came back: No gas main ever laid in that area. 'That wasn't southern fried chicken I smelled,' I told them in the office.

"The next Sunday morning the apartment building next to the station blew up, with a wedding party going on on the third floor. The bride was blown to bits, the bridegroom was maimed for life, the best man had a leg blown off and one of the bridesmaids got her spine snapped in two.

"I owe it all to that army doctor who done such a good job operating on me. I give him full credit."

"You must have gotten a pretty good raise," I suggested.

Smith began to revolve his head gently, trying to decide whether I was serious.

"Not exactly," he told me, "I got fired the next week for intermeddling with Department of Gas Historians."

JULY 6TH

SOUTH CHINA SEA, TWO DAYS FROM THE PORT OF HONGKONG. DINGDING, HINKLETINKLE, THE FINKIFIED LASAGNA AND THE MAN TOO TIMID TO DAMN.

I once went to New York for the skating at Rockefeller Plaza and was sharpening my skates when the telephone rang. A woman's voice, sounding like a cross between a crow's and a barbed-wire fence, informed me, "Alfred Bovine would like you for dinner."

"I don't blame him," I assured this charmer, and hung up. The phone rang right back.

"Don't you *like* lasagna?" the same voice inquired.

Realizing that Bovine had altered his plan of attack, I went down to the lobby with my skates under my arm.

They were waiting for me. I didn't place him right off, but he had the air of a pool-hustler who works days in an embalming parlor. He liked me too.

All the way to the restaurant they took turns recommending the lasagna.

"I'm a meat-eating mouse," I had to let them know.

We entered one of those Italian joints where all the waiters look like they want another crack at Ethiopia.

"Three orders of lasagna," Bovine decided.

"I'll eat anything that won't eat me," I corrected him, "but I draw the line at the cheese-and-flour route. Give me an oyster stew, filet mignon rare with several well-chosen champignons."

A lull like the grating of pebbles being dragged, against their common will, by an ebbing wave, ensued; yet the place was two miles from the sea.

"What do *you* do?" I asked the blonde just to see if she did anything but recommend lasagna.

"I work at Doubleday," she told me, "but I don't like it. Nobody laughs at Doubleday."

I could see how things might work out that way. "They laugh at Random," I assured her.

"I don't see anything funny in *that,*" she assured me.

"I didn't think it was anything riotous myself," I had to admit. "I just thought it was better than sitting around looking at one another. After all, I'm not Zero Mostel."

"I wish you were," she told me.

"I wish you were Dorothy Loudon myself," I told her resignedly, "but there are people in hell who'd like ice-water too."

Bovine was chomping lasagna as though cheese were going out of style. If there was going to be any further conversation I'd have to make it. I'd finally placed him as a distributor of well-packaged precepts whom a friend of mine had once described as "too timid to damn and too stingy to applaud." But all that had been before my time.

"Have you seen any plays here?" he asked me. There was a dab of lasagna on his chin.

"I saw one about a fellow in jail," I recalled, "that reminded me of a fellow named Hinkle, who was once doing time in the machine shop at Jefferson City. He began eating bolts, nuts and washers with the notion that if he got enough metal inside himself he'd get sent to the dispensary. He got so much junk inside him that you could hear him tinkle when he walked, so the other cons called him Hinkletinkle. When they put him under the X-ray there was so much metal inside him they had to operate and the operation was a success."

"What is the point?" the lady inquired.

"Why, the operation was a success because the warden said 'We're transferring Hinkletinkle to the mental ward—'mental,' not 'metal,' and I thought that was pretty good for a warden. Though I admit," I added hurriedly, "it isn't nearly as comical as the time when Judge J. Daniel Dingding tried a kid for getting out the hook-and-ladder on a false alarm."

"I'm doing a *critique* on Hemingway for *Commentary*," Bovine let me know. "Where are the *great* writers?"

"I read your papers on the Failure of Steinbeck, the Failure of Faulkner, the Failure of Fitzgerald, the Failure of Wolfe, and the Success of Irving Shulman," I filled him in. "I can hardly wait to read this one."

"All the great ones are gone," he mourned.

Somebody had put an oyster stew in front of me.

"There was this Chicago judge we called Dingding," I continued, "because once, long before he was elected to the bench, he'd turned in a false fire-alarm and gotten the hook-and-ladder dashing about looking for something on fire; only there wasn't anythng on fire. They couldn't do anything much about it except put him on probation and keep him away from matches because he was under-age. Dingding promised never to pull another firebox, and was so true to his word they made him a judge; and he has kept his word to this very day. To this day, if Dingding says he'll dismiss a case for five hundred dollars, he'll *dismiss* it."

"Your stew is getting cold," the lady told me.

"Wait till I finish the story," I promised her. "You'll howl. Because even though His Honor doesn't pull fireboxes any more, he still thinks like a man who'd like to own his very own hook-and-ladder—you ought to have heard him holler at this kid accused of setting fire to a school. 'We have to keep Chicago strong and America mighty! Bury this terrorist! Hard labor! No parole! Take him away!' But the kid jumped up and hollered as loud as Dingding, 'Your Honor! This case has been fixed'—and his lawyer jumped up and knocked the kid down right there in court!

"'*What* did he say?' Dingding asked the kid's lawyer.

"'Your Honor, he said 'I'm only a kid from the sticks,' the lawyer answered as quick as that. Dingding looked at his bailiff and the bailiff gave Dingding a wink.

"'In view of the defendant's extreme youth and it being a first offense we recommend mercy and suspend sentence until after lunch,' Dingding announced, 'go and sin no more.'"

"There's nothing funny in that either," the lady felt.

"But that isn't the end of the story," I explained to her, "because when the lawyer took this kid home and told his father what the kid had jumped up and said, the father knocked the kid down too."

"So?" she asked.

"So that same evening the bailiff dropped by and talked to the boy more like a father than the boy's own father.

"'I feel so bitter about being knocked down in public,' the boy told the bailiff.

"'Well,' the bailiff told him, 'we're in private now'—and knocked the kid down *again!*"

"Are you making this up as you go along?" she wanted to know.

"Well, Dingding came in later, wanting to know what the bailiff thought he was trying to get away with fixing a case behind his back, and the bailiff said he'd been afraid to mention it because he was afraid Dingding would be furious at the idea of fixing a case. 'I don't blame you,' Dingding acknowledged, 'I like a good thief—but a man who'd pull a fire-alarm in cold passion'—and he swung around and hit that poor kid so hard the kid went out cold right there on his own parlor floor."

"What *is* the point?" the lady demanded to know.

I looked at the last lonesome oyster in my stewless, drained and drying bowl. And the oyster looked back up as baffled as myself.

"The point is that, when it came *his* turn, Dingding hit the kid harder than anybody," I explained.

"What did you think of the play you saw?" Bovine asked.

"It was by an Irishman who'd spent eight years in an English prison," I recalled—"It was about Capital Punishment."

"O, this killing, killing, killing," Bovine grieved, "O Castro! Enough violence! Enough killing!"

"I just can't see how *anyone* can object to capital punishment for traitors," the lady sailed in.

"They used to hang eleven-year-olds for sheepstealing," I remembered reading, "but it didn't put a stop to sheepstealing."

"I wasn't talking about *stealing*," she corrected me, "I was talking about *treason*."

"A person's habits are pretty well formed by the time he's old enough to be a spy," I decided to go along with her, "now if they'd string up a couple of ten-year-olds for snitching as a preventive measure, it would put a short quick stop to selling atomic secrets later. And there'd be more sheep for the rest of us. As it is there's hardly enough to go around."

Conversation somehow slowed down after that, being mostly about whether Theodore Dreiser was a Great *Great* Writer or just a pretty good old sport. I maintained that the pen is mightier than the sword.

Then, having disposed of the filet, I took a toothpick and began trying to pry my gums loose.

"Put that *away!*" the lady commanded me.

I'd *thought* that would get her.

I went to work so furiously that a fragment of filet pirouetted off the toothpick and taxied in on Bovine's spumoni. The lady was halfway to the door before, half into his coat, Bovine caught up with her. I had just time to grab my skates and catch up with them both as they went through the door, wedging the three of us tightly for one moment. Then the wedge broke, they fled into a waiting cab and wheeled off trailing a scent of finkified cheese.

A light snow was falling. I stood alone but for my toothpick and skates. Somewhere down on Sixth Avenue a siren wailed.

Making me wonder whether Dingding's disappointment wasn't the same as that of any critic, or critic's mistress, for whom all triumphant hook-and-ladders fade.

Until nothing is left along cold streets where nothing can ever catch fire again.

I understood why the critic preferred dead writers to living ones.

CONCANNON GETS THE SHIP IN TROUBLE
or
ASSY-END UP ON HO-PHANG ROAD

The blood on my shirt is not my own. It never worked for me. It was last employed by Manning. If he wants it back all he has to do is to wring out the shirt.

Manning won't be wringing anything out of anything until the swelling below his left eye subsides. Has anyone informed you that Communications Officers have *very* fast hands?

Traveler! You too can be the only man aboard sporting a Kowloon Shiner! A fast bust in the face, delivered with all the elements of total surprise, can be yours without provocation. Southeast Asia has the action because everybody coagulates faster there. Even children coagulate. Anything goes in a free-trade port.

Kowloon was the town for Japanese transistors and Ho-Phang Road was the street for lovely girls. We would find a bar leaping with merriment was THE PLAN: There Quong and I would wait while Concannon purchased transistors for one-third of what we would be able to sell them for in Bombay.

Time was of the essence. The *Malaysia Mail* would stand off Hongkong for four hours, including the minutes that would be taken by the ship's shore-launch. So Concannon asked the driver to put in at Kowloon when we boarded the launch. The motor was going when Manning climbed in. Nobody had sent for him: he just climbed in.

"We're not going to Hongkong," Concannon told him. "We're going to Kowloon."

Manning didn't reply. He just sat at the end of the launch by himself. It looked as if he had it in mind to follow us around Kowloon to see whether we were buying Japanese transistors.

Concannon was our leader. Transistors was our mission. Lovely girls would be our reward. But how was Quong, who sometimes took as long as half an hour to fall in love, going to find time to fall in love twice in Kowloon? If he didn't it would be the first port in which he would fall in love only once. Concannon, of course, held the ship's record by falling in love five times in two hours. But there was a fifteen-minute limit in that whorehouse.

"You don't have a wife in every port because you're a seaman," I reminded him, but he cut me short.

"You've used that bit before," he told me dryly.

When we stepped onto the Public Pier, the heat hit us straight out of the airless vault of a Chinese slum—and straight down into that vault we went.

Multitudes: multitudes: haulers of carts and bearers of water, bicyclists, pedicabs, taxis, drivers of jeeps, honking vendors of fish in a heat the hue of a yellow dream. Ho-Phang Road lay between tenement terraces festooned with clothes drying in the scorching air.

Concannon milled ahead of us. Sparks never picked a boulevard to stroll when there was an alley to prowl. He wasn't content simply to make his way somewhere—if he didn't have to force his way he was unsatisfied. We had to hurry to keep the crown of his head, where the hair had thinned, in view. His object being to lose Manning, he dodged into a bar under a sign that said: *The Lion of Kowloon.*

A wave of cold air rushed over me as soon as the door shut behind me. After the murderous heat of the street, this air-conditioning felt like a plunge into a pool for seals. When the dimness lifted I looked around.

The whores of that cave were waxen horrors transfixed by times long gone. One Chinese hooker loomed so huge, flesh enfolding flesh, that her eyes began melting helplessly as her belly began to swell. Beside her sat one so gaunt that her shadow had bones. I felt the wind of a cold depravity.

A Japanese girl on a bar-stool in a bright dirndl swung about darting her pink tongue-tip at me and then smilingly spread her legs. She wasn't more than sixteen and her dress was high on her black-mesh thighs. The Lion of Kowloon growled low. We took seats either side of her.

A Japanese seaman left a drink standing to come over, take the girl by her arm and lead her out. Protectiveness turns fast to love.

His move left the cave looking more like a wax museum than ever.

"This looks worse than Korea," I accused Quong, "you told me things were going to get better."

"Wait," Quong promised me.

"Wait for *what?*"

Quong, out of the memory of his seaborne years, began searching for some port where I would be happier.

"*Sitagong!*"—he hit on it—"Ooo-ooo—When you get to Sitagong! *Muts* better gel, Sitagong."

"*Really* better in Chittagong, Quong?"

"*Betta? Ooo-ooo!* Pretty gel come *get* you in Sitagong! Very pretty Sitagong gel take you home! Sit on lap! Fan you! Kiss-kiss! *Ooo-ooo*—How pretty Sitagong gel kiss-kiss!"

"How much is this going to cost me, Quong?" I inquired calmly.

"*Cost* you?" He looked at me incredulously. "Not cost *you.* Sitagong gel, she not *like* Pakistani man—*American man for Sitagong gel!*" He started swinging his right hand over his head as though he were pitching for a girl's indoor softball club; and a girl took the bar-stool next to mine as if she wanted to play catcher. Quong whispered into my ear, "*And* give you bath! Put you in perfume-bubboo! She get in perfume-bubboo *with* you!"

"Quong!" I tried to stop him by sternness. "You aren't expecting me to believe that this girl is going to get into the bath *with* me?"

"Sure!" he insisted. "Very pretty sixteen-year-old Sitagong gel, she get in, scrub back, you foat."

"I *float?*"

"Sure, when she hit you on head, you foat. Assy-end up you foat."

I got to my feet. "Why should she hit me on the head for God's sake?"

"Wha' *for?* For take you pants. For take you shoe. For take you money. Hit one time real good you foat down River Tsangpo." He threw back his head in a Chinese convulsion and almost fell off the bar-stool. "Assy-end up! Assy-end up in River Tsangpo!"

The humor of the Oriental is apparently based upon the superstition that, no matter how preposterous a premise, mere repetition entails comedy. Although I could visualize a corpse floating down the River Tsangpo I failed to see that it was funny if it were mine. Assy-end up indeed! I turned to face the girl who'd joined us.

"What the hell *you* laughing at?" I asked this fool.

"My name Suzi," was her stupid reply.

"Where you from?" I asked her magnanimously.

"Sumatra."

"Meet Suzi Sumatra," I introduced her to Quong, "Frank's sister."

Now, if any, was the moment for hilarity.

Nobody laughed.

"Buy Lady-Drink?" Suzi—she had eyes of taximeter brown—inquired.

"She wants you to buy her a drink," I assured Quong.

"Lady-Drink," Suzi insisted. And what do you know, the bartender already had it poured!

I tasted it. Suzi drank it. Quong paid for it. It was my turn to buy.

"Short-term?" Suzi asked, "long-term?"

"This girl has fallen in love with you," I assured Quong, and left the pair of them to make a closer inspection of the whores of Ho-Phang Road.

One woman was so thin I paused to see whether she was a vertebrate. She thought I was flirting but all I was doing was trying to see whether she was held together by wire or string.

Lashes by *Maybelline,* talc by *PX—Even in the dark you know.* She wore one earring of amber and one of jade. Those things have a way of working loose in bed. Then you try to match one of each as best you can. For a ghost she had attractive cheekbones.

"Me Alina," she told me so tenderly that I decided to buy her a drink if she could swallow. "Two beers," I instructed the waiter.

"Wee-skee," my tender ghost corrected me.

I looked for marks on her arms but she didn't have veins. We went to a table. Quong and Suzi left to find short-term happiness.

What I found so winning about Alina was her combination of unearthly reflexes with a deathlike pallor. "Must be on muggles," I thought. But where could she hide a pipe beneath her dress without poking out some honest seaman's eye? If she weren't sniffing cocaine she must be taking heroin in her earlobes. It would have been nice to have found an opium-eater; but old-fashioned girls are hard to find.

Yet it has to be admitted that Kleenex, flesh-colored talcum and sixteen-gauge hypodermic needles have improved hygiene in free-trade ports. A girl who used to have to sneak down to a dirty opium pad at risk of her social standing, can now carry a sixteen-gauge hypodermic needle manufactured in New Jersey, in tissue manufactured in Ohio, and keep herself presentable on heroin brought in by American seamen. The exchanging of the poppy for the hype has brought the Orient closer to the Free World. More than one opium den has been swept out and now boasts a neon sign, saying MOM'S GOOD EATS; where you can get anything from redbirds to yellow jackets.

"Me Nepal gel," my ghost informed me. I had to keep an eye on the door for Concannon.

"Nepal gel very strong," she added, "make good pong-pong."

"You don't look too strong," I had to tell her.

"In Nepal me no make The Bad Busyness," Alina explained, "Bad Busyness no good for Nepal gel."

"How long you do Bad Busyness?" I asked just to get a line on her age. She looked so young yet so old.

She studied her fingers and finally held up two: "By Railroad Station, Madras, two year." She held up another: "By Suklaji Street, Bombay, one year. Me get sick, go home Nepal, one year." Now all she had left was one thumb.

"You tell," she asked me, "in your country, do priest kiss priest?"

"Why do you ask *that?*" was all I could think to answer.

She took it for confirmation of what must have been an old suspicion. "My country best," she decided, "there we don't know *anything.*"

When who walks through the door but The Unacknowledged Champion of Everything, Ship's Fink W. McAdoo Manning. And headed right for our table.

"Meet Miss Sumatra," I invited him.

Nobody laughed again.

"The ship-launch leaves in an hour," Manning informed me. "I just wanted to check it out with you."

He just wanted to get me out of the Lion of Kowloon, that was all.

"I'm waiting for the radio officer," I explained.

"Do you consider *him* reliable?" he asked me at the precise moment that Concannon, loaded with boxes, bottles and bags, loomed in the doorway.

"*Very* reliable," I told Manning.

Concannon began ambling about in the dimness—his eyes were weak even in the light of day. I guided him to our table. Manning waited until

Concannon had dumped his packages on the table. I knew he hadn't yet seen Manning.

Suzi and Quong returned. That had been *really* short-term.

"*Loot!*" Alina cried happily. "*Loot! Loot!*"

"You're going to get the ship in trouble, Concannon," Manning spoke at last.

Concannon surveyed him without surprise.

"Are you coming?" Manning asked me sternly. He couldn't get over the idea that I was his charge.

I didn't answer. Yet he waited.

Sparks embraced both girls and kissed each in turn. Revulsion shadowed Manning's face like a wind rippling water. Why didn't the man leave?

A waiter came whizzing around the bar with a tray of drinks. Alina poured the gin.

Concannon extracted a transistor from one of the boxes, pulled out the aerial, and a hillbilly voice came droning in from some army base—

> *All the good times are past 'n gone*
> *All the good times are o'er*

Manning left in a high-wheeled huff. He actually thought the good times were o'er.

Concannon didn't think so. The whores of Ho-Phang Road didn't seem to think so. I'm sure *I* didn't think so. Alina sat on my lap.

"You look out," Quong told me, smiling his everlasting smile, "you not wait to foat in River Tsangpo—you foat, *here*."

I didn't know what Quong was driving at.

"He means the slouch at the bar," Concannon informed me casually, "that's *his* old lady on your lap."

The Slouch, across Alina's shoulder, looked like one of those men so ineffectual you think he's English until his accent sounds Greek; and sure enough, he turns out to be Italian. I rotated Alina's skull toward him.

"Who *him?*" I inquired fluently, and unrotated the head.

She giggled Chineasily.

"Him nutty-nut," she told me. The Slouch came over with a slouching motion.

"I am *sea*-man," he told us, and we had to take his word even though he looked like he'd been putting in more time trailing John Gielgud than swabbing decks. Nonetheless I asked him to sit down and nonetheless he coldly declined. It wasn't, apparently, roaring good fellowship he was after in the Lion of Kowloon.

"May I have con-were-sation?" he requested me politely—putting this down with an injured air.

"Sure," I let him know.

"*Private* con-were-sation, if you please," he asked me.

I put Alina down and followed The Slouch into a stockroom back of the bar. I let him slouch in first. It was dark in there.

I followed.

"I am not *offended*," he assured me, "I wish all Americans to have joyous time."

I'll just bet you do.

"Good time, happy time"—and he gave me his hand as though he'd completed his message. Then he choked up, twitched, clasped his hands and unclasped them.

"My fiancée," he finally came out with it, "*good* woo-min."

"*Alina?*" I asked. "You wish me to enjoy myself but *not* with Alina?"

That I'd gotten the message relieved him; while his admission of jealousy left him more miserable than ever.

I didn't tell him that I'd invited her to have a drink only because I feel sorry for ghosts in need of somebody to haunt. I'd had no idea she was haunting *him*. He held my arm.

"A *great* woo-min!" He dropped his voice to a confidential whisper—"*Do not offer her money—you will only wound her feelings.*"

By making a determined effort, I felt I could suppress the impulse to hand Alina my wallet and watch. My lust for his hipless, breastless, stenciled, penciled, pseudo-Caucasian heroin-head was also governable.

"Our ship leaves in an hour," I informed him, putting my hand on his shoulder reassuringly, "may the shoes never be made that'll walk over your grave."

"The past is done," he announced as if, were it not for him, it would still be here. "What she once was she no longer is!" If it was Alina he was talking about that was a change for the worse, it seemed to me.

We returned to our table linked arm in arm.

"Wh*ee*-sk*ee!*" he demanded loudly, "wh*ee*-sk*ee!*" and a waiter came whizzing with a bottle and glasses.

"To Alina!" The Slouch raised his glass, and we all raised ours but Alina.

"Me no drink longside nutty-nut," she told us.

"He's jealous of you," I urged her, "he wants to marry you."

The thin crimson line of Alina's lips broke into a grin.

Her teeth had gone bad.

"*Me* no marry nutty-nut. *Him* no give Alina money. Him all the time say *pong-pong, pong-pong*—but him no pay one goddamn dollar! Me say, 'Go longside ship, nutty-nut, I make *busyness*—him say 'love, *pong-pong*, love, *pong-pong*'"—she threw a slanty glance at him with sufficient fury— then drank to him all the same.

Concannon began heaping the packages. We had just time to make the ship.

The Slouch liked the idea of our leaving so much he helped to speed us to the dock. When Alina picked up a shopping bag, he took its other handle. He wanted to be certain we wouldn't abduct her.

This pair were leading the loot parade, Concannon toting the gin, Quong the Scotch and Suzi and I bringing up the rear with the transistors, when the door opened from the outside and here was Manning blocking our way again.

"I *can't* let you get the ship in trouble, Concannon," he announced.

Concannon put his bottles down and, with ominous care, rested his hands on Manning's shoulders.

"*That* won't do you any good," Manning assured him confidently.

Concannon spun him aside, picked up the bottles, and again led us forth. It *had* done some good after all.

"The old man is going to hear about this!" Manning warned us. "This isn't the end of this!"

We fell inside the cab every which way. I had Alina on my lap and Concannon had Suzi Sumatra upon his and Quong was sitting on somebody that couldn't be anybody but The Slouch.

"To the docks!" our leader ordered and toward the docks we wheeled.

"*Looooot!*" my mascaraed ghost cried out, her head poking out of the window to the throngs of Ho-Phang Road—"*Looooot! Looooot!*"—while The Slouch fingered the hem of her skirt secretly, poor slouch.

"I hope the sonofabitch misses the ship," was Concannon's only reference to the purser we'd left behind us.

Riksha and trolley, bus and jeep swerved, skidded and reeled, beggars
fled and an American seaman threw beer cans at us. "*Big fis' in river!*"
Quong threatened him. A policeman whistled, fire broke out in a tenement and a Chinese child waved goodbye to us with a blue balloon.

Goodbye to the girls of Ho-Phang Road, goodbye to all wives left on
the beach, goodbye to all Slouches madly in love and all Americans gone
bamboo. Goodbye to Hum Hong Bay and the Chinese Y.M.C.A., the
Kowloon Cricket Club and the Yaumati Vehicular Ferry. Goodbye to
ancestral Kowloon and farewell to old Hongkong. I'm glad I saw your
waxen whores may I never see them again.

The shore-launch was rocking at the dock. Suzi and Alina rushed the
bags into the launch—and then sat down for the shore-to-ship ride. The
Slouch tried to climb in beside Alina.

"Nutty-nut go home!" Alina cried out, so I shoved him back onto the
dock—now here comes Manning breathing hard. As he clambered in he
took command.

"Let's *go!*" he demanded of the driver—yet the driver wouldn't go.

"Letty go!" Quong commanded him too.

Yet he wouldn't go.

"What's he waiting for?" Concannon asked.

"He wants pay," Quong explained.

"Company pays for ship-to-shore transportation," Concannon remembered.

"The company launch went to Hongkong," Manning reminded us,
"you went to Kowloon."

Manning was right. Manning was *always* right. I paid the driver.

"You fuckin' purser," Concannon told Manning.

"Nobody calls *me* a fuckin'—" Manning began and Concannon
hooked a short right to his face. Instead of pulling back, Manning doubled forward with his forearms across his head, leaving himself wide open.
Concannon slammed his left into the stomach and Manning went face-
down, his arms still quaintly protecting his ears. Bottom up and face
bleeding onto the boards, Manning looked like a fish whose gills have
been ripped.

Concannon began kicking.

Alina came at him with her spindling arms straight out, her face still a mask—the boat lurched and Concannon teetered.

I got between him and Manning.

"You won," I announced. "See?" I asked Suzi and Quong, "*See?* Sparks won!"

Suzi turned her face toward the dock as though regretting having left it. Quong looked solemn.

"*You* stay out of this," Concannon warned me. He was hot, but he couldn't get at me because of Alina kneeling, in front of him, beside Manning. She gave Manning a handkerchief to hold to his face and had gotten him into a half-sitting position before Quong and I had the sense to see he was too heavy for her. We got him to the end of the boat and let him sit with his face toward the water. Alina held his head so he could throw up. Then she cleaned his mouth with her scarf and threw it over the side.

She sat beside him, protectively, until we hove to the *Malaysia Mail.*

Captain Karensen was hunched over the rail so mad he could spit: had it not been for not having anyone to replace Concannon he would have been gone half an hour. We let Manning get up first. He dimbed painfully. I let Sparks go up right behind him in case Manning should fall. Quong scrambled up after Concannon. Not one of these fools remembered our loot. Karensen didn't look ready to delay his sailing hour in the interest of our black-market investment. I heard the anchor being raised.

I shoved one transistor under my belt and got one under either arm. The hell with the booze. "You take," I told Alina what to do with the rest of the loot. How a man could climb a two-story rope ladder with only teeth and fingertips I hadn't figured out, yet I made it all the same. Bridelove and Muncie helped me over the rail.

Manning was stretched on the deck. That had been a perfectly dandy shot to the stomach and a fairly good kick in the eye. It had started to bleed again. Well, that's what comes of mixing with foreigners.

Bridelove, Muncie, Smith, Danielsen and Chips were more interested in my shirt than Manning.

"Wash it out with lukewarm water," Chips advised, "hot water'll shrink it."

When I looked at my bloodied shirt I understood: they assumed by it that it was myself who'd whipped Manning.

"How'd it start?" Bridelove asked.

"Ask Sparks," I suggested.

The launch below was wheeling about. Alina was at the rail no larger than a child, looking up. Only the mascara shadowing her eyes showed it wasn't a child's small face.

I waved, but she didn't wave back. Just stood looking up while I looked down; until I could no longer see her face.

Her face so young yet so old.

❋   ❋   ❋

Manning opened the store for an hour that night just for the honor of the thing. But he was wearing dark glasses.

I didn't ask him how he was feeling. I went down to see whether the crew had any questions they might care to ask.

Smith was at his green-baize board, sitting slantwise to favor a boil he'd been developing on his behind, and shuffling a deck, but he had no players. A few seamen were sitting around, but none expressed curiosity about my bloodied shirt: my moment of glory, that had struck so brilliantly, had been too brief.

"Believe me when I tell you," Smith began, "the Marquis of Kingsbury, you can have him. Did you know his own son whipped him? I'm glad he did. I wish I'd whipped him myself. I could have, too. I beat better men than the Marquis of Kingsbury."

It wasn't easy to visualize Smith, with his jaw jutting upward from a neck fixed at angle, maneuvering an opponent around a ring.

"Did the bob-and-weave type of opponent ever give you any trouble, Smith?" I inquired tactfully.

Smith stopped shuffling. "What you're trying to ask is how could a man with his neck on one side be a fighter," he read me—"I took it up after my career as a gas-smeller was ended. In fact I contracted this hitch from such a terrible blow in the Adam's apple that it ruint *another* highly promising career."

"Were you *really* any good, Smith?" I asked.

"To tell you the truth, no, sir, I wasn't," Smith admitted. "But I *did* have color."

"How do you mean?" I wanted to know.

"Well one thing I done was I always wore a cap with the peak over my eyes into the ring. It worried my opponent not to see my face. I'd keep it on till the ref made me take it off just before the bell. Once a ref forgot and I had it so low I couldn't see my opponent and he knocked me cold. After that I just depended on my natural skills of which I had only two."

"Which two were they?" I asked to be obliging.

"One was how I never threw a low punch without following through with a fair one—they can't take a knockout back, can they? No fight crowd would stand for a referee doing that even if he could. This also had the effect of making the fight look to be on the level. My other thing was how I never pulled my head back when I butted, so's I wouldn't get butted back."

I waited.

"Once I was fighting a fellow with a skinny neck. He hit me low right off and, when I held, he hit me a short one in *my* neck. At the bell he had his entire glove in my eye. So I dropped my hands and he hit me a clean shot that nearly took my head off. I realized then he had the referee so I didn't foul him back—I was afraid the ref would take the round away from me. And I didn't want to lose because I wanted to buy a Chevrolet. I had to beat him fighting fair or lose the Chevvy.

"When he came out for the second round he made as though to touch my gloves but I didn't accept his offer. So he bent me over a ring-post and laid his full weight on me till I thought my spine would crack before his referee took him off. Then he banged both my ears at the same time and backed off with his gloves up as if he had just been *boxing* somebody.

"I looked at the referee for help and that was another mistake, because this fellow immediately punched me in the neck again. It was the second fair punch of the fight and he had thrown both.

"Wouldn't you think the crowd would be proud of him for throwing two fair punches? They weren't. They booed. They thought punching a man in the neck was a foul. 'If he hits me in the neck a couple more times,' I thought, 'maybe the referee will take the round away from him.' When I went back to my corner I knew I would never be able to finish on my feet. So I said 'Goodbye Chevrolet.'

"I went out head down and butted him in the stomach. He went '*Oof.*' I brought my skull up against his right eye. He went '*Jzzz.*' Then I got my left glove around *his* neck. It was so skinny I could feel his windpipe through my glove. While he was choking to death I stepped on his foot.

'How does it feel?' I asked him. 'I'm disappointed in you,' he told me. My butt hadn't opened his eye so I dragged my laces across it and it opened fine. The referee noticed I'd changed my style. 'If you boys want to fight like this it's all right with me,' he told us.

"I pulled up my trunks and went to work. I butted him again and said, 'O, Pardon Me.' I scraped his back against the rope and said, 'O, Pardon Me.' 'Stop saying "O, Pardon Me,"' this fellow told me, and chopped me in the neck so hard I felt something come loose, so I drove my left five inches into his groin and I guess it must have stung him because he didn't express disappointment. He just doubled over like he was looking for something. I straightened him up with an elbow and hooked a *clean* left to his jaw. It was the fairest, cleanest punch I ever threw in my whole life. He went out like a light.

"But that referee! It took him eighteen seconds to count to six. He gave him six more to get to the count of eight. If he gave the man another half-minute it looked like he might get up. In fact, he rolled over at the count of ten. I held up my own hand before the ref could call it a draw. Then I went back to my corner and put on my cap and—"

"*Hold* it," I interrupted him, "hold it right *there*, buddy. You didn't go to your corner until the man was counted out? *No* referee, *nowhere,* ever started a count until a man got back to his own corner."

I had Smith cold.

"Sir," he reproached me gently, "when I told you I came into that ring wearing a cap I assumed you understood we weren't fighting according to the Marquis of Kingsbury. How could I have won by holding up my own hand if we're going by the rules? But you know—" he resumed quickly— "that fellow took so long to come to, that by the time he got back to his corner his handlers had left? That poor guy had to carry his own bucket all the way back to his dressing room. Nobody in that whole house offered him a hand. Isn't that a *shame, sir?*"

"It wasn't the Marquis of Kingsbury," I answered irritably, "it was the Marquis of Queensbury."

"Thank you," Smith answered, "I stand corrected. My point was simply that, whoever he was, you could have him. The reason he made up a set of rules about fighting fair was to cover up ways of fighting dirty. If he wasn't a dirty guy why did his son wait till he had him on the street to whip him, where the people could see? Why didn't he take the old man on at home? Believe me when I tell you, the Marquis of Kingsbury, you could have him."

"Let me ask you something else, Smith," I told him. "When a sailor dies at sea and is sewn up for sea-burial, does the last stitch go through his nose?"

"That's right," Smith assured me, "an old sea-tradition."

"*Why?*"

Smith studied me. When he studied you he rotated his head gently before reaching his decision.

"I'd like very much to fill you in on this, sir," he decided at last, "but the way I look at it is that any man who knows that the Marquis of Kingsbury was really the Marquis of Queensbury knows all there is to know. So what would an ignorant seaman like myself be doing trying to fill him in?"

He began dealing himself a hand of solitaire.

Sailors are a touchy lot.

INDIAN OCEAN: "I CAN SEE YOU HAVE BEEN WOUNDED"

Had Jeannie With the Light Brown Hair died the same day as Ernest Hemingway, it would have been difficult to distinguish her work from his by some of the summaries.

"Hemingway's prose was as chaste as a mountain stream," one Magoo claimed of a stream bearing mules with their forelegs broken, stiffs floating bottoms-up and the results of several abortions.

"He was dedicated to Truth and Beauty," another mad groundskeeper claimed of a man who had always disposed of both abstractions in his "built-in shockproof shit-detector," as he described it.

The overpraisers were judges as useless after his death as had been the begrudgers before. Of whom one, describing a critical anthology about Hemingway, wrote: "He is still a sacred cow, and readers will look in vain through these pages for any sustained and fundamental attack on the American master. This must be accounted a reverential weakness in the editor's principles of selection. True we are given Barea's notable assault on *For Whom the Bell Tolls*—but this is an attack on only one book and only from one angle. The total considered rejection will not be found in these pages."

I hadn't known of Barea's notable attack. Indeed, I hadn't even known Barea was sick. Yet the reviewer's own affliction is plainly the same as that of the man who once explained to me why he opposed equality of opportunity for Negroes—"God-*damn* it, I feel inferior enough already!" It wasn't Hemingway's prose, but his life, which demanded "total and considered rejection." It wasn't his economy of language which made them feel small-it was his free-handedness. To men whose self-doubt put them in need of formal respect from others, the ease with which Hemingway earned the informal respect of workaday men and women felt like an accusation. It certainly never ceased to raise the hackles of such a domesticated peacock as Dwight Macdonald. Macdonald couldn't even bear Hemingway's beard.

"He was a big man with a bushy beard,"* Macdonald wrote upon Hemingway's death, "and everybody knew him. The tourists knew him and the bartenders knew him and the critics knew him too. He enjoyed being recognized by the tourists and he liked the bartenders but he never liked the critics very much. He thought they had his number. Some of them did. The hell with them. He smiled a lot and it should have been a good smile, he was so big and bearded and famous, but it was not a good smile. It was a smile that was uneasy about the edges as if he were not sure he deserved to be quite as famous as he was famous.

"He liked being a celebrity and he liked celebrities. At first it was Sherwood Anderson and Ezra Pound and Gertrude Stein. He was an athletic young man from Oak Park, Illinois, who wanted to write and he made friends with them. He was always good at making friends with celebrities. They taught him about style. Especially Gertrude Stein. The short words, the declarative sentences, the repetition, the beautiful absence of subordinate clauses. He always worked close to the bull in his writing. In more senses than one, *señor*. It was a kind of inspired baby talk when he was going good. When he was not going good it was just baby talk. Or so the critics said and the hell with them. Most of the tricks were good tricks and they worked fine for a while especially in the short stories. Ernest was fast and stylish in the hundred-yard-dash but he didn't have the wind for the long stuff. Later on the tricks did not look so good. They were the same tricks but they were not fresh any more and nothing is worse than a trick that has gone stale. He knew this but he couldn't invent any new tricks. It was a great pity and one of the many things in life you can't do anything about. Maybe that was why his smile was not a good smile.

"After 1930 he just didn't have it any more. His legs began to go and his syntax became boring and the critics began to ask why he didn't put in a few more subordinate clauses just to make it look good. But the bartenders still liked him and the tourists liked him too. He got more and

---

* © 1962 by Dwight Macdonald. Reprinted from *Against the American Grain* by Dwight Macdonald by permission of Random House, Inc.

more famous and the big picture magazines photographed him shooting a lion and catching a tuna and interviewing Spanish Republican militiamen and fraternizing with bullfighters and helping liberate Paris and always smiling bushily and his stuff got worse and worse. Hemingway the writer was running out of gas but no one noticed it because Mr. Hemingway the writer was such good copy. It was all very American and in 1954 they gave him the Nobel Prize and it wasn't just America any more. Hemingway's importance is almost entirely that of a stylistic innovator."

Style is that force by which a man becomes what he most needs to become. When this need is one common to multitudes and the man's force suffices, we call him an artist, because in saving himself he saves others.

Ernest Hemingway's need was not to write declarative sentences with a beautiful absence of subordinate clauses. It was not to meet celebrities: he was on speaking terms with Georges Clemenceau, Benito Mussolini and Mustapha Kemal before he had heard of Ezra Pound and Gertrude Stein. He was one of the most highly paid correspondents in Europe.

Therefore the man had at his disposal a lifetime of meeting celebrities, while living comfortably with his wife and children in the capitals of the world; enjoying that degree of fame a foreign correspondent earns.

It was a lucky way of living—but he didn't want it. He didn't want it because, to him, it wasn't living at all. To Dwight Macdonald it would have been living. To have a respectable name with the Establishment and be a dissenter too! What *more* could a man ask than to have it both ways?

Hemingway didn't care for it either way. He wasn't an athletic young man from Oak Park. He was a soldier whose life had been broken in two. He didn't come to The Moveable Feast as to a picnic begun in Kansas City now being continued in the Bois de Boulogne. He had seen the faces of calm daylight looking ashen as faces in a bombardment. He had been the man who did not know where he went each night nor what was the peril there; nor why he should waken in a sweat more frightened than he'd been in the bombardment:

> "But I must insist that you will never gather a sufficient supply of these insects for a day's fishing by pursuing them with your hands or trying to hit them with a bat. . . . Gentlemen, either you must govern or you must be governed. That is all, gentlemen. Good-day."
> "I can see you have been wounded," the adjutant said.

Hemingway had felt his life fluttered like a pocket-handkerchief by the wind of death. In the watches of the night he had heard retreat beaten. Out of dreams like Dostoevsky's, endured in nights wherein he had lost his life yet had not died. Hemingway forged an ancestral wisdom in terms usable by modern man: that he who gains his life shall lose it and he who loses it shall save it; into a prose magically woven between sleep and waking.

Those were the nights the river ran so much wider and stiller than it should and outside of Fossalta there was a low house painted yellow with willows all around it and a low stable and there was a canal, and he had been there a thousand times and never seen it, but it was there every night as plain as the hill, only it frightened him. That house meant more than anything and every night he had it. That was what he needed but it frightened him especially when the boat lay there quietly in the willows on the canal, but the banks weren't like this river.

"Life is everywhere life," Dostoevsky had written after hearing himself sentenced to hard labor. "I am not dismayed. Life is in ourselves, not in outward things. There will be people beside me, and to be a *man* among men, and remain a man forever, not to falter nor fail in any misfortune whatever—that is what life is, that is where its task lies." Like Dostoevsky, Hemingway was a moralist whose waking resolutions were drawn from nocturnal visions. And in this he is much closer to the writers of the American twilight—Hawthorne and Poe—than he is to the image of the blood-and-guts adventurer that he projected—and *Life* swallowed whole.

"The critics had his number," Macdonald wrote. But it was Hemingway who had the critics', and particularly Macdonald's, number. Because Macdonald, who apparently has never read anything of Hemingway unless *Life* printed it," fell for the myth that Hemingway was a reporter of the bullring, the fight-ring, warfare, fishing and safari expeditions, but no more. Yet he was much more. Otherwise how explain these death-drawn visions?

They shot the six cabinet ministers at half-past six in the morning against the wall of a hospital. There were pools of water in the court-yard. One of the ministers was sick with typhoid. Two soldiers carried

him downstairs and out into the rain. They tried to hold him up
against the wall but he sat down in a puddle of water. The other five
stood very quietly against the wall. Finally the officers told the sol-
diers it was no good trying to make him stand up. When they fired
the first volley he was sitting down in the water with his head on his
knees.

Hemingway only began to write like this after he had learned how to
sleep again. His life that had been broken in two, had healed strangely. As
though his hold on life, having been loosened, now took a grip that possessed iron control. And from it derived a tension that fixed scenes
dead-still as in dreams—yet that flowed with a secret life of their own:

Jack's sitting on the chair. I've got his gloves off and he's holding him-
self in down there with both hands. When he's got something
supporting it his face doesn't look so bad.
   "Go over and say you're sorry," John says in his ear, "it'll look
good."
   Jack stands up and the sweat comes out all over his face. I put the
bathrobe around him and he holds himself in with one hand under
the bathrobe and goes across the ring. They've picked Walcott up and
they're working on him. There's a lot of people in Walcott's corner.
Nobody speaks to Jack. He leans over Walcott.
   "I'm sorry," Jack says, "I didn't mean to foul you."

"Memory remains," Dostoevsky wrote, "and the images I had created
but not yet clothed with flesh. These will rend me to pieces, true, but my
heart is left to me."

This conviction, so close to Hemingway's own resolve, explains why
he had no more need of being a professional dissenter than he had for
ingratiating himself with the powers that be. It wasn't his syntax, but the
man inside the prose, that makes Macdonald struggle and fret to secure a
hold on the man. For, to one so devoid of inner sinew as Macdonald, literature is explainable only in terms of declarative sentences; his own life
being invested in syntax. He must of necessity assume that Hemingway's
style was a matter of being an athletic youth sufficiently clever to pick up
some tricks from Gertrude Stein to serve his ambition.

Hemingway's emulators thought so too. For his art was so hidden it seemed easily imitated: one had only to talk tough and cut it short. Some imitated him boldly, some secretly, some mockingly and some slavishly.* But what they wrote had no tension: his prose was invulnerable.

Though his prose was invulnerable, his life was not. He flaunted a personality as poetic as Byron's and as challenging as Teddy Roosevelt's; before timorous men whose lives were prosaic. It was necessary, no, absolutely *essential*, to get his number.

"He thinks like a child," someone remembered Goethe saying of Byron. So Norman Mailer said "Hemingway has never written anything that would disturb an eight-year-old." So Professor Fiedler said it and Professor Podhoretz said it and Professor Edel said it and Professor Macdonald said it. First they said it one by one. Then, gathering courage, they all said it together in chorus: Now we have his number: Now we *really* have his number.

And of all our thinkers, from Paul Goodman to Ronald Reagan, who has given us a passage so certain not to disturb an eight-year-old as this:

"If you serve time for society, democracy, and the other things quite young, and declining any further enlistment make yourself responsible only to yourself, you exchange the pleasant, comfortable stench of comrades for something you can never feel in any other way than by yourself. That something I cannot define completely but the feeling comes . . . when, on the sea, you are alone with it and know that this Gulf Stream you are living with, knowing, learning about, and loving, has moved, as it moves, since before man, and that it has gone by the shoreline of that long, beautiful, unhappy island since before Columbus sighted it and that the things you find out about it, and those that have always lived in it are permanent and of value because that stream will flow, as it had flowed, after the Indians, after the Spaniards, after the British, after the Americans and after all the Cubans and all the systems of government, the richness, the poverty, martyrdom, the sacrifice and the venality and the cruelty are all gone as the high-piled scow of garbage, bright-colored, white-flecked, ill-smelling, now tilted on its side, spills off its load into the blue water, turning it a pale green to a depth of four or five fathoms

---

* See *Something of Value* by Robert Ruark, a novel slack as a severed clothesline.

as the load spreads across the surface, the sinkable part going down and the flotsam of palm-fronds, corks, bottles, and used electric light-globes, seasoned with an occasional condom or a deep floating corset, the torn leaves of a student's exercise book, a well-inflated dog, the occasional rat, the no-longer-distinguished cat; all this well shepherded by the boats of the garbage pickers who pluck their prizes with long poles, as interested, as intelligent, and as accurate as historians; they have the viewpoint; the stream, with no visible flow, takes five loads of this a day when things are going well in La Habana and in ten miles along the coast it is as clear and blue and unimpressed as it was ever before the tug hauled out the scow; and the palm-fronds of our victories, the worn light-bulbs of our discoveries and the empty condoms of our great loves float with no significance against one single lasting thing—the stream."

Call that baby talk.

RAFTS OF A
SUMMER NIGHT

Every morning of that lost summer came as a fresh surprise: a sallow youth wearing a bright red sweater practiced walking a tightwire right next door! He traversed the air from his back porch to his little garage, glided to the ground, then trotted lightly. We cheered as though the circus had come to our neighborhood. Nothing like it had ever happened on our street before.

He never spoke. My father called him "The Greenhorn"—but from what green country he had come he never told.

Yet we knew that the green country to which he went was Wisconsin. In the first hours after Friday night had fallen, when every back porch wavered, like rafts of a summer night, with the pinpointed flares of sticks of punk; that we burned, and moved as we burned them, to ward off mosquitoes, Greenhorn cranked up his Model-T and wheeled off to some county fair. I went to the backyard gate to watch him go: his taillight winked *Goodbye Forever* to me.

Goodbye to summer, goodbye to fun: goodbye to the weekday-morning sun.

Until a triumphant Monday-forenoon honking and a neighbor's cry— "Greener back! On wire going up!" brought summer back in a Model-T.

He rode the air and we rode the fence and the very air seemed daring.

Strangely, I anticipated scenes yet greater to come.

They came.

Greener soldered a pulley onto an ironworker's helmet, turned himself upside-down in it and rolled, upsy-downsy, along a cable to his garage!

A burst of applause—then he hit the ground on his face. Bashing his forehead and bending the hell out of the pulley.

"Greener's balance is so good upside-down he can't walk to the garage straight up anymore," my mother commented—and rapped me one that spun me half across the kitchen—"let that be a warning to *you!*" A warning not to walk straight up to a garage or not to glide upside-down to it I didn't know.

Yet in that week nobody walked the wonderful wire. Greener had holed up in his garage. He was sleeping in there now.

"He hasn't come out for two days," my mother reported to my father.

"He's *thinking*," I assured them.

What Greener thought of was a double-cable, one length tightened from porch to garage and a lower strand drawn from garage to porch.

I saw the problem: how would he make it to the lower strand? When, through his garage window, I saw him somersaulting on an old mattress, I got an idea.

He came out of the garage somersaulting. Cheers—then apprehensive silence as he clamped on the helmet, slid on the cable straight-up to the garage; balanced himself upside-down on the wire—then somersaulted onto the lower strand and glided triumphantly home!

I stood on my head in upside-down joy. My father whacked the upside until I put it down—"Why can't you be a good boy like I like I was when I was a boy?" he wanted to know. I didn't know why, but no whacking could lessen my joy: a man had but to be foolishly daring and the world was changed, from sunlessness to sun, for everyone.

Hard times returned to the back porches of home. Greener had to travel farther, and take greater risks with his neck, for less money. One Monday the Model-T ran out of gas five blocks from home and we had to push it—half a dozen other kids and myself—to his garage. He did not wheel away to a county fair the next Friday evening: no gas.

"Greener will think of something," I promised my mother.

"May it be to walk on his feet," she hoped.

Greener thought of something. He jacked up the Model-T and crawled underneath it. He was converting it to a kerosene-oil burner. My father took alarm.

"The Stanley Steamer has already been invented!" he called the news down to Greener through the car's open hood—"It doesn't work out!"

Greener crawled out, looked up at my father, shook his head—yes— for *him* it would work out. And crawled back under the hood. His will was forged of the same stuff as his tightwire cable. But it wasn't as flexible.

Now he lay against the November earth. In the slant yellow light of the last of day, coldly framing his garage door, we glimpsed the soles of his ragged sneakers, and saw his toes twitching with the cold. After dark he worked on by candlelight. It looked like the good times were over.

"If that boy had a mind he'd be dangerous," my father felt.

"He's only saving electricity," my mother hoped.

"He'll wind up in a room without corners," my father decided.

"May he never lift anything heavier than money," my mother wished.

Her washing was whipping whitely in the bright blue winter weather when a long, low, dripageous pall of coal-oil smog, sufficiently light to clear fences but too soggy to clear a clothesline, emerged from the hood of the Model-T, enwrapping sheets, shirts, petticoats, panties and pants, blankets and handkerchiefs, pillowcases and flannel underwear, leaving line after line dragging blackly toward earth.

Some Stanley Steamer.

Through this belching pall two policemen groped, with flashlight and gun, ready for anything. When Greener did not respond to a billy rapping the soles of his sneakers, one cop seized one naked ankle and the other seized the other, and dragged him forth, looking more like a miner coming up from a cave-in than an acrobat. Under the coal-oil his face was ashen. On the step of the hurry-up wagon he stumbled. I laughed.

It was like seeing a cat trip over itself.

Ten days later he returned, with a shuffling, brokenhearted walk. The Room Without Corners had done for that pale youth.

For neither upright nor upside-down, Greener never walked another wire. Nor wheeled off to farewells waved by small pinpointed flares from back porches on either side of his steering wheel. Nor ever in honking triumph returned.

Greener went to work in a neighborhood factory that manufactured endless belting for other factories. The acrobat stood at an endless belt making belting endlessly. He grew thin.

First he worked on wide-belt belting, but, as he grew still thinner, he was transferred to narrow-belt belting. There he began to gain weight. Greener had begun drinking.

He began drinking as soon as he had finished making belting endlessly, and his drinking went on all night without end. When he began drinking as endlessly as he tended to belting, he was replaced by a beltless machine that makes machines for manufacturing endless belting.

Greener never tried anything again. His summer had been brief, the applause only fleeting, the good times soon done. The first heavy frost split the kitchen pane of the house in which he had once lived. One of the cables, that he'd drawn so tightly, snapped under its burden of ice; entangling itself with the lower cable. At last both wires hung uselessly dangling. I felt disappointed in everything. In March I shattered the window of his garage.

From time to time, in winters that followed, I saw Greener, diminished to a beer-drinking fly of the tavern corners, again. On the kind of night when cats freeze on fire escapes, I watched him shuffling about a bar with a shot-glass of whiskey on his head, inviting somebody to knock it off and make the whiskey run into his eyes, because some of it ran into his mouth. Once a bartender put him down on all fours and rode him across the floor, standing up in the saddle and then bringing his full weight down on his horse. Greener sprawled, rolled over laughing, onto his back, and lay with his mouth wide until the bartender paid for his ride with a shot of bar whiskey; that he sloshed down Greener's throat.

There was simply no end of the fun when Greener was in good form. People don't know what good times *are* any more.

                      ❂   ❂   ❂

Wandering about a Mammoth Cave of the paperback trade, through a fluorescent basement mist a few days before I boarded this ship, was what had brought the memory of Greener back. For it returned a phrase I'd read long ago—"We don't even know what living is now"—as though, watching men and women adrift through an underground glow, it wasn't titles of books we were seeking, but the names of our true selves.

Even the titles seemed adrift: *The Quest of Meaning, The Quest of Man, Man's Quest, The Quest of Being, The Meaning of Man, Meaning and Existence*—they began revolving as on some endless unseen belt. I closed my eyes and held on.

When I opened them the titles had steadied, yet they were still there: *Man's Destiny, Man's Hope, Man's Fate, Man's Place, The Past of Man, The*

Path of Man, Hillbilly Nympho—now how had *that* gotten in Man's path?—*Be Glad You're Single, Be Glad You're Neurotic, Be Glad You're Ugly, Be Glad You're Paraplegic, Be Glad You're White*—isn't anybody *pleased* to be black anymore? *Be Glad You're You, Be Glad You're Absurd, Growing Up Absurd*—is Paul Goodman arranging our booklists? What is more absurd than to be so grown-up that the Meaning of Man concerns you more than men and women? Since when does abstracting the life from the poetry of living entitle a hollow hack to the honorable name of thinker?

I saw three biographies of Melville but not a copy of *Typee*; four studies of Dostoevsky but where was *Crime and Punishment*? About D. H. Lawrence the safest statement anyone can now make is that yet another "definitive edition" of his work will be issued within the year, although eleven of his books are out of print—definitively. Who hooked *that* tightwire up? Would their publication dump all "definitive editions" onto the remainder tables? Who's standing on his head now?

"*Where are they? Where are they?*" were Dylan Thomas' last coherent words.

They went thataway.

Our most daring minds, from Mailer to Murph the Surf, are now so high above ground with no net below, that the only people still looking up are those on pot.

"What I really object to," one Home Ec thinker claims, "is the writer who offers me the world's horrors without offering a solution";* thus advising us that Flaubert behaved badly in sending *Madame Bovary* to the publisher without appending a solution to small-town adultery. (That the world offers hardly a horror more deadly than a bourgeois antiquarian imposing a merchandiser's morality upon all art not subserving his personal comfort, he is too complacent to suspect.)

Dostoevsky's underground man, born from an idea instead of a father, lost and confused when left alone without books—a creature who did not know what living was—has strangely risen bearing a critic's credentials.

And the word to the Pfc instructor, wherever faculty brass and their wives compete for captaincies, is *publish, publish, publish*. Riding an endless belt of useless information, he becomes confident that the footnote is the road to fame and fortune. The present imbalance of books *about* writ-

---

* Edmund Fuller in *Saturday Review*.

ing, to those written from direct experience, is sufficient evidence of this. And sends throngs of young people to believing that literature derives from other books rather than from life.

They are duped by a presumption: that the truths which can sustain them can be handed down by educators, critics, analysts, anthologists and professional distributors of safe precepts: all those who, like Greener losing his sense of life under the hood of a secondhand Ford, lose theirs in a world where terminology embalms alike the living with the dead. The man whose passion attained its peak in a course in cost accounting now emerges as a shaper of American letters.

How else to explain that a compilation of literary allusions such as *Herzog*, possessing no value beyond cuteness, can be mistaken for a living book? The explanation is that dedication to accuracy no more suffices to make criticism true than does correctness in a novelist: lacking a sense of poetry, all creative work becomes false.

"What I have termed 'evasion' in his work," another big-spender-around-campus explains Hemingway, "will be borne out if we search for its roots in his life, from which an artist's work always springs. To be able to cope with emotion only by indirection [is] like escaping from life by big-game hunting or watching violence in the bullring. These are fascinating pursuits for our hours of leisure when given proper perspective. When they become a substitute for other forms of life they become an evasion of life."*

This is spite-burning; not criticism. When my father scolded me— "Why can't you be a good boy?"—he was being quite as critical while being more just. And his English was better. But then he wasn't a terminologist whose morality depended upon personal security.

That "always and everywhere the proper study of mankind is man" doesn't mean to annotate Man but to live like one. The critic's resentment here is that which the small shopkeeper has always felt for the restless wanderer. What business does anyone have, he is asking, following bullfighters from arena to arena when he could be having a rich, full life teaching young women iambic pentameter? Why go bumping in a jeep across a battlefield when one can go wheeling contentedly to class in a Porsche?

---

* "The Art of Evasion" by Leon Edel, in *Hemingway. A Collection of Critical Essays* edited by Robert P. Weeks.

There, *there,* between the "definitive edition" and the bursar's office, between the hard cover and the soft, between an LL.D. and his next *critique,* is where annotated man faces up to a life of no evasions.

Hemingway's life could be told solely in terms of his hostility toward the *petit bourgeois* demand that neither love nor death be real. That he overstates his proofs does, not now lessen the usefulness of his voyage. He began with *Nada,* he ended with *Nada:* but he knew those ports-of-call where life conflicts with death. He made the voyage.

For the risks he took were not unmeasured. Both physical and literary, they were the calculated chances of a pro. His risks were of the kind that, failing, the taker fails alone; but succeeding, succeed for everyone. To be qualified to pass judgment upon his style, therefore, a critic would himself have to be a man willing to take similar risks. Since no such man appeared during Hemingway's career, his work remains to be judged.

Villon, writing in the fifteenth century, brings Hemingway to us more justly than any modern critic:

> *In my own country I am in a far-off land*
> *I am strong but have no force nor power*
> *I win all yet remain a loser*
> *At break of day I say goodnight*
> *When I lie down I have great fear of falling*

More than any other contemporary, Hemingway put the ancestral warning, that he who gains his life shall lose it, into terms usable by modern man. Of many American writers who represented their own times, Hemingway alone made his times represent him.

For the painter no longer in touch with people who don't look at pictures begins to die as a painter. The actor whose life has moved from the marketplace to the studio acts falsely. The novelist, grown remote from people who don't read, becomes untrue to those who do read. The thinker who loses contact with those who never think at all, no longer thinks justly.

As the critic whose only wellspring is the work of other men at last gets to know all there is to know about Literature.

Except how to enjoy it.

ARABIAN SEA

Between the ceaseless rocking of the sea and the ceaseless wordiness of the critics, I divided the hours until afternoon. Then I decided to visit the officer's lounge for a cup of coffee and witty conversation.

A ward for catatonics would have been as lively and the coffee might have been better. First Mate, Third Mate, First Engineer and Second, each sat by himself looking straight ahead with his assigned cup before him. Each had his rating, so no more words were needed. What was there to do the rest of one's days but avoid gonorrhea?

William Gibbs McAdoo Manning, Chief Purser, was the philosopher of this likable group. When I came in he had just finished not replying to something the First Mate hadn't said. The Second Engineer appeared to be in agreement.

I noticed that the sugar-shaker was empty but, rather than ask for sugar, I drank the coffee black: why stick *my* neck out?

The thinking seemed to be to take death's mouth softly to one's own, in order to escape the risk of living. This, in the flesh, was the American affliction of living incommunicado even to oneself.

One deck down the seaborne sadsacks, foulups and misfits from every state in the union were lounging around reading comic books. Chips was listening on a transistor to the Dodgers playing the Giants.

Smith motioned to me.

"You remind me of a fellow I knew once"—Smith adjusted his neck and shifted a hip (to favor his Monstrous Boil) in order to get me into his sightline—"because his face was purely honest, but all he was good at was stealing."

"Thanks," I acknowledged Smith's flattering way.

"His name was Zekl," Smith went blithely on, "and the way he was most different from you was that *he* was *fat*. Zekl was *all* fat. He carried an outfielder's mitt on his hip from the time he'd played semi-pro ball but now he could barely waddle. We called him 'Hippo'—now ain't *that* a diller?"

I didn't see any diller.

"Hippo Zekl was a good center-fielder on Sundays and a good Saturday-Night-Mover. A Saturday-Night-Mover is a fellow who helps cops move stuff out of back-doors Saturday nights. This was in the days before night baseball so his athletic career didn't interfere with his criminal life."

Smith hitched his neck: it was going to be a long story.

"One Saturday night he helped move 10,500 dollars' worth of office furniture out of an office-furniture place, and the next day I was playing center and Hippo was in right. It was the last of the ninth, we were one run behind, there was two out 'n nobody on. Zekl came to bat.

"He sliced the first pitch toward first 'n should of been out by five feet, except the first-baseman waited for the pitcher to field it and the pitcher waited for the first-baseman, then both made the move together just as Zekl slood—"

"He *what?*"

"Slood. Slood into first. He was trying to beat the baseman to the bag with the ball. So he slood."

Smith looked perfectly guileless.

"Go on," I encouraged him.

"He brought up such a cloud of dust that nobody could tell what had happened till the dust cleared. Then we seen Zekl standing on the bag and the first baseman looking for the ball.

"He made sure the baseman wasn't trying the hidden ball play on him. Then he took off for second. This time he slood spikes-first."

Smith glanced at me to see whether I had any objection. I had none.

"When Zekl made second, he seen that the pitcher was helping the first-baseman find the ball, so he said to the second-baseman, 'I guess you fellows just don't want me'—and took off for third. This time he slood right *under* the baseman. When he got up and begin dusting hisself off, the right-fielder came in to help find the ball before Zekl took off again, because now there was nobody left but the catcher to stop him. But Zekl just stood on the bag as if we didn't have four dollars apiece going on him.

"'Home!' we hollered at him. 'Home, Hippo! Home!'"

Zekl began *strolling* toward home like he had all day.

'*Slide, Zekl! Slide!*' everybody began hollering."

"And he *slood?*"

"No *sir,*" Smith told me reproachfully, "he *didn't* slide. He took the ball out of his own pocket and tossed it to the catcher when he was still ten feet from the plate. The catcher got so excited he put Zekl out by shoving the ball in his face. Zekl *sat* down in the middle of the base-path saying the same thing over and over."

"What was he saying over and over?"

"'I had it coming,' Zekl kept saying, 'I had it coming.'"

Smith looked at me smugly confident I would be unsatisfied with the story.

"What was the final score?" I wanted to know.

"Five-four. We lost."

I turned away, but felt his hand on my shoulder lightly. I turned back.

"That wasn't what you were supposed to ask, sir."

"What was I supposed to ask?"

"You were supposed to ask why this fellow got hisself throwed out and then just sat there saying he had it coming."

"Why did he get hisself throwed out and just sat there saying the same thing over and over?"

"Well, he said, 'I had it coming, I had it coming,' because his conscience bothered him about trying to steal a baseball.

" *That's* what he *claimed* later."

"And what about the ten thousand dollars' worth of office equipment he'd moved the night before?" I asked.

"'*Everybody* moves office equipment on Saturday nights,' was the way Zekl felt about *that*—'but no *good* guy,' he told me, 'no really *good* guy *ever* slides into first. Nobody *ever* slides into first,' he went around saying. That's what he'd meant when he kept saying 'I got it coming, I got it coming.' It wasn't office equipment on his conscience. He'd got hisself throwed out at home because he didn't think a fellow who slood into first *deserved* to score a run."

"Frankie Frisch did," I reminded Smith.

Smith jerked his neck a notch inward.

"You're putting me on."

"I'm not putting you on," I told him irritably, "he *slood* fingers-first, on his chest, into first, at the Polo Grounds. It started a riot."

Smith studied me.

"If it started a riot," he decided thoughtfully, "then he must have."

He put out his hand and I took it.

"Thanks for telling me that. I feel better now."

"Because *you* were the guy who slood into first?"

He grinned.

"You G-Twoed it, sir," he told me with fresh respect—"you hit it right on the head. Never was *nobody* called Hippo Zekl. I made up the name because I was ashamed of what I done. You've took a weight off my conscience. Thank you. I appreciate it. Any time I can do anything for you, sir, you have only to let me know."

"You could fill me in on why the last stitch goes through the nose any time you feel in the mood," I suggested.

Smith nodded as though he'd anticipated my question.

"Let me make a *suggestion,* sir," he told me without seeming offended, "ask Chips. It's *his* job, not mine."

We were three days from the port of Bombay.

Port of Bombay

I. INTO THE GALA DAY

This street, when the land was British, was named *Saféd-Galli:* Avenue of the White Whores. Today it is the Street of the Hundred Cages. Not everybody went home.

Those who stayed do a lot of spitting. The walks in front of their cages are streaked by ropes of spittle of blackish red. A platinum blond with purple lips puts out her tongue; and her tongue is a deadlier purple yet. She smiles and the smile fills with blood: these ominous splatters marking the public ways are betel. The girls of the public cages chew it to dull hunger.

Some go into the cages for shelter. Some are waifs who were snatched off the streets to earn their keep as servants until they grew big enough to be used. Some are working off fines for husbands and brothers. Betel is easier to spit out than debt.

India's bureaucracies are accused of using too much paper; around the cages of Suklaji Street it uses none at all. Any tourist can become an official jail visitor just by pausing long enough to say, "Hello, Baby." By dispensing with paper-work entailed in making out visitors' passes, an enormous saving is being effected for the nation. What India will do with the money is India's problem.

The areaways, where boys wearing saris wait, seem less streaked by betel. "*No mama, no papa—you give,*" one cries in light mockery after me. His sari looks wound in mockery of himself; and of all Bombay's grinning amputees, contented bearers of incurable afflictions, flaunters of unnamed and unnamable diseases; and rouged gimps who plead languidly.

Yet the woman extending her palm upturned to me through bars of wood, while giving suck to her infant, isn't mocking me. Her breasts are wrinkled.

Nor that lank youth naked to his loincloth, balancing a bicycle against himself and shading his eyes with his hand while standing in cow dung.

He ducks into a doorway, emerges with a red umbrella hooked to his cloth, mounts the bicycle and wheels merrily away. When you work for Western Union it doesn't matter *what* you're standing in.

The girl's voice bouncing in from an American army base, through shop, taxi and bazaar, is that of Pat Suzuki—

Daddy, I want a diamond ring—

"The proper season for rain is the present, sir," a voice in low-rolling thunder warns me—"yet the entire month, we are empty!"

Two eyes, threaded by yellowish filament and filmed by cunning, looked up at me from under my armpit like two olives in a bowl of buttermilk. The man was almost as wide as he was high, and as dark as he was sweaty; with the head of a lion so long caged its mane has fallen to ruin.

"O, Bombay is a great city, my friend—nobody knows how many people there are in Bombay, sir—multitudes!"—here The Lion daubed at his forehead with a handkerchief, taking care to flutter it against my lapel so I could see it was silk—"a great city and one with much traffic! Yet not a drop of rain! Nature finds herself scourged: friendship falls off: brothers divide. In cities, mutinies. In countries, discord. In palaces, treason. Bonds cracked between son and father"—I sensed his touch go down my belt then lightly withdraw. I'd never been frisked before by anyone who could quote *Lear* while doing it. It was my first time.

Anyhow the transistor was on my other side.

"A hundred and fifty inches of rain once fell in five days at Cherripunji! Yet *here*"—he turned his palms so wide yet so empty up to a blind sun—"Empty, sir, a city of empty multitudes! '*We must do something i' the heat!*'"—and closed his pitch with a smile so snaky it wriggled out of his perspiration.

The girl giving suck to her infant still had her palm upturned at me through the bars. The platinum blonde again put out her tongue. The lank youth on the bike was lost in the traffic's endless pleading. The dreadful day of big Bombay burned on.

While Pat sang on and on—

Daddy, you got to get the best for me . . .

Yet Daddy never replied.

"Sir!" The Lion introduced himself with a command that sounded like "*Atten-shun!*"—"Sir! *I* am Baliram! Thirty-five years in Customs!"—then coyly waggling a warning finger playfully at me—"Beware, my American friend! I may come aboard *your* ship! Baliram may inspect *your* quarters! O, you won't know Baliram in uniform! Baliram knows the tricks! Watch out, my friend, or your visit may cost you a pretty penny!"—then that smile like a pang gone yellow with servility.

Suddenly shifting to a man-to-man approach, The Lion became all manliness and candor—"Baliram is no angel to be sure. Baliram knows the places seamen go. It has not been so long that Baliram has forgotten his own sins. Baliram too was young"—I had to keep turning slightly from him as he moved, to keep him off the transistor—"*A man may see how this world goes with no eyes*" he assured me—"but have you ever spent an evening in an Anglo-Indian parlor, my friend? Have you seen the little ones playing contentedly on the kitchen floor while the Anglo-Indian mother cooks and the father reads Dickens aloud?" I wondered who was listening to father reading in the parlor while everyone else was busy on the kitchen floor. "Have you seen a home God watches over, my friend?"

"No," I had to admit, "but I once knew a girl who roomed with the Alton Giant."

The Lion pretended to laugh. "You *are* pulling my leg, my friend— How can there be trust between men unless they begin with respect?" His fingers brushed a corner of the transistor.

"Sir, my car is at the corner. Let me *show* you an Anglo-Indian home." He linked my arm in his. This old boy really wanted me.

He waved a taxi to the curb, climbed in beside the driver and began giving directions in the tone one would use to one's chauffeur, with a condescending hand on the driver's shoulder.

"O, my friend, you don't know our people," he resumed, "you hear nothing but cries of *baksheesh! baksheesh!* so you think we think of nothing but *baksheesh*. My friend, let me tell you. We do not *all* live as you see the ones of Suklaji Street live. We are the most spiritual of peoples. In our humble Anglo-Indian homes you will see The Golden Rule come true!"

I looked out the window to see if there were a good movie in town. Under a sky stained by betel we wheeled midst the blind, overtaking the maimed, and abandoning the dying. Come to The Land of the Golden

Rule! Opportunity knocks in bustling Bombay! Here at last, I perceived, was a city where I might not only get a start in life—but a *headstart!* For I outweighed almost everybody and even the ones my own size were non-violent. Nothing stood in my way.

"Madam"—I began practicing a pitch of my own—"Do you find cataracts troublesome? This little bottle of Magic Chalmugra Oil cures cataracts, leukemia, leprosy, the falling sickness, hernia and gangrene—only seventy-five rupees per bottle. Thank you, madam. You need a small loan in order to marry, sir? Happy to help you—leave your wife at the fourth cage from the left, Falkland Road and Suklaji Street. You say you are well known as The Cha-Cha Queen, young woman? How would you like to give private dancing lessons to American seamen on long- or short-term rates?"

Come to The Land of Non-Violence! The One Democracy where everyone has the same opportunity of leaping into a taxi beside its passenger and saying "*Sssssss—you like nice gel, sor?*" If he looks like he'd prefer riding alone, get hold of a finger and *smile. Breathe* on him. If he still doesn't break try "*Sssssss—you like nice boy, sor?*" Then claw him lightly, blow in his ear and *get out.* Americans solve spiritual issues violently and *we* are a non-violent people.

Never forget—*no violence, no violence, no violence.*

There's big money to be made in India mugging the mutilated. Earn while you learn! A pretty penny can be picked up robbing the lame when they're sleeping. Something for everybody in bustling Bombay! Learn to fall headlong in front of a gharry! Dad! Be a leper and own your own bell! Sis! Be a girl *devi-dasi* and give suck to your young behind bars! Junior! Learn to make friends with seamen and wear jade earrings! Granny! Be an old abandoned *ayah* and scratch strangers from a prone position! Get your left arm sliced off at the elbow and pick up alms with your right! Did somebody leave the knees out of your legs? Stick your foot in your mouth and learn to roll! Make a pile overnight stuffing hashish into condoms! Come to The One Democracy that squats to pee! But: *no violence   no violence   no violence.*

I couldn't be sure that I wasn't still in Chicago.

Miracle of Todd-A-O, I saw, was showing at the Strand. Jerry Lewis was due at the Regal. *Kwality Ice-Creams with Soft-Recorded Music* flashed past between chop suey joints and hamburger stands. Where the hell *was* The Mysterious East?

"The offense of throwing articles at members of the judiciary," Baliram saw fit I should know, "is increasing in Bombay, sir. Only last week Mr. Sarjero hurled a shoe at President Magistrate Chinoy in the Mazagon Court. Fortunately it struck an advocate. Persons of this type menace our society, sir. I am of those who feel that, unless deterrent sentences are imposed, it will not be long before disorder will reign in our courts."

"What happened to the nut who threw the shoe?" I asked.

"Two years' rigorous imprisonment. He was fortunate. He might well have received five."

A kid with his left arm sliced off raggedly at the elbow climbed into the seat beside me and shoved the elbow into my face. It was festering nicely.

"*Papa! You give!*"

I gave him a dime to take it away. He handed the dime back: not enough.

"Now you don't get anything," I decided firmly.

After all, *I* hadn't sliced it off.

The kid began working up a spittle and in no time at all had a great froth going. I handed him a quarter and he leaped out laughing. The old man smiled. He knew, I knew, everybody knew I *had* sliced it off.

What India specializes in is chicken curry and redemptive beggary: the Indian takes such contentment in affliction he wants to share it. All that yummy agony, all that festering horror is yours as well as his. When he lays it on you, it *stays* there. Then leaps out laughing.

Yet: no violence. No violence. No violence.

Anthony Quinn in Carl Foreman's GUNS OF NAVARONE flashed past. Hi, Tony. Hi, Carl. How's Greg?

"Do you see that innocent-looking hack-Victoria?" Baliram cut in. "Do you notice the bales of hay beneath for the horses? Only last Tuesday the Yellow Gate police found a radio transistor at the Red Gate, concealed in just such innocent bales!"

"What the hell are the *Yellow Gate* police doing at the *Red Gate?*" I asked him—"Why don't they stay in their own precinct?"

A face framed by shoulder-length hair and fever obtruded itself into the cab window, but at my shout of dismay—"No! No!"—it withdrew looking shocked. *That's* how to deal with interviewers from *Time.*

I poked my head out to see if anyone from *Playboy* was around but couldn't see a soul wearing a pith helmet.

"And only yesterday the police stopped a gharry on Falkland Road—at the very point where we met today—and discovered not one transistor in the hay—but another in the tool-box!"

You're cutting in closer all the time, Dad, I reflected. I may have to jump ship and pan elsewhere for gold. But so long as I was seeing the city I might as well keep riding away from the madding throng, I decided.

Even though my guide seemed more of a fink every minute.

The throng got more and more madding. The nearer to his little Anglo-Indian nest Baliram got, the finkier he sounded and the worse the American movies got.

The cab stopped for a light and I crouched, but a *rap-rap-rap* on the door straightened me up—a boy selling balloons, with his left leg tied back to a pole. It was the pole he was using to rap the taxi-door, leaning on the car to do so. I grabbed a balloon, handed him a dime and the Sikh started the car and the kid fell in the road before I could get my change.

He sprawled on his face holding fast to his balloons. This was also my fault.

"Don't start up so fast," I scolded the Sikh—"I had a nickel coming."

And away we wheeled without a woe into the gala day.

Five Branded Women was at the Rex. Would they show the actual branding? That was one show I didn't plan to miss.

"A curious incident of only last Sunday," the old man's low rumble resumed, "a spider was discovered in an aerated bottle! Now the Health Officer has asked the people to consume aerated water only after the most careful examination!"

I liked my balloon. It wasn't young any more but I liked it all the more for that. It was fever-red stippled with small yellow disease spots but they weren't malign. I could tell because they weren't festering. Not yet.

A cat raced across the street grinning with glee at the possibility of being squashed under wheels. He made the curb by a whisker and then stood on the curb looking disappointed: he was going to make another try.

"Nonetheless, the situation is good for The Free World," The Lion assured me, "your General Taylor saw that in South Viet Nam last week and had the courage to say so."

A girl put her head in the window and howled, "*Bly-eye-nd brother! Blye-eye-nd* brother!"

She wasn't lying. When I put my head out the window I saw him. He wasn't just *blind:* he was the Blindest. He didn't even have to roll his eyes to show *he* was blinder than anybody. Somebody had left his irises out.

"Get him contact lenses," I advised, and gave her a nickel. I would have made it a dime but I didn't want to corrupt her.

Geraldine Page was at the Alexander in *Summer and Smoke.*

I became absorbed in watching a man so thin his bones cast shadows: six feet high, with a growth of beard and hair, holding a bit of burlap across his genitals. Except for that burlap he was bare-ass naked in the middle of town. What a market for burlap!

"Sir," the old man insisted, "only today my friend Ayub Sardar Mulani was arrested by the General Crime Branch for breach of trust—what a dishonor to come upon gray hairs! Over a thousand pounds embezzled since the first of the year!—and admits everything freely! 'Now that God is dead, my Mistress is my Heaven,' he told the arresting officer, but his mistress threatened to leave him if he didn't move her to a more respectable heaven. She may be an angel to Sardar, she told him, but people were looking at her as though she were a whore. So he stole to save his angel's honor. We are a people who prize honor over everything, sir."

"So long as he didn't spend anything on himself they can't touch him," I assured my old man as the cab wheeled up before a yellow cabaret.

Baliram projected his great bulk backwards out of the hack and waddled, frontwards, to a door beside the cabaret; leaving me to settle with his "chauffeur." I followed his monstrous bottom up a flight of careworn stairs into a room crowded with fixtures of another day. There was faint music, as of someone playing a piano only for himself, from the cabaret below. Overhead a wooden ceiling fan beat monotonously. My balloon tossed in its breeze—I'd have to be careful not to get it caught in *that.*

"I want you to meet my wife," Baliram assured me, "*Pawm!*" he bawled, "*Pawmela!* We hawv a gist, *Pawmela!*"

All the pictures around the room were of the Stations of the Cross; and of such size that the room itself was diminished. The old man had a bigger stake in the legends of Christianity than in its real estate, it looked like. I wondered whether anybody was being crucified in the kitchen.

"*Pawm,*" he called out in a tone most affected, "*Pawmela dee-*ah! We have a *gist,* Pawmela deeah!"

The girl who emerged from the kitchen was another Caucasianized slant; one, I guessed, from the hills of Burma or the plains of Assam, with eyebrows penciled high to make her eyes look round. Her name would, more appropriately, have been Kai-Li. She didn't crack a smile at sight of an American holding a red balloon. This was to show me she was British to the bone.

"Do you like our little home, sir?" Baliram asked me.

No farther than I can throw my old balloon, I thought.

The girl nodded coldly once; then slipper-sloppered back to her kitchen-station.

"*Pawm* deah. *Pawm*ela. I would like you to *welcome* ouah gist."

So here comes Pawm slipper-sloppering back. If she'd put in as much care on her dress as on her eyebrows, two buttons wouldn't have been askew. Pawm wasn't more than twenty-two but she walked like sixty-six. Pawm just didn't *care*.

"How do," she acknowledged both me and my balloon, and started away again.

"*Pawm*ela, our guest would like a bit of Anglo-Indian cheeah with us— *Would* you mind stepping out for it?"

"Where's the bread?" Her English was faultless.

"O, I'm suah ouah guest will be glad to contribute a few rupees toward some Anglo-Indian cheeah," the old man decided airily.

I extended a five-dollar bill toward him, and when he reached for it I gave him my index finger instead.

Immediately he feigned great amusement. "*Pawm*ela! Did you see the trick? O, *will* you teach me how *that* is done, sir? See, deah—he offers money but then gives nothing but a finger! It is done to reprove persons who act greedily—O, but wasn't it neatly accomplished!"

The girl blushed. He was too much for me too.

I gave her enough change to buy a bottle and she shuffled out into the hallway.

"I'm interested in radio engineering," Baliram informed me, indicating a radio disassembled on a mantel—"on occasion I buy old sets in hope of repairing them for resale. Unfortunately," he shrugged—"I have little skill along mechanical lines. Perhaps you would care to trust me with your balloon long enough to take off your coat? You'd feel more at ease."

Sitting down at the table and letting the balloon catch the breeze from the fan, yet not letting it get too near the blades, I indicated I was at ease already.

Pawmela returned with a bottle. Baby, I thought, that was a fast trip to the still, considering you didn't even use the stairs. Either you went down the side of the building or the Liquor Permit Office is in the hall.

"*Pawm!* May we have *glaw*sses?"

Pawm slid a couple glasses across the table and turned back to the kitchen before they stopped sliding. I knew they'd like me in Bombay.

Baliram filled my glass, then his own. I waited to see whether he'd drink it or quote *Lear* to gain time. I gave him time and he downed the drink, so I followed: a rich blend of Jamaican rum and rotting bananas.

"We would *both* feel more at home if you took off your coat, my friend," he urged me.

The balloon was a problem. When I tried taking off my coat I found it wouldn't go through my sleeve. Finally the old man held it for me until I got my coat off. When he handed it back I pulled the transistor out of my belt, extended its aerial and tuned it in—all with one hand.

It isn't fair for you to want me—

a tenor's voice came in pleadingly—

You only want me for today—

"That's Tokyo," I assured Baliram so he wouldn't think it was Atlanta.

"What price are you asking, my friend?" he asked me.

"Sixty dollars American."

"I'm only a poor broker," he explained. "I can't buy it myself."

"I don't care who I sell to."

He examined the brand name, fussed with the aerial, tuned in another station, expressed doubt, shook his head regretfully. He wanted to tune it in again; so I drew the aerial down.

"I *can* get sixty dollars for it," he decided, "but no more. That leaves me nothing for the risk I take in your interest."

"Everything you get over fifty-five is yours," I compromised. "If you don't get over fifty-five you take the risk for nothing." Some compromise.

"And if I get less?"

"Then you deduct the difference between what you got and fifty-five and that much is what you're out."

"You drive a hard bargain, my friend."

"I can get seventy-five for it myself," I lied.

He stood up wiping his forehead in anticipation of the heat of the street, went into the kitchen, and returned with a shopping bag and two loaves of French bread. He put the set in the bottom of the bag with the loaves sticking out; and left walking more heavily than before.

I was left alone with a pint of cheap rum and Kai-Li.

The girl waited till the old man's heavy step had died away before she came out. She'd tidied her hair, touched her lips and eyebrows; but still looked sullen. I invited her to share the rum.

"Me no drink," she explained; but sat down all the same.

I waited.

"Papa no good," she told me at last, "Mama no good. Everybody no good."

Then merely sat looking at me as though suspecting I was probably worse. There wasn't a thing she could do for me and there wasn't a thing I could do for her. Except to listen to her woes.

That she plainly wanted to tell. For they were the kind one can safely tell only to a stranger.

I tied the balloon to my finger.

"You like the old man?" I encouraged her.

She wrinkled her nose. "I do like he tell," she told me, "I got no paper."

"No passport?"

"No nothing."

"Where did you come from?"

"Macao. My real papa Chinese gambler-man. Mama Russki. Both no good. He sell her. Then he sell me."

There was a long silence.

"You're a long way from Moscow," I pointed out to be helpful.

The overhead fan deepened its whirring roar.

"You know *Cages?*" the girl asked me.

Yes, I'd seen The Cages. What about The Cages?

"Is where old man find me."

So the old man had bought her out and now was trying to get his money back.

"How long ago did he take you out?" I asked her.

"Two year," she told me. "First year, me *good* to Old Man. I no tell he steal because he no tell I got no paper. He no tell on me, I no tell on him. *Steal, steal, steal.* Custom-Man do too *much* steal. 'Old man,' I tell him, 'you stop steal now; you do too much steal, old man.' Old man no stop. Old man get catched." The girl clutched her hair to mimic the old man's fright—"'O-O-O, your little daddy gonna get rig-or-ous labor now! O-O-O your little daddy gonna die in jail—O-O-O'"—her eyes, that had been so leaden, came pleasantly agleam at the recollection of the old man's panic—then dimmed with disappointment: "Old man no get rig-or-ous labor. Old man no go to jail. Old man pay. He go free. Then he make sailor-busyness. Old man buy what sailor got—watch, ring, radio. Then old man say, 'You like nice Anglo gel, sailor?' he no ask *me.* He tell *sailor—sailor* say, 'I pay good money for you, Baby'— How you like *that?*"

I couldn't say I cared for it. But I could see how things could be worse. I waited.

The girl studied me curiously.

"You like short-term?" she asked at last.

I shook my head: no short-term.

"You like long-term?"

I shook my head: no long-term.

"Mama no good!" She began one of those demonstrations of absent-minded anguish which, by inflicting sufficient misery upon the innocent bystander, permit the anguishee to make plans of his own for the following day. "Papa no good! Me got no paper! Me got no little baby! Me got no *baksheesh!*—Me got no home! Me got nothink! You no want short-term, you no want long-term—O! O! O!—You no good too!"

There, I'd done it again. Every time anybody in Asia tried improving his difficult lot, there I'd be throwing my weight against his chances. I was certainly going out of my way to foul people up.

"Old man t'row me out!" she howled.

"Why should he do that?"

I only wondered.

"Because *you* no want short-term, *you* no want long-term, *you* not give poor girl nothink!"

Nobody loves The Good Guys anymore.

"Back to Cages!" she concluded the demonstration. "Me die! You no good. You no *damned* good."

"Whenever things seem to be darkest, honey, is just before they get worse," I consoled her.

She put her head down on her arms and began shaking her shoulders. It was the most theatrical exhibition of fraudulent guilt-placing I'd had put on me since James Baldwin accused me of complicity in the lynching of Matt Parker.

"I was at a ball game in Comiskey Park that night," I'd tried to wriggle out; but when James lays down a charge, he *lays* it.

"You were there all the same," he put it right on me—"your Northern indifference triggered the Southern gun. The men who did the lynching merely acted out the will of the white community—and there is no Mason-Dixon line to *that* community. You are as much a part of it in Chicago as any Mississippi sheriff."

"I don't follow you," I had to admit.

"Because you don't *dare* follow," he challenged *me*.

"Where would I wind up if I did?" I asked curiously.

"By finding that your father and your father's father conspired in the lynching of Matt Parker a hundred years before the lynching."

"My old man came from Indiana," I felt I ought to explain, as James plainly had me confused with somebody else, "and *his* old man came from Europe."

"Europe raped Africa, let me remind you," James informed me.

"You mean we were in on *that* too?" I asked.

"Everyone in the crucible of Western Civilization was in on it," he assured me.

What could I say except that I was *terribly* sorry?

"I'll have to take responsibility," I finally confessed to the lynching of Emmett Till as well as of Matt Parker, "so long as you'll stop denying you set the Reichstag fire."*

The girl had stopped shaking her shoulders. She had a new thing going.

---

* "The white community," Mr. Baldwin commented recently upon the murder of Malcolm X" "must share the responsibility for this thing no matter who pulled the trigger; for whoever did it was formed in the Crucible of Western Civilization."

And whoever did it was also formed in the crucible of the American Negro community. If that community's claim to equal justice in the company of men is to have validity, it will have to assume responsibility for its own acts. Putting responsibility on Ol' White Massa for every act of violence of our times affords the Negro a convenient cop-out; and also means he wants to hold on to the immunity of being a slave.

She was trailing her fingers down the front of her blouse, smiling seductively; and every time she touched a button the blouse opened a bit wider. This interested me as I thought that if she got the blouse open entirely it would mean she was going to wash it. By the time she had it open I saw that her bra needed washing even more. I took my bottle and stretched out on the divan.

And felt the beat of the city's terrible heat on rooftop, alley, bazaar and wall. The balloon tied to my finger rose toward the blades of the fan as though irresistibly drawn; then swung like a weightless pendulum there, four swings every half-minute.

My watch ticked off the swings and the beat of the fan slowed to the throb of engines hauling deep below-deck. Seamen were coming down the hall but they didn't know which door was mine. Yet they stopped and began whispering just outside.

"He's trying to get the ship in trouble," one began informing on me.

"It isn't any of his business," a half-familiar voice agreed.

Then the whisperers conferred: they were going to come in on me. I tried to waken but could not. Someone was standing in the door.

"The last stitch is through the nose," he announced. His face was bleeding and his cap was afire. It was a matter of life or death that I waken before he touched me and I did.

And heard Baliram's heavy step upon the stair. He came into the room awash with sweat.

The girl had left her blouse and bra on a chair. Baliram saw it at the same moment that I did.

"Did you enjoy my wife's company, my friend?" he wanted to know.

"Where your wife hangs her underwear doesn't concern me," I assured him. "What did you get for the set?"

"I earned nothing for myself," the old man told me—just as my balloon touched the blades and exploded as though exploding his lie.

"I was forced to sell without profit for myself, because I could not risk carrying it around any longer. I'm becoming too well known, my friend. I know you will not let my services go unrewarded."

A tiny fragment of rubber, all that remained of my balloon, drifted downward toward the floor.

"What did you get for the set?" I asked him again. "Fifty dollars," he lied in his teeth.

"Count it out," I asked him.

He counted out fifty dollars in rupees. Close enough. I pocketed it.

"Not even cab-fare, my friend?" he begged.

I didn't bother to answer.

Passing down the dimness of the hall I was almost past the girl before I discerned her huddling against the wall.

"Old man think I cheat him," she whispered, "old man think *everybody* cheat."

"Well," I asked, "*doesn't* everybody?"

She held her palm out to me.

"Was it you who informed on the old man?" I asked her.

She wriggled her fingers to tell me her hand was still empty.

"*Did* you?" I asked her; for I really wanted to know. And she wasn't getting a dime *until* she told me.

She nodded her head in confirmation and I put a dollar's worth of rupees in it. She examined the money.

"If you don't give me another dollar," she told me, "he'll hit me."

"Hit him back," I suggested, and turned down the stair.

Into the gala day.

II. KAMATHIPURA

"Do priest kiss priest?" Alina had wanted to know in *The Lion of Kowloon*—"Do men kiss men?"

Between the abounding sensuality of the Hindu and the Puritanism of the Muslim, betwixt one race whose gods are all lovers and one whose God is a celibate soldier, an ancestral conflict is renewed each night in Kamathipura.

The women and girls who stand in stalls, with pitch-black eyes and brows blackened in ash-white faces, looking silently out at the street beneath the glare of sixty-watt mazdas, are merchandise as open to the view of buyers of the night as canned fish to buyers of the day. But the glare overhead keeps them from seeing the faces of those who stand and look.

They hear laughter of men but cannot see who is mocking them. They hear cries of defiance from girls in other cages; sometimes one curses one of the lookers and he swears back at her laughingly.

Other times the laughter comes more lightly by, from areaways where boys wearing earrings wait. By the light of flares that blow upward, like yellow saris in a twisting wind, old men move among them. Kamathipura is less mocking of earringed boys than of imprisoned girls.

For the Koran is terribly hard on a whore. "If any of your women be guilty of whoredom," it teaches, "then bring four witnesses against them and shut them up in their houses until death do release them." Early Islam simply walled the woman up alive—an unconscionable barbarity it later sternly revoked in order to stone her to death without qualms.

It looked more benignly upon the male sinner and looks more benignly yet: "If two men among you commit the same crime, then punish both, but if they turn and amend, then let them be, for God is He Who Turneth Merciful."

Turneth Merciful is a God who turns on the mercy for men only. From

Woman He Turneth Away. Soldiers always give themselves the benefit of any doubt and Islam was a race of soldiers: women are for one thing only and now let's get back to barracks.

Weakness being shameful and Woman being weak, an open contempt of her is one means of feeling oneself a full man; and may disguise the fear of being inadequate. Islam lacked nothing of making a Playboy club in Mecca a going concern except affluence. It was so rich in disdain that there must have been enough inadequacy for everybody in town to have a bunny all his own.

Yet holding Woman in contempt contains the risk that, if you surrender to her, you yourself become contemptible. Holy men who would not harbor in their hearts neither fear of man nor contempt of woman beat the game by sleeping with one another and billing the bit as "Pure Love." And what was pure enough for a priest was pure enough for a general: the process of purification spread down through the rank and file to the flaring areaways of Kamathipura.

The Koran went down before the *Mahabharata.* Yet the Muslim aristocracy maintained its tradition of homosexuality by keeping pages. That these young studs solaced the master's harem as often as they solaced the master can be safely assumed. And that some resisted the master altogether is recorded by a seventeenth-century traveler, Jean-Baptiste Tavernier, telling of a singular occurrence at Patna:

"An officer disgraced a young boy who was in his service. The boy, overwhelmed by grief, chose his own time to avenge himself. Being out hunting with his master, and removed from other attendants, he drew his sword, came up behind the master and severed his head with a single cut. Then, crying aloud he had slain his master, he rode full speed to the governor's house; who placed him in prison. Although relatives of the slain man demanded the page's execution, the sympathy of the people for the boy was so strong that, after six months, the governor pardoned him."

As the Moors, whose deserts had lent them ferocity sufficient to conquer Spain, became so softened when cut off from their deserts that they changed to a race of scholars, so the desert-men of Mohammed were softened by the grandeur and reverence with which the Hindu civilization surrounded womanhood.

The Indian prostitute was not originally, like the Muslim, an abandoned woman, but a dedicated one. The Devi-Dasi was a temple harlot dedicated to the service of a god. When she was married to the god, the marriage was honored by a festival. As a dancing girl the Devi-Dasi served both man and god, and the man who shared her bed shared it with a god. Rather than feeling corrupted by woman, the Hindu felt uplifted.

Prostitution became womanhood organized. The elaborateness and efficiency with which the king of the Hindu state of Vijanagar had set up the establishment of prostitution stunned Abd-Er-Razzak, an ambassador of a fifteenth-century Persian Shah:

"Opposite the mint," he wrote, "is the house of the governor, where are stationed twelve thousand soldiers as a guard, who receive every day a payment of twelve thousand *fanom,* levied upon the receipts of houses of prostitution. The magnificence of places of this kind, the beauty of the young girls collected therein, their allurements and their coquetry, surpass all description.

"Immediately after mid-day prayer they place before the doors of the chambers, which are decorated with extreme magnificence, thrones and chairs, on which the courtesans seat themselves.

"Each of these women is bedecked with pearls and gems of great value, and is dressed in costly raiment. They are all extremely young, and of perfect beauty. Each one of them has by her two young slaves, who give the signal of pleasure, and have the charge of attending to everything which can contribute to amusement. Any man may enter this locality, and select any girl that pleases him, and take his pleasure with her. Each of the seven fortresses contain places of prostitution, and their general proceeds amount to twelve thousand *fanom."*

The proceeds of the holy whorehouses, it would appear, were turned over to the military before midday prayer and spent back in the houses in sacred copulation that same night. If the girls were thus kept content while the state was being protected, everyone shared in the general prosperity, nobody got up before noon and all were too busy screwing after to dissent from anything, is it any wonder that the king kept laughing his head off?

A Portuguese traveler, Duarte Barbaso, perceived, behind this grandeur, a fearful savagery. (It must be borne in mind that he came of a Christian country which denied womanhood to women: either she married for the advantage of her house or was locked into a deathly vise of enforced chastity.)

"Many women," Barbaso reported, "through superstition dedicate the maidenhead of a daughter to one of their idols here; as soon as she reaches puberty she is taken to a house of worship, accompanied, with exceeding respect, by all her kindred holding festival for her as though she were to be married. Outside the gate of the church is a square block of black stone of great hardness of the height of a man, shut in by gratings.

"Upon these oil-lamps burn all night; and they are ceremonially decorated by many pieces of silk that folk outside may not be able to see within. Upon the said stone is yet another, the height of a stooping man; in the middle of which is a hole into which a sharp-pointed stick is inserted.

"The maid's mother takes her daughter, and other kinwomen within the grating. After ceremonies have been performed the girl takes her own virginity with the stick and sprinkles blood on the stones. Therewith the idolatry is accomplished."

How Barbaso found out so much without putting an eye under the grating is a problem only posterity can resolve.

What seems more pertinent is that these idolatrous women knew that the vagina was intended for *use:* an idea which now so completely confounds the American woman that she attaches it to a two-car garage instead. And then can't understand why years of searching for her femininity through analyst's offices end by leaving through the same door by which she came in—except that her husband is less masculine than when she entered. *Wow.*

The correlation between our rising incidence of homosexuality and our increasing indifference to the suffering of others is partially accountable by the proximity of cruelty to effeminacy; these shade into each other because both overvalue pain. And both are rooted so deeply in Puritanism that we have become more tolerant of homicide than lovemaking.

The thirty-eight witnesses to the murder of Miss Genovese were not uniquely worse than any other thirty-eight window-watchers between Schenectady and Sausalito—had a couple been making love on that walk instead of a woman being stabbed to death, there would have been a surge of outraged citizens upon them like buffalo stampeding.

Of the ancestral savagery of India much remains in Kamathipura; but nothing at all of the grandeur. The tradition of the temple harlot has brought the devi-dasis to the stalls and the sons of the poor to the areaways.

Between the areaways and the stalls, peddlers of ices and toters of pots, seamen going up stairs that lean and other seamen coming down, sellers of condoms and hawkers of gum, riders of bikes between fly-buzzed cafés, taxis, gharries, hay wagons, drivers and bringers, changers and criers, all are borne past the cages in a diffused light lit by occasional flares. And carried on waves of sound now loud, now soft, now far, now near: of rock-'n'-roll from jukeboxes, transistor-jazz amid a thin bleating of dying balloons; and of a doorbell being buzzed again and again and again.

And all move on a tide of cheap perfume pervaded by urine, face powder, onions frying, burning oil and decaying fruit, a sea of smells, scents and odors diverging; then merging into the single smell of thronging humanity.

Between hush-hush whisperings of the night—"*Come to me here you— Papa you give—Short-term-long-term—You speak-Joe-you-like-nice-boy—Papa-I -show-you-good-place-you-do-what-you-like-Papa*—I heard a whole night-universe begging Americans for their lives.

Between the cold white glow of the stalls and the hotter light of the areaways, I saw a woman coming toward me; whose eyes, I saw, were crossed.

I'd never before been accosted by a cockeyed whore. It was my first time.

We sat down at a rickety table in front of a café that cast a pale blue light. When a boy came out bowing and scraping I ordered tea before he could start saluting.

She would have been passably good-looking but for those incredibly crossed eyes: I mean this girl was *completely* cockeyed. And wearing a smile so foolish it was pitiful.

"No short-term," I told her, "no long-term." And shook my head with infinite regret.

She shook her head regretfully as well.

Then took my hands as though to read my palms. But, instead, began matching my fingers with hers, finger for finger. When she had ten apiece, and had established that we both had the same number, I cocked my head toward her to see what she had in mind.

She cocked her head at me in turn.

If this kid wasn't demented then she had a going sense of humor.

I stuck out my tongue.

She reddened, rose and was gone in the misty light of Kamathipura. I called the waiter out to pay him for the tea.

"That girl no can talk, sor," he assured me.

"Why can't she talk?"

"Her Papa very rich Arabian, sor."

"Why can't she talk?"

"Her name, Kusum, sor."

"Why can't she talk?"

"She Singapore gel, sor."

"*Why can't she talk?*"

"Japan soldier take her from Papa. When give gel back to Papa, gel no can talk. Japan soldier cut off tongue. Papa no like gel no more. You think she *see* out them eye, sor?"

I spent the rest of that night talking to the women of the cages of Kamathipura, of whom many spoke English brokenly. Some spoke not at all, but merely held out a palm.

Several spoke of Kalyani, the woman who'd spoken for them to Ghandi. And who still spoke for them to the continual parade of reforming committees which visit Kamathipura. Men and women of goodwill who come to take count of incidence of the V.D. rate to see whether syphilis is on the rise or declining; to determine the percentage of women who become prostitutes of their own will or by kidnapping; and to determine from what provinces of India these women have come. Because there is nothing to do about Kamathipura except to chase the pimps off the corners for an hour and take a fresh count.

A light rain was falling, as the light of ordinary day was breaking, when I left Kamathipura. Suklaji Street, Falkland Road and Foras Mews were deserted but for a few taxis in which bearded Sikh drivers were asleep at their wheels. Even the pimps had given up. All the café tables had been taken in but one; and at that a woman slept with her head upon her arms.

As I passed her I realized it was my mute and mocking friend of the blue-lit café.

> Idling the night in blue cafés
> Mid roar of cab and cabaret
> Wand'ring the flares of Foras Mews
> The girl Kusum whose eyes are crossed,
> Whose eyes indeed lean each to each,
> Walked smiling among the alien crews.
> Fists matter little to a whore,
> *Baksheesh* matters more.

When doors are locked to all cafés
And morning slants along the street
Sailor and soldier alike have left
And pimps have made a night of it
Then Kusum, after all have gone,
Dreams yet of seamen on the beach.

In a rain that lightly rains regret
Lamps along the long gray street
Bend, wearied out with all-night love
Like cockeyed lovers each to each.

Fists are no matter to a whore,
Baksheesh is what matters more.

III. KALYANI-OF-THE-FOUR-HUNDRED

When Mahatma Ghandi came to the south of India he was met by four hundred whores of Bombay.

"How may we become good women once more, Master?" their spokeswoman, one Kalyani, asked the Mahatma.

"Go to the spinning wheel, my children!" the Master instructed Kalyani-of-the-Four-Hundred.

"How is the wheel to save us, whom the loom has brought such shame?" Kalyani asked The Master.

CAGE I

Kalyani's parents were weavers. They owned their own looms, upon which Kalyani's parents, her two brothers and herself worked. They also owned their own house.

When Kalyani was sixteen she married a man from Bombay, who did not have living space for a wife. So Kalyani went to live with her mother-in-law until her husband found accommodations.

Kalyani's mother-in-law mistreated her, as she had wanted her son to marry another girl; yet Kalyani could not go back to her own home. So she lived unhappily with her mother-in-law, hoping her husband would soon send for her.

After a son was born to her, an older woman advised Kalyani to take the child to its father in Bombay, and offered to accompany her there as Kalyani had never been to the great city.

When they reached the city the woman took Kalyani to a brothel and sold her for four hundred rupees. Kalyani at first refused to give herself to men; yet she had no choice, for there was no way of getting out of the place. She gave in to the keeper at last.

CAGE 2

Seeta was brought up by her widowed mother who worked as a farm hand. She had an easy childhood and was married to a farmer at the age of eleven. After puberty she lived with him for four years and bore him a son. Then her husband died. Seeta lived alone as she did not want to burden her mother.

She worked as a domestic for paid Rs. 5/- per month plus food and clothing. When the other members of the family went out, the master of the house used her sexually. This continued until her mistress found out and dismissed Seeta.

She was now a spoilt woman; she went to Bombay to become a prostitute.

CAGE 3

Parvati's parents were very poor. Her father was a porter and her mother a blind beggar. She was the eldest child and had eleven siblings, all younger than herself. With her family she lived in a *Harijan* colony amongst the poorest people. Parvati picked wastepaper, rags, and bones from the garbage pails and sold them. She used to roam the streets alone at all hours. Men took advantage of her. Parvati had sex experience from the age of eight. At fourteen she was happy, with the approval of her parents, to join an aunt in a brothel.

CAGE 4

Prema's parents were industrial workers and she was their only child. When the parents were away for work, Prema was left alone. When she was fourteen, Prema fell in love with a lorry driver and eloped with him to Bombay, where they lived together for four years.

The man started drinking and beat Prema every day. She ran away and came to Kamathipura, where she found shelter and an easy way of life.

"We are prepared to take any number of men, but they don't come," Prema now complains.

CAGE 5

Sarasa's family lived contentedly, as they had their own farm and house. Sarasa played a lot with the children of her locality and passed a happy and comfortable childhood. At the age of nine she was married to a farmer. Later, she lived with him. Two years passed happily. Then her husband died of a fever.

Sarasa continued to stay with her in-laws, who asked her to remarry; but she felt that her marriage had been broken by God. So it was no use marrying again.

At eighteen Sarasa returned to her own home. She worked on her father's farm for four years and then she saw women from Bombay who appeared to be happy and well-to-do. So she went to Bombay. At Victoria Terminus a *gharwalli* took her to Kamathipura.

"Why do you make me think of days that are now gone?" Sarasa wants to know.

CAGE 6

Sheela was brought up by her widowed mother, a domestic. Her mother loved her and Sheela helped her mother; When Sheela was twelve her mother died of a short illness. She took up her mother's job.

Sheela fell in love with a young man of her neighborhood and married him at thirteen. Within a few months, her husband died. Sheela felt alone and lost. An elderly woman from Bombay persuaded her to return to Bombay with her, where the woman sold her. At first Sheela refused to work. When she found out she could not leave, she capitulated.

CAGE 7

Anjana's parents died when she was ten. She and her sister started working as domestics. When Anjana was fourteen a man from Bombay showed the sisters sympathy, and they went with him to Bombay; where he sold them to a *gharwalli* for Rs. 500/-. The sisters cried but had to give in.

"Everything is left to God," Anjana believes.

CAGE 8

Usha was the only daughter of a sailor who died when she was ten; her mother was a domestic.

Usha's time was her own, and she spent it roaming with friends. By the time she was eighteen she was completely out of her mother's control. Tired of her incorrigible daughter, her mother no longer cared whether Usha came home or not.

The girl stole some gold ornaments from her mother and went to Madras, where an actor's agent obtained work for her in films, as an extra. He harassed her for sexual favors, but she despised him. She preferred to sleep with a film director. The agent began threatening her life, and the director no longer wanted her. Usha migrated to Bombay and became a prostitute.

CAGE 9

Krishna's father died when she was six and her mother found it difficult to earn enough to maintain the family. The mother used to weep that she could not give enough food to her children. Krishna was married at the age of five, when her father was living, to a grown man who had a mistress. He refused to take the girl when she grew up because he was attached to his mistress. Her mother felt sorry that she could not get her married again because of poverty. Krishna came to know a woman from Bombay who explained to her about prostitution. Her mother gave her permission to go with the woman to Bombay and enter the business "because it is better to live comfortably at any cost than to starve."

CAGE 10

Nancy's parents died when she was an infant and she remembers nothing about them. She was brought up by farmers. They gave her enough food and clothes, but treated her like a servant. When she was ten, her guardians left her with a Christian family as a domestic. When her employers left Bombay Nancy was abandoned. She begged on the streets and slept in doorways until she came to windows where women sat with their faces painted. She served as a domestic in a house where most of the women were Chinese. At ten she began accommodating men.

A superstition was then prevalent that a venereal disease could be cured by making love to an under-age girl. By being put to the use of this superstition, the girl suffered several early infections. Although she has now, she claims, effected a partial cure, she has no doubt but that she has infected a number of men.

CAGE 11

Padma was three when her parents died. An old friend of her father, a petty businessman who had no family of his own, brought her up as his own daughter. He was very affectionate toward her and fulfilled her needs till she came of age. She was fourteen when he died.

Padma was left alone. She was attractive to men and was without obligation to anyone. She took up prostitution of her own will, without being seduced into the trade.

"It is just as well not to marry," she feels. "If a woman falls in love with her husband, and is foolish enough to let him detect it, he will deceive her. If she does not fall in love, then she is a slavey. I meet new gentlemen every night, every one of whom swears he loves me. Of course they are all lying. But then that is what I am being paid for—to pretend to believe gentlemen. I would rather be lied to by a variety of gentlemen whom I respect than by a husband I despise."

CAGE 12

Maya's earliest memory was of begging on the streets of a city she now thinks must have been Pandharpur. She remembers a railway station, and of begging through railroad carriages. She remembers a train beginning to move before she could alight and that she was not frightened.

The train came to Bombay and Maya came begging to Kamathipura. She was not yet ten, but a *gharwalli* took her in. She worked in a brothel, as an *ayah,* until she attained puberty. Her *gharwalli* then turned her over to the trade in young girls.

"Just you wait," she stands at the bars of her cage and tells men who are passing, "just you wait, you child-killers."

CAGE 13

Girija lived in an abandoned hut and worked for her neighbors to have food. Girija had nobody in the world. She was grateful to a man who came to her and made love, though she was too young to feel or to understand the act. He used her regularly, sometimes giving her money, and was later replaced by other men. One of these brought her to Bombay and sold her for four hundred rupees.

CAGE 14

Indira grew up tending younger children in a missionary orphanage. Her lot was the storing of water and cleaning of floors. She was nine years old when this routine was interrupted by a trip to Bombay. The child was so charmed by the city that she ran away from the orphanage to return there. Since she spoke only Kannada, it was inevitable that the friends she found were the Kannada-speaking women of Kamathipura. She has since picked up a number of other languages.

CAGE 15

Sundari's parents were weavers who owned their own looms. She was an only daughter, and was brought up strictly. At sixteen she married a man from Bombay, but he did not bring her back to Bombay with him as, he claimed, he did not have living accommodations for her. When he finally brought her to Bombay she had to live there with his mother, who mistreated Sundari because she had wanted her son to marry a widow who owned property. Sundari's husband was afraid of his mother.

When Sundari gave birth to a son, the husband's mother began to beat Sundari at will while the husband stood by. The girl came to Kamathipura to avoid more beatings. The husband now visits her house regularly, and regularly pays the housekeeper for the privilege of sleeping with his own wife. He makes love to her passionately, Sundari says. But after he is through making love he reproaches her: "If I had listened to my mother I would never have married you."

CAGE 16

Sukla's parents were sellers of toddy, and Sukla was the youngest of several toddy-toddlers. She was married, at ten, to a farm-laborer, and began living with him when she was fourteen.

Six months after her first experience of sex, her husband took a mistress whom he refused to give up, although she begged him desperately not to abandon her for the other woman. To this he responded by refusing to have anything to do with her.

"How can I, a young girl, live without a sex-life?" Sukla thought, and left her husband for Bombay.

She has now been a prostitute of Kamathipura for three years, and confesses to be weary of the love of men. She has not practiced Lesbianism; but has felt herself tempted.

"I cannot say I will not drink of that well," Sukla admits, "sooner or later, of that well I will *have* to drink."

CAGE 17

Kamala's father was a mill hand. After her mother died of tuberculosis he married Kamala to a farmer of their native village. Within a year of their marriage she had borne a son to her husband, and he had begun beating her. She carries the scar, on her forehead, of a blow he gave her that knocked her unconscious. When she recovered from this blow she walked out of his house with nothing that belonged to him, carrying her child and wearing only a house-dress, to return to her father.

Her father became wild with her, claiming she had brought a terrible shame upon her family. Kamala left her father's home and has never seen either her child or her father or husband since.

At 4 A.M. the landlord wakens her for his rent of one rupee. At 4 annas as per man, this means she has to take four men merely to make the day's rent. Then the brothel owner collects two rupees from her—eight more men. Thus Kamala has to accommodate twelve men before she has enough to buy food.

"A poor life," Kamala says, "but better than no life at all. God has more than He has spent."

CAGE 18

Long before Ghandi came to the south of India, Kalyani was held in a brothel of the lowest order, against her will. But she succeeded in getting a note out addressed to her husband, advising him of where she was being held.

Kalyani's husband came immediately to that place, and fought bitterly (though no actual blows were exchanged) with his wife's *gharwalli*. He finally got Kalyani out of the place by giving the *gharwalli* a promissory note covering Kalyani's debt to the house.

"As I am now deeply in debt," her husband then told Kalyani, "I will put you in a much better house."

He was as good as his word. The house in which he put her, and in which Kalyani remains to this day, is one of the best in Bombay.

But she is still in debt. It is now plain that no spinning wheel will get her out.

This was why Kalyani asked The Master, "*How is the wheel to save us whom the loom has brought such shame?*"

ARABIAN SEA

Crying hoarse warnings to a soundless sea, the ship slides and dips in the trough of the waters, under a weighted sky. Rail, rigging and deck break out in a coldclinging sweat: the ship is afraid of the sea.

Two hours out of the Port of Cochin, we are running into heavy weather. Somewhere below, behind ladder or beam, Manning lurks, ready to pounce on contraband.

Chips is the party I'm salty about. He hasn't paid me the fifty he promised to return in Bombay.

I discovered him heaped beneath a G.I. blanket on the fantail, pretending to be asleep. I yanked the blanket off him. He was lying face-down naked to the waist, hugging the pillow, like a man dreaming he's having a woman. I kicked the sole of his big fat foot. He opened one great pale eye.

"I want that fifty in Calcutta," I told him.

"You'll get it when I get a draw," he told me, and shut the great pale eye. He looked like something fished from the deeps that hadn't been slit and hung to dry because the Captain thought we'd hooked something of interest to science.

"I'll get it draw or no draw," I promised him, and walked away.

I went up to the radio shack. The door was shut. Within, the ceaseless jot-jot-jot of Morse code informed me Sparks was on the job. When I opened the door he turned his head, headphones clamped, toward me.

"It wasn't any of your business," he told me.

"What business is *that?*" I wanted to know.

He turned back to his work. I knew what he meant alright. He was still salty about my getting between him and Manning to keep him from kicking the man to death. Let him stay salty. I went down to see what the seaborne winos were up to.

Where had I read that seamen had faces bronzed by sun and salt-sea air and that their eyes scanned far horizons? The only horizon I'd ever seen a seaman scan was a clothesline on which damp socks moved in the wind of a small electric fan, deep in the bowels of a ship. Their mugs were the hue of gin except for those who'd been born sunburned.

According to the script, they got homesick in every port. But I'd never seen one hit the beach, with money in his pockets, whose thoughts weren't cutting in closer to the closest whorehouse than to home. Nobody goes for a life on the roving deep whom life on the beach hasn't first made seasick.

Crooked-Neck was the only man in the crew's lounge; he was stretched on his side to favor The Monstrous Boil. A deck of cards was scattered along the mess table. I shuffled them and began dealing myself make-believe draw poker.

"I heard you wrote a poem," Smith began his usual game.

"My trade is writing," I told him defensively.

"Say a poem," he ordered me.

The first hand I dealt held a pair of deuces, a pair of fours and a five. I threw away the five; rather shrewdly, I felt. The strongest hand left was a pair of eights with a pair of aces and a deuce. There goes the first guy's full house, I reflected, and took time out to accommodate Smith.

" The Assyrians came down like a wolf on the fold—"

I remembered—

> *"And his cohorts were gleaming in purple and gold*
> *The sheen of his spears was like stars on the sea*
> *When the blue wave rolls nightly on deep Galilee*
> *Like the leaves of the forest when summer is green*
> *That host with their banners at sunset were seen*
> *Like the leaves of the forest when summer hath flown*
> *That host on the morrow lay withered and strewn—*

"That's all I remember," I told him, drew one card face-down, one to a possible straight, one to a possible flush and one to the aces and eights. The first card I turned up was a deuce: well what do you know, a full house with the case card. The other hands missed, every one. I dealt around once more.

"Come again," Smith ordered. I waited till I had five cards to every hand—

> *"They went forth to battle*
> *But they always fell*
> *Their eyes were fixed upon their sullen shields*
> *Bravely they fought, and nobly*
> *But not well*
> *And on the hard-fought field they always fell."*

I looked at my players' hands while Smith thought *that* one over. The first two hands were dead, but the third needed only one diamond to flush, the fourth held three sixes and the sixth hand held four clubs with a pair of jacks. I drew one card to the first hand, kept a king kicker to the three sixes and split the jacks on the last hand. The first hand missed the flush, the trips didn't improve, but what do you know, the club came in to the last hand! Toward morning the farmer gets lucky.

"It goes this way for days sometimes," Smith began to grieve, "then it gets worse. Every time a man tries to do the right thing the world turns against him, sir."

When Smith added a "sir" he was planning a touch.

"Don't try me for a nickel," I warned him, "I won't bend."

"It isn't money on my mind," he complained, "it's the clap. I developed a drip the morning after we went ashore in Bombay and reported it to Manning. He made me promise to pick up the girl I'd been with and take her with me to the company doc."

I kept dealing.

"It took me half the morning trying to find her. She was living with another hooker and they were both friendly girls. But I couldn't come straight out with my story because I didn't want to get my old-lady-of-the-night-before in Dutch.

"'Do you feel like taking a walk with me?' I asked her. 'No, but if you do, bring back another bottle of rum,' she asked me, and put on an old Johnny Ray record, all about a little white cloud that cried. I began dancing with my old lady's friend.

"I got along *good* with that one. It looked like I had me a new old lady, and my Night-Before-One jumped salty—'We're out of rum,' she told me— 'How about it?' 'Are you coming down to get it with me?' I asked her. 'Get it yourself or blow,' she told me. That made *me* salty.

"'I have to blow anyhow,' I told her, 'account I picked up a dose off you last night and I'm now on my way to the doc, so put on your hat and come with me unless your mind has snapped.' She came at me like gang-busters. She shoved me halfway down the stair—'And don't come back!' she hollered after me.

"I done the best I could, didn't I?" Smith asked me. "After all, I'm not a Health Officer. Then the company doc tells me to use a condom next time and sends me on my way. I didn't have a thing!"

"So what's your beef? I should think you'd be happy to find out you're not sick after all."

"I *was* happy about myself, but not about bugging that girl about being Infected. The only thing I could do was go back and tell her I was wrong. I wouldn't sleep that night if I didn't un-bug her. I went back."

"That was very decent of you, Smith," I told him.

"Wait till I tell you," he cautioned me. "I went back and she was out— maybe gone to her own doctor—and the other girl was just sitting around looking restless. I asked her if I could wait for my Night-Before-Old-Lady and she said sure, and brought out rum and Cokes, and we had a couple of drinks. Then she put on Johnny Ray singing about that little white cloud, and before the cloud had finished crying we were in the sack mak-ing it—that girl was wound up so tight it felt like she never *would* unwind. But when she began unwinding she unwound so fast I had to hurry to catch up: it was absolutely The Greatest Lay—Ouch!"

Smith sat up grimacing with pain—he'd shifted onto The Monstrous Boil a moment. Now he shifted off it with such enormous care that, by the time the move had been made, he'd lost the thread of his story.

"Where was I? Oh yes—there we were, absolutely *out*. I had just strength enough left to fall off that girl and she was already asleep when in walks my Night-Before-Old-Lady—'*What the hell is going on here?* Why you clappified double-backing sonofabitch'—she hauled me off the bed, straddled me and began banging my skull against the floor. She would have beat my brains out if she hadn't reached to grab a hairbrush off the dresser so I could tumble her off. I grabbed my pants and shoes and got through the door with her after me with the hairbrush and down the stairs buck-naked. She came halfway down the stairs, pitched the brush and did a u-turn back into the room. I heard the door slam. I put my pants on in the street."

"What about The Greatest Lay?"

"Either she was completely out or just pretending to be. All the while we were battling she didn't stir Inch One. What happened after I don't know, but I don't think my Night-Before-Lady was hot at *her.* It was the idea she had that I was making out when I had a dose, and I didn't get a chance to tell her I had the doc's okay."

"Don't let it get you down, Smith," I consoled him, "we're all human. We all make mistakes."

"We don't all make mistakes like mine," Smith grieved. "I've caught the worst dose I ever had in my life off The Greatest Lay—and all Manning will do for me is give me pills."

"Don't worry," I told him cheerfully, "maybe it's only congenital."

Night in the
Gardens of
Horn & Hardart

HEMINGWAY AND LARDNER

The god of the Middle Border was a Now-you-see-me-now-you-don't-scratch-my-back-and-I'll-be-back-Sporty-O-Jehovah, propitiable by prayer. So long as you gave him an hour of hymning on Sunday morning and provided an organ with a heavenward trump, he'd vibrate your soul with an I-Shall-Quit-This-Mournful-Vale sensation then let you sleep it off on apple pandowdy all Sunday afternoon.

A God who wouldn't stick needles and pins in your little ones because you cut a corner or two on a real estate deal. What was wrong with speculation so long as you didn't use your own cash? Long before the Pentagon devised the phrase "military dialogue" the owners of the Middle Border knew there was nothing wrong with any war you didn't go to yourself.

If you didn't make trouble for Him, He wouldn't make trouble for you, this God-of-Good-Dividends who never tossed pebbles at your midnight window just to whisper "*Hey you! He who gains his life shall lose it.*" Nor ever tossed a rock through an Oak Park window wrapped in a warning— "*Man shall not live by bread alone, man.*"

Hard times on the rivers and hard times on the plains, hard times on the farm and hard times in town, had bred a midland generation of Righteous Grandfathers who'd stayed right with *Him*. And now, by God, Grandpa had the property to show for it.

Risks that were narrow had all been taken; times that were hard were over at last. What was there left to do in the world now for winners except to keep out losers?

"They built high walls, not only about the walls of their houses," Booth Tarkington observed, "but they walled up their associations with one another as well."

393

Coming from one Righteous Grandfather who owned a good piece of Indiana pandowdy himself, it is curious that Tarkington's observation touches upon that of Chekhov, writing, of Russia's landed gentry, that "there is poverty all around and the footmen are still dressed like court jesters."

For it was not only their homes, and their associations with one another that the winners of the Middle Border walled, but their mills and factories as well. This was not only a means of protecting private property, but also a way of removing their lives from those of the men and women who worked for them. They thus effected a separation of their lives from the life of American multitudes; and subsequently created a dream-world more real to them than the world of struggle going on in the streets. The men that their power and wealth nominated for public office, therefore, were consistently men who prided themselves upon their "practicality."

A practicality as wholly dedicated to keeping their dream-world inviolate as it was to keeping trespassers off their property: they had more success in keeping the violators of property out than in keeping out violators of their dreams.

Among the footmen of literature dressed like court jesters, defending a world in which property and prestige were more real than love and death, were such writers as Tarkington, Clarence Buddington Kelland and William Dean Howells; whose classic comment was that literature should be written for maiden eyes alone.

But American literature has not been made by writing about lives undeflowered. Literature is made upon those occasions when a challenge is put to the legal apparatus by a conscience in touch with humanity.

When the city clerk of Terre Haute refused to issue warrants for arrest of streetwalkers despite his sworn legal duty to issue warrants for arrest of streetwalkers, and instead demanded of the Terre Haute police, "Why don't you make war on people in high life instead of upon these penniless girls?" that little sport performed an act of literature.

For he was sustaining the great beginning Whitman had made when he wrote "there shall be no difference between them and the rest." A beginning marked by an exuberant good humor; that yet sought darkly for understanding of America.

And sought through New York's Bowery and down Main Street of Winesburg to the edge of town; where the last gaslamp makes all America look hired.

A search past 4 A.M. gas stations upon nights when cats freeze to death on fire escapes and chimneys race the moon; down streets that Sister Carrie knew.

Beyond the grandfathers' walls there began to flow a bloodcolored current of vindictive life; that was fed into America's heart by violators of the grandfathers' dreams.

These were impractical men who lived upon a street for whom nobody prayed; where the cries of the sick, the tortured and the maimed had gone unheard.

They were the accused with whom Whitman had taken his stand when he wrote "I belong to those convicts and prostitutes myself." Guilty or not guilty, Whitman pled the defense.

As Stephen Crane had taken his place beside Maggie; as had Dreiser beside Clyde Griffiths. As had O'Neill beside Anna Christiansen; as had Richard Wright beside Bigger Thomas. As had Tennessee Williams beside Blanche DuBois. And where James Baldwin made his still-unanswered challenge: "If you don't know my name you don't know your own."

What these writers shared was the perception that the owners of their society had not only lost touch with one another, but with their own true selves. The youth who had early armored himself against love became the man who found greater gratification in property than in love; the girl who began by evading the touch of the propertyless man became the woman demanding that Robin Hood be banned from the local library. For the prophets and preachers of this midland bourgeoisie damned the basic act of love as piggishness; while dignifying acquisitiveness, if succeeding on a scale sufficiently grand, as virtuous. Thus marriage consummated more for increase of property than for physical gratification seemed, to this strata, to be morally higher.

"When one is peacefully at home," Chekhov had seen what all these impractical men had also seen, "life seems ordinary. But when one goes into the street and questions women life becomes terrible."

It wasn't Tarkington but another Hoosier who heard, below the roar of ballpark crowds with a doubleheader sun striped across them, cries for help from beneath the stands. Ring Lardner left the park laughing strangely to himself. And later sat drinking alone.

Lardner's women come out of that same suburb of hell wherein Eliot's women waited in parlors for husbands with headpieces made of straw.

Indeed those splenetic vixens, whom W. C. Fields feared perpetually to confront, occupy the kitchen of the same house. Lardner's marvelous mimicry barely concealed his dread.

Though all his marriages are desperate, and all his Women prepare to cry to have their own way, their tears are never from disappointment of the flesh. Lardner's woman weeps because another woman's husband is succeeding faster than her own; because a daughter married beneath her, or because her son failed to make a certain fraternity.

The desolation of her view is reflected by that of Lardner's aging husband looking out the window of a Miami-bound Pullman:

"First we'd see a few pine trees with fuzz on 'em and then a couple acres of yellow mud. Then there'd be more pine trees 'n more fuzz and more yellow mud. And after a while we'd come to some pine trees with fuzz on 'em and then, if we watched close, we'd see some yellow mud."

The God of the Middle Border had avenged Himself. He had let the Righteous Survivors sleep untroubled only to waken to a nightmare: the wills by which men and women had been divided from their true selves now divided them from conscience. The men they named to speak for them were men whose morality was no more than a projection of consciencelessness in the name of a whole class. Saith the pandowdy Jehovah: "If you're well-to-do you don't need a soul."

The heart had been made fat and the ears heavy. They heard but understood not. They saw yet perceived not.

Nada was a sea of yellow mud seen through a Pullman window.

Ring Lardner discerned the myths. He heard the cries. But he didn't know what to do about the lies. In a mock-biography he reported himself as a radio enthusiast who had designed his own set:

"At first he was unable to get any station at all and this condition held good to the day of his death. But he was always trying to tune in on Glens Falls, New York. It was not until his last illness that he learned there was no broadcasting station in that place."

There was no broadcasting station in America. Lardner ended with nothing to tune in on. Hemingway's own set did not begin to work until he was in Paris.

II. HEMINGWAY HIMSELF

The surprising thing, next to their progressive corpulence, is the amount of paper that is scattered about the dead. Their ultimate position, before there is any question of burial, depends on the location of the pockets in the uniform. In the Austrian army these pockets were in the back of the breeches and the dead, after a short time, all consequently lay on their faces, the two hip pockets pulled out and, scattered around them in the grass, all those papers their pockets had contained. The heat, the flies, the indicative positions of the bodies in the grass, and the amount of paper scattered are the impressions one retains.

Out of the scattered letters of that field, Hemingway wrote his own letter to the world.

He wrote to the woman whose life, she had been told, had been complete by having her own checking account. To her, the death of Catherine Barkley brought a fear that she who guards her life too well might lose it. A strange unease surrounded her heart. Was it possible that one had to earn one's death in order to become alive? And should no tragic pour strike for her, would it not mean that her own death would be nothing more than a mere sloughing off into earth of a husk no sun had warmly touched?

> *And light was all it needed*
> *And a little cleanness and order.*

To this woman, watching her husband waving goodnight to friends in his well-lit door, he seemed unaware of that dark precipitous edge whereupon both endured their days and nights together. She had no way of knowing that he, too, was secretly afraid.

> *What did he fear? It was not fear or dread*
> *It was a nothing that he knew too well.*

If an increasing awareness of the precariousness of life is increase of wisdom, the death of Catherine Barkley made this woman wiser. And if the belief she had sustained in an afterlife was thereby shaken, it was because her own life began to feel like a sieve through which living hours kept draining.

Hemingway liked to say that he wrote on the principle of the iceberg that has seven-eighths under water for the one part showing above. And how aware he himself was of his own depths can only be guessed.

He knew he had the critics fooled, those who, like Macdonald, swallowed the image put out by one *Esquire* illustrator, depicting him machine-gunning sharks. That he would take a machine-gun to sea is as preposterous as it would be to take a howitzer on safari. That was the image all the same: The Violent American, the man of no memory all muscle and blood, standing with one foot on the head of a slain lion.

Among the critics, only Malcolm Cowley and Maxwell Ceismar have perceived that what Hemingway appeared to be—the Byronic reporter of the bullring, the boxing ring and battle—was only the surface of this writer. If he had been no more than this—had he been only the writer who most represented his time—he would never have provoked the attacks of the begrudgers. It was his submerged sources which troubled them so. For he did not represent his time at all: he made his time represent him. Because within him the whole buried burden of America's guilt, the self-destructiveness of a people who felt their lives were being lived by somebody else, found expression.

In a sense of longing and a sense of loss, Hemingway identified himself with the victims of America; as though those most unworthy of love were the most worthy of it.

His sketch, called *A Pursuit Race,* in which Campbell, an advance-man for a burlesque show, wearies of trying to stay one town ahead of the show, demonstrates Hemingway's early commitment to those who resigned not only from war, but from the race for Success.

"I'm hopped to the eyes," Campbell tells Turner, his boss, when Turner finds him under the sheets in a cheap hotel. Then, rolling up his sleeve, Campbell reveals a line of purple blue punctures from elbow to wrist.

"They've got a cure for that," Turner assures Campbell.

"They haven't got a cure for anything," Campbell contradicts Turner.

Then, caressing the sheet with lips and tongue: "Dear sheet, I can kiss this sheet and see through it at the same time . . . Stick to sheets, Billy. Keep away from women and horses and eagles. If you love horses you'll get horseshit and if you love eagles you'll get eagleshit and if you love women you'll get a dose."

"Are you alright?" Billy asks.

"I was never so happy in my life."

This is not merely a story about drug addiction. It is a report on isolation as an American affliction.

Hemingway came of a strata so afflicted. His great innovation was not the devising of a literary style, but bringing to this class a realization of what was real and what was unreal. A realization for which he went back to the Old Testament.

> *The sun also ariseth, and the sun goeth down, and hasteneth to the Place where it ariseth . . . and there is no new thing under the sun.*

The reason that the critics failed Hemingway is simple: they didn't read Hemingway. They read, instead, other critics of Hemingway.

"I did not try to see behind the façade," an Italian critic admits with contentment, "nor what view of life was beyond that depersonalized style. This has been done, however, in Mr. Savage's essay." He doesn't tell us what critic Mr. Savage went to to understand Hemingway.

Nevertheless—we have his word on it—that "Mr. Savage shows how the entire extrusion of personality into the outward sensational world makes Hemingway's characters the inwardly passive victims of a meaningless determinism; how the profound spiritual inertia, the inner vacuity and impotence, which is a mark of all Hemingway's projected characters, ends in a deadening sense of boredom and negation which can only be relieved by violent, though still essentially meaningless, activity; how the final upshot of it all is the total absence of a sense of life, so that life is brought into a sensational vividness only by contrast with the nullity of death."

I never cease to be astonished when I see someone like this dealing with half a deck and nobody calling him on it. "The most essential gift for a good writer," Hemingway told an interviewer, "is a built-in, shock-proof, shit-detector." Almost any kind of detector would serve to detect what the above critic is spreading around.

Another charge the critics made against Hemingway consistently was that he was a man who wrote as though he had no memory. And yet it was Hemingway, and none other, whose memory was adequate enough to give new life to John Donne's sermon that no man is an island. For his memory worked in terms of a race-memory; whereas theirs was limited to the dates of their own reviews.

Nor was his style a clever trick, an acquired device that a clever young man, panting to get along in the world, picked up from Gertrude Stein, as Macdonald claims. It wasn't Hemingway who needed to follow Miss Stein around Paris with notebook and pencil poised, but Miss Stein who needed the pencil. His style was the means by which he fulfilled a need uniquely his own; thus filling a need of the company of men.

This need was for light and simplicity. In achieving it for himself he achieved it for others enduring a murky complexity. By strength of his own love he forced a door. That opened into a country in which, for those willing to risk themselves, love and death became realities.

For Hemingway, in his life as well as in his writing, always left a door wide for others to enter.

Robert Frost, at his 75th birthday party, found himself being introduced to Gene Tunney.

"How did it happen that Hemingway bloodied your nose?" Frost asked just that fast.

Tunney took a step back as though he'd just walked into a stiff jab.

"I was trying to teach him something," Tunney remembered, "but you had to watch him every second."

What Macdonald means, in saying that *he* had Hemingway's goat, is merely that Hemingway never considered him a worthy opponent.

Why should he? There's one in every crowd.

III. THE REAL THING IN KITSCH

I once observed another bearded man trying to force another door: one of those little glass jobs of Horn & Hardart's. In the days when you had either to smash the glass or put in some nickels.

As a man of force, this one might have smashed a lemon chiffon pie without leaving an imprint unless he were using both hands and chocolate would have stopped him cold. He was a critic whose passion for nickels was barely surpassed by his concern for his corpuscles. Precisely, his passion was so corpuscular that, once had he announced himself as "The Diagnostician of our diseased culture," the self-congratulatory tone was justified; as he himself was a charter member of the affliction.

At the moment, this curious fellow had a salad in hand and was trying to get the attention of someone behind one of the little windows. Something had gone wrong at Horn & Hardart's.

The girl who was witnessing this scene beside me was from out of town. She was from so far out of town that she called the place "*L' Automatique.*"

"Does your friend have a difficulty?" she wanted to know. For the Diagnostician of a Diseased Culture had now put his salad down as if it were contagious. He was dissenting from somebody who was behind the window; judging by his expression, his dissent was sharp.

"He says that American culture is a pudding of mediocrity," I reported, "if you call that 'a difficulty.'"

Now he picked up the salad he'd put down and tried to insert it into the open window—it shut so fast he had just time to withdraw his fingers. But the fringe of his beard caught and there he was, trapped with a salad in one hand. He was a tall man and he'd been caught bending. He rapped the glass and waved the salad until the window was opened, releasing him. Then it shut. He inserted a nickel. It reopened, he drew out a second salad and returned to our table, carrying both.

Yet he appeared perfectly composed.

"Is it not permitted to make exchange of salads in *L'Automatique?*" the girl asked about the rules.

"When God is dead, *all* is permitted," the critic quoted Dostoevsky contentedly; in a kindly tone.

"Providing one puts in an extra nickel," I pointed out.

He was a critic with a beard that appeared to be more of an appendage fastened with Elmer's Glue-All than anything growing from skin. He was a de-corpuscled diagnostician who preferred riding the subway to taking taxis unless he was pursuing a celebrity. His pleasures were few and riding in a taxi with a celebrity was an experience as rich to him as riding a passenger train.

Bartenders regarded him without enthusiasm because The Dram Shop Act discouraged them from throwing him out. They didn't mind his mixing Coca-Cola and Scotch so much as they did his using half a case of Cokes to one shot of Scotch. Celebrities seldom minded him because they were never sure which one he was.

"What kind of writer is he?" my friend inquired, after the critic had left his two salads for us to guard, pending his return from another visit to the little windows.

"A kind difficult to define," I decided, "his field seems to be that of deriding Philistines for exploiting the *avant-garde.*"

"And *do* Philistines exploit the *avant-garde?*" she inquired.

"No. The *avant-garde* exploits the Philistines."

The Diagnostician was now in a dispute with the handle of a faucet that pours a nickel's worth of milk into a nickel's worth of coffee, this combination then being purchasable for a dime. Assuming that a man who could measure an entire culture could tell at a glance that he'd gotten only nine cents' worth, the faucet was obviously in the wrong.

"Is it not against the rules, exploitation?" the girl asked, eyeing the begoggled wretch suspiciously.

"It is," I tried to bring her up to date—"but they keep changing the rules. It used to be *against* the rules for an artist to become rich. He was *supposed* to live in extreme poverty and remain unknown until he died of exposure. Upon which event his fame would become widespread and great sums would be made out of the beauty found in his paintings or his books or his songs. Now he doesn't have to die to become famous. He doesn't, in fact, have to create a work of beauty. In fact he doesn't even have to be good. All he has to be today is become *avant-garde.*

"You see, so many people have become rich, and so few people are recognized *avant-gardists,* that it is like a country run by electricity where there is a shortage of electricians. There are simply not enough *avant-gardists* to go around.

"So many people have become rich so easily that they can't get enough of books that tell them how rotten they are. This provides a neat way for the *avant-gardist* not only to denounce culture, but to get rich by doing it. And the Philistines are so afraid that someone will catch them *not* applauding, that a writer, like our friend, not only makes money by being against *kitsch* but earns a reputation for being *avant-gardist* too."

"I do not understand this *kitsch,*" the girl admitted, "is it the pudding of no plums?"

"Not exactly," I told her. "It is a pudding that *pretends* to have plums. It is any song, or play, or book, or painting, or film that pretends to be profound although it is shallow, and true although it is false."

"Then it is good that your friend is against *kitsch*—is it not?"

"It would be *if* he were. But where *kitsch* comes in, he is the country's widest distributor of it."

"Again I do not understand."

"I will try to be more precise," I promised her, "*par example:* our friend expresses extreme distress at the thing that Hollywood writers do to a good novel, when adapting it to film, which they term 'licking a book into shape.' He claims that what this means is to drain the novel of all reality and offer its corpse on the screen."

"This is a dreadful deed indeed," the girl exclaimed.

"Be patient," I reproached her, "I am still *par-exampling.* Because at this dreadful-deed-indeed called 'licking a book into shape,' no writer in America is more skillful than is our friend."

"I cannot bear to hear more," she whispered in my ear.

"Try all the same," I asked her, "you will be fascinated by its unimportance."

I was keeping an eye on our Diagnostician—whom we shall henceforward refer to, Dear Reader, simply as 'Macdonald,' as that is shorter than 'Diagnostician'—and saw he was now tied up in an argument with the woman who changes quarters into nickels. I assumed he was trying to get six.

"*Par example*": I continued, "during the Spanish Civil War an American actor named Flynn arrived at the Spanish border accompanied by his studio's publicity department. He was photographed in a Spanish Republican militiaman's uniform, being greeted by a Spanish Republican militiaman, and the photograph was sent to newspapers all over the world with the story that the actor was now fighting against Facism. When the stunt was over he returned to his yacht, anchored in French waters, and had a party."

"I am disgusted with your Flynn," the girl assured me.

"Don't bother," I suggested. "For one thing, he is dead; and, for a second, he wasn't *my* Flynn."

"Then what is the point of telling me?" she wanted to know. She was a child of a strong curiosity.

"The point is that when Hemingway became just as dead as Flynn, and Macdonald made it his business to sum up the man's life, it wasn't necessary for him to compare Flynn's adventure in Spain with Hemingway's in order to create the impression that there was no difference. The picture of Flynn fighting Fascism by shaking hands with a Republican militiaman and that of Hemingway doing the same thing, made it necessary for Macdonald only to comment about how much Hemingway loved being photographed.

"*Kitsch* is a way of implying when one lacks the courage to speak directly. He thus created an impression that Hemingway, too, was faking. All he omitted was that Hemingway was on the Spanish front, in the worst part of the fighting between Madrid and Barcelona for two years. All he omitted was that Hemingway endured battle, wrote the best dispatches on the fighting, assisted on a movie called *Spanish Earth* and, later, wrote a novel about that war which brought the necessity of defeating Fascism in Spain to multitudes in America."

"What was the pudding-man doing at that time?" she wanted to know.

"An excellent question," I congratulated her, "he was discovering a way to be a dissenter against the way we live and at the same time to earn good dividends."

"How is *this* done?" she asked me.

"I'm *trying* to tell you," I scolded her—"it is done by being extremely careful about disapproving of the society in which one lives while at the same time being *very* angry at its art. By doing this one is not at all likely to be subpoenaed by a Congressional Committee asking what organizations one belongs to. Congressmen do not consider organizations of intellectuals to be dangerous. In another country, yes. Not here. Here it is the men who organize unions that must be watched. And by knowing this, Macdonald is able to be against things as they are in *Dissent* and for things as they are in *Encounter,* and to make as much money by saying things *against* them one week, as he does by taking them all back the next. This he has learned from watching Hollywood writers lick a book into shape. Only he goes farther—he knows how to lick a *writer* into shape."

"He sounds terribly confused," the girl observed.

"On the contrary," I insisted, "he is very clear-headed."

"But does not this kind of process have a poor effect on the writing of the *avant-garde?*"

"It leaves the *avant-garde* with no distinction between themselves and the Philistinism except to change their own name to 'hipsters' and that of the Philistines to 'squares.' And makes it possible to have both garlic dressing and roquefort."

"In the pudding of mediocrity," the girl said thoughtfully—and this was a most thoughtful girl—"I think Macdonald is no plum."

At which moment the Diagnostician materialized beside us with a face full of explanations.

"I didn't mind paying the extra nickel," he advised us, "but I prefer roquefort to garlic and it looked to me like an even trade." He drew the salads closer, for purposes of comparison. "How do they look to you?"

I failed to see the trap.

"Frankly," I told him, "the garlic salad looks better."

Immediately he put it in front of me. "I can't eat both," he assured me, "it's only twenty cents."

Had it not been for wanting to make a strong impression on the girl I *might* have pushed it back. Instead, I found a twenty-five-cent piece and handed it to Macdonald.

He pocketed it and evaded my gaze while a triumphant flush rose in his cheeks at the realization that he had recouped the difference in price between garlic and roquefort.

Only he hadn't. I fixed him with an eye so steely that at last he reached into a small dime-store wallet, unhooked a brass clasp and brought forth a nickel.

He ate the roquefort with a disappointed air. And left us, immediately after, with the same aura of silent reproach. There was no doubt we were both *kitschers* now.

Yet I could not help but marvel at what I had seen: a man recognized as an arbiter of literary style who himself did not possess ordinary grace sufficient to see him through a meal in an Automat.

"In *L'Automatique*," my friend observed after he had left, "*all* seems *automatique*."

Well, I *told* you she was from out of town.

BAY OF BENGAL

"Never let a woman get so worldly-wise that she loses her leadership," Smith glanced up at me from the table where he'd been shuffling a beat-up deck, "I took a seventeen-year-old bum named Gracie and made a fast-stepping queen out of her, but she lacked leadership. The minute you let a woman feel she don't need you to lean on, she's off and away."

"What's our next port?" I wanted to know.

"Calcutta. Gracie got so near to perfect I changed her name to Old Faithful. She kept herself that clean, and kept our apartment that neat, she cooked so good, and done whatever I told her without asking questions, and all the while bringing in five hundred to seven-fifty a week, I had to belt her now and then for being *too* perfect—what else *was* there to belt her for?"

"Was she good-looking?" I asked.

"The doll of the world. One hundred and four pounds of redheaded ravishment, that was all."

"You should have married her," I suggested.

"The truth of the matter is, Mister," Smith assured me, "was that taking out papers on Gracie was *exactly* what I had in mind. When a hustling woman has had as many chances as Gracie had to put me in the pen and didn't, she deserves to work out of a home instead of a bar."

"How's your boil?" I inquired.

"You see, I owned the bar Gracie was working out of—and it wasn't a bar—it was a taproom."

"I didn't know there was a difference," I admitted.

"You would if you had to run one in Santa Vaca," Smith informed me, "where all the bars had to shut down at twelve o'clock but a taproom could stay open till four. That made a difference when a ship was docked in town. That was why I called my place *The Fantail*—like it was someplace you just hung around off duty. I know you think I'm a bum, sir, but that's only because you met me at sea. On the beach I'm a first-class operator and I know my trade."

"Every time I talk to you you have a new trade," I had to point out to him.

"I had a three-piece combo going for me, and the drummer had one of those rubber deals we used to slip over a gearshift for when things got out of hand. The piano player wore knucks. The trumpet man was unarmed because he was a sissy. Gracie kept a pound jar of Pond's cold cream in her handbag, and we had an old spade called Bull who took care of the men's room. Bull was very dignified and wore a high white collar and tie, but I never called on him except in ex*treme* emergency because he was on probation and hadn't ought to be working where liquor was sold. We were *ready.*"

Smith began that slow rotation of his skull which betokened inner agitation.

"I left the joint early one night—about twelve—and left Gracie in charge. It was breaking daylight when she came in. I was in bed. She put eighty-five bucks on the dresser. Then she took off her slipper and put two c-notes on top of the eighty-five.

"'Where're *they* from?' I asked her.

"'A new trick,' she told me.

"'I didn't notice him—he must have come in after I left,' I told her.

"'No, he was there when you left. The Bosun's Mate,' she told me.

"'*Him?*' I asked her. '*Him?* Where would *he* get two bills to blow so free and easy?'

"'I don't know, Daddy,' she told me, 'but the man is ready to beat.'

"'You don't know where the money is from but you think the man is ready to beat?' I tried her.

"'Not if *you* don't think so, Daddy,' she told me, coming into bed.

"I let her go to sleep. I didn't mind beating a Bosun's Mate but I didn't want to undertake whipping the American navy. What if it were ship's funds the man was spending?

"'I don't want you to rap to that new trick,' I told Gracie the first thing in the morning. 'Don't even say "hello."'

"'Whatever you say, Daddy,' she agreed.

"Things never start the way you think they're going to. Gracie shook the Bosun's Mate off, wouldn't even drink with him, and he left without a beef. After he left I relaxed because, what I hadn't told Gracie, the reason I was scared of the man wasn't that he might be a thief so much as I was afraid he *might* be law. I was sitting there with a couple old-time hookers, thinking about this move to myself, when one of the hookers says, of a sudden, 'All I want to do is get married.' 'What in God's name you hangin' around *here* for then?' I asked her. 'To give the joint a little class,' she answered me. 'You wouldn't add class to a geek-show,' I let her know, 'every time you come in that door the joint is brought down.' 'In that event I'll leave,' she jumps salty. ''N don't come back'—I threw that in just to speed her on her way and she stops dead at the door—'Just for that last crack,' she tells me. 'I am coming back.' 'We'll wait,' I let her know, not worrying about a thing.

"It wasn't half an hour before the door flies open and in comes a flying wedge of so many seamen I thought the S.S. *Idaho* must be in port—at least forty of them lined up at the bar and here comes the Bosun's Mate—250 pounds of him in new whites acting like he never been in the joint before.

"'Who's the head-pimp here?' he wants to know, coming directly to me to put that question.

"'I am,' I told him, 'you looking for work?'—and he slugged me so fast I went ass over teakettle and landed against the bar.

"'And now,' he tells me while I'm still sitting there trying to clear my head, 'we're going to wreck this joint.'

"'Let me lock the door,' I asked him, 'and we'll help you wreck it.'

"I made it through that mob of sailors to the door, even though my head was still swinging from that sock he give me. I got the door locked. Then *we* went to work.

"I wrapped myself around one of the Bosun's arms, the drummer got the other, and the sissy rapped him with the gearshift-cover. The man didn't even shake. 'I'll kill you a hundred times!' the sissy hollered, and rapped him again. He shook, but didn't go down. 'Give *me* that thing,' I told the sissy, and I brought that rubber down flat on the man's skull. But he didn't go down.

"'Let *me* try,' the drummer asked, and I handed the rubber to the drummer. He tried it from the back on the very point of the man's skull. That worked better. The man went down.

"But he got right up.

"'Get Bull,' I told the sissy.

"Bull came out in his high collar and tie, grasped the situation and made a sign for us to step aside. Bull backed up a few feet, then came on skull first right into the Bosun's middle. The man made a sound like *Wuff-ooooof* and went down doubled up. Then we went to work on the others.

"By the time the shore patrol got there we had fifteen sailors laid out. The rest had fled. The Bosun's Mate had come to, but all he could do was sit in the middle of the floor and hold his middle.

The next day the navy hung an OFF LIMITS sign on us. I was as good as out of business. I went to see the Commandant.

"'Sir,' I told him, 'I've served my country's armed forces too.'

"'What has that got to do with it?' he asked me.

"'Sir,' I tried another tack, 'I realize we hospitalized one or two of your men.'

"'Six of them are still in traction,' he told me, but I think he was exaggerating."

Danielsen came in wearing that lonesome smile; without saying what he had in mind in coming down to the crew's lounge.

"No game tonight," Smith told him, "the guys aren't taking another draw until we hit Calcutta."

Then, since Danielsen merely stood there smiling wanly, Smith concluded his wandering tale.

"I was shut down for twenty-three days. Gracie had to start working out of a joint called *The Club Gayety.* I went to see the Commandant every day. 'I'm sorry as can be, sir,' I'd tell him, 'that we put your men in traction. But, in a manner of speaking, sir, you have *me* in traction too. I can't move either.'

"'In that case we'll take you out of traction when my men get out,' he told me.

"'But that may be weeks,' I beefed.

"'Might be months,' he told me.

"'I'll be out of business by that time, sir,' I told him.

"'Your old lady will help make ends meet,' he tells me just like that.

"'Can we leave her out of this, sir?' I asked him.

"'Well,' he tells me, sitting back comfortably in his big navy chair, 'you *are* a pimp, aren't you, Smith?'

"'I'm not sure what you mean by that, sir,' I told him, staying cool as possible. "'I run a bar where seamen come looking for women and I don't stand in the way of their wishes, that's all.'"

Smith glanced at Danielsen to see whether the man had decided what he wanted; but all Danielsen did was to smile remotely.

"You see," Smith addressed himself once more to me, "I realized that what the man was doing was trying to provoke me. He was being straight-on insulting so I'd flip and try to slug him, only I didn't flip. I set myself to let anything he said roll off me.

"'O,' he tells me, 'I *beg* your pardon—I thought one of them red-headed whores was your wife.'

"That *almost* did it—but not quite. I felt my throat go dry and felt my face burning. But I gave him a kindly smile all the same.

"'Sir,' I asked him, gentle-like, 'has it ever occurred to you that anyone of us *might* have been the Christ Child?'

"He lost color because he hadn't expected me to turn sweet on him. Then he started getting red. I saw it was the moment to reach him.

"'I'm afraid my wife will leave me if we don't get the place open soon, sir,' I told him—and got out of there fast.

"The next day the shore patrol came by in a jeep, took down the OFF LIMITS sign, gave me a paper to sign releasing the navy from any legal responsibility, and wheeled away."

"You and Gracie must have had a ball *that* night," I surmised.

"It wasn't merely a ball," Smith assured me—"it was a *celebration*—only Gracie wasn't there."

"Gracie wasn't there?" I asked, with the uneasy feeling I've been had again.

"O no," Smith assured me lightly, "she took off with the Bosun's Mate. Like I told you—never let a woman get so worldly-wise that she loses her leadership. Always remember that you can always treat a woman too good—but you can never treat one too bad."

"Look, Smith," I had to protest, "you got a boil on your ass as big as your mouth and you got plates in your mouth that don't fit. You owe everybody aboard and you've got chronic clap. Manning has your dis-charge papers ready to hand to the company as soon as the ship hits Long Beach and who do you think is going to give a man in your condition a job? You are absolutely the most-fouled-up man I've ever known on land or sea and the worst of it is you don't even seem to know it."

Smith hitched his neck a notch outward to indicate he was giving serious reflection to my reproach.

"You left something out, sir," he told me after a minute, in the humblest voice I'd ever heard him employ—"my wife is in and out of the loony-bin like a fiddler's elbow. Every time I send her an allotment the neighborhood winos take it out of our mailbox, sign it with her name and cash it. The poor thing is lucky if she gets a bottle out of it for herself. I can't do anything about it because my sister-in-law has a rape warrant out on me. And you understand that anyone with a chest as weak as mine can't afford to get into violent situations—to see my brother again would be to risk tuberculosis. Could you let me have five dollars till I get my draw in Calcutta, sir?"

I found myself examining my wallet and, finding it had nothing in it but a ten-dollar bill, showed it to Smith in order to prove that I didn't have five to loan him.

"I'll be right back with your change, sir," I heard him say and noticed that I wasn't holding the tenner anymore.

"What did he mean?" Danielsen asked me.

"Mean by what?"

"By saying that anyone of us might have been Christ?"

"Your guess is as good as mine."

Danielsen turned to leave, but I had a question of my own. He waited.

"Sparks told me that when a sailor is buried at sea and the ship's carpenter sews him up, the last stitch goes through the nose. Is there anything to it?"

"An old sea-tradition still faithfully observed," Danielsen assured me, and again turned to leave.

"*Why?*"—I stopped him—"*why?*"

"Your guess is as good as mine."

That irritated me.

"What the goddamn hell is all the stupid *secrecy* about?" I demanded to know. "You're the fourth man I've asked and everybody ducks like I'm asking a woman about her wedding night or something. There *has* to be a reason."

"There is," Danielsen told me, but lowering his voice and regarding me somehow remotely: "Seamen live between water and land and belong to neither, their whole lives. They can't rest at sea and they can't get rest on land. So they get to thinking that, after death on the ocean bottom, they'll rest forever. But if a dead man's nostrils are left open, he'll take in too much water to get all the way down. He'll float, as he has in life, between bottom and top and never rest for all eternity."

"You're putting me on," was all I could think to say.

The change in Danielsen startled me. It looked like genuine anger. I'd never seen even the hint of that in him. Then his color returned, and he left without a word.

"They'll like me in Calcutta," I assured myself.

The Quais
of Calcutta

A low half-moon came nodding toward our rigging; then nodded quietly away. A moon at rest, half-wearied yet uneasy, returned and still retreated. A moon for payday lovers, regretting passion spent.

Deep below-decks the seaman lies; whose whore sleeps well in Pusan or Kowloon. The orange-red lamp that lit his pleasure in Ho-Phang Road, burns for another seaman's joy tonight. Seaman who sleeps not well below: the moon is on the beach and broke again.

The tides of night still promise love from all earth's Bamboo Alleys. Women wait, in places called *Club Frisco* and *Sam's New York Bar,* for youths from Denver, Philly and The Bronx. All seas swell with women's longing, ceaselessly. Great fish are sleeping on the waters.

While the moon wanes slowly to ash-white.

Dock-hawks, pretending to be owls, followed us upriver; till our rigging severed the night's last star.

A smear across a dungsmoke pall became the ordinary day.

And dogs of those quais never bark but run away.

Then cowdung cooks, where their barge-fires burned beside our hull, blew smoke across our rails and readied for their day. We tied into a jungle of masts and jutting spars.

Whatever they were cooking was too pungent to be fried eggs: that had just occurred to me when the mad head of Crooked-Neck Smith, crowned with hair like feathers afire, thrust itself eye-level to the passenger deck; where it had no business being thrust. Seeing me he came up all the way; his head only one notch awry.

"Notice anything conspicuous about me?" Smith wanted to know.

His shirt, transparently thin, was jutting with contraband.

"Nothing but two cartons of Pall Malls," I told him, "the other looks like Chesterfields."

"Man!" Smith feigned astonishment, "how old are you?"

"Past fifty," I had to admit.

"And with the eyes of a twenty-year-old Cheyenne!—God, I bet when you were *my* age you could see right *through* people!"

"I can still see through you," I let him know, "I won't let you have a dime."

"How about ten bucks?"

"Not ten cents and not ten bucks either."

"You doubt I'm good for it?" Smith's tone accused me.

"No doubt whatsoever. I *know* you're not good for it."

Smith's head jerked half a notch out: he was getting hot. Then he decided he'd just be hurt.

"I can borrow from any man aboard this ship, sir. You *know* that. But as you're our only passenger I wanted to give you first crack."

"I don't deserve it," I told him, "give my chance to Manning."

"Smith," Manning came bellowing down-deck as though he'd been called—"Smith! *Don't move!*" But Smith was already to the ladder. Manning watched him skipping down.

"You're going to get this ship in trouble, Smith!" Manning warned him, then stood looking down at something on the dock. I went over and looked too. It was a young Indian woman in dirty robes, hair matted and eyes sunken. She held one palm upward toward us.

"Papa!" she pleaded, "you give!"

Both Manning and I stared at this sight of living starvation: and living starvation stared back at Manning and me.

"Don't call *me* your papa," Manning called down—"I'm not *your* father."

And when I looked at him he was ashen-pale.

I recall tossing a coin onto the dock and seeing a uniformed guard bearing down on the woman to take it from her. When I looked at Manning again his color had returned.

"Caught Chips with nine cartons," he reported to me briskly, "three Camels, three Old Golds, three Kools."

"Congratulations," I told him.

"Seamen *never* learn," he explained, "just because Customs is soft in one port they think Customs is soft everywhere. I have to protect them from themselves."

Glancing across his shoulder I saw four white-uniformed men drive onto the quai. The only officers who wear white in India are customs cops. As I watched, another car, with four more, joined them. All eight waited in the cars. Manning turned to see what was transfixing me.

"What are *they* up to?" I heard him ask himself.

"Waiting to come aboard," I told him as though nobody else could possibly have guessed.

Manning took off his officer's cap and began running a finger around its sweatband.

"They usually only send Sirdar," he complained.

"Who's Sirdar?" I asked, but he didn't answer.

I left him running one finger around and around his hat.

I found Concannon half stripped at his mirror and preparing to shave. A pair of new whites lay on his bunk.

"*Accentchuate the positive,*" he was singing or bawling "*Ee-liminate the negative / Latch on to the affirmative—*"

Sparks was feeling better.

"Going ashore, Sparks?" I inquired.

"Not *about* to stay aboard."

"You're going to be delayed."

Concannon went to the rail, took one look and began pitching bottles and cartons into the depths of the receiving set that ran the length of his shack. In its vasty deeps he had receivers hidden within receivers.

"I once crammed a little whore in here—she was cramped but she came out okay. All she needed was a shower. Paid her extra. Now," he paused, "was that in Macao or Saigon?" Then he remembered our transistors.

"*Get those sets,*" he commanded me, and I was off straight down into a hell of boilers, pistons and furnaces, barometers and engines, that got hotter and deeper as I descended. At the bottom of that broiling pit I took one moment to look up, down, and all around lest Manning be lurking behind a boiler. We'd hidden the sets behind a red warning: DANGER: HIGH VOLTAGE. I began the ascent, with two sets under each arm, two steps at a time. By the time I reached the deck I was pouring sweat.

The deck was clear. I made the run to the radio shack—followed in by Smith, breathing as hard as I was.

"I only followed you halfway down," he apologized. "I was protecting you against Manning."

What Smith was after was a place to hide his own contraband. Concannon took his cartons and dumped them after our transistors.

"Stay away from Smith ashore," Concannon advised me.

I went to the officer's lounge to see what was happening.

The customs cop questioning the Captain seemed to sense that Karensen couldn't afford to lose another ship.

"Your ship has a bad name, Captain." His accent was Oxford.

"I don't gather your meaning, sir," Karensen answered.

"No meaning was intended for your gathering. That your ship has a bad name is a mere statement of fact." He paused. "You are now free to deny the statement."

Karensen wiped sweat off his face. The more he wiped the more he sweated.

"I deny the statement," he said at last.

The officer shoved a paper in front of Karensen, turning it around so he could read it.

"Five," the officer announced, and took the paper back.

"Five *what?*" I inquired from where I stood.

"I beg *your* pardon?" the officer asked me.

"I wondered five what," I answered.

"Who are you?" he wanted to know.

"A passenger."

"Would you mind waiting outside until we are ready for passengers?"

Across the rail the lamps of Calcutta shone through a curious haze: the city burned like sacrifice lit by a memorial light.

When Karensen came out he looked miserable. I returned to the lounge and handed the officer my passport.

"Did I ask you to show me that?" he inquired coldly.

"Come to think of it, you didn't," I admitted, and replaced it in my pocket.

"Will you sit down?" he asked me.

I sat.

"May I see your passport?"

I took it out and handed it to him once more.

Then, after examining my declaration: "Where is your typewriter?"

"Which one?" I boasted, "I have an electric and an un-electric."

"There is only one declared here," he went for it.

"I didn't bring the electric. I was afraid India wasn't ready for it."

"Where is the other?"

"In my stateroom."

"May I trouble you to bring it here?"

I went up to my stateroom, returned with the machine, placed it on the table before him without opening it. As soon as I did he was going to tell me he hadn't asked me to open it.

"*Would* you mind opening it?"

I was pleased to do so.

"Would you mind closing it?"

I was pleased to close it.

"Your passport will be returned to you before the ship sails," he promised.

Going down the ramp with my typer banging my knees I ran head-on into another high-minded, bullet-headed official.

"Where going?"

"Ashore."

"Has been *in*spected?" He pointed to the machine.

"Yes."

"Show certificate of *in*spection."

"I wasn't given any. You can inspect it yourself."

"Is not my duty to inspect."

"What do you want me to do?"

"Get certificate."

I hauled the damned box back up to my stateroom and came back down the ramp without it. Now the only move he had left was to stop me because I *didn't* have a typewriter. He let me pass reluctantly. What they've failed to learn from the British about soldiering, these people have more than made up for in snobbery.

Danielsen, the loneliest-looking sailor since Alexander Selkirk, waited on the dock clasping one wrist with the other; as if trying to keep from arresting himself. His usual aspect was that of a man with the blues. I noticed he was now carrying a full set. For his voice, normally a whisper, was now lowered to a mere movement of the lips. Things that always went wrong with him had now gone even wronger: the customs cops had come on him while he was dressing, found three twenty-dollar bills on his bed, and snatched the lot. He was dead flat broke in Calcutta.

"Why didn't you declare your money?" I asked him.

"Because it worries me for people to know how much I'm carrying," was his peculiar explanation.

"I promise not to tell anybody you're broke," I tried cheering him up.

When I loaned him fifty, joy shook him so powerfully that he gave me a barely perceptible nod. Then he dodged to one side to let a beggar pass. You're supposed to shove them out of your way. Danielsen just wasn't made of the stuff that makes great empires.

"If you let the gate cop take that fifty off you, you might as well go back to the ship," I threatened him.

The gate cop stood beneath beacons so bright that it looked a simple matter to slip past him in the darkness behind the beacons. But he had a gun on his hip, even though no Indian soldier has yet hit a target smaller than a cow from further than four feet, this one might be just lucky enough to have a bullet ricochet off a buffalo and kill us both with a single shot. He decided to capture Danielsen first, as the most dangerous-looking, and escorted him to a dimly lit shack to be examined by one final bureaucrat.

I stood outside and watched Danielsen's papers being examined, stamped, restamped, and his passport re-examined, restamped; until at last he was dismissed and came out shaking his head as if he'd just been robbed and insulted again.

I entered and showed my shore-pass but did not so much as lay it on the desk.

"That's all," this one informed me quickly.

"That's *all?*"

"Yis"—and began a smile so downright fawning that I thought he was going to his knees— "Yis. You *gentleman.*"

Well what do you know. I was tickled pink.

"You didn't take long," Danielsen observed as we finally got into Calcutta.

"Because *I'm* a gentleman," I reminded him.

He smiled so wanly I knew I'd made a wildly hilarious joke. "What are our plans?" I asked him, when we'd gotten into the cab.

"Ezekiel's," Danielsen instructed the driver.

❖   ❖   ❖

Tribesmen through endless Chinese ages, by foot and by horse, fought across the wastes of Asia down to the plains of Assam. What frozen heights, what burning valleys, what marshes, flights, descents and pursuits they endured, achieved this ultimate victory: their good-looking daughters boarded trains to get into a Calcutta cat-house.

Welshman, Cockney, Scot and Irisher, nobly volunteered to help the British put India under their Queen. Sikh and Hindi, Ghat and Gurka, had to yield or serve: simply to bring forth a new tribe on earth even loopier than the tribes that had come before. An estranged race, as unrooted in India as in England; detached from Calcutta and Southampton both: congenital expatriates called Anglo-Indians.

Nonetheless I remain enormously gratified by the concern of Sikh and Mongol footmen, Scots Guards, Welsh Grenadiers, Irish Cannoneers, Cockney cavalry and litter-bearers from Wessex, in preparing a field of lovely girls a full furlong long for me, some dusky as twilight with green half-slanted eyes, dressed for Eighth Avenue if not for Fifth; as well as those of rosier flesh, with hair dark blond or orange-red; dressed in the robes of Kashmir and Bengal. Who had told these kids I was coming?

Somebody must have because not one was missing. Between the bar and the bartenders, a three-piece combo and an air of haste, a welcome-home party was in progress for me at Ezekiel's; the classiest abyss in Calcutta.

Its class derives not merely from the profoundly bad taste of its décor and its genuine phoniness, but also from its practice, unique in Calcutta, of serving Scotch to patrons requesting Scotch and bourbon to those preferring bourbon, without watering either. When you ask for English gin you get English gin and not Indian gin, and nobody puts knockout drops in it in order to rob you later. You make your own arrangements for that.

Between the tables and the bar a pushing throng of seamen and whores, the seamen all drunk and the whores all sober, lent such a cheerful, homey air, what with a brawl of two jolly Englishmen trying to kill one another on the floor, I didn't see how anyone could help but be happy here. The scent of cheap whiskey mixing with cheaper cologne lent a woodland tang to the air, like early fall in Miami when ryebread trees throw out their first dark blooms. A seaman wearing a single earring pinched me and I would have seized him by his hair, but he was bald. The friendliness of the people and the air conditioning made me feel like going for a little stroll; which I did simply by shoving people aside.

The air is conditioned, the drinks expensive, the women good-looking: and the drop from booths to brothels so fast that any of these women might have a gala night and yet be over the edge the night after.

Over the edge and down is an easy drop, where everyone lives on a ledge. It's only a bit more sudden for her, and only a bit more steep, than it is for the red-collared bellboy, leaping for tips on the red-plush rugs of the Grand Hotel: let a desk clerk catch him picking up a few rupees changing money on the side and it's back to the walks, but leave your little red collar behind. Calcutta is the place, whatever your job, where the drop is steepest; and the drop from the bars is steepest of all: always some baby-face never seen before hustling your tricks before your eyes. And just that fast the knowledge comes: you're waiting for men other women don't want.

The darker women of Ezekiel's seem less estranged than those of the Anglo strain. The girls from Assam, Nepal and Kashmir belong to themselves because they belong to India. But, despite her Indian robes, the Anglo who feels she truly belongs to Essex or Oxford or Kent, belongs neither to India nor to the West. She belongs only to the seaman who mounts her.

That's how it is in The Orient, men. That's how it *really* is.

A tug on my sleeve turned me to face an Anglo in Western dress, her reddish-blond hair worn long; and her eye-shadow trying to hide the tiredness of her eyes.

"See that bloody nay-gur?" she confided—"the very nerve of 'im—awskin' me to drink with the like of 'im. O, I thanked 'im like a lydy—'Thank you ever so kindly all the same'—but would you mind sitting by me here so's he won't come back—there's a good chap. Bartender! Two whiskeys straight!"

I'd heard fake-cockney spoken before, but this one went at it as though she'd been listening to Audrey Hepburn.

She kept on and on about that "bloody nay-gur" until, turning my head from her, I found myself eye-to-eye with a woman whose eyes were warm with light. Her hair, piled high, was so black it had a bluish sheen. One of the dusky kind of a country I could not place.

"Of what country are you?" I asked her.

"I am of Assam. We are a hill people."

"Your name?" I asked.

"Martha."

"Can you leave here?"

"Cannot now."

"I'll wait."

She shook her head: no, that wouldn't do. Instead, she took a stub of a pencil from her handbag and wrote, on the inside of a book of matches:

Martha. Kanani Mansions. Apt. 872.

"You come there midnight," she instructed me, swung herself off the stool and slipped away into the mob of milling seamen.

"Now there's some say a nay-gur's all one and the same, but how *I* were brought up—" the red-haired monologist's voice kept turning like a barber's pole, stripe after stripe, getting nowhere at all. I decided to walk back to the ship and show up, around midnight, at Kanani Mansions.

      ✿   ✿   ✿

This was in that twilit Indian hour when bazaars are shadowed and beggars rest.

The voices of Calcutta, that great city, change then from the loud cries of the workaday world to murmurous pleas of evening. Nobody knows how many people there are in Calcutta.

Nor how many cats died yesterday there.

Nobody knows how many cats were born in Calcutta yesterday.

All The-Committee-For-Counting-The-Cats-Of-Calcutta is certain about is that there are going to be more cats in Calcutta tomorrow than there are today.

Nobody knows why it is that crows pursue hawks on the quais of Calcutta; while in every other port it is the hawks that pursue the crows.

All The-Committee-For-Counting-The-Hawks-Of-Calcutta is sure about is that, if the crows keep it up, there are going to be fewer hawks in Calcutta tomorrow than there are today.

Nobody knows how many cows there are in Calcutta. All The-Committee-For-Counting-The-Cows-Of-Calcutta is sure about is that some are standing up but others are lying down. It looks like the work of The-Committee-For-Counting-The-Cows-Of-Calcutta will have to be divided into a Committee-For-Cows-Standing-Up and a Committee-For-Counting-Cows-Lying-Down.

Nobody knows why the dogs of Calcutta never bark, but run away. All that The-Committee-For-Counting-The-Dogs-Of-Calcutta can report is that you have to catch a dog before you can count him—and how can you count him when he runs away?

At this writing it appears that there are going to be more people on

The-Committee-For-Counting-People-In-Calcutta at this time tomorrow than there are today.

We plan to tackle that as soon as The-Committee-Dividing-The-Work-Of-The-Committee-For-Counting-Cows has been organized.

A bureaucrat of nine fell into step beside me, wearing only a pair of ragged shorts. His arms, thin as reeds, had been tattooed with a butterfly on one arm and a cobra on the other.

"Go to ship, Papa?" he wanted to know.

I nodded yes.

"You go wrong way to ship, Papa."

I was going the right way. But if I believed I was going wrong I would hire him to guide me, and he'd take me to the ship by another route. He took my hand. I took it away.

"You want to go to American movie, Papa?"

I didn't answer. He kept stepping right with me. I increased my pace. He increased his.

"You want to go to library, Papa?"

I made no answer. His hard little fingernails clawed my arm. I came to a dead stop.

He deadstopped too.

I made a feinting movement to the right.

He feinted to my right.

I feinted to the left. He feinted to my left.

I made a fast u-turn and hurried in the opposite direction. He hurried with me. I broke into a run. He ran with me. I stopped to get my breath. He stopped too.

"Don't you have a home?" I asked him.

He nodded. Yes. He had a home.

"Why don't you go there then?"

"Cannot go to home without *baksheesh,* Papa."

I offered him a dime. He shook his head. No.

"What's wrong with a dime?" I wanted to know.

"*Quarter,* Papa."

"Go to hell," I told him, and reversed my direction back toward the ship.

He stayed beside me. I broke into a run. I was six feet long and he was four, but he maintained the pace. I ran faster.

We ran along a wall. What was on the other side I had no idea—but it would only take a moment to scoop him up, toss him over and lose him forever. He seemed to divine some such intention; because he put himself out of reaching distance without losing stride.

I ducked, between hacks, across a street: he ducked between hacks with me. I raced back across the same street: he raced with me. Now I had only a few yards to go to a gate he could not enter.

I reached it and leaned against it, knees shaking, heart racing, chest heaving, sweat pouring. He wasn't even out of breath—merely stood there regarding me curiously.

"Eckersize, Papa?"

It *could* be put that way. It felt more like the wildest workout in town.

"*Baksheesh*, Papa?"

I handed him a cigar.

"Match, Papa?"

The *Malaysia Mail* loomed ominously at the quai. A line of porters were toting sacks of flour off her into a warehouse. Danielsen was leaning over the rail. He watched me climbing the ramp as if waiting to tell me something.

"I thought you were at Ezekiel's," I told him.

"Customs are questioning the old man," he explained, "they found a thousand watches behind Manning's medicine cabinet. He thought his medicine cabinet had immunity from inspection."

I started to feel elation; then my elation died. "What do they want with the old man?"

"They want to know whether he was in on it."

"Do you think so?"

"No."

"How much could he have gotten for the loot?"

"At least thirty thousand."

"I'd never have given him credit for the nerve," I had to admit.

It came to me, at last, how strongly fear had been driving Manning.

In my stateroom I picked up an accusation of Hemingway, yellow with years, written by a critic named Rascoe, now forgotten, in the thirties. Hemingway was infantile when he had written *The Sun Also Rises* and had since grown increasingly childish, Rascoe had decided. On the other hand, James T. Farrell had reached the full flowering of his maturity. Well, good.

I found another review, of a decade later, entitled "The Dark Night of

Ernest Hemingway," which proclaimed Hemingway's failure "because there is no freedom in work when it becomes compulsion. The word for that is anarchy—a strange God to put before God. Personally, I would settle for just one story in which the Ten Commandments did not get kicked all over the place." When Billy Graham came along Hemingway lost *this* critic for certain.

If Hemingway hadn't written himself out in the twenties, as Rascoe had announced, he'd certainly written himself out in the thirties—left-wing critics were agreed by the forties: the writer to watch, however, was no longer Farrell. Now it was Howard Fast.

Somehow or other Hemingway *must* have managed to keep writing through the forties, because, by the fifties, it was clearly understood that now he had *really* written himself out. There was always somebody else who was more mature, someone more profound; someone more promising. Someone more true.

Yet the forties had passed, and the fifties had passed, and new critics came on and old critics passed; and new writers came on, and old writers failed and still Hemingway stood them off. Like Sal Maglie, he had nothing left and yet he won ball games. And still he went to the wars and still he went to the bullfights and still he enjoyed his life against all the rules: until he had not only the full pack of American Podhoretzes in pursuit, but European Podhoretzes as well.

"I do not like that old man," one boy, withered by bitterness, because others were richer, wrote for *L' Express,* "for certain reasons I have simmered all along in the reading of his books. This man is a comedian who during all his life walked around with his testicles for a necklace. But I do suspect that he has none, and that he is a comedian whose literature, by means of tricks, realizes nothing more than the assumptions of *Reader's Digest.* Ernesto's virility is wine and literature. Don Ernesto is afflicted with an awfully sly and wicked look. Hiding behind his beard, Don Ernesto has a mischievous air, mischievous, *very* mischievous."

I remembered this withered boy. He'd once petitioned Jean-Paul Sartre for employment as a secretary, but had later to be dismissed for selling old manuscripts of Sartre's on the sly. The game worked so long as buyers were interested only in collecting—when one began publishing, somebody had to go. He went. Apparently in pursuit of Hemingway. Some people can't wait to get rich.

"In nearly all of Hemingway's books we feel his sympathy with those who are worthy of it," one faint-praiser observed; failing to realize that the great thing about the man's books is their sympathy for those unworthy of it.

"There are no *women* in his books!" Professor Fiedler exclaims. "If in *For Whom the Bell Tolls* Hemingway has written the most absurd love-scene in the history of the American novel it is not because he lost momentarily his skill and authority. It is a giveaway—a moment which illuminates the whole erotic content of his fiction."

Catch that "if." Because when the Professor himself revealed a homo-sexual relationship between Huck Finn and Nigger Jim, he extended absurdity in love scenes into naked asininity. Thereby illuminating nothing but the Professor.

Well, there's one on every campus. In Fiedler we have the classic mediocrity avenging itself for its deprivation. His method is the equivalent process, in academic terms, of Hollywood writers in "licking a book into shape."

Fiedler employs symbolism to drain art of its life. He does not criticize: he adapts. By transferring the writer's meaning into arbitrary abstractions, he can leave any work for dead. We find, for example, that Hemingway's description of Mount Kilimanjaro, in *The Short Happy Life of Francis MacComber*, as "wide as all the world, great, high and unbelievably white" *really* means (says the Professor) "the whiteness from which the American author tries so vainly to flee, the bland whiteness of the irrational taboo in Melville, and antarctic whiteness of polar disaster in Poe, the whiteness of the White Goddess herself—who having been denied as giver of life and source of love, must be recognized as dealer of death!"

All he overlooked is that Hemingway wasn't talking of anything but snow. All the rest of the stuff is simply the Professor earning a living. Talentlessness, like asexuality, is never passive, but finds another outlet.

The Professor's trouble is simply that he himself cannot react to womanhood unless it is wrapped in erudition enfolded in a symbol tied by a ribbon made of concepts. What he demands is one of those Puritan euphemisms about "the mystery of femininity." Hemingway disposed of the mystery and presented a woman.

"What Hemingway's emphasis on the ritual murder of fish conceals," the Professor continues, "that it is not so much the sport as the occasion for immersion which is essential to the holy marriage of males. Water is the symbol of the barrier between the Great Good Place and the busy world of women."

He boasts of wounds who never bore a scar: he disbelieves that the earth can move who has never felt it move.

What is saddening about this piggish jargon is that young people with a love of literature pay for courses to learn how to speak it.

I was glad to be interrupted by a knock. It was Danielsen. "Manning bought the watches in Kowloon," Danielsen told me, "the merchant tipped off the Customs police. They make a good raid now and then to cover bribery. This was their good one."

"What happens with Manning?"

"If the company stands by him with an American lawyer he'll get the case transferred to the States. If the company fires him he might have to do time here—I wouldn't wish that on the worst dog that ever lived."

"Can't he get his own lawyer?"

"Manning doesn't have a nickel. In debt. Alimony. More fouled up than Crooked-Neck."

"I have to get back into town," I told Danielsen, "are you coming?"

"I'll see you at Ezekiel's," he told me.

"The hell you will," I thought.

Chips, wearing a Hawaiian shirt, was lounging outside the door of the stateroom in which Manning was under arrest.

"I want to see *him* getting *his*," he told me, "*with* the manacles."

He crossed his wrists to be sure I understood what manacles were.

"When am I getting mine?" I wanted to know.

"When I get a draw," he promised me again.

The quai was full of old shadows. Out of one came a nine-year-old bureaucrat.

"Hello, Papa."

He was smoking a cigar. "I paid you to go home," I reminded him, "no more *baksheesh*."

He skipped along as confidently as before.

"Cigar, Papa?"

When I got through the gate I jumped into a cab and slammed the door on him hard.

"Kanani Mansions," I told the driver.

KANANI MANSIONS

Black-market rascals came and went, sedate Sikhs moved Sikhishly about their Sikhish business; American seamen rapped all the wrong doors and *ayahs* skittered like withered leaves down the careworn corridors of Kanani Mansions.

The whores of Calcutta don't live like the whores of Bombay. In that bootlegging, Puritanical, black-marketing, dreadful Bombay, there are no bars for a seaman to find a wife for a week or a month. There are only the great cat-houses (more like curtained cow-houses) run on short-term love. These; and the animalized women of the cages of Kamathipura.

But in Calcutta's flashing bars, thronging with attractive girls from every port of Asia, a seaman can find long-term love. This circumstance makes it possible for such a woman as Martha to keep an apartment of her own with civilized appointments: Martha had a high bookshelf lined with books and records—mostly American—as well as her own bedroom, bath, kitchen and a small parlor. She supported an *ayah,* an infant son and her mother.

Martha's mother, Anna, did not live with her. Although Martha's trade was of her mother's devising, and Anna would have preferred to live with her daughter, Martha kept her at a distance in a small apartment down the hall.

A certain looseness in her look and a cleverness in her eyes distinguished mother from daughter more than her years. Anna's coldly whorish air left Martha seeming to be the more motherly woman of the two.

Martha was darker. Anna hennaed her hair and powdered her face too heavily; to make herself look less Asiatic. Every afternoon she came in dressed for a ball, with a copy of the trial of one Commander Nanavati, a naval officer who had shot and killed his wife's lover.

She would insist on reading excerpts of the trial to us whether we would or no.

Martha's little *ayah* ran for cover as soon as Anna came in. These homeless old women who serve as maids-of-all-work in return for a corner of a floor to sleep on and the leftovers of a table to subsist on, can be obtained anywhere in Calcutta simply by going down the street and finding one, already starving, on the curb.

"Get rid of that one," Anna would command Martha, "she'll steal the carpet while you're asleep."

"She is honest," Martha defended the old dry leaf huddled, listening, behind a chair.

This *ayah,* whose past had no meaning, whose future no one cared about, knew that Anna was speaking of her unfavorably.

"Send her back to the street," Anna urged.

"She is good with the boy," Martha replied.

So many autumns had blown down from the north, since this wisp out of the hills of Assam had first come begging into the heat of Calcutta, that they were now beyond counting. Yet the old cracked brown grandmother had a life of her own along the floor; that she shared with Martha's infant son.

While Martha and I and Anna lived among records, shelves, chairs and windows, the infant boy and the very old woman crept in and out of caves made of pillows; or hid together under the divan.

Music, the sound of voices, arguments, orders, food and tea all came down to them mysteriously from somewhere above. And although the *ayah* did not understand what was being said when we spoke in English, she sensed enough to stay in hiding while Anna carried on about this "fair-looking person of thirty-seven and Commander of I.N.S. *Mysore,* who was accused in the murder case of PREM BHAGWANDAS AHUJA, an automobile dealer."

Martha retired to the bedroom when Anna began reading.

Even The-Ayah-Who-Lived-On-The-Floor stopped crawling about when Anna got into the heart of the matter of Commander Nanavati.

But after a while Anna herself would grow bored with this endless Nanavati. Then she'd go for the Scotch.

The Scotch was *The Best Procurable,* the same brand that Hemingway had once offered me. A Hollywood producer, I remembered, also used to keep a bottle of the same handy—but *he* wouldn't open it.

"You are of New York?" Anna wanted to know while she was pouring. "Do you want ice?"

"Yes. I mean no. I mean yes, I want ice, but I am not of New York. I am of Chicago."

"Is that far from Los Angeles?"

"As far as the width of India," I answered; with no clearer notion of India's width than she had of Chicago.

"I understand you have written a biography of Frank Sinatra," Anna told me. "He *must* be a *wonderful* person."

"A *great* human being," I assured the poor creature—why disenchant her?

"*All* that money," she marveled, a dream all of glass spinning behind her eyes—"he must spend a great deal on women."

"He gives most of it to charity," I decided. As long as I was Frankie's biographer I might as well be on his side.

"He must give wonderful parties," the woman dreamed on, "in Colorful Los Angeles."

"The last one wasn't in Los Angeles," I seemed to recall, "he threw it in the cove below Niagara Falls."

Anna clasped her hands—"What *that* must have cost!"

"A pretty penny," I guessed, "but the man has such marvelous luck he *always* ends up ahead. Somebody started a dice game when the guests started to leave, and Frank won more than enough to pay for renting the cove. I lost everything I had," I added defensively.

"I'm sorry," she told me.

"Small matter," I assured her, "it's easy come easy go in Colorful Los Angeles."

My mind returned to that bottle of *The Best Procurable* that I couldn't get the producer to open in Los Angeles. That city of Good Procurers.

There I'd lived in an encrusted crypt entitled The Garden of Allah Chateau—which ought to indicate how far ahead of the rest of the world L.A. was. It was already orbiting in 1950.

Most of the residents of The Chateau were independents—actors, writers and producers; and several were not only independent as artists but independent of the entire human race. The Chateau at sunset, in fact, looked like a reunion of the garden party Alice's Wicked Queen once gave. There were several wicked queens on the premises and a few wicked kings as well.

The Wickedest of any was the Wicked Producer. I knew he was wicked because he toted this huge bottle about, tucked resolutely under his arm as if firmly determined to get everybody drunk. I saw immediately I would have to be careful.

I knew he was a producer because he wore sunglasses tinted chartreuse and open-toed sandals whose protruding toes were tinted a matching shade.

His name was Schlepker. Otto Schlepker.

It wouldn't be fair to call Otto grasping as he often let me hold his bottle for minutes at a time.

"*Read* that label," he would say, and, after a moment—"Read it out *loudt.*"

"*The Best Scotch Procurable,*" I would read aloud, looking at him appealingly.

"Let me be open with you," he offered, taking the bottle back and looking hooded, "you have noticed I am not a happy man?"

"Well, I didn't think of you as being downright happy so much as just gruesomely smug," I had had to confess.

"I *force* myself to look contented," Otto confessed, "actually, I am a tragic person. All my life I have thoughtlessly devoted my life to selfish interests and now I am paying the price—I have pangs of guilt so secret only my analyst knows where to find them. But unless I begin doing things for other people right away the secret pangs will destroy me. As I have already spent over three thousand dollars on my analyst I cannot afford doubt. That would be throwing money away. I'm going to start living for others if it kills me. I will make a movie that will show the terrible suffering of drug addicts that will make a million dollars."

A human soul stood before me naked and imperiled. I would give him succor in his spiritual struggle. Nothing short of that was going to get him to open that bottle.

I ought to explain that I was in California on a Hollywood Fulbright. That is the kind whereby a studio will allot five hundred dollars to an independent producer toward the entertainment of an out-of-town writer upon the assumption that a week's free feeding will so fill the recipient with gratitude that he will sign anything just to show he is a good old sport.

When the word got around that a studio was picking up my tabs at Romanoff's, a marvelous change came over the occupants of the Chateau.

Where they had heretofore appeared indifferent to my career, they now began competing good-naturedly with one another to give me friendly advice. When my allotment ran out we were blocking traffic.

With the allotment run out and still no signature, there was a danger that the Wicked Independent Producer would find himself merely Independently Wicked. He did not wish to threaten me, he threatened me, but unless I signed he would blacken my name with everyone in Schwartz's drugstore.

"'Whatever am I to do in this crisis?"—I turned to my agent who was dealing himself a solitaire hand with mutuel tickets. "I am depending on your wisdom, acquired by long years of toiling in the vineyards of Art."

"Jump ship and pan for gold," the agent advised me, and won the hand.   .

At that moment the large producer materialized, accompanied by a small gimp.

"I want you to meet a Dedicated Fan," the producer introduced him.

"To whom, sir," I inquired courteously, "are you dedicated?"

"Why," he told me, "to *you*. May I see some identification?"

"You want me to *identify* myself?" I asked.

"I can't risk dedicating myself to an impostor," the friendly fellow explained.

I showed him my library card and my army serial number. These distinctions satisfied him. For he handed me a packet of attractively colored papers and left looking even more dedicated.

As any process server ought when leaving a client properly subpoenaed. So this was Hollywood.

Otto handed me the bottle of the best procurable as if to apologize for threatening me with the law. It was the first time I'd been invited to a party and ordered to jail by the same man with a single gesture. I didn't know how to react to Otto. This may have been because Otto didn't know how to react to himself.

He turned on his heel in a lurching safari with myself lurching solemnly after him, my benefactor; clutching my subpoenas and my Scotch to my breast with equal ardor.

He did a hard right and braked. I almost ran the man down. He drew himself up and, literally striking his own breast, declaimed, "I'm a *nice* fellow! I do *good* for everybody! *Why do you make me act so damned cheap?*"

Transfixed by the realization of what I was doing to a fellow human being, my guilt was self-proclaiming.

"Open the Scotch!" he roared at me. "*Or isn't the best procurable good enough for you?*" And handed me the contract he'd been begging me to sign.

"It is surely the *very* best procurable," I confessed meekly, hurrying to put my signature down while he still permitted me to make such a small atonement, "so it will have to do until we can get a bottle of the best that is unprocurable," I added hopefully.

Martha came out of the bedroom dressed to go out.

Anna picked up *Commander on Trial,* determined to resume the story of Nanavati's trial. But a low growl from the corner where the *ayah* hid, protested. Every time Anna began to read, the *ayah* growled.

"She is stealing the brandy," Anna warned Martha, "I smelled it on her when I came in."

How a person so soaked in *The Best Procurable* could tell what anyone else had been drinking was something I couldn't figure.

"I want you to leave," Martha told Anna.

Even the *ayah* was glad to see her go.

Martha seemed contented, most of the day, to lounge about in Indian robes, idling the hours between her record player and her son.

She had been married, at sixteen, to a man of Shillong; who had deserted her shortly after their son had been born. She'd had one letter from him, postmarked London; that had contained neither money nor a promise of it. It had sounded as though he had remarried.

The photograph on her bookshelf was of a middle-aged American wearing a maritime officer's cap. It was signed: *With all my love to Martha—Jeff.*

When she'd put on her Western clothes we'd wheel about Calcutta for an hour.

We both looked forward to that late afternoon hour when the sun softened the city's ancestral walls to amber. Then we rode into the first flares of the night past trees like clouds at rest. We'd have dinner at a restaurant as far from Ezekiel's as I could take her; and buy her roses—one rupee per bunch—before we had to go back.

Her father had been a physician of Shillong. Anna had spent a great deal of money entertaining men younger than herself. The physician had at last divorced her and remarried, severing all connection with his first family.

Anna had then pressed Martha to leave Shillong and come to Calcutta until Martha had given in.

Anna had brought an American home with her.

He was a seaman of twenty and had been displeased with the older woman. Anna had taken money that belonged to him while they had been drinking.

"A man who wants to make love to *me,* must pay," Anna had justified herself in taking the boy's money.

"I don't want to make love to you, old dog," the seaman had answered.

"Now you insult me, you cannot have your money back," Anna had decided.

"Give the man his money, Anna," Martha had instructed her mother.

"He gets nothing," Anna had been stubborn.

"I ought to whip you," the seaman had threatened her.

"You want to beat somebody?" Anna had picked up the threat—"beat her—*she's* the one you want to make love to, *isn't* she?"

The sailor had not denied it. It was Martha or his money back. Anna wouldn't give up the money.

Martha had taken him into the bedroom.

"I gave you life," Anna reproached her after the seaman had left, "now you take away my sweethearts."

"I do not like to sell my bud-*dee,*" Martha would say at the same hour every night. As if, just by saying it, she could delay the night at Ezekiel's.

She was disliked by Ezekiel's other B-girls: they mistook her contempt for this trade as contempt for themselves, and her beauty sharpened their resentment.

Yet she was not truly a beauty. The bridge of her nose was a bit too broad, and she lacked perhaps half an inch of being of average height. Yet her face was abundant with warmth and light.

"They are all like Anna," she told me of the other women of Ezekiel's— "they think I take their sweethearts."

I knew she didn't need to take their sweethearts. Seaman and tourist alike were drawn toward her, and not merely for her looks. This woman had such inner calm that her presence lent others a sense of repose.

One night, after she had come in late and had fallen asleep immediately, I wakened, later, to feel her arms come around me. Yet it wasn't love-making on her mind. She needed to talk.

"I do not like to sell my bud-*dee*," she wanted me to understand, "because if I do this, how am I to belong to the child?"

"Don't you feel you belong to him now?"

"I belonged to him in Shillong. I belonged, also, to my father. I belonged, then, to Shillong. Now I belong to nothing. And I cannot go back to Shillong. I thought I belonged to Jeff, but then Jeff go. I think maybe I belong to you; but soon you go. How can I belong to the child when I do not belong to myself? I belong to Ezekiel's, nothing more." She began to cry softly.

I did not try to console her.

✿   ✿   ✿

I hadn't been aboard the *Malaysia Mail,* nor seen any of the crew, for over a week. I'd avoided going into Ezekiel's, when I dropped Martha off there, and waited for her at home.

I got along well with the Ayah-Who-Lived-On-The-Floor by means of such small gifts as the butts of cigars or a nip of brandy. It was like spending the evening with a small, intelligent, domesticated monkey. Sometimes, without a word, she would bring me tea.

I would feel a touch on my knee and she would be crouched, holding the cup and saucer out to me and grinning from ear to ear. The old woman had beautiful teeth.

When Martha and I took a cab in the evening, I would have the driver stop by the quai, just to make sure that the ship was still in port. There would always be a great crane unloading cargo off the deck, and a line of porters carrying fresh cargo into the hold. I had no idea either of what was being unloaded or of what was being taken on. Sometimes I caught glimpses of Sparks or Chips or Danielsen or Bridelove or Muncie. I didn't see Manning. Sufficient unto the day, I thought.

"What kind place is Shy-Ann?" Martha asked me on one of these evening spins. "What kind place in America?"

"Shy-Ann?"

"Shy-Ann in Why-O-Ming."

"Oh. Wyoming is in the West of America."

"Why people of Why-O-Ming call me monkey?"

"Why should people call you monkey?"

Martha touched a finger to her cheek: "Dark."

She was brooding about her American engineer. Whoever he was, he was a kuke; he had bewildered this girl.

His letters, that she'd asked me to read, were dense with endearments and plans for bringing her to Cheyenne.

"I wait many day," she remembered now. "Jeff come at last. Him very good to me and boy. I not have to sell my bud-*dee*. Then, middle of night, big knock on door. I turn on light. Jeff not in bed. Jeff *outside* door making big noise. 'Whore!' he speak at me—'Whore! Open door!' *What* I gonna do? I not open, police come. I open. He hit. Keep hitting. I fall. He kick. Jeff *dronk*."

Now the letters of endearment had begun again; filled with the same old plans. The desperation of her situation was tempting Martha to believe that, if she gave Jeff a second chance, he might mean it after all and take her to America. Whatever might happen to her in Cheyenne could hardly be worse, she felt, than what was happening to her in Calcutta.

"You think this man *love?*" she asked me.

"He love alright," I assured her, "for sure."

"Then why he *hit?*"

"Because to be in love makes a man no longer free, and not to be free makes him angry. He would rather give you money and go away."

"In Why-O-Ming, will I have to sell my bud-*dee?*"

"As the wife of an American engineer making eight hundred dollars a month I shouldn't think so," I told her; but the way things are changing I couldn't be sure.

Jeff, I felt, had problems.

One was the hard time he was going to have convincing his neighbors in Cheyenne that his wife wasn't a squaw.

The other was tougher, being within himself. My hunch was that Jeff was a churchgoing, college-educated middle-class man who believed in being sorry for whores and kind to Indians—but to fall in love with an Indian whore! Wouldn't that be degrading himself? The man was in the switches without a doubt. If he weren't he'd come and get her and take her home and be damned to the neighbors; instead he was turning destructive.

The cab wheeled us to Ezekiel's. I never hung around Ezekiel's long after I'd taken Martha there, and she didn't want me standing by. If I saw anyone there from the ship I'd have a drink with him, then get out. Danielsen, sitting by himself as he always sat, looked like he was waiting for somebody.

"Your girl friend have a friend?" he asked me.

"She lives by herself," I explained, "what's the matter with the stuff walking around?"

"I don't go for the short-term deal," he explained. "I'm not like Sparks, a new thing every night. I want the same thing. We may be here another week."

"Don't look now," I changed the subject, "but did you notice what just came in with a jug in his hand?"

It had to be Crooked-Neck, his head slowly revolving; and carrying a gin-fifth simply by a finger thrust into it for a stopper. By that continuous slow rotation both Danielsen and myself had the apprehension that Smith was getting in shape to surpass himself in fouling himself up as well as everybody within fouling-up distance.

"Hi-*ee*," he greeted us with one hand on Danielsen's shoulder and his bottle-hand on my own, "shall we bound a bit on the waves, my boys? Shall we zig? Shall we zag? What course shall we steer?"

"I'm thinking seriously of getting laid," Danielsen announced like a Papal Edict.

I wanted to shake off Smith.

"Kanani Mansions is *swarming*," I suggested.

"Let's go," Danielsen said quickly. He wanted to shake Smith too.

"See you on the ship, sailor," I told Smith, to make our departure final.

Danielsen wouldn't ride an Indian taxi unless it were driven by a Sikh. We found one that was satisfactory because the Sikh had a white beard.

"Smith," Danielsen advised me in the cab, "is dangerous."

"So I've been told," I answered.

Although Anna must have been a couple of years older than Danielsen, she appeared ten years younger. Fairer than Martha, with an oval face where Martha's was square-jawed, her hair dyed red and worn in bangs— befitting the green that flecked her eyes whenever she thought about money—she made a strong impression upon him. When she led him to a pink settee and began brushing his colorless hair with her hand, she cinched that impression. A pink blush rose to Danielsen's cheeks that matched the settee's strange hue. He was in good hands.

I was fixing the drinks when the knock came.

Crooked-Neck stood in the open door, still gently revolving his ominous skull, his bottle still attached to the finger.

I'd said "Kanani Mansions" too loudly.

Yet Anna welcomed him warmly. An American was an American regardless of the angle at which his head might be attached was her thinking. When she went into her small kitchen, I followed.

"Sick," I whispered in her ear, spinning a finger at my temple and indicating her new guest, "a Crazy."

"All Americans are Crazies," Anna told me. "You are a Crazy too."

Smith declined the drink she offered, preferring to unstop his own bottle, wash gin between his cheeks for a minute, then swallow it down with great boggling jumps of his Adam's apple.

Danielsen's set of the blues began darkening. He never held a fleeting doubt that *anyone,* who wanted to take the trouble to do so, could take *any* woman he wished away from Danielsen.

"I was batting the breeze with this Anglo chick in a bar on Ho-Phang Road," Smith began relating cheerfully, "and it got toward closing time. She told me if I wanted to spend fifteen dollars I could come up to her place and stay all night. I said I'd like that only all I had was thirteen. She said 'That'll do.'

"'But I have to get out early,' I told her, 'to get back to my ship.' She said, 'That's alright, I'll set the alarm.' I said, 'Well, alright, but I'll need cab-fare to get back.' She said, 'I'll see you get back alright.' 'I feel awfully crummy,' I said, and she said 'I'll draw you a bath.' 'This shirt is like a rag,' I told her. 'There's a couple of new shirts at my place you can have,' she told me. I said, *'Gee,* Honey, that's swell, but we can't go up there and just *look* at one another.' So she said, 'We'll pick up a couple of bottles on the way.' So we got a cab and picked up a couple of bottles and went to her place and she cooked up ham and eggs. There was a suit of my size hanging in the clothes-closet. She says would I like to see her dance with nothing on but her shoes and stockings, so I said, 'Gee, Honey, that would be great.' So she mixed the drinks and turned on the record player and danced naked holding her hand between her legs. Wonderful figure. After a while we went to bed. I could still kick myself when I think about it."

"What are you kicking yourself about?" I obliged Smith—"It sounds like you got a pretty fair shake."

"I wanted to see if she made good on her promises," he explained, "but she didn't."

"What happened?" I asked.

"I forgot the suit in the closet," Smith explained, "and she forgot to remind me."

"Why didn't you go back and pick it up?" I asked.

"I didn't have the time. I phoned her. I asked her to bring it down to the dock."

"Did she?"

Smith looked at me cynically. "Did you ever know a broad to keep her word?"

"Why should any woman keep her word to anyone like you," I heard Danielsen asking quite distinctly, "no woman in her right mind could respect you."

Anna stopped stirring the ice in her glass and looked over at me curiously. I looked out the window at the roofs of Calcutta. I hoped Smith would have the sense to let it pass.

He did. "You're kidding," was all he said, and laughed uneasily; knowing Danielsen wasn't kidding at all. I forced myself to glance at Danielsen.

He looked positively gaunt. And the shadow of an old determination lent his face an expression too fixed. Yet he'd had only two drinks.

Anna rose, put a record on, and went to Danielsen with her hands outstretched.

He didn't take them.

"Dance with your boy friend," he ordered her.

"I don't even know the woman, Danielsen," Smith said, trying to sound casual.

Anna wore a sheepish look, like anyone who doesn't know her next move.

"I told you to *dance* with him," Danielsen let her know what her best move was. "I *told* you. And I'm getting pretty well fed-up waiting."

"I'll dance with her if you want me to, Danielsen," Smith offered amiably, and added, as he ought *not* to have added, with the pair dancing stiffly under Danielsen's eye—"I just don't see what you're getting so cocky about."

Danielsen put down his glass too carefully.

"Turn off that record," he commanded me. I turned it off.

"I'll *tell* you what I'm getting cocky about, sailor," Danielsen told him, "you're a clap-ridden forty-year-old degenerate running a crooked card game, *that's* what I'm getting cocky about."

Smith sat down across the room. He wasn't going to precipitate a fight. But he was going to draw a real firm line.

"Alright," he told Danielsen. "I *do* have the clap. Since *you* say so, I'm a degenerate. And I *do* run a crooked card game. But I'm *not* forty. I'm only thirty-nine. And that makes you out a liar."

Danielsen swung into the kitchen and swung back with a bread knife. We were in business.

Smith stood up, looking toward me yet watching Danielsen. Anna waited dead-white under her rouge.

I got a chair in front of me.

Danielsen looked ridiculous, but he was holding the knife right. He began tiptoeing, then sprang—Smith leaped clean over the pink settee, tilted it in front of him, holding it by its springs, with his back to the wall: as perfect a fort as I've ever seen constructed in two seconds. There was absolutely no way of Danielsen getting at him.

Danielsen's eyes, glazing around the room to find where Smith had gone, skipped across Anna and found me. It was *my* move.

All I had was the chair behind which I was standing. Smith put his nose over the top of the red settee.

"Don't throw the chair," he advised me conversationally; and pulled his nose back.

The settee moved an inch toward Danielsen; Danielsen didn't see it move. Smith was holding it, a bit off the ground, by its springs. Even at that moment I realized how much strength that required.

Danielsen began trying to ask me something. I could tell only because his lips were moving.

"I can't hear you, Danielsen," I told him with my hands on the chair's back. He raised his voice.

"The last stitch," he told me—"you're asking for it."

I shifted my eyes. He followed the shift, saw the settee coming and came at me blade first as Smith lunged with the settee—and missed. I thrust the chair upward to block the blade. It went into the chair's rattan bottom and stuck.

Smith lay sprawling. I leaped across him and got to the door while

Danielsen was extricating the knife. As I opened the door he turned and leaped across Smith.

It was me he wanted.

I knew I was running only because two long dark walls, on either side, kept passing me. I knew I'd fallen because the walls weren't moving. I rolled over onto my back just in time to get both hands on the wrist that held the knife.

Danielsen was astride me with the blade four inches off my heart.

I held.

I was the strongest man in the world. I held it and cried up to the blind eyes looking down:

"*Danielsen! Danielsen!*"

Through a dark and distant land he heard his name called once—and called again.

The blindness faded from his eyes.

But not the rage.

Now he knew who he was. He *knew* who I was. He saw the knife. And knew he could kill me.

And he didn't know why he shouldn't.

He switched the knife to his free hand.

There was nothing I could do. The decision was Danielsen's.

"You asked for it. You *want* it now?"

"No," I assured him, without knowing what *it* was, "I *don't* want it."

Then he smiled that ever-so-wan, ever-so-lonesome, terrible smile.

"You've got me," I assured him. "You win."

"Get up," he commanded me.

I got up.

"*Run for your life.*"

I ran. For my life.

I ran for Anna's door. I shut the door and locked it. I turned.

Smith had Anna spread-legged on the naked springs, her dress over her head, screwing like a madman.

I went into the kitchen and found whiskey and a cup. I had to hold the cup with both hands to bring it to my lips. Then I had another. My shakiness diminished to an interior quivering: I was going to quiver inwardly for some time to come, I realized.

When I came out of the kitchen Anna was huddled on the floor, her dress ripped down the middle. Smith was sitting on the edge of the settee buttoning his pants.

A high shrill shout challenged us from the other side of the door.

"Anyone *one* of us! Last stitch! Last stitch!"

"Go back to the ship, Danielsen," I called.

"Last stitch through your nose!"

Then his step fled lightly down the hall.

Anna had recovered sufficiently to sit up, holding her dress together while shifting her dazed look between us: she didn't know which one of us had raped her.

"Don't leave me with him," she decided, looking at me.

The night's events were just a series of cheerful little coincidences to Smith, but they'd left me exhausted; the only thing that kept me from leaving was the fear that Danielsen might be waiting in the hall. I waited until Smith was ready to leave too.

He was taking his ease by cracking peanuts between his palms and spitting the shells out onto the carpet.

"After you get through picking up the shells, sailor," I suggested, "we'll set the settee rightside up."

Smith studied me thoughtfully.

"For a man whose life I've just saved you don't sound overly grateful," he reproached me. And spat another shell onto the carpet.

"*Don't* leave me alone with him," Anna repeated.

But I waited at one end of the settee until Smith felt sufficiently obliging to get his can off of it long enough for me to upend it. Then he sat down again.

"Didn't you know that Danielsen is beach-nuts?" he asked me.

"I know now," I told Smith, tossing him his cap.

"What do you think you'd have if you put Danielsen's brain in a cat?" Smith wanted to know. "That's a riddle, son," he explained, grinning contentedly. He'd enjoyed every minute of the row, it was plain.

"*Don't* leave me alone with him," Anna said again.

"She don't want to be left alone with you," Smith told me.

"What do you think you'd have? *Guess.*"

"Why don't you *both* go?" the woman asked weakly.

Smith jammed a finger into his bottle and got up.

"Coming, Pops?" he asked at the door.

"I'm coming."

"Just want me to wait out first, eh?" he asked, grinning.

"You're cutting in close," I admitted, "after you."

There was no shadow, in that long hall, of Danielsen.

"What's the next stop, Pops?" he asked me, more ready than ever for anything.

My own next step was bed and that bed wasn't far. But I waited till I had the key in the lock before I let Smith know how close to home I was.

"See you on the ship, sailor," I told him; let myself in and barred the door behind me.

If Danielsen was waiting down the hall, Crooked-Neck Smith had a problem. It no longer interested me.

"Wait till Anna gets Martha's ear tomorrow," I thought.

Martha's boy was curled up on the couch.

I helped myself to the brandy on the bookshelf.

There was a knock on the door.

"What do you want?" I called through the door.

"What you'd have *is a crazy cat!*" Smith whooped—and I heard him walking off laughing his head off all the way.

I lit a cigar and began reading *Commander on Trial:*

> *A car running at a stormy speed on the Flora Fountain Road turned suddenly towards a magnificent building in the beautiful city of BOMBAY, knows as "JEEVAN JYOT." The gate of the Car was opened with a zerking sound and a hand-some man of dominating personality exactly six feet tall came out, pushing the door back and rushed straight towards the upper stairs, a Place well known to him.*
>
> *It was a hot afternoon of April 27, 1959. People were gasping for wind. Pitch on the road was melting, the sea was calm, which was the clear indication of some unexpected storm.*
>
> *BANG . . . ! BANG . . . !! BANG . . . !!! was the sound which naturally diverted the attention of the passers-by. This unusual gun shot in a residential flat made people curious to know about the reasons for. this unfortunate event. Before the persons assembled outside could know the reason they saw the dramatic turn of an Officer looking man, running down with a naked revolver in his hand. Automatically, it created a curiosity among people assembled outside*

the gate to know what actually had happened. The well dressed man wearing a spotless Fawn colored shirt and a pair of dark colored trousers appeared. From his very appearance it looked as if his excellent character was blotted with some undesirable act, which was clearly reflected from his perplexed appearance. The Durwan of the building tried to stop him but he could not.

POLICE! POLICE!! cried the mob, but the man did not care for police, got into the Car and without properly answering the queries of DURWAN and others, he went on, though he uttered something but exactly he could not remember as his conscience was guilty.

Taking a sharp turn he drove fast assuring the people outside, in hurry and went to a Police Constable on duty. He slowed down his car. It was Government House Lower Gate where he stopped for a while and asked the Constable, who was on fixed post duty, the nearest Police Station?

I looked up, feeling I was being watched. There was only an infant sleeping. I resumed reading:

"Will you take me to the Police Station" asked the man.
"No, I am on fixed post duty and cannot move from here" told the Constable.

After enquiring of the Police Station and being told that the nearest Police Station was GAMDEVI P.S. he drove away. Now the man was totally undecided and was in half-haphazard state of mind, completely perplexed and could not ascertain his further steps. He was under the impression as some thing unpleasant had happened. He had never imagined the consequences which actually happened because only an hour and a half before he was the man who was seen at METRO CINEMA dropping his beautiful blue-eyed English born wife and his three kids. What a tragedy it was? That the wife was enjoying a film show on the screen and husband was playing a prominent role in another practical life drama outside the auditorium which was even more powerful and packed with thrills and followed by unexpected events. How for a fate can play with a man no body can guess?

It was Commander Samuel's Office, where Commander in his

white official dress was busy with his office routine. Suddenly he was diverted from his official work to an unofficial one, when another officer of same rank stepped in the office. He was well acquainted with him.

"I do not know exactly but I think I killed a man" said the man and asked his advice in this matter where the matter of accident according to his own belief was to be reported. The fact that the Smith & Mason .38 Service Revolver was used in this unfortunate event created an anxiety in Samuel's mind but he advised him the proper way and asked him to see Deputy Commissioner LOBO a C.I.D. Officer.

Actually this was an extraordinary event which happened for the first time in Commander's pleasant life.

"She is not faithful to me! She is not faithful to me"!! were the repeated words which were rotating in his mind and even the whole picture of past was coming by and by to his mind, which he could not avoid. Thinking it better to submit himself to Police, he did so and relied upon the theory of accident and struggle.

The accused in this case, Commander Kavas Maneckshaw Nanavati, a handsome well built man of 37, was a man of three battle fronts and had spent eighteen and a half years of his life in the Navy Service.

I glanced about the room and saw nobody but the sleeping infant. I got up and looked into the bedroom. Nobody. Then the bath. Nobody. The windows were secure. Danielsen had frightened me more than I cared to admit to myself, I began to think, when I saw her.

She was squatting like a watchful fox in a corner, that old *ayah* who lived on the floor. And what had gotten her nose up was my cigar.

I held it out to her and she came a-scuttering, snatched it out of my hand, puffed at it twice while squatting, thrust it back to my hand and, holding in the smoke she had inhaled, held it until she'd scuttered back to her corner: there, her eyes bright with pleasure, she let the smoke out. I'd never seen anyone so old take so much joy out of so small a pleasure.

I returned to reading:

Nanavati married Sylvia in England in 1949. The couple had three children, the youngest being of three years. They came to stay in a flat at Coloba in Bombay in December, 1957, as a Naval Officer Nanavati had to be away from home for long periods of duty at sea. During 1958, Nanavati was away from Bombay for about six months.

Mr. Trivedi said that Nanavati was introduced to Ahuja by another naval officer, Lt. Cdr. Yagnik, in July or August, 1950. During the absence of Nanavati at Sea, his wife used to visit Ahuja's house to see his sister, Miss Mammie Ahuja. She also happened to meet Ahuja during those visits. Actually, Nanavati visited Ahuja's house along with his wife only twice or thrice.

During these visits, the Prosecution said, "some intimacy appears to have developed between Ahuja and Sylvia." On April 18, 1959, Nanavati returned to Bombay. He took ten days' leave from April 19 and stayed in Bombay. It was during this leave period that the murder of Ahuja was committed.

The prosecutor told the jury that just before the return of Nanavati, Sylvia, it appeared, had written "some sort of a letter" to Ahuja. During the leave period Nanavati noticed a "sort of inexplicable coldness" on the part of Sylvia towards him. He was unhappy about this change in her attitude, but could not find out the exact reason.

On the morning of April 27, 1959, the date of the offence—the couple got up early and took their sick dog to a veterinary surgeon. Later they went to a picture house to reserve some tickets for the afternoon show. They returned home after buying some vegetables at the Crawford Market.

At breakfast that day, Nanavati asked her the reason for the change in her attitude, but failed to get any answer. He raised the matter again during lunch. As he approached Sylvia, the Prosecutor said, she asked him to keep away. Further questioning elicited a reply from his wife.

To a query as to how she happened to lose her love for him and whether there was anyone else for whom she cherished her affection, she said "yes." Nanavati then asked Sylvia if that person was Ahuja. To this too she replied in the affirmative. This naturally upset Nanavati.

She even acknowledged that she had not been faithful to her husband. This stunned Nanavati. From that moment Nanavati was hot.

*"This gentleman in the dock is one of the ablest officers in the Navy
and the Victim happens to be a flourishing Business Man dealing in
motor cars." By these words public Prosecutor Mr. C. M. Trivedi,
broke the silence of the Court and opened the case for the prosecution.*

I glanced up: she was waiting for another chance at the cigar. It was hardly
more than a butt but, when I held it toward her, she came and returned
to the corner with it: now it was *all* hers.

In the corner she puffed the dying butt with her eyes closed, as if she'd
lived her whole life for this moment. She didn't open her eyes till the butt
went dead. Then, as though she'd known my eyes had been on her, she
looked up at me with a mischievous air.

"*Brrrr-andy,*" she demanded, in a low, long growl.

Martha had put the stuff too high on the shelf for the *ayah* to reach. Well,
I could stand a snort myself.

When I brought the bottle down she crouched beside me, eyes alight
with apprehension lest I drink it all and leave her not a drop. I had one
drink but I didn't trust this one with the bottle. She understood and put
her mouth up like a baby lamb. I let her have enough to stagger a ewe and
drew it away. The stuff ran down the corners of her mouth, brown as her
brandy-colored hide. She flashed me a smile white as milk and scrambled
back to her corner. I put the bottle on the shelf and went back to the trial
of Commander Nanavati:

SYLVIA'S EVIDENCE

*Clad in pure white, Indian style, 28-year-old Sylvia Nanavati, Eng-
lish wife of Commander Nanavati, gave her evidence for the defence
in the Bombay Sessions Court, in clear low tones, which had a touch
of sadness at times and told the court "I was infatuated with Ahuja."*

*Sylvia's evidence was eagerly awaited by the parties as well as the
public because it was she from whom some extraordinary story was
expected. She was refused by the prosecutor to be called as a prosecution witness as prosecution did not place any reliance on her.*

*Examined by the defence counsel, Mrs. Nanavati said that she was
married to Commander in July, 1949 and had three children, aged 9
½, 5 ½ and 3. She came to know Prem Ahuja three years ago. Before*

she knew Ahuja, her married life was perfectly happy. Her friendship with Ahuja resulted in intimacy with him, roughly speaking about the beginning of 1958.

Mrs. Nanavati did not disclose this intimacy with Ahuja to her husband till April 27 last (1959). Describing her activities on that day, witness stated that in the morning, she and her husband went to the veterinary hospital at Parel, and on the way back to their residence at Colaba, she purchased from Metro Cinema one ticket for herself and three tickets for three children. Then she did shopping at Crawford Market and returned home at 12-30 P.M.

Before lunch, they were sitting in the sitting room when Commander Nanavati came and touched her. Witness asked him not to do so because she did not like him.

Defence counsel: Why did you not like him (husband)?

Mrs. Nanavati: At that time I was infatuated with Ahuja.

Witness, continuing, said that Commander Nanavati asked her why she was so cold and why she did not like him. She replied that she did not want to talk about the matter.

After lunch Commander Nanavati went to lie down in the bedroom and witness was in the sitting room. After a time her husband came out and told her they must talk this matter out. He further said that for the last few months "you have been cool to me." He also asked for the reason, and said, "Don't you love me?"

Witness did not give any reply. Commander Nanavati then asked her whether she was in love with anyone else . . . and she said yes. He then wanted to know who the other person was, but witness said nothing.

Witness continued: When he asked me whether it was Ahuja I said yes. He asked me whether I had been faithful to him. I told him I had not been faithful to him.

Commander Nanavati just sat dazed. Suddenly he got up rather excitedly and said that he wanted to go to Ahuja's flat and square things up. Witness became alarmed and put her hand to her husband and said, "Please don't go there, he will shoot you."

Commander Nanavati said: "Don't bother about myself. It does not matter, and in any case I will shoot myself."

Witness then caught hold of his arm and tried to calm him down.

She told her husband "Why should you shoot yourself? You are the innocent one in this."

After this, witness said, her husband cooled down a bit and asked her whether Ahuja was willing to marry her and look after the children. She avoided answering that question, because she was too ashamed to admit that she had felt that Ahuja was trying to avoid marrying her. Thereupon her husband told her that he was prepared to forgive her if she promised never to see Ahuja again. But witness hesitated to give an answer.

Witness: I was still infatuated with Ahuja, so I hesitated to give the answer. As this was question which affected my whole future, I could not give an answer at the moment.

Continuing, witness stated that in the meantime, the doorbell rang and the neighbour's child came in for going to the cinema. Then they got ready for the cinema and her husband said that they should not talk about it any more and that they would talk about it the next morning.

Witness went to the cinema with three children, her husband driving the car. Though she requested Commander Nanavati to go with her for the show, he did not go, but just took them to the cinema. Counter foils of the tickets, which were taken charge of by the police were then tendered.

After leaving them at the theatre, her husband told her that he was going to the ship, I.N.S. Mysore, to get some medicine for the dogs.

Witness identified a silk shirt and coloured pants as having been worn by Commander Nanavati at the time her husband told her that he would return and pick them up at the cinema, the show ending at 5-30 P.M.

When she came out of the cinema she did not find her husband, but she was picked up by a relative of her husband. When she reached home, she came to know as the incident in the case. Her husband had taken the keys of their flat.

Question: I am definitely suggesting that your husband never said that he would kill himself?

Witness: My husband clearly said that. Asked how she was indifferent to that statement of her husband, she replied:

"I was myself in a state of upset. So I did not think clearly, but I was not indifferent to my husband shooting himself."

Question: Despite all that happened you went to the Cinema on that day?

Witness: It is difficult to explain things to the children. So as I had promised them, I took them to the Cinema.

Question: Where are you staying?

Witness: I am staying with the parents of my husband.

Question: "I am suggesting that you have agreed to oblige your husband now that lover is no more."

Witness: It is not true. I am stating what I actually know.

I fell asleep over the sorrows of Nanavati; and slept so soundly I did not hear Martha let herself in. I did not waken until she called to me from the bed.

My tactic was to make no love to her until she took the initiative: had she been making love, my approach would be tolerated only because I was supporting her for a short while.

So now, when she fell to sleep on my shoulder, I merely held her.

The drumming of the overhead fan began to drum to a slower beat; like the throb of great engines hauling below deck. They were whispering the same warning over and over—or was it a seaman, whispering to himself while he listened, on the other side of my stateroom door? Baliram, in a white uniform and his face bloodied, stood, smiling knowingly, above me.

"Bombay is a great city, my friend," he said sorrowfully—and bent so low above me I felt his breath on my face and wakened.

It was Martha's breath, while she slept with her head on my shoulder. She had thrown her arm across me, and on the nape of my neck I could feel her fingers lying lightly. Her breasts, crushed against me, yet felt firm. She moved her thigh across mine and caught the calf of my leg with her heel, pressing herself against me. Her fingers tapped my nape: she was awake and waiting. I swept my hand down her back to the fullness of her hips and gently backward till she joined her hands about my back. Then joined her thighs.

When her breath began coming harder I took her mouth till her lips went cool in release. A moment later she had fallen back to sleep; her head upon her palm.

All night, in voluptuous gravity, this woman of Assam, wearing golden earrings, slept; her cheek upon her palm. All night the ceiling fan above her whirred. I saw her purchased breasts: their rise and fall.

While four roses made a shadow, as of many roses, on the wall.

Beyond the door her ancient *ayah* slept upon the floor.

All night, along the flaring street below, I heard the cabareting taxis'
roar.

A night that roses, at one rupee for four, made a shadow, as of many
rupees, on the wall.

✿   ✿   ✿

I wakened to a tremendous crash, flinging my hands across my eyes—I
thought the overhead fan had fallen.

Martha was pulling on a robe. There came a long low wail of fright. I
got up and stumbled into the living room.

The top shelf of the great bookcase had crashed to the floor on top of
the *ayah,* lying prone and wailing with the brandy bottle smashed across
a litter of broken records. That she had tried to climb the shelves for the
bottle and had gotten high enough to reach it before the top shelf crashed
was plain enough. Martha was rocking the baby while keeping up such a
flow of abuse—in a tongue I'd never heard—that the kid was becoming
more frightened than ever.

The *ayah* came crawling toward her on her belly, but Martha ignored
her, joggling the baby in her arms. She paced up and down, strode to the
bookcase and, with one hand demonstrating the enormity of the old
woman's crime, shook the lower shelves angrily—and down they came
with a louder crash than the one the old *ayah* had caused. In this fresh
plunge every record, that had not fallen in the first fall, was smashed
utterly.

And the *ayah,* as though sure now she must be responsible for *all* the
bookshelves in the world, emitted a howl like a terrified child. She
clutched, in her misery, at the hem of Martha's robe and Martha slapped
her off so forcefully I felt I myself had been struck.

The old woman lay howling face-down in the rug.

"She's honest. You said so yourself," I reminded Martha.

Martha didn't seem to hear.

"She's too old to get work," I insisted, "she'll die in the streets."

"Let her die," Martha decided.

In the morning the *ayah* was gone. Anna would be pleased, I knew.

It was time for me to leave as well.

So farewell to Ezekiel's and Ezekiel's creatures: goodbye to slicky-boy mackers with paralyzed mugs—may their ricepaddy angels all turn out to be carhops.

Good fortune for keeps to old ruined customs-men asweat in the noon bazaars: may police never entrap him in his Anglo-Indian home. And farewell to slipper-sloppering snitch-on-Papa girlfinks: may they wind up in such cages as have room for one more.

Goodbye to all Mama-sans of low-voltage ports whose girls sell their clothes when no ship comes to dock. Farewell and soft blessings on all mascaraed ghosts who subsist on green ladydrinks along old Ho-Phang Road.

Farewell to the flares of Kamathipura and its sixty-watt night-bulbs burning all in a row. May all cockeyed whores, the whole wide world around, find rest under lamps that lean each to each.

Farewell to poor girls who put up with everything: and to upside-down tightwire walkers who wind up on all fours in fly-buzzing bars.

Good riddance to all cheesified, praise-me-and-I'll praise-you bone-deep begrudgers, whittling their words to gain six more floppy-hats at the next lecture—small-time cross-indexing annotators: Fiedlers, Kazins, Pod-horetzes, Macdonalds and such, sniffing the wind while counting the house—mere nosedrops in the nostrils of literature—screw the whole spiteburning lot.

Goodbye to all seamen whose heads are on crooked as well as to those whose heads are on straight. Goodbye to dead pursers who kept their ships out of trouble; and to radio officers, headphones clamped, who can't remember whether it was in Macao or Saigon.

Forever farewell to all mariners, beached or ashore, adrift between lonely hotel rooms and the shifting floor of the ocean's deeps.

Goodbye to all seamen who fear those deeps: yet fear the shore even more.

Goodbye to that ominous tenement—goodbye most of all and good-bye for keeps—goodbye to the woman of Assam.

Wherever she sleeps.

❈   ❈   ❈

The *Malaysia Mail* was swinging out of the Port of Calcutta.

It was that hour when the ship, leaving the quais lighter for cargo discharged, seems heavier than ever with a weight of regret. Those short-term loves that might have been long-term; those glimpses of the Might-Have-Been that never would be now, leave officers and men alike feeling low. I needed a drink myself.

Concannon's door was open; the radio was beep-beep-jotting. But all to be seen of Sparks was two big feet, with shoes unlaced, stretched on his bunk. He opened one eye when I came in and rolled face to the wall. I helped myself to his gin, sat down and waited.

Fantasies, of having Martha with me in Chicago, came and went; in each of which she was companion and lover. Coming down one level of fantasy, she became faithful servant in a spacious house, with living quarters for herself and her son: the boy was growing up to share his mother's everlasting gratitude to the magnanimous American who had rescued them both from a life of shame, all of that. How to fit this into a sixty-a-month walkup in Chicago I hadn't quite resolved, when Concannon came awake at last.

"That was the worst one yet," he concluded.

"You look it," I assured him.

"I feel like it," he acknowledged, splashing cold water across his temples. He was already beginning to get his color back.

"What's the story on Manning?" I wanted to know.

"You know as much as I do," he told me, "a thousand watches worth fifty apiece, and twelve thousand dollars, American, in undeclared bills."

"I didn't know about the money."

"It's a break for him, as it turns out," Concannon filled me in, "he'll be tried in the States instead of here."

"You mean he's still on board?"

"Karensen got hold of the American embassy—they wouldn't let the customs cops take him off the ship. He has to face charges on the twelve thousand first. Then India can extradite him. They didn't like it one bit."

"What becomes of the watches?"

"Customs confiscates them, then sells them at auction. The merchant who tipped them off will be allowed to get them back for a token bid."

"Do you think the old man was in on it?"

Sparks shook his head, no. "But he'll have trouble getting another ship all the same. Drink up."

He slipped the headphones on to indicate he had to get to work.

"Watch out you don't get the ship in trouble," I warned him.

I glanced into the officers' lounge on the way down to the crew's quarters. Danielsen, stirring something in a cup, seemed to be waiting for me. He gave me a faint bird-like shuttering of his eyes to indicate he wanted to say something. I tried a hearty, "How's things? What's your story?"

I had to put my ear down toward his mouth to catch his answer.

It sounded like "I'm not going ashore anymore."

"I don't blame you," I assured him, "if I'd had a gun I would have had to shoot you."

"I know," he smiled weakly, "I know."

"Has it happened before?" I asked, sitting down across from him.

He started to nod, yes. "But never aboard ship," he assured me, "never at sea."

There was an awkward silence.

"It's why I never go home at Christmas," he told me, "I *always* ship out."

"Something about Santa Claus does it?"

He shook his head. "I can drink at sea but not ashore."

"Well," I told him, "I thought I'd had *my* last drink, at sea or on shore, you can believe me."

"I'm sorry," he told me wistfully, "I apologize."

I didn't like it. His fury had diminished, yet had not died. When the light of sanity had come back into his eyes he had *still* wanted to kill me.

What I represented to him, that he needed to kill it, I surmise, had something to do with being—or seeming to him to be—of some specially privileged order.

"Have you seen Manning?" I asked, to change the subject.

"I haven't seen him," Danielsen told me, "the First Mate was taking care of the store when I was down there. Either Manning is ashamed to show his face or afraid to."

"What does he have to be afraid of?"

"The men won't get a draw again until we hit Long Beach. He was using their money to buy watches. There goes Smith's funny poker game."

I left Danielsen stirring whatever-that-was in a cup.

Cutting through the narrow Officer's Galley I had to squeeze past Smith and Captain Karensen in front of Manning's stateroom. Had either recognized me I would have exchanged greetings. But, as both moved aside to let me pass without a word, I took it as one of those small snubs that men at work put on the man who has nothing to do but stroll idly about.

"Mister Manning!" I heard Smith call loudly as I left the galley. I continued on, down the ladder and into the crew's quarters.

Nobody was around but Bridelove and Muncie, playing call rummy for matches. Bridelove looked to be winning.

"What's our next port?" I asked him.

"The Philippines," Bridelove informed me. "I don't know whether we'll hit Tacloban City. Probably Ilo-no and Cebu."

"Why not Manila?"

"Not this trip," Bridelove was certain.

Crooked-Neck Smith stood in the doorway, his head as far out on his neck as I'd ever seen it. It was really *stretching*.

"Manning just killed himself," he told us.

And turned and walked off.

✿   ✿   ✿

Manning had been not only a scandal himself, but a cause for others to behave scandalously. The overdose he had taken had not been, necessarily, fatal. Had there been a single person aboard who cared, in the slightest degree, whether the man lived or died, he could have been saved.

Nobody had reported to the Captain that the purser hadn't shown up for duty. The Third Mate had rapped the man's door at six that morning and, receiving no answer, had informed the First Mate; who had simply dismissed the matter until ten, and had then opened the ship's store himself.

It had remained for Smith—who else?—on his customary round of making everybody's business aboard his own, to bring Karensen down to Manning's door. It had been Smith who'd broken in and dragged the man, without help, into the galley.

He'd tried mouth-to-mouth breathing, but the man's lips had turned blue even while he was trying. The Captain and the First Mate had had to carry the body down to the engine room.

There was no other place aboard to keep a corpse. Manning could not be buried at sea because the cause of death had not been determined. Karensen could scarcely risk an investigation like that on top of the one he was already facing because of Manning's black-market operations. Beyond sending a radio cable to the next of kin, Karensen could do nothing about Manning's body until he could turn the body over to a company doctor at Tacloban City or Ilo-Ilo.

That meant keeping the body in ice for a full week.

Whether Smith volunteered or was ordered to it I wasn't told: yet he seemed the logical man for the job.

"Talk about getting the ship in trouble," I heard Smith mourning the loss of his poker game, "I'm going to freeze the fat bastard's balls off!"

At first they distrusted his style. Then they distrusted his lack of politics. Then they distrusted his politics. Then they distrusted his drinking in public while they drank in secrecy. Or—worse yet—didn't drink at all. They distrusted his adventures. They distrusted his beard. Finally they distrusted his smile.

Yet they never came out with what they really distrusted. Because the big thing with them was the money; and he never went for the money. He made the money, he liked the money, he spent the money. But he never went for the money.

They had his goat, they said. Because, sooner or later, they felt sure, he'd go for the money. He bought leisure and travel and adventure and houses and boats and sporting days and easy good times. Yet he never went for the money. Had he gone for the money they would have had his goat. As long as he didn't he had theirs: because it left them with nothing to get hold of except his beard and his smile.

The big thing with him was neither the money nor yet that mystic stream of time, eternal and serene; nor yet those long beautiful islands. Nor yet the changeless and changeful seas.

He was the historian who noted how many letters littered the field where the Austrian dead lay face-down in the sun with their hip pockets emptied: and he was the Austrian facedown in the sun. He was the English girl dreaming herself dead in an Italian rain. He was the advance man with purple wounds from elbow to wrist hiding beneath the sheets in a cheap hotel. He was the chronicler of mules with their forelegs broken drowning in the port of Smyrna.

It wasn't the gulf stream of time, but the deep-floating corset borne upon it and the student's notebook that, in the end, were most important to him.

Hemingway was the picker with the long pole.

"Life is the greatest left-hander we know," he said—"unless it was Charlie White of Chicago."

And of the American writers of our time now dead, which one, given a single choice, would you bring back to life?

For myself it would have to be Hemingway.

Hemingway *all* the way.

EPILOGUE

QUAIS OF CALCUTTA

Our rigging severed the moon the night we sailed
Into that jungle of cranes and jutting spars
The smear in that dungsmoke pall was merely day
Lighting impossible multitudes; that stirred as one.
Then rose, between the No-Beef Restaurant
And the Family Planning Store
Crying *No Mama No Papa No Baby No Chowchow Papa You Give.*

Kanani Mansions someone had named that ominous tenement
Where a woman of Assam wearing golden earrings slept
Her cheek upon her palm
Her ancient *ayah* slept upon the floor.
And all night long the ceiling fan whirred on.

O night so starred, with trees like clouds at rest
With lamps that leaned in pairs
And roses black as red—
I saw her purchased breasts
Their rise and fall.
A night that roses—one rupee per bunch—
Made shadows as of many rupees on the wall.

O chasmed love, with thighs that locked so sure
O deep-joyed dark, that makes the world come true:
Her roses choked within the burning air.
Yet in voluptuous gravity she slept on
Above the cabareting taxis' roar.
O night that sanctifies
The seaman's whore.

Dock-hawks followed our rigging to the sea
Then let us sail our ways alone.
Yet far, far out
With all docks gone and daylight swiftly going
Two messenger crows came cawing from the sun
Accusing me—
No Mama No Papa No Baby No Chowchow Papa You Give.

NELSON ALGREN (1909–1981) wrote of the despised urban underbelly of America before it was fashionable to do so, and stands as one of our most defiant and enduring novelists. His novels include *The Man with the Golden Arm*, winner of the first National Book Award; *A Walk on the Wild Side*; and *Never Come Morning*.